Divorce and Separation

DIVORCE
AND
SEPARATION

---

*Context, Causes,
and Consequences*

EDITED BY

GEORGE LEVINGER

AND

OLIVER C. MOLES

Basic Books, Inc., Publishers   *New York*

Library of Congress Cataloging in Publication Data
Main entry under title:

Divorce and separation.

    Bibliography: p. 337
    Includes indexes.
    1. Divorce--United States--Addresses, essays, lectures.
I. Levinger, George Klaus, 1927-   II. Moles, Oliver C.
HQ834.D56   301.42'84'0973   78-19815
ISBN: 0-465-01682-0

CONTENTS

PART IV

PART V

CONTRIBUTORS

SHIRLEY J. ASHER is an advanced graduate student in the doctoral program in clinical psychology at the University of Colorado at Boulder.

MARY JO BANE is Associate Professor of Education at Harvard University and Associate Director of the Harvard-M.I.T. Joint Center for Urban Studies.

JESSIE BERNARD is Research Scholar Honoris Causa, Pennsylvania State University.

BERNARD L. BLOOM is Professor of Psychology at the University of Colorado at Boulder.

CAROL A. BROWN is Associate Professor of Sociology at the University of Lowell.

ROBERT F. CASTO is Graduate Research Assistant in the College of Human Development at Pennsylvania State University.

ANDREW CHERLIN is Assistant Professor of Social Relations at Johns Hopkins University.

MORTON DEUTSCH is Professor of Psychology and Education and Director of the Social Psychology Laboratory at Teachers College, Columbia University.

ROSLYN FELDBERG is Assistant Professor of Sociology at Boston University.

FRANK F. FURSTENBERG, JR., is Associate Professor of Sociology and an Associate of the Population Studies Center at the University of Pennsylvania.

KELIN E. GERSICK is Assistant Professor of Psychology in Psychiatry at Yale University School of Medicine.

PAUL C. GLICK is Senior Demographer in the Population Division of the United States Bureau of the Census.

CHARLES T. HILL is Assistant Professor of Sociology at the University of Washington.

DENNIS T. JAFFE is a staff member of the Center for Counseling and Psychotherapy in Santa Monica, California, and is Adjunct Assistant Professor of Psychiatry at the UCLA School of Medicine.

ROSABETH MOSS KANTER is Professor of Sociology and Organization and Management at Yale University.

JANET A. KOHEN is Assistant Professor of Sociology at the University of Massachusetts at Boston.

KENNETH KRESSEL is Assistant Professor of Psychology at Rutgers University, New Brunswick.

GEORGE LEVINGER is Professor of Psychology and Head of the Social Psychology Program at the University of Massachusetts at Amherst.

CYNTHIA LONGFELLOW is an advanced doctoral student at the School of Education at Harvard University.

MARTIN LOPEZ-MORILLAS is a doctoral candidate in the social psychology program at Teachers College, Columbia University.

OLIVER C. MOLES is Leader, Home and Community Studies Team at the National Institute of Education.

CHARLES W. MUELLER is Associate Professor of Sociology at the University of Iowa.

ARTHUR J. NORTON is Chief of the Marriage and Family Statistics Branch of the United States Bureau of the Census.

LETITIA ANNE PEPLAU is Assistant Professor of Psychology at the University of California, Los Angeles.

HALLOWELL POPE is Associate Professor of Sociology at the University of Iowa.

ZICK RUBIN is Louis and Frances Salvage Professor of Social Psychology at Brandeis University.

JOHN SCANZONI is Professor of Sociology and of Child Development and Family Relations at the University of North Carolina, Greensboro.

GRAHAM B. SPANIER is Associate Professor of Human Development and Sociology at Pennsylvania State University.

JANET WEINGLASS is a doctoral candidate at Teachers College, Columbia University.

ROBERT S. WEISS is Professor of Sociology at the University of Massachusetts at Boston and Lecturer in Sociology at Harvard Medical School.

STEPHEN W. WHITE is a doctoral candidate in the clinical psychology program at the University of Colorado at Boulder.

FOREWORD

BY JESSIE BERNARD

THIS informative and thoughtful book comes at a most opportune time. The fast pace of change, as Bloom, White, and Asher note, renders research reported more than a decade and a half ago almost anachronistic, as though from another era. As a result, we are having a hard time readjusting our picture of marriage and divorce to the reality of what they are—actually, now, today, at the present moment. As a consequence, we have so little consensus with respect to marriage and divorce that we cannot even organize a White House conference on the family. In the face of all these changes, this book succeeds admirably in its goal: to help us understand what is happening. And, as Norton and Glick, Pope and Mueller, and Furstenberg show, a great deal is happening.

Different people will read the trends differently. Some will read them as a headlong plunge toward Armageddon;[1] in this they will join a long tradition.[2] Others will read them, as a woman writing some fifty years ago did, as an index of the rising status of women.[3] Most will fall between these extremes. Few would forbid divorce altogether nor would many advocate it as a good and beneficial goal. Most would undoubtedly prefer all marriages to be loving, supportive, and mutually enhancing. Lacking such a reality, we have to try fine-tuning the pros and cons for both partners with respect to leniency and severity in the rules regulating divorce. Historically, as Scanzoni makes abundantly clear, the rules governing marriage have favored husbands and penalized wives. Perhaps for

1. "The value system that used to hold families together has been turned upside down. . . . This breakdown of the family is going to prove to be the most powerful, the most destructive and the most enduring of all the changes . . . young adults are bringing into society" (Interview with James Coleman in *U.S. News & World Report*, reproduced in the *San Francisco Chronicle*, March 31, 1978).
2. Thwing and Thwing (1887) noted that the rising divorce rate was awakening "grave apprehension for the perpetuity of important institutions" (p. 153).
3. Mary Burt Messer was seeing divorce "as essentially a mode of redress for women" (1928, p. 332). It raised their status. The growing economic independence of women put marriage to the test; it had to survive on its own merits or not at all.

that very reason divorce seems to be more stressful for men than for women—as Bloom, White, and Asher point out.

The nursery rhyme—"Peter, Peter, pumpkin-eater, had a wife and couldn't keep her; put her in a pumpkin shell and there he kept her very well"—encapsulates Scanzoni's perceptive sketch of Peter's pumpkin shell; that is, the legal, religious, customary, and ideological structure of marriage and divorce in American history. He illustrates vividly how disadvantaged women have been in marriage. His discussion makes clear how strong were Levinger's constraints on marital breakup. He shows that women had to endure a great deal before they found marriage intolerable. And they did endure. Battered wives are by no means a new phenomenon. Scanzoni shows us the changing nature of Peter's pumpkin shell. It worked fairly well for him if not for his wife. It kept women in the pumpkin shell under almost any and all conditions. But it has now worn thin. It keeps fewer and fewer women in.

Peter has to do more now to keep his wife. Or even, in fact, to get her in the first place. He has more competition. For example, young women with jobs show, age for age, a lower marriage rate than women without jobs. And the better the job, the lower the rate. Norton and Glick in their survey of trends note a recent decline in the overall marriage rate, or at least a delay in marriage, most likely among career-minded women. There was a time when the career costs of marriage were taken as a matter of course. Women had to choose one or the other; it was not possible to have both. Almost a hundred years ago a book on marriage was already noting that "the sacrifices of personal ambitions and pleasures which she [the wife] makes are far greater than his [the husband]" (Thwing and Thwing, 1887, p. 118). Today the costs may be reckoned in opportunities for career advancement rather than in terms of a career itself, or in terms of a woman's overload in combining home-making and career. It is not likely that women will ever forswear marriage altogether, whatever the cost. But they are more and more trying to reshape it to a more egalitarian pattern before they enter it, as well as leaving it when the costs become insupportable.

The high divorce rate today does not imply that marriage has become worse for women nor that wives in the past were happier in marriage than they are now.[4] It is not argued that women suffer more in marriage today than formerly. It would, in any event, be hard to document such subjective states. But we can now see how disadvantaged wives have been. They remained even in brutalizing relationships because there were, in effect, no genuine alternatives. When there was no place in the social

---

4. When asked in polls, married women almost all reply they are happy in their marriages. Epidemiological studies of depression, on the other hand, find a high prevalence among married women.

structure for women outside of established families, women had few if any bargaining chips. They had to settle for what they could get. Nor does the rise in divorce reflect a deterioration in the character of women. Neither women nor what they want in marriage has changed all that much—including the companionship and affection Scanzoni tells us became part of the bargaining in his "head-complement" conceptualization of marriage. The high divorce rate reflects neither a worsening of the nature of marriage nor of the character of women. It reflects rather the fact that there are now better alternatives to give women a chance to express their dissatisfaction—to "vote with their feet"—as they literally had to do in colonial times. The alternatives are offered in the form of independence by way of labor-force participation. Alternatives involve choice which, in turn, calls for the weighing of costs.

Marital viability, as Levinger, Scanzoni, Jaffe and Kanter, and Kohen, Brown, and Feldberg—each with slightly different conceptualizations but still with converging paradigms—note, is a function of "costs" and "rewards" or "benefits." Levinger classifies both the rewards and the costs of marriage as material, symbolic, and affectional. Weiss suggests that marriage in-and-of-itself, happy or not, is rewarding, that it contributes to the well-being of its members; and separation, even from a bad relationship, has emotional costs.

The material costs of divorce are considerable for both parties since stretching one income for two households reduces the resources of both. It is not often that research findings using different approaches, different conceptual tool-kits, different models converge as clearly as do those dealing with the influence of the wife's economic resources on the probability of divorce. Rarely are they as unequivocal as those reported by Cherlin, Levinger, or Kohen, Brown, and Feldberg: women with potential for economic independence are more likely to leave a marriage than those with none, especially if low income or unemployment of the husband nullifies the economic benefits of the marriage. Such potential reduces the cost of divorce. Now that more and more women are entering the labor force they are increasingly willing to leave the marriage. We see now that until recently there have been numerous marriages that persisted at enormous cost to the partners, especially to women, because the costs of divorce were even greater than the costs of remaining in the marriage. Physically and psychologically battered wives who now come "out of the closet" in the past might have remained indefinitely closeted rather than admit their situation since there was no feasible alternative. Even today most women are economically worse off after divorce—as Bane and Kohen, Brown, and Feldberg show—and a marriage must be pretty bad before a wife walks out.

The benefits and the costs of divorce have changed over time. The social costs of divorce, for example, have been greatly attenuated. If or when the stigma is great and society is inhospitable to divorced women, the social costs may well be assessed as high.[5] When etiquette books said divorced men and women meet socially as strangers, as Emily Post's did well into the 1920s, or when they made no provision for divorced women on the social scene, costs were high. Today the stigma of divorce has become so attenuated that in some circles it has completely vanished.

Nor should the nitty-gritty costs of divorce be overlooked. Spanier and Casto remind us of the hum-drum practical costs that accrue, however light may be the economic and social costs of divorce. But for all of the authors of this book, it is the psychological or emotional (Levinger's "affectional") costs of divorce that overshadow all the others.

If the economic and social costs of divorce seem often higher for wives than for husbands, the same does not seem true for psychological costs. These seem to be higher for men. For example, in most cases they suffer from loss of close contacts with their children. As Gersick shows, for men who did not have custody the loss of children seemed a high price to pay for ending even an unsalvageable marriage; and for those who did have custody the emotional demands of fatherhood in a one-parent family were great and often constituted an interference with their work.

Data on hospitalization also suggest that the costs of marital dissolution—as well as the benefits of marriage—tend to be higher in the case of men than of women. The data presented by Bloom, White, and Asher, for example, imply that moving from the never-married status to the married state greatly reduces the probability of hospitalization for men but does so much less for women.[6] Conversely, moving from the state of marriage to the status of either divorced or widowed increases the probability of hospitalization for men considerably more than for women.

5. The purely social costs of divorce to women in the upper classes and how they were changing in the early years of the century were poignantly portrayed by Edith Wharton in a story published in 1916, "Autre Temps." It was about a mother who had become déclassée because she had divorced her husband. Now she has returned to attend the remarriage of her divorced daughter who has been obliged to pay no such price; the daughter is accepted socially without penalties.

6. Admissions to institutions are an admittedly gross measure, but the findings are buttressed by a considerable corpus of epidemiological research on mental health which documents unequivocally the benefits of marriage for men, and somewhat less unequivocally, for women. Among never-married women, those who are economically independent seem to be better off than married women so far as depression is concerned, but the same is not true for never-married women who are not. Thus, for example, Lenore Radloff (1978) reports that never-married female heads of households with incomes of $16,000 or more, and hence presumably independent, showed as of 1971–1973, the lowest depression scores of any marital-status category, lower even than married men, the best-off so far as depression was concerned of any of the marital-status categories. Some of the older data on the relative welfare of married and never-married men and women were summarized by Bernard (1972). Work on depression since then has corroborated the older findings. Under the age of, say, thirty, comparisons between never-married and married are contaminated because many of the never-married will marry later on.

Granted that the remarried men are not included among the divorced-widowed, which blurs any conclusion arrived at, still the very fact that more men than women remarry after divorce suggests that they need marriage more and benefit more from it.[7] Thus, in this rough measure, both the costs of divorce and the benefits of marriage in 1975 were greater in the case of men than of women.

Neither hospital admission rates nor community surveys can, of course, reveal the subtler affectional components of the marital relationship. Scanzoni quotes Wollstonecraft who as early as 1792 was pointing out that the wife even then was being "defrauded" of her husband's caresses. He refers also to Cott who shows that in the head-complement model wives were entitled to socioemotional gratification.[8] And he cites Gadlin on the growth of the importance of expressive rewards in marriage. Granted that the data on marriage of the past is fragmentary, we conclude that women's sphere, the home, was the "realm of the heart" and that women did supply expressive support for their husbands. Their gift of "heart," however, was not reciprocated. American men were not socialized to be emotionally expressive. Tocqueville attributed this lack of affection to their preoccupation with business which engendered a matter-of-fact mentality. Whatever it was due to, this lack of affectional expressivity was hard on women, and no doubt limited the communicative ability of men as well.

Thus, for example, Scanzoni tells us that more men than women in colonial times advertised for runaway spouses; Spanier and Casto tell us that in nine out of the eleven suddenly separating couples they studied it was the woman who wanted out; Hill, Rubin, and Peplau tell us that more women than men opt out of premarital relationships; and we know that more divorce actions are brought by women than men. Although such indexes are subject to severe limitations, they do suggest that the psychological "costs" of marriage are greater for women than for men.

Why, in the face of such a relatively low return, have women married at all? The pressures on women to marry have been overwhelming. "Better dead than unwed" has been the lesson hammered home to them. A rhyme sung by schoolgirls in a parochial school a generation or two ago ran: "St. Catherine, St. Catherine, oh lend me thine aid, and grant that I never may die an old maid! A husband, St. Catherine! A good one, St. Catherine! But anyone better than no one, St. Catherine! A husband, St. Catherine! Handsome, St. Catherine! Rich, St. Catherine! Young, St. Catherine! Soon, St. Catherine!" Such pressures were understandable when there was little place for women outside of marriage (Watt, 1957). When there was no way for a woman to support herself outside of a

7. In addition, men have more eligible women to choose from than vice versa since brides are generally younger than their grooms.
8. For systematic data on the current scene, see Bernard (1976).

household, the spinster came to be an object of mirth or contempt. So women felt they had to marry.

But times have changed. The old principle that the one who cares less in a relationship has an advantage over the one who cares more (see Ross, 1920 and Waller, 1938) could not operate equitably until another chip was added to the woman's resources—potential economic independence outside of marriage. And now there is another alternative to marriage, living together without marriage, as Norton and Glick have noted.

So what is the upshot of all the knowledge offered in this data-rich book? What answers does it supply to questions of policy? Not, it must be admitted, a great deal. It is pitched from neither Mt. Olympus nor Mt. Sinai. Although its authors offer hints and suggestions for policy, they pretend to no final solutions. Unfortunately, research findings do not automatically translate into policy. Moles shows how hard it is even to determine what the results of specific policies actually are. Knowing the variables associated with divorce is not the same as being able to reduce it. Totalitarian states do not have to consider independently competing interest groups as much as democratic societies do in setting policy. When totalitarian states are concerned about the birth rate, a policy change may encourage women to stay home and have babies; when they are concerned about the labor force, they can encourage women to enter it. When they want both a high birth rate and also female labor-force participation, they can attempt to reconcile the demands of these different goals—often, it should be noted, at high cost to the women involved in the form of overwork. But Americans are jealous of their family prerogatives, and at least in this democratic society, government policy generally avoids direct attempts to influence the form of the family.

Furthermore, there are some aspects of marriage and divorce that are far beyond the realm of policy. How, for example, can husbands be encouraged to cultivate the expressive role that would give the affection women so long for? Can we change the sex-role stereotype which idealizes the "strong, silent" kind of man? The efforts now being made to overcome such sex-role stereotyping in the schools may be a step in the right direction. Research has told us how important the expression of affection in marriage is; so far it has not told us how to achieve it.

In the meanwhile, until we know better how to translate research into policy and action, there is a lot that is possible for mitigating the costs of divorce. We can make intervention in the divorcing process as supportive as possible, as sketched by Kressel, Lopez-Morillas, Weinglass, and Deutsch. We can try to protect children from the worst trauma of divorce, as discussed by Bane and Longfellow. We can attempt to make the adjudication of child custody as untraumatic as possible, as proposed by Weiss. And we can make it possible for fathers to continue their parenting after divorce, as suggested by Gersick.

It is not often that a joint effort proves to be so well integrated as this volume is in theoretical approach, complementarity of data, and congruence of conclusions. This book is considerably more than the sum of its parts, excellent as is each of them. It may not have all the answers about divorce and separation; but it has more answers than we have had so far. It will prove indispensable to all researchers, policy makers, and activists interested in the subject.

NOTE

From the Society for the Psychological Study of Social Issues

FEW social institutions in Western society are as ubiquitous as the institution of marriage. The 1970 United States census, for example, indicates that more than 90 percent of all women and men 35 or older have been married at least once. Many marriages prove to be enduring arrangements, a source of growth and satisfaction for their participants. Other marriages, with increasing frequency, are considered a "failure" by one or both parties, and are eventually dissolved through separation or divorce. Thus, just as the institution of marriage has touched the lives of most Americans, so too have many Americans been affected, directly or vicariously, by the process and the consequences of marital dissolution. During 1977 alone, almost 4 percent of American married women, 14 to 44 years of age, became divorced. Marital dissolution is thus a widespread phenomenon, whose importance as an object of study is dictated in part by its long reach into the corners of so many lives.

Beyond the frequency with which separation and divorce now occur is the fact that both their experience and their social acceptance have changed dramatically in recent years. The breakup of a marriage, once considered to be sign of personal defect, a state of having fallen from grace, and a cause for social ostracism, has come to be viewed as a commonplace event for which there are socially approved explanations. Moreover, people who have experienced marital dissolution may be regarded as innocent victims, and sometimes even as courageous "survivors." In these changing times, it therefore seems increasingly important to bring scientific scrutiny to bear on the new realities of separation and divorce. This book represents just such an effort, and it is a most welcome and successful effort at that.

This book is sponsored by the Society for the Psychological Study of Social Issues. SPSSI is a nonprofit organization comprising one of the most active divisions of the American Psychological Association, and consisting of more than 3500 members in the United States and around the world. Since its inception some 40 years ago, SPSSI has attempted to adhere to Kurt Lewin's dictum that "there is nothing so practical as a good theory." SPSSI's business, in effect, is the identification and analysis of social issues, particularly those issues amenable to clarification through social theory and research. Separation and divorce are issues of precisely this genre, and their insightful treatment in this volume epitomizes SPSSI's perspective and values. It is therefore with considerable pride and pleasure that SPSSI sponsors this book, and in so doing consummates a marriage among authors, editors, and the SPSSI organization that promises to be an enduring source of satisfaction.

MARILYNN B. BREWER, *Co-Chair*
JEFFREY Z. RUBIN, *Co-Chair*
Publications Committee (1978–1981)
The Society for the Psychological Study of Social Issues

PREFACE

CHANGE has become a central expectation in our century. Not only in America but also in other industrialized lands, people have come to expect a high rate of change in most aspects of their lives—in the underlying technology, in production and consumption, in family life, in personal aspirations or paths toward self-fulfillment. This is the day of the marketplace ethic, of the renegotiable contract, of the continual search for options.

Changes in the meaning of marriage and the rise in the divorce rate in Western countries are part of this larger picture. Yet despite the dramatic increase in divorce and separation and their important impact on social and personal well-being, the topic has received only scattered attention from social scientists. Over the years there has been an accumulation of descriptive data, of anecdotal reports from the formerly married, and of exhortative or clinical advice. But, until recently, there has been only a trickle of systematic research.

In the present volume, we have pulled together some of the best recent work on the topic. Its nineteen chapters focus on the societal context of divorce and separation, as well as on antecedents and consequences for particular pairs of individuals. The chapters present a variety of approaches. They range from the broadly demographic to the narrowly personal, from statistical analyses of censuses and surveys to individual reflections of participants in small sample studies. Several chapters include reviews of important literature and several deal explicitly with aspects of social policy.

Our book is divided into five parts, dealing consecutively with the general context, the causes, and the consequences of divorce and separation. Part I presents a contextual overview regarding recent trends, historical implications, and social psychological theory. The next two parts present a variety of approaches and findings concerning the determinants of couple breakup; Part II deals with social and psychological antecedents of separation and Part III with largely economic factors. The last two parts consider the consequences of breakup; Part IV pertains mainly to the lives of the ex-spouses themselves, while Part V extends the focus to the families and children of the separating parents.

Throughout, our purpose has been to illuminate critical issues so as to stimulate further thought and study. We believe that our selections represent the best current thinking among psychologists and sociologists. Our own training was in social psychology at the University of Michigan, where we learned to value the importance of interdisciplinary approaches to social problems. In this instance, it has helped us appreciate the diversity of possible perspectives for examining marital dissolution, a topic which often evokes more impulsive emotion than factual thinking.

Our book grew out of a set of articles originally written for the *Journal of Social Issues* [1976, 32 (1)], published by the Society for the Psychological Study of Social Issues. The editors of Basic Books asked us to expand that publication into book form, and the Society agreed to sponsor the present volume. In this book, chapters 3, 4, 5, 6, 7, and 12 are slightly revised versions of the 1976 articles. Chapters 1, 14, and 16 have each been considerably rewritten or brought up to date. The remaining chapters contain entirely new material.

A book such as this is based on the work of many people, few of whom can be acknowledged by name. The author index recognizes the names of many persons whose work has contributed in some way to our total enterprise. We are also grateful to our chapter authors for their fine cooperation and their willingness to allow all royalties to go to the Society for the Psychological Study of Social Issues. We owe a particular debt to Jacqueline Goodchilds, who was editor of the *Journal of Social Issues* during both the inception and the publication of the original papers; we thank her for her support, her critical reactions, and her editorial help. We are also indebted to Robert S. Weiss for his interest in developing this volume, his readiness to make suggestions and to react to particular pieces; he has been a valuable informal consultant. Andrew Cherlin, Marylyn Rands, and Pat Thompson each have helped by commenting extensively on one or more chapters. We also appreciate the work of Julia Strand at Basic Books who helped to oversee final production to ensure that the various pieces would fit into a coherent whole. Finally, we want to thank Ann Levinger and Pat Moles for their perceptive comments and their continuing support during the long time that we spent on this project.

GEORGE LEVINGER
University of Massachusetts, Amherst

OLIVER C. MOLES
National Institute of Education,
Washington, D.C.

December 1978

---

* The views expressed in this volume do not represent positions or policies of the Institute.

Divorce and Separation

PART I

Perspectives on Marital Dissolution

D IVORCE is at a record high and little change in the rate of marital separation appears in sight. This situation touches each of us, whether we are single, married, or formerly married, and whether we come from an intact family or from one torn by marital disruption. It seems important to try to understand what is happening. How common is separation, divorce, or remarriage, and what changes have occurred over recent years? What clues are provided by people's experience with divorce over longer American history? Furthermore, is it possible to formulate some integrated explanation for understanding why couples stay together or separate?

Part I is concerned with such questions. Its first two chapters present accounts of divorce trends in America during recent decades and the farther past. They consider both the number of divorces and reasons for changes in the rates over the years. The third chapter provides a theoretical explanation for divorce.

In the first selection, Arthur Norton and Paul Glick present a demographic overview of U.S. population statistics. Their examination extends from 1920 to 1977 and attempts to project past trends into the future. Recent divorce rates are shown to be more than double those of even fifteen years ago. Although there was a peak in the divorce rate following World War II, it then dropped to a lower level during the 1950s. In the mid-sixties the rate began to rise sharply again, and by 1977 almost 4 percent of American married women aged 14 to 44 were divorced during one year alone.

Norton and Glick's data indicate that the first marriage rate has remained fairly stable over the past half century—except for a rise just after World War II and drops during the Depression and during the 1970s. The remarriage rate for many years paralleled the divorce rate, suggesting that divorced persons were rejecting their first marriage partner but not marriage itself. Recent statistics, however, show a drop in the remarriage rate; since 1970, it has diverged dramatically from the divorce rate. It appears that previously marrieds have begun to accept their single status and have become less prone to quickly formalize new bonds.

In chapter 2, John Scanzoni provides a longer historical perspective on marital bargaining power and instability. Beginning his account in the Colonial Era, he suggests that husband-wife relations at that time paralleled "owner-property" relations; divorce was rare, and desertion occasionally resorted to in extremely unpleasant situations. The nineteenth century saw a change first to a "head-complement" form of marriage, followed by a "senior partner–junior partner" arrangement. Over the course of the century, wives were increasingly expected to become expressive toward their husbands, and their marital bargaining power also rose.

Scanzoni suggests that contemporary times are encouraging an "equal partner" approach to marriage. This shift to equality of power is one of the more important reasons for the rising divorce rate. He argues that it is neither necessary nor inevitable, however, that equality produce divorce, especially if husbands and wives learn how to coordinate their individual and their mutual interests in the total marital bargain.

Chapter 3 sets forth a social psychological perspective on processes of marital dissolution. Spotlighting the marriage pair, but also attending to its outside relationships, George Levinger uses two concepts derived from Lewinian field theory in order to examine the psychological forces that affect a couple's cohesiveness and its dissolution. He suggests that any given relationship continues as a joint function of its attractiveness for the partners and its constraints or "barriers" against their leaving it. Conversely, it may break up if its internal attractiveness compares unfavorably with some competing alternative at a time when its barriers are too weak to deter dissolution.

Levinger is concerned with the pair's ongoing reward-cost balance, as is Scanzoni, but he also considers the additional costs of termination. He applies his theoretical framework to a wide range of research findings on marital satisfaction and marital separation.

Together, these three chapters introduce the analysis of separation and divorce in this volume. Each chapter is an attempt to explain the phenomenon, either by accounting for recent changes in marriage and divorce patterns, by interpreting long term trends in American husband-wife relations since Colonial times, or by theorizing about the bonds that hold together marriages in any society. While the research in this volume is directed at the American experience, its implications have a far broader reference. As societies industrialize and urbanize, they tend to develop comparable family patterns (Goode, 1963). Divorce rates have been rising elsewhere in both the West and the East, and many of the findings reported in this volume have cross-cultural significance.

[1]   *Arthur J. Norton and Paul C. Glick*

Marital Instability in America: Past, Present, and Future

A demographic analysis of trends in marital instability may be made with better factual support if the study features divorce rather than separation. Annual statistics on divorce for the country as a whole are published from vital records, but corresponding statistics on "separation events" are not available. Moreover, the annual statistics on currently separated persons that are published by the Bureau of the Census regularly show a far larger number of women than men reported as separated. In addition, the statistics on separation would be much more meaningful if there were a way of identifying, at a given point in time, the separated persons who would eventually become divorced, those who would become reconciled in their existing marriages, and those who would remain separated. Accordingly, the present discussion focuses attention primarily on probable connections between changes in dissolution of marriage by divorce and concurrent changes in social and economic variables that tend to have an impact on divorce in the United States.

A previous version of this chapter appeared in *Journal of Social Issues*, 1976, 32 (1).

Historical Perspective

Historical trends in American marriage can be traced in terms of patterns of change in vital rates since the early twentieth century. The historical movement of the incidence (or rates) of first marriage, divorce, and remarriage is well documented in the publications of the National Center for Health Statistics (Plateris, 1969; Hetzel and Cappetta, 1971) and in the publications of the U.S. Bureau of the Census (1976, 1977c). Table 1-1 and Figure 1-1 show the estimated annual rates of first marriage, divorce, and remarriage in terms of three-year averages for the periods 1921–1923 through 1975–1977. The first marriage rates were calculated with single women under 45 years old as the base, the divorce rates with married women under 45 as the base, and the remarriage rates with widowed and divorced women under 55 as the base. These bases include

TABLE 1-1

Number and Rate of First Marriage, Divorce, and Remarriage: United States, Three-Year Averages, 1921-1977

	First Marriage		Divorce		Remarriage	
Period	Thousands	Rate[a]	Thousands	Rate[b]	Thousands	Rate[c]
1921-23	990	99	158	10	186	98
1924-26	992	95	177	11	200	99
1927-29	1,025	94	201	12	181	84
1930-32	919	81	183	10	138	61
1933-35	1,081	92	196	11	162	69
1936-38	1,183	98	243	13	201	83
1939-41	1,312	106	269	14	254	103
1942-44	1,247	108	360	17	354	139
1945-47	1,540	143	526	24	425	163
1948-50	1,326	134	397	17	360	135
1951-53	1,190	122	388	16	370	136
1954-56	1,182	120	379	15	353	129
1957-59	1,128	112	381	15	359	129
1960-62	1,205	112	407	16	345	119
1963-65	1,311	109	452	17	415	143
1966-68	1,440	107	535	20	511	166
1969-71	1,649	109	702	26	515	152
1972-74	1,662	103	907	32	601	151
1975-77	1,508	85	1,070	37	646	134

[a] First marriages per 1,000 single women 14 to 44 years old.
[b] Divorces per 1,000 married women 14 to 44 years old.
[c] Remarriages per 1,000 widowed and divorced women 14 to 54 years old.
  Source: Glick and Norton, 1977.

FIGURE 1-1

Rates of First Marriage, Divorce, and Remarriage for U.S. Women: 1921-1977

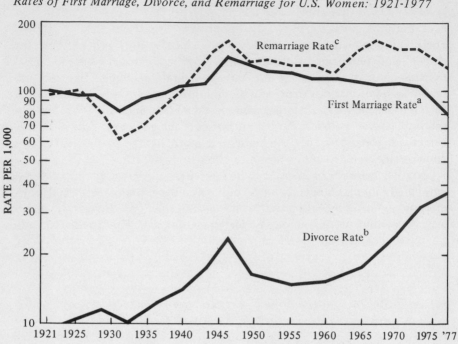

[a]First marriages per 1,000 single women 14 to 44 years old.
[b]Divorces per 1,000 married women 14 to 44 years old.
[c]Remarriages per 1,000 widowed and divorced women 14 to 54 years old.

about 99 percent of all single women who marry, 85 percent of all married women who became divorced, and 80 percent of all women who remarry in a given year.

When observing trends in marital behavior over an extended period of years, rates for women are generally used because they present a more consistent population base, less affected than rates for men by fluctuations in service in the armed forces. For example, in 1977 there were roughly 8 million veterans who had served in the armed forces during the Vietnam War and who subsequently returned to civilian life. Although many men in the armed forces marry before or during their military service, those who live in barracks or who are stationed overseas are not covered by the Bureau's Current Population Survey.

The trend lines for each of the three measures display similar patterns until the late 1950s. Each shows low points during the economic depression years of the 1930s, followed by a gradual climb that accelerates to peak levels in the immediate post-World War II period, succeeded by declines into the 1950s. The first marriage rate continued its rather steady decline through the 1960s and into the 1970s; it has now reached a low level similar to that shown for the latter years of the Depression. However, both the divorce rate and the remarriage rate turned upward around 1960 and increased dramatically during the ensuing decade; by then, the divorce and remarriage rates were higher than any previously recorded for this country. The rising remarriage rate might reasonably be interpreted as a corollary of the rising divorce rate, inasmuch as an estimated four out of every five divorced persons eventually remarry (U.S. Bureau of the Census, 1976). Since 1970, however, the divorce rate has continued its steep upward movement while the remarriage rate has declined sharply.

Another measure of the rise in marital disruption was derived from a special survey on marital history conducted by the Bureau of the Census in June 1975. The assumption was made that the future divorce experience of young women will produce future increments in the percentage divorced that are the same as those for successively older cohorts of women in the early 1970s. Using this procedure, a projection was made indicating that four out of every ten marriages contracted by women born between 1945 and 1949 would eventually end in divorce, a figure substantially higher than the estimated three out of every ten for women born just a decade earlier (U.S. Bureau of the Census, 1976). However, the decrease in marriage rates and increase in divorce rates cannot continue indefinitely because the pool of divorce eligibles would eventually be used up.

Inspection of the rates in Figure 1-1 confirms the undeniable connection between the disposition of people to marry, divorce, or remarry and the contingencies of particular time periods. Apparently the Depression of the 1930s caused a downturn in all of these vital rates, whereas the period of relief and release experienced in the immediate post-World War II era gave rise to a temporary but substantial increase in all these rates. The rapid increase in the level of divorce during the 1960s came at a time when divorce laws were being liberalized and when the social structure at large was in a transitory state, a time when basic social institutions, values, and ascribed roles were being questioned and alternatives were being tested. Some have characterized the 1970s as an era of social uncertainty marked by a movement toward individualism which could be partly responsible for the continued increase of the divorce rate and the overall decline of the marriage rate.

Among the variables that have been shown to have an impact on marital stability are age at first marriage and level of education and income. Reports on several studies have demonstrated that divorce after first marriage was inversely related to age at marriage, education, and income considered separately, but without regard to interaction between these variables (Glick and Norton, 1977; U.S. Bureau of the Census,

1977c). Bumpass and Sweet (1972) reported a high correlation between early age at marriage and marital instability among white ever-married women under the age of 45. They also reported that the effect of education on marital disruption is minimal when age at marriage is controlled, but early marriage and low educational attainment are closely correlated among white women (U.S. Bureau of the Census, 1973a).

The results of the 1970 census showed that among persons who first married between 1901 and 1970, the proportion of men who were divorced after their first marriage was more than twice as high for those who married before the age of 20 as for those who married in their late 20's; it was more than twice as high for women who married before 18 as for those who first married in their early 20's (U.S. Bureau of the Census, 1973a). A substantial proportion of persons who married at a later age had delayed marriage while attending college. Among both men and women who had ever married, the highest proportion who were known to divorce after their first or last marriage (or both) was of those with an incomplete high school education (U.S. Bureau of the Census, 1972a).

Similarly, men on the lower rungs of the income ladder in 1970 had a greater proportion known to have been divorced than those with higher incomes. For females, however, the opposite was true; divorced women with a relatively high personal income level tended to delay remarriage or to remain unmarried, whereas those with relatively low incomes tended to remarry within a short time (U.S. Bureau of the Census, 1972a).

The median age at first marriage for men and women in the United States was first computed for 1890 when it was 26.1 years for men and 22.0 years for women (U.S. Bureau of the Census, 1977a). There was a fairly constant decline in the ages at which men and women married from the turn of the century to the mid-1950s. The median ages at first marriage for men and women in 1956 were the lowest recorded in the history of the United States—22.5 years for men and 20.1 for women—and remained at about the same level until the mid-1960s. Since that time, however, the median age at first marriage for both men and women has increased by approximately one year, so that in 1976 the median for men was 23.8 years and that for women 21.3 years.

The increasing tendency during the last decade for men and women to marry at later ages may reflect, in part, the demographic phenomenon referred to as the "marriage squeeze" (Parke and Glick, 1967). This phenomenon depends on the presence of two conditions: (a) a changing level of births, and (b) a traditional differential in the ages at which men and women marry for the first time. In the United States both conditions have been present. Women have traditionally married men a few years older than they are, and the birth rate in this country has been subject to fluctuations that varied from moderate to radical.

The squeeze situation in the mid-1960s arose because more women 18 and 19 years old in 1965 were entering the marriage market than were men 20 and 21 years old in that year; the women were members of large post-World War II birth cohorts, whereas the eligible or targeted men were members of smaller birth cohorts conceived before the end of the war. In addition, the scarcity of young men was intensified by the large increase in the armed forces during the war in Vietnam and the simultaneous acceleration of college enrollment.

Available data suggest that the squeeze was partially resolved by a process whereby many young women in the vanguard of the "baby boom" either postponed marriage as they moved into adulthood or ultimately married men more nearly their own age.

Thus, the marriage squeeze may have been an initial contributor to the establishment of a pattern of delaying marriage, particularly among young women, beyond ages traditionally considered the prime ages for first marriage. The extent of this delay may best be seen by pointing out that in 1960, 28 percent of women 20 to 24 years old were single, but in 1976 the corresponding proportion single had increased to 43 percent (U.S. Bureau of the Census, 1977a).

Concomitant developments associated with this delay in marriage among young adults are far-reaching. Especially among young women, postponement of marriage has occurred along with the pursuit of advanced education or career experience, as a prelude to entering into a family living situation, thus providing women with the basis for role expansion beyond that of wife and mother. Increasing postponement of first marriage has been a major aspect of the emerging pattern of transitional living arrangements among many young adults after they leave their parental homes, but before they marry conventionally and form their own families.

College enrollment of both men and women increased markedly during the sixteen years from 1960 to 1976, after being fairly stable during the 1950s. For example, 11 percent of all persons 20 to 24 years old in 1960 were enrolled in college as compared to 23 percent in 1976. For men aged 20 to 24, the enrollment rate was more than half again as large in 1976 as in 1960, and for women in their early 20's it more than doubled in those sixteen years (U.S. Bureau of the Census, 1964, 1977b). In addition, there was a sharp upturn in the labor force participation of young women over the last quarter century, a change almost entirely due to the participation rates of young married women. Among women 20 to 24 years old who were married and living with their husbands, about 26 percent were members of the labor force in 1950, as compared to 57 percent in 1975; similarly, for women 25 to 29 years old of the same marital status the comparable increase was from 22 percent in 1950 to 50 percent in 1975.

relatively small because this measure disregards the fact that about three-fourths of the women and five-sixths of the men remarry after divorce. Furthermore, the 1970 census shows that 3.8 percent of all ever-married men and 5.0 percent of all ever-married women were currently divorced at the time of the census, but that more than 14 percent of both the men and the women were known to have obtained a divorce. This means that only a small proportion of the adults who had ever experienced a divorce were still divorced at the time of the 1970 census. Nonetheless, revealing comparisons showing the convergence of divorce by social level between 1960 and 1970 can be made by the use of proportions of persons currently divorced.

Between these two dates the proportion divorced among men 35 to 44 years old tended to converge among the educational, occupational, and income groups. As mentioned above, men in the upper status groups continue to have a below average proportion divorced (but not re-married). However, the rate of increase in the proportion divorced was more rapid among men in upper as compared to lower status groups between 1960 and 1970 (U.S. Bureau of the Census, 1967, 1972a). These results become even more meaningful when one recognizes that the extent of remarriage among the divorced is greater for men at the upper status levels than for men at the lower levels.

Among women 35 to 44 a general trend toward convergence among status levels of the proportion divorced also occurred between 1960 and 1970, but in the opposite direction from that for men. The proportion divorced among all women 35 to 44 went up by nearly one-half during the 1960s; however, among women who were professional workers or who were in the highest income categories (where the proportion divorced for women, unlike men, has been characteristically quite high), the percentage divorced rose by a smaller proportion than among other women. Thus, for upper status women the percentage divorced was converging with that for other women by increasing more slowly than the average, whereas for upper status men the percentage divorced was converging with that for other men by increasing more rapidly than the average.

Data from the June 1975 marital history survey indicate that the trend toward convergence in the proportion divorced among different levels of educational achievement for both men and women has continued through the first half of this decade (U.S. Bureau of the Census, 1977c). In fact, by 1975 the proportion divorced for men with one or more years of college had risen to the level for all other men. However, men and women with four years of college still had the lowest proportions divorced.

The important conclusion that can be drawn from these trends is that the recent increase in divorce has been pervasive with regard to social and economic level, but that socioeconomic differences in divorce are now smaller than they used to be.

Although blacks and whites display generally similar patterns of divorce by social and economic characteristics, the incidence of divorce is uniformly higher for blacks than for whites. In 1975, 25 percent of ever-married black men and women 35 to 44 years old were known to have had a divorce. The comparable figures for white men and women in 1975 were 19 percent and 21 percent, respectively.

A further indication of the higher rate of marital disruption among blacks than among whites is the difference in the proportions of people reporting themselves as separated but not divorced. In 1976, 10 percent of all black men 35 to 44 and 15 percent of all black women 35 to 44 were reported as separated, whereas 2 percent of white men and 4 percent of white women of the same age were separated. Between 1960 and 1976, the proportion separated and the proportion divorced increased among both black and white men and women 35 to 44 years old; however, the rate of increase for each race and sex group was larger for the proportion divorced (Glick and Mills, 1975; U.S. Bureau of the Census, 1977a). This finding brings out the significant fact that decreasing proportions of those with marital problems are leaving them legally unresolved and increasing proportions are resolving them by becoming divorced.

Despite an increasing similarity in the form of marital disruption displayed by the two racial groups, major differences continue to exist. These differences seem to be linked with both the overall level of disruption and the promptness with which divorce and remarriage follow separation. Findings from the 1975 marital history survey showed that although whites and blacks had similar durations of first marriage before divorce, white men and women remarried much sooner than their black counterparts (U.S. Bureau of the Census, 1976). But even though blacks have a generally higher rate of disruption through marital discord than whites, the estimated rates of disruption for those with racial intermarriages is even greater. Using data from the 1960 and 1970 censuses, Heer (1974) reported "clearly the black-white marriages are shown to be less stable than racially homogeneous marriages."

Another characteristic reflecting recent changes in divorce is the presence of children among couples involved in a divorce. The U.S. National Center for Health Statistics (1977c) reports that an estimated 1,123,000 children were involved in divorces and annulments in 1975, an average of 1.08 children per decree. Although the estimated number of children involved in all divorces has been increasing steadily (logically enough, given the overall increase in divorce), the average per decree has been declining in recent years; in 1964 the average reached a peak of 1.36 children per decree. Perhaps the main reason for the decline is the recent decrease in the birth rate. Other reasons include a slight increase in the proportion childless at divorce, although six out of ten divorces in 1975 were among couples who had children and the estimated interval between marriage and divorce decreased from 7.2 years in 1960 to 7.0 years in 1968, and to 6.5 years in 1975. The estimate of the percentage of divorcing couples who were childless was published by the U.S. National Center for Health Statistics on the basis of data reported for the divorce-registration area (DRA) which in 1975 was composed of 29 participating states, each of which used closely conforming certificates of divorce or annulment and cooperated in testing for completeness and accuracy of divorce registration.

The recently declining fertility rate may have contributed to the rise in the divorce rate. Women with small families are more likely to be in the labor force and, therefore, financially independent of their husbands. And as family size has declined, the proportion of children in the family who are of preschool age has declined. This additional development has tended to free the time of the potential divorcee for work outside the home.

Among other factors which may have influenced the recent rise in divorce are an increase in premarital conceptions and the so-called "incentives" toward family disruption found in the present welfare system. As Davis (1972) points out, premarital conception is conducive to divorce, and an increase in family formation in such circumstances tends to increase the divorce rate. The impact of the welfare system on family and marital disruption is open to debate. Various social scientists have studied this problem and have arrived at conflicting or opposing conclusions (Cutright and Scanzoni, 1973; Honig, 1973; see also Moles, chapter 10).

Other possible contributors to the rising level of divorce include the prevalence of intergenerational divorce, the effects of intergenerational mobility up and down the socioeconomic ladder, and the problems faced by veterans returning from the war in Vietnam. The returnees are of special interest because they came back from an unpopular war and were sometimes made to feel that they personified the official war policy. This atmosphere must have affected their ability to adjust to traditional life styles.

Since divorcing has always been largely confined to relatively young adults, the lifetime behavior of persons born during the high fertility years that spanned the period between 1947 and the early 1960s will be of major import in this context. As we have pointed out," the experience of this population subgroup—largely because of its size—is different from that of any other in the age spectrum. During their lives they have faced, and will continue to face, greater competition for fewer opportunities than their predecessors did or their successors will. They are finding that traditional institutions have not been able to respond effectively to their needs, and their patterns of action have begun to deviate in certain ways from past norms" (Norton and Glick, 1976). Thus, it is clear that their decisions involving marriage, divorce, and living arrangements will have a profound and lasting impact on future lifestyles. As the vanguard of this group has reached adulthood, patterns of change have already become evident. Along with a postponement of first marriage has been an increased tendency to leave parental homes in favor of setting up nonfamily households either as lone individuals or as sharing partners. The latter group includes the often-discussed "living together" couples who have more than doubled in number since 1970 (Glick and Norton, 1977). Whether these developments represent a prelude to entering into more traditionally conventional family living arrangements or herald the beginnings of a new concept of family living is not clear.

Conclusions and Future Perspectives

The variables influencing the marriage and divorce behavior of people in this country are numerous and tend to interact with one another. In general, socioeconomic variables such as education and income which have been regarded as predictor variables have become less discriminating.

Youthful marriage has been found to correlate with a high divorce rate: there is an approximately two-year younger average age at first marriage among those who obtain a divorce before middle age than those whose first marriages remain intact to this age (U.S. Bureau of the Census, 1973a). However, one can only speculate about the future level of age at marriage and its continued usefulness as a short-term predictor of marital stability or instability.

There seems little doubt that a basic transformation of the institution of marriage is underway and that many variables are influencing the direction of the change. This transformation appears to be predicated largely on a restructuring of the roles which men and women play within the traditional boundaries of marriage and family living. Some people can confront this type of change and adapt to it without much difficulty; others find that the process of adjustment is much more difficult and leads ultimately to marital conflict and disruption. Fundamental to the understanding of this change is a comprehension of the redefinition of expectations of individuals involved in a modern marriage.

"More personal fulfillment in marriage," a common current demand, is an elusive idea which can take many forms depending on the individuals involved. It is possible that one of the problems encountered by marriage partners is that many men and women have inadequately defined the happiness they are seeking. This is not an unusual situation in a period of transition. New ideas and values can only gradually replace old or traditional ones. Thus, eventual general recognition and acceptance of a newly established set of rules for marriage may cause expectations to conform to "real-world" conditions. Viewed in this manner, the high rate of divorce can be interpreted as an understandable pursuit of happiness. This does not necessarily mean that people are marrying and subsequently divorcing without care or concern, but rather that there exists a new awareness that a marriage which is subjectively viewed as not viable can be dissolved and—hopefully—replaced by a more nearly viable one. The means to introduce alternatives are ever so much more widely available today than they were 20 years ago. As Davis (1972) puts it, current marriage "is not premised on the condition that wedlock is rigidly determined for the rest of life."

To the extent that the married state—but not necessarily being married only once—is a preferred status, some available indicators may portend a relatively optimistic future for married life. The high divorce rate coupled with a high remarriage rate appears to signal a strong desire for a compatible marriage and family life. In support of this line of reasoning, findings from two separate studies conducted by the Institute for Social Research of the University of Michigan (ISR, 1974) on subjective social indicators (studies of people's perceptions of the quality of life) showed that "marriage and family life are the most satisfying parts of most people's lives and being married is one of the most important determinants of being satisfied with life." Thus, there appears to be a generally high regard for the ideal of being married and living as a family member, but a current inability on the part of growing numbers of couples to achieve and sustain a high level of satisfaction in this sphere without making at least a second attempt.

One might hypothesize that the recent trends away from early age at marriage and the decline in the remarriage rate are indicative of more careful mate selection among those marrying for the first time, as well as among those marrying for a second or subsequent time. Perhaps more persons considering marriage now are influenced by the large number of current marital failures and consequently are making their own decisions in a more serious and cautious manner. At the same time, however, others may be postponing divorce because of the presently uncertain national economic situation. As previously stated, both marriage and divorce behavior appear to be sensitive to major political and economic events. The practical financial constraints imposed by an economy troubled by inflation and recession, coupled with a high unemployment rate, may force individuals contemplating divorce to rethink their positions and possibly to make marital adjustments based on more tolerance of the status quo between themselves and their partners for a longer time, if not permanently.

Speculations regarding the future of marriage and divorce in this country are tenuous; nonetheless, the authors have called attention to those factors which seem likely to have an impact on marital behavior over the next several years. Additional observations of marital behavior from year to year will surely provide the students of marriage and the family with better explanations of the current situation than anyone can give with confidence today.

A Historical Perspective on Husband-Wife Bargaining Power and Marital Dissolution

This chapter works toward a theoretical explanation for divorce that is historically valid and which might also apply to Western nations besides the United States. Its conceptual approach, to be called reward-cost theory here, has its roots in perspectives that in recent years have gained attention under labels such as exchange, conflict, or equity theory (see also Levinger, chapter 3; Hill et al., chapter 4; and Jaffe and Kanter, chapter 7).

Reward-cost theory assumes that persons (Actors) have goals that bring them into interdependence with others. At times, the interdependence exists in the form of "peaceful exchange," in which both the Actor and the Other perceive their association to be fair and just; each believing that he or she is receiving the benefits they *should* receive *relative* to their input in the relationship. At other times, the interdependence is better characterized as a "regulated conflict," or a situation where, by virtue of greater power, the Actor is able to impose a reward-cost ratio that the Other deems unjust.

An additional element in sociological approaches to reward-cost theory is the larger social network or context of the association. For instance, married persons generally have relationships outside their marriage. The significance of external associations is manifold, but here I shall mention only two. First, they are potential sources of benefits and costs alternative to those derived from the spouse. Second, the wider network helps shape, define, and reinforce definitions of what is just or fair. Thus, partners to an association such as marriage do not alone define what is equitable.

Instead "prevailing social norms" (Blau, 1964) play a definite part in that process.

These comments provide a springboard to the discussion that follows. The discussion itself will serve to elaborate and illustrate the ramifications of this theoretical perspective for the marital relationship.

First, I examine the seventeenth century roots of present attitudes toward divorce, and then the emergence of divorce patterns in Colonial America. From there I trace the dynamics of wife-husband bargaining power until the present. My aim is to show how shifts in their respective bargaining stances have been related to changes in divorce patterns.

Divorce in Seventeenth Century Europe

Marriage and divorce are arrangements that grow out of wider social contexts. Prior to the sixteenth century Reformation, marriage throughout Europe was a sacrament that fell under the jurisdiction of ecclesiastical rather than civil courts (Mollenkott, 1977). Divorce was granted by Roman Catholic courts for only three reasons: adultery, cruelty, or heresy. Moreover, remarriage was not permitted for either spouse.

Subsequent to the Reformation on the Continent, the Calvinist and Lutheran churches redefined marriage as nonsacramental. It then fell under the control of civil courts. Adultery and desertion became grounds for secular legal divorce, and remarriage was permitted—but solely for "innocent" or "wronged" parties. In England, however, the Reformation did not place the control of marriage into the hands of civil authorities; the Anglican Church retained its ancient prerogatives, refusing to allow desertion as a ground for divorce and prohibiting remarriage.

In the seventeenth century, John Milton set out to bring Anglican Church doctrine into line with that of the Continental Protestant Church. Indeed, he went even further than they, actually laying the groundwork for what would one day be a widely recognized justification for dissolving marriages: he argued, first, that incompatibility was by itself a proper ground for divorce; and second, that divorce should be a "private matter" (Mollenkott, 1977; Farber, 1967). The first of Milton's four essays on divorce was published in 1643, just after Parliament had passed a resolution asking the governing body of the Anglican Church to revise various aspects of ecclesiastical law. Although Milton aimed to influence the Church to moderate its divorce posture, the radical character of his proposals had precisely the opposite effect (Mollenkott, 1977).

The conservative divines of the Westminster Assembly reacted very negatively to the ideas set forth in his essays and pulled back from whatever inclinations they had had to "Europeanize" English divorce laws.

Divorce in Colonial America

The contrasting social norms of Continental and English Protestantism appear to have carried over into early American divorce patterns, as detailed by Cott (1976). Since the Puritans were Calvinists, they held that marriage was a *civil contract* which could be dissolved by *secular authorities* for reasons of adultery, desertion, or cruelty (p. 589). Cott reports that, while divorce records from the seventeenth century are "probably incomplete," there is evidence that even by then the civil authorities had already granted some divorces. But though the Massachusetts colony was Puritan-dominated, it did after all remain a creature of Parliament and King, and therefore of the English Church.

Thus Massachusetts, along with some other colonies, Cott says, found itself in conflict with the Crown over the enactment and execution of divorce laws. In 1773, King George ordered "all royal governors to withhold consent from any divorce act passed by a colonial legislature" (p. 591). Unlike several of its sister colonies, however, Massachusetts had based its customs regulating divorce less on formal legislative acts, easily reversible by the King, than on informal powers simply assumed by the Governor and his Council. Such powers, in their very informality, were difficult for the Crown to contravene. As a result, while the King's edict "halted divorce in the Colonies other than Massachusetts until the Revolution, . . . in that province both petitions for and grants of divorce continued to multiply" (Cott, p. 591).

The multiplication to which Cott refers, to be sure, starts from a very small base. Through almost the entire eighteenth century (1692–1786), only 122 wives and 101 husbands filed 229 divorce petitions in Massachusetts (6 wives petitioned twice). Despite the modesty of those numbers, the *rate* of divorce did increase substantially toward the end of this era. More than half the petitions occurred after 1764, and more than a third between 1774 and 1786. To explain this increase, Cott suggests that there was a "modernization of attitudes," which she defines as "individuals . . . asserting control over the direction of their lives and . . . refusing to be ruled by unhappy fates . . ." (p. 593).

In other words, what Milton had sought to promulgate as revised theology begins here to find expression through a secular consciousness. His idea that neither ecclesiastical nor civil law should hinder the individual's well-being in matters of divorce and (re)marriage was apparently finding some acceptance throughout Britain and America. Therefore, as Cott says, while the norm of individual well-being sought for by Milton by no means prevailed in eighteenth century Massachusetts, it had at least begun to permeate the decision making of some wives and husbands. Perhaps for the first time since the days of liberal divorce laws of ancient Rome, ordinary citizens began to consider it legitimate to exit from marriages in which they judged their reward-cost ratio to be unfavorable. Subsequently, "the more divorces were allowed, the more likely it became for a discontented spouse to consider the possibility. . . . News of divorces being obtained must have encouraged more men and women to petition" (Cott, p. 593). Thus divorce actions increasingly became justified by earlier divorce actions, at the same time becoming further legitimated as the norm of individual well-being was more accepted.

In spite of evolutionary "modernization" of the norms governing marriage and divorce, the difference in social status between men and women continued to greatly favor men and their interests. This was true for those men who wanted to maintain their marriage, as well as for those who might want to dissolve it. Whatever restraints prevented eighteenth century men from petitioning for divorce, they applied doubly to women. "Male domination of colonial public life suggests . . . that men were less shy of the authorities than were women, better able to stand adverse publicity about their marriages without risking their entire reputation, significantly more independent economically, and better equipped than women to pay legal expenses. A man could also take the initiative in acquiring a second spouse" (Cott, p. 594). More generally, men had access to more resources than did women—and to the *power* that resources "buy" (Heath, 1976). Husbands, in other words, were in a far better bargaining position than their wives.

As a practical example of male advantage, Cott reports that half or more of the female population in Massachusetts were illiterate, "compared to [only] 10 to 20 percent of the male population. But significantly, almost 75 percent of the female divorce petitioners could sign their names" (p. 595). In short, literacy seemed very much to be a factor in enabling or "causing" some women to petition for divorce. Very likely there were numerous other women who were equally dissatisfied with their marriages but who, because they were illiterate, possessed neither the skills nor the courage to petition for divorce. In other words, female petitions for divorce might have been greatly increased had more women of the eighteenth century been able to read and write.

It seems safe to say, then, that the reported incidence of divorce tells only part of the story. There probably existed a far higher incidence of marital dissatisfaction (or unfavorable reward-cost ratios) than shown by the records of divorce petitions.

WOMEN'S DISSATISFACTIONS

Moreover, there is some ground for believing that more women than men were dissatisfied with their marriages. Men made the laws and possessed more power and privileges; they were the dominant group. Women were the subordinate group. Since men controlled the conditions of marriage, they were more likely to structure it to their own satisfaction. Women, on the other hand, having relatively less control over the conditions of marriage, were less able to satisfy their wishes in the marriage relationship. Naturally, means to assess differences in men's and women's marital satisfaction in the eighteenth century are not readily available. However, Lantz (1976) has presented material from which certain reasonable inferences can be made. He examined eighteenth century colonial newspapers for advertisements "renouncing debts or announcing desertion on the part of a husband or wife" (1976, p. 12). The relatively high incidence of such ads during the pre-industrial era provides evidence for a great deal more marital dissatisfaction and "incompatibility" than had previously been imagined. Furthermore, Lantz reports that "in all states throughout the entire century it was the husband [in more than 95 percent of the cases] who was responsible for placing the ad, not the wife. . . . There is little evidence to show that men abandoned their wives. . . . The reverse . . . is true. It was the husband who stated that his wife had left him. . . . This picture of female discontent in the home is certainly at variance with the [usual] picture of [contented] early American women. Indeed, such behavior on the part of women suggests an assertiveness that has not been recognized and possibly has been underestimated" (p. 16).

It is also possible that many husbands may likewise have deserted their wives but that the wives did not bother to advertise the fact. Since women were apparently not legally bound by their husband's debts, they would have been less motivated to advertise his departure. Consider also the high illiteracy rate among women. In addition, persons of either sex may, for various reasons, often have failed to advertise desertion.

While we cannot be certain about the pervasiveness of desertion, the mere evidence for it is instructive. It seems that prior to 1800, both in America and in Europe, desertion of one's spouse was a real option open to members of either sex. Thus despite the fact that prevailing norms and laws prohibited marital dissolution, the same kinds of social processes that have come to account for legal dissolution may, historically, have also accounted for nonlegal dissolution. Women may have deserted because, say, their husbands beat them; husbands, on the other hand, may have deserted because they were unable, or unwilling, to provide for their usually large families in the face of the wives' demands to do so. These demands were, of course, backed by community norms making the husband's financial support a sacred duty.

Desertion being a practical recourse, stringent divorce laws may historically have been as ineffectual in assuring marital stability as Rheinstein (1972) claims they are in modern times. I am not suggesting that marital dissolution was as common prior to modern times as it is today—if only because women in general lacked the alternative economic and social resources that would permit them to obtain rewards outside of marriage. Even if a marriage was punishing, the alternative open to women may have seemed worse or at best uncertain. But beyond this, compared to the present, pre-modern women on the whole lacked the impetus to individual, autonomous action. Though the idea of female autonomy had been enunciated as far back as Milton, it took nineteenth and twentieth century feminism to legitimate that idea and make it more widely accepted. (This point is again discussed later in the chapter.)

To the degree that eighteenth century women actually resorted to desertion, one reason they may have done so was the virtual impossibility of a woman's obtaining a divorce even if her spouse committed adultery. No Massachusetts woman petitioned for divorce by reason of adultery before 1773. "Unless we assume that husbands displayed much more virtue than wives, the difference [in adultery petitions] suggests a deeply entrenched double standard of marital fidelity. . . . Women did not expect to obtain divorce for that reason alone and so did not petition" (Cott, 1976, p. 601). Unable to end their marriages by divorce on that ground (or on others, including cruelty), they simply opted to desert. The relative sex differences in the ability to divorce can be seen from the following comparisons. Throughout the entire century, 68 percent of male petitioners were successful in obtaining dissolutions, as compared with 58 percent of women (p. 596); more significantly, 67 percent of successful husbands also "gained freedom to remarry, in contrast to only 45 percent of the wives" (p. 596).

The last quarter of the eighteenth century, however, saw women successfully petitioning for divorce on the grounds of adultery (p. 605). Indeed, more women than men began to petition for divorce on all grounds. Cott argues that the new willingness of male officials to respond to women's grievances was not out of repugnance for the sexual double standard, but was politically motivated. Leaders of the infant republic felt that the "sexual vices" of the English had led to their general "corruption," and that America must avoid that fate by insisting on the letter of Puritan morality, that is, sexual fidelity by *both* partners (p. 606).

Marriage Types and Bargaining Power

OWNER-PROPERTY

Elsewhere, I have called marriage arrangements similar to those described by Cott as the *owner-property* type of marriage (Scanzoni, 1972; Scanzoni and Scanzoni, 1976). In this kind of marriage, aside from the requirement that the woman be kept alive, she had virtually no formal rights. By law and by powerful custom she was the property of her owner-husband. Now, to change an owner-property relationship in marriage so that it becomes less costly and more rewarding requires a certain degree of bargaining power. The Actor's power to alter the situation depends on certain sets of "resources" or valued rewards that the Other wants. Prior to the advent of the factory system, a married woman had few resources that she controlled independently of her husband. Although she worked side by side with him on the farm or in a small shop, whatever meager capital was generated by their joint efforts legally belonged to the husband, not to the wife. Even though he would have had great difficulty subsisting alone, there was no way she could gain, or even share, formal control of their resources in order to achieve her own goals.

Even so, wives were not completely without resources. If they were healthy, their physical strength was a resource. They were valued workers for their husbands. Rubin and Brown (1975) define bargaining or negotiation as a process of give and take where each party gets something, but not everything, he or she originally wanted. Fox (1974) uses the term *spontaneous consensus* to describe situations where no bargaining takes place: parties simply come to the already existing "fully structured" arrangements and conform to them (Brickman, 1974). No doubt the majority of eighteenth century married women conformed to the prevailing "spontaneous consensus" surrounding the owner-property arrangement. They did not negotiate to remove perceived injustices.

Nonetheless, the fact that women did have at least some resources, especially that of a "valued worker," makes it reasonable to suppose that certain limited kinds of negotiations did take place. Women may have bargained about how the shop or farm should be run, about the children, or about their own and their husbands' nonwork activities (church involvement, for instance, or drinking and gambling) when there was time for such activities. The fact that some couples divorced or that some mates deserted, and that others suffered from low marital satisfaction means that bargaining deadlocks were not unheard of. For some people the only way to end their deadlocks was to dissolve their association. Others endured it because they had no viable alternative.

Therefore, even during the eighteenth century we may postulate, albeit in embryonic form, the essential elements of a model of marital stability/instability centered in negotiation over desired goals, based on the possession of valued resources, and set within a larger context of prevailing norms. Norms govern, among other things, how tough a bargainer one should be: a tough bargainer makes high demands and grants few concessions while a soft one makes low demands and grants many concessions. The degree of toughness or softness is one bargaining element that is strongly influenced by interested third parties.

The eighteenth century woman, if she bargained at all, was, in general, socially constrained to be soft and consequently achieved little. Nevertheless, as in any intimate relationship, a certain amount of marital negotiations did exist during the eighteenth century, even though most women were distinctly disadvantaged. The history of marriage and divorce patterns since that time is, in essence, the history of alterations in the bargaining positions within that relationship.

HEAD-COMPLEMENT

The nineteenth century witnessed the emergence of a second type of marriage and the gradual eclipse of the owner-property type. As early as 1792, Wollstonecraft argued that the wife of her day was being "defrauded of her just rewards; for the wages due to her are the caresses of her husband" (cited in Scanzoni and Scanzoni, 1976, p. 208). Cott cites several historical sources to show that, during the late eighteenth and early nineteenth centuries, prevailing norms were changing regarding wives' rights to receive emotional gratification from husbands and, concomitantly, wives' obligations to provide the same to their husbands. Perhaps for the first time in history, "friendship, complementarity, and emotional bonds" (Cott, 1976, p. 613) were factors that entered significantly into husband-wife bargaining processes. Wives who played a complementary role in marriage could hold expectations for men that had been precluded by the owner-property type of relationship.

By the same token, husbands could begin to expect expressive rewards from their wives, which went beyond the sexual gratification that men had always expected. For instance, Gadlin (1977, pp. 18–19) points out that the early and mid-nineteenth century witnessed "the burgeoning of a whole popular literature addressing itself" to the question of "how to" get more expressive rewards. However, that literature made sharp distinctions between friendship and companionship as desirable marital benefits, and sex, which was considered suspect in the Victorian fashion (Gadlin, 1977).

As *head*, the man continued to hold greater power over the instrumental dimension of marriage, including economic production and decisions affecting the social status and overall well-being of the family. In that realm there remained the clear-cut "spontaneous consensus" that had always existed. As *complement*, the woman's "submission" was evidence of her "feminine virtue" (Welter, 1966, p. 160).

Nevertheless, the following description of head-complement roles indicates that the complement's bargaining power exceeded that of the property-type: "The man [is] all truth, the woman all tenderness . . . , acknowledging his superior judgment she complies with his reasonable desires, whilst he, charmed with such repeated instances of superior love, endeavors to suit his requests to her inclinations" (Cott, 1976, p. 614).

Notice that his "desires" (requests) are assumed to be "reasonable," and moreover that he makes requests that "fit" her inclinations (goals). The bald coercion of the owner-property relationship becomes replaced by a consensus arrangement in which the husband is supposed to bargain in such a way as to respect the wife's interests. The wife now has at her disposal a potent resource—her "love"—which enables her to gain certain ends. As a result, the wife's bargaining "power" increases. She now holds the expressive rewards that her husband wants, while she also expects *both* economic support *and* expressive benefits in return.

Simultaneously, prevailing norms were shifting throughout the nineteenth century and into the twentieth, permitting the wife to be a somewhat "tougher" bargainer than she was as mere property. The validity of her toughness lay in the growing legitimacy of using divorce as the ultimate bargaining threat. In effect, the wife had an increasingly legitimate alternative to unsatisfactory marriage. Furthermore, the alternative became open to her not solely because of his adultery or cruelty— he may have been guilty of neither. It was also available (à la Milton) if he failed to supply enough of either set of expected rewards, or if she thought his demands on her were "unreasonable."

Cott observed that by the late eighteenth century women were becoming more likely than men to petition for divorce (p. 613). Starting from that era and extending throughout the nineteenth century that pattern accelerated. By 1870, 65 percent of all divorces (in the United States) were granted to the wife (USDHEW, 1973, p. 50). By 1916, that figure was 67 percent; in 1950, 72 percent; in 1965, 73 percent (Norton and Glick, chapter 1).

The long-term increases in women *formally* leaving costly situations that in prior decades and centuries they had merely endured (or fled from informally) can be readily seen by these comparisons. In 1867 there were 10,000 reported divorces in the United States, a rate of 0.3 divorces per 1,000 persons. One hundred nine years later (in 1976), the number of divorces stood at 1,077,000 and the rate had increased to 5.0 per 1,000 persons (USDHEW, 1977a).

Transition to the Contemporary Scene

A recent study suggests that the head-complement arrangement, which, throughout the twentieth century has been the most common form of marriage, still retains its predominance (Scanzoni, 1978). However, at least two other contemporary marital structures can also be identified. And while the model of bargaining power and its implications for marital stability remain basically the same in these newer forms, they nonetheless display significant differences. These two newer forms have their roots both in nineteenth century feminism and in the factory system which emerged during that era. In a very real sense feminism provided what Max Weber (Bendix, 1962, pp. 44–48) called *ideal* interests, or values and goals; the factory system supplied *material* interests, or the economic resources to enable women to achieve their goals. The historical convergence of the ideal and the material has had profound impacts for women's bargaining power and thus, ultimately, for patterns of marital stability or instability.

SENIOR PARTNER—JUNIOR PARTNER

Let us examine wives' bargaining power and marital stability within one of the two newer marriage arrangements—that in which the wife is now *junior partner* to her husband. In this arrangement, the expressive dimension remains substantially the same. Each expects the other to be companion and friend. (In recent years high levels of sexual gratification have been added to the expressive component.)

The major contrast between the head-complement and the junior-partner relationship lies in the wife's independent access to the developing factory and business system. That sector provided wives with power that historically few women had ever enjoyed, a power based on the production of economic resources independent of the husband. This new situation stood in contrast to farms or small shops where men controlled capital though wives helped earn it.

At the beginning of the twentieth century only 5 percent of married women had some earnings (Cain, 1966). By 1975 the figure was 51 percent of women living with their husbands (U.S. Bureau of the Census, 1977e, p. 116). This century, therefore, has seen the rapid evolution of the marital arrangement in which the wife participates in the paid labor force. For many decades, census data have shown that the lower their husbands' income the more likely wives are to work; furthermore, low husband income results in wives' being less economically satisfied (Scanzoni and Scanzoni, 1976). Hence, their major motivation for working is to help supplement husbands' earnings. Also, the lower their husbands' earnings, the less satisfied wives are with their marriage or its expressive rewards (Scanzoni, 1975a). It should, therefore, come as no surprise that male earnings are positively related to the likelihood of marital stability, and that because of economic discrimination marital dissolution is more frequent among blacks than whites (U.S. Bureau of the Census, 1977c; see also Cherlin, chapter 9).

In short, the wife in the junior-partner marriage, as compared to the one in the complement marriage, bargains with her husband from a position of relative strength. Her bargaining power, including the ultimate threat of breaking the relationship, is not inconsiderable since she has the option to support herself. Furthermore, she often bargains with a man who supplies relatively less of the two major gratifications (economic and expressive) that are his "duty" to provide her. An additional variable that contributes to lower marital satisfaction, and also to higher dissatisfaction with the husband's income, is the number of children in the household. In the past, numbers and ages of children imposed negative constraints on the likelihood of women's employment, thus weakening their bargaining power. Recent census information suggests that numbers and ages of children are less likely than ever before to keep women out of the paid labor force (Hayghe, 1975).

Census data have, for many years, revealed that divorced and separated women are more likely to be working than are married women living with their husbands. But it has been difficult to know whether their working itself causes dissolution, or whether marital dissolution forces women to work. On the basis of their recent investigation, Ross and Sawhill (1975) conclude that the former causal sequence has greater validity: "new economic opportunities for women are one explanation for rising divorce rates" (p. 62). Another study finds that women who were more inclined to egalitarianism as to gender or sex roles in 1971 were likely to work a greater number of months between 1971 and 1975 (Scanzoni, 1978). Furthermore, women who became divorced or separated by 1975 had also been more role egalitarian and were more likely to have worked in 1971. In short, it may be that some egalitarian women are both more likely to work and also to be at greater risk of marital disruption.

In sum, compared to the complement type of marriage, the junior-partner marriage is more prone to experience separation or divorce. And since the number of junior-partner marriages has increased rapidly in recent years, it is not surprising that divorce rates have risen correspondingly. In Levinger's (1965) terms, their internal situation is relatively less satisfying (lower levels of economic and expressive rewards), and the external situation is relatively more satisfying (her alternative occupational resources). Therefore, if her spouse cannot or will not negotiate an equitable arrangement, her potential threat of dissolving their marriage often becomes a reality.

EQUAL-PARTNER

With the revival of feminism, in a form much broader in scope and more intense in the pursuit of its goals, there has emerged a fourth marriage form that has been called the *dual-career* marriage (Fogarty, Rapoport, and Rapoport, 1971) or the *co-provider* arrangement (Scanzoni, 1972). A recent study found that slightly more than half of working wives in a regional household sample of younger married white women (aged 22–33) were classified as dual-providers along with their husbands (Scanzoni, 1978). Those particular women considered it just as much their own duty as their husbands' to provide for the family. This role interchangeability is a major feature that distinguishes the *equal* from the junior-partner wife. The latter defines her husband as the chief provider, and she is thus more likely to transfer in and out of the labor force in response to any variety of domestic contingencies. Recent data show that over a period of years the equal-partner wife remains much more consistently involved in the labor force, and consequently earns significantly more money than the junior-partner wife (Scanzoni, 1978); the latter are also significantly less inclined toward sex role equality than the former.

Because of her higher income, the equal-partner has greater bargaining power than the junior-partner. But even more important, the unique feature of this marriage form is that *nothing is non-negotiable*. Unlike in other marriage forms where certain things remain prearranged, all issues are open to bargaining. There is nothing that is *not* open to question, whether it pertains to occupational involvement, sexual exclusivity, and so on. The husband does not come to the situation knowing *a priori* that his occupational interests will remain pre-eminent, or that the couple will have children, or that the wife will be primarily responsible for child care or for the household, or that she will live with him during the week instead of commuting home on weekends.

Because the equal-partner possesses a high degree of individualism that predisposes her to bargain very strongly on behalf of her own interests (Scanzoni, 1978), because her income disadvantage is narrower) some wives earn as much or more than their husbands), and finally because she no longer recognizes any fixed rights or inherent authority which he can plead, the potential for marital dissolution may be quite high. In view of recent evidence showing general increases in the levels of sex role egalitarianism, or individualism (Mason, Czajka, and Arber, 1976), it is likely that part of the sharp increase in divorce rates over the past 15 years can be attributed to the development of the equal-partner marriage. Therefore, the *general* model that accounts for marital stability/ instability is the same as that examined in connection with the three prior types. But there are radical differences in the substantive content between this one and the others. All four are in a very real sense variations on a theme, but the equal-partner type is also pushing beyond that traditional theme. It is also the beginning of a very different marital and familial life style.

Moreover, it is likely that such marriages will increase steadily. One indication is that increasing numbers of women are getting more schooling, including college (U.S. Bureau of Census, 1977d), which is positively associated with sex role modernity or individualism (Scanzoni, 1975b). Between 1960 and 1970 there has been a substantial increase in the proportion of highly educated (beyond four years of college) women who have experienced marital disruption (Houseknecht and Spanier, 1978).

Individual versus Social Interests

Focus on the emerging equal-partner form of marriage, and on its potential for marital disruption, raises the question of whether or not this form has a negative impact on society. Interestingly, the general issue of whether changes in marital roles have negative or positive societal consequences has been with us for a hundred years. Throughout the late nineteenth and early twentieth centuries as divorces increased substantially, and women more frequently initiated them, those whom O'Neill (1973) calls "divorce-conservatives" (both men and women) publicly protested that those changes represented a decay that would ultimately lead to the downfall of American civilization. "Most conservatives recognized that divorce stemmed, at least in part, from the altered temper of American womanhood" (O'Neill, 1973, p. 62). Feminists came under particular attack for their vigorous advocacy of the right of divorce. In one such attack, it was charged that feminists did not appreciate that "the victims of unhappy marriages could not be allowed divorces, because permanent marriage was not only the one institution which distinguished man from the beasts but the very foundation of civilization. . . . If marriage was to be saved, young women must understand that men were instinctively promiscuous and their lapses from grace were no excuse for divorce. Indeed, male weaknesses offered women splendid opportunities for spiritual growth through suffering" (O'Neill, 1973, pp. 70–71). Feminism was also attacked because "it encouraged women to compete economically with men [thus undermining their duty to be subordinate to their husbands] although women lacked the equipment to succeed in such a struggle" (pp. 76–77).

Those inegalitarian perspectives were certainly at odds "with the liberal ideas beginning to emerge at the end of the nineteenth century. It was hard to argue that women should be freer, moral judgments more humane, and happiness a goal to be pursued, while at the same time denying relief to the maritally oppressed" (p. 69). But perhaps the major issue that troubled the "conservatives" is the same kind of question raised by contemporary manifestations of women's rights and their uncertain impact on the future of the family *qua* institution. "Emancipated women [have] an imperfect sense of social responsibility. They selfishly obtain divorces without regard for the common welfare. . . ." (p. 73). The "conservatives" issued a call for the "suppression of the individual in favor of the community" (p. 74). In condemning divorce, Felix Adler is quoted as accusing Rousseau of being "the individualistic villain who had propagated 'false democratic ideals' at the expense of social order" (p. 74).

Adler's position is reiterated today by many who fear that as women press for their own interests, family and social order will suffer. As women get more education they become more egalitarian. As they become more egalitarian they become tougher bargainers. Their education also gives them access to a wide range of rewards alternative to those supplied by husbands. If these trends continue, to what heights might we expect divorce rates to climb?

The first response to that question is to recall O'Neill's (1973) arguments to the effect that divorce *per se* does not undermine family. Instead, divorce may be thought of as a "safety-valve," apart from which the institution might indeed undergo convulsive spasms. In short, divorce is merely a symptom and not the fundamental issue. Furthermore, were there no formal exit from marriage, we could expect heavy use of the kinds of informal exits employed historically, such as desertion.

A second response is that in spite of those intertwining trends (education, gender roles, tougher female bargaining) recent government data reveal that "the rate of [divorce] increase [has] tapered off in the early seventies. The increase in divorces for 1974 to 1975 was 4.3 percent, the smallest annual increase since 1967" (USDHEW, 1976, p. 13). The increase in divorces from 1975 to 1976 was an even smaller 4 percent (USDHEW, 1977a). And, compared with the first eight months of 1976, January through August of 1977 registered an increase in divorces of less than one percent (USDHEW, 1977b). Finally, during the twelve months ending August 1977, 2,000 *less* divorces were reported than during the preceding twelve-month interval (USDHEW, 1977b).

No one can tell whether this deceleration will continue; or, if it does, whether *annual* divorces and divorce rates might actually drop; or, if they did, whether they would once again begin to climb. The rate (5.0 divorces per 1,000 population) for the first eight months of 1977 remained the same as it had been throughout 1976 (USDHEW, 1977b). At the least, these data demonstrate that we may expect no automatic effect of the trends connected with women's individualism. The image of divorce rates inevitably spiralling upward owing to women's pursuit of self-interest is not necessarily valid.

One possible explanation for the deceleration is the fact that increasing numbers of younger women are postponing marriage—some until their late twenties and early thirties (U.S. Bureau of Census, 1976). For a long time it has been known that the older a woman is when she marries, the less is her likelihood of ever experiencing marital disruption. Further, better-educated women wait longer to marry. Putting these factors together it is possible to suggest that better-educated, younger, unmarried women (both never and once-married) are becoming more cautious about striking marriage bargains. Unless they can find men with whom they may negotiate equitable arrangements they tend not to marry. Hence, by delaying entry into marriage, emerging patterns of female individualistic reward-seeking may actually tend to deflate increases in marital dissolution.

A third response to the question of individual versus group interests must take into account male interests. Throughout this discussion, men have been cast as the dominant group resisting the increasing encroachment of the subordinate group. It turns out, however, that, like women, men with more years of schooling are more egalitarian in regard to their sex roles (Scanzoni, 1975b). And younger men are more egalitarian than older men (Scanzoni, 1976). Therefore, it can be argued that younger, better-educated men are more willing than older ones to negotiate marriages in which both partners experience "maximum joint profit" (Kelley and Schenitzki, 1972). Men of today and of the near future may be better able to cope with the egalitarian demands that, for the past 15 to 20 years, faced males who were unprepared for them. The inability or unwillingness of those men to recognize their wives' demands, and the strength of women's growing power, may have contributed substantially to the doubling of the divorce rate between 1965 and 1976.

In the last few years, in contrast, an increased male egalitarianism may have contributed to the leveling of the divorce rate. However, the connection between marital dissolution and male sex role egalitarianism and willingness to negotiate seriously over women's interests is in need of empirical investigation.

There is no logical reason why the modern woman's pursuit of self-interest must rule out male self-interest. Modern marriage is not a zero-sum game. And if that is so, it follows that if couples today can negotiate on the basis of "maximum joint profit," the threat of familial and social disruption commonly attributed to *women's* pursuit of their own interests becomes less problematic. In other words, even if one should grant that women's emerging individualism negatively affects the social order (which I do not), it could be countered that the social order will be improved if members of the two sexes negotiate with each other so as to meet the goals of both (Gerson, 1976, p. 799). I believe that would hold for two related reasons: first, divorces owing to women's self-interest would presumably decline, and second, the overall satisfaction with both the economic and the expressive aspects of marriage would be greater than in its three other forms.

Summary

My purpose has been to outline a model of marital stability that applies to Western societies across time. The model spotlights the relative bargaining power of women and men, temporal changes in such power, and changes in social norms regarding the legitimacy of "tough" bargaining and of divorce.

Prior to the industrial era and the emergence of feminism, marriage was characteristically an owner-property arrangement. Divorce was not unknown, but rare. Although women had only limited bargaining power to affect their marital arrangement, they did have the option to leave it. Some wives deserted, as did some husbands. The actual frequency of desertions is unknown, but its incidence indicates that marital stability was hardly universal prior to the legitimation of divorce. Persons with high cost/low benefit marriages did tend to leave them upon occasion.

The nineteenth century saw gradual changes in the relative bargaining power of the sexes. Such changes centered around the new obligations imposed upon males. With no lessening of their traditional duty to provide economically, they also were expected to supply emotional gratifications to their wives. To be sure, women had to reciprocate emotional benefits, but for them this was largely an elaboration of their age-old support function. For men, it was something new and different. Compared to the past, men's new obligations limited their bargaining power.

Simultaneously the wife, whose role was complementary though still subject to her husband as head, could legitimately ponder dissolution if he failed to supply both economic and emotional benefits. Her bargaining position was supported by the development of feminism, with the result that divorce rates rose steadily throughout the latter third of the nineteenth century.

Factories and businesses made it possible for married women to increase their power still more through production of economic resources independent of husbands. The increase in junior-partner (working-wife) marriages has continued throughout the twentieth century, as has the increase in divorce rates.

The contemporary era is witnessing the emergence of equal-partner marriages in which there are no ultimately fixed patterns nor rights closed to negotiation and renegotiation. The woman is generally involved in the labor force and her contribution to family income is substantial. Given her high bargaining power the potential for marital dissolution is considerable.

Despite the increase in well-educated, egalitarian women, however, there need not be a further increase in the divorce rate. Husbands can themselves benefit from their wives' pursuit of their own interests. Both partners can learn to negotiate with each other so as to achieve marital arrangements based on equity and mutual satisfaction.

George Levinger

A Social Psychological Perspective
on Marital Dissolution

The cycle of life is inexorable. What rises eventually descends. What grows eventually perishes. Closely knit interpersonal attachments, too, sooner or later dissolve.

Why do couple relationships dissolve? The grounds are often complex. Determinants of disruption vary on a continuum ranging from entirely voluntary to entirely involuntary. At the involuntary extreme is death. At the voluntary end, either or both partners may clearly choose to break the bond, as occurs in some instances of withdrawal, estrangement, separation, or divorce.

Divorce generally is the end product of a process of estrangement (Goode, 1956; McCall and Simmons, 1966). It is often preceded by numerous little acts that cool the relationship. Before the actual breakup, a sensitive observer can note stepwise detachments or withdrawals:

The parties to a progressively less rewarding relationship are allowed simply to give it correspondingly less salience in their respective agendas. . . . The two parties thus begin to fade out of each other's lives. [McCall and Simmons, 1966, pp. 198–199]

Intimate relationships are not easily broken. If they do break, however, they seem already to have declined to a point where one or both partners see an alternative state that is more attractive. The more attrac-

Work on this paper was facilitated by Grant GS-33641 from the National Science Foundation. For their valuable comments on an earlier draft, I am indebted to Ann Levinger, Oliver Moles, Phillips Cutright, Marylyn Lacey, and particularly to Zick Rubin.

A previous version of this chapter appeared in *Journal of Social Issues*, 1976, 32 (1).

tive alternative is not necessarily another lover; it may be going it alone or living in groups other than a nuclear family.

There are few actual data on processes of dissolution. Existing data about the afflicted system are generally based on retrospective reports of single spouses or ex-spouses (Goode, 1956; Weiss, 1976) or of ex-members of premarital pairs (Hill, Rubin, and Peplau, chapter 4). Process data about couple interaction are difficult to obtain, and neither researchers nor couple members themselves are in a position to view such pair processes objectively.

Most instances of pair dissolution, however, contain a mixture of perceived volition and coercion through circumstance. Events inside the relationship, such as poor communication or intermember coordination, are usually only partly accountable for its breakup; external events also exert powerful effects. Discussions of marital disruption must recognize such external factors. For example, one indirect contributor to the increase in voluntary marital separation during the past century has been the decrease of involuntary separation through death (Bane, chapter 16). Spouses today see only a distant prospect of death parting an unsatisfying union; thus they may have a greater need to consider other forms of separation. External determinants can also be the source of marital conflict or deficiency. One important source is inadequate income; low family income has been a significant correlate of divorce (Cutright, 1971; Norton and Glick, chapter 1). The private lives of marriage partners are intertwined with events in their surrounding social and economic environment.

A Social Psychological Perspective

This discussion of divorce will view the marriage relationship as a special case of pair relationships in general. In doing so, it builds on two lines of my earlier work—a decade-old integrative review of the literature on marital cohesiveness and dissolution (Levinger, 1965) and a more recent conceptualization of the development of attraction in dyadic relationships (Levinger, 1974; Levinger and Snoek, 1972). Although cognizant that the events affecting marital durability emerge out of the broader sociocultural matrix, I here consider the marital relationship mainly as a dyad. And even though most data about marriage and divorce derive from the work of demographers and family sociologists, my present view will be mainly social psychological.

Thus, my conceptual framework focuses more on the marital dyad than on the subtleties of its context. Its constructs are simple, and the complexities of existing data do not arrange themselves easily into its structure. Nevertheless, the approach serves as a heuristic strategy, the limits of which will be considered at the end of the empirical review.

COHESIVENESS OF THE MARRIAGE PAIR

One approach to the determinants of marital breakup is to conceive the marriage pair as a special case of all other social groups, and to consider its continuation in terms of its cohesiveness:

The marriage pair is a two-person group. It follows, then, that marital cohesiveness is analogous to group cohesiveness and can be defined accordingly. Group cohesiveness is "the total field of forces which act on members to remain in the group" [Festinger, Schachter, and Back, 1950]. Inducements to remain in any group include the attractiveness of the group itself and the strength of the restraints against leaving it; inducements to leave a group include the attractiveness of alternative relationships and the restraints against breaking up such existing relationships. [Levinger, 1965, p. 19]

A second approach focuses on gradations of interpersonal relationship. Pair relationships are distinguished according to degrees of interpersonal involvement, from the unilateral impression of another to the deeply mutual attachment (Levinger, 1974; Levinger and Snoek, 1972). Consider, in particular, the continuum of interpersonal involvement ranging from superficial contact to profound closeness—as indicated by varying degrees of cognitive, behavioral, and emotional interdependence.

Most pair dissolutions occur long before two acquaintances ever reach any appreciable depth, but data about dissolution pertain almost entirely to the breakup of established pairs. The ending of superficial encounters offers few research problems. In contrast, the phenomena of marital separation and divorce pertain to couples who have had high involvement, sufficient for them to enter into a long-term commitment; yet, at the moment of breakup such involvement may be either low or charged with negativity. My social psychological perspective does not make categorical assumptions about the phenomena of separation or divorce. Without knowing a pair's location on a continuum of relatedness, one can say little about the meaning of its breakup.

An image of the pair. Figure 3-1 depicts a relationship between Person (P) and Other (O), interpretable according to the above two views. The size of the intersection between P's and O's life circles refers to the degree of their interdependence—substantial in this instance. It refers to a complex of joint property, joint outlook or knowledge, capacities, behaviors, feelings, joint memories and anticipations.

The arrows marked "+," "—," and "b" pertain to different aspects of pair cohesiveness. The positive and negative arrows refer to forces

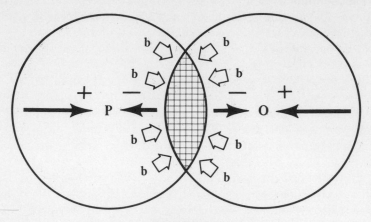

FIGURE 3-1

Schema of a Person-Other Relationship

that drive a person either toward or away from a relationship—positive "attractions" such as feelings of comfort or admiration, and negative "attractions" such as discomfort or irritation. It is assumed that one usually has both positive and negative feelings toward an intimate partner. P's net positive attraction tends to be higher, the larger the size of the P-O intersection. Nonetheless, we can imagine persons who feel large interdependence with their partner, but whose feelings are predominantly negative. Resentment or hatred are also forms of bondage or, conversely, being forced to remain together may itself raise negative feelings.

The "b" arrows in Figure 3-1 refer to barrier forces that act to contain the P-O relationship. Barriers—or psychological "restraining forces" (Lewin, 1951)—affect one's behavior only if one wishes to leave the relationship. In a marriage one's feelings of obligation to the contract or one's fear of community disapproval at its termination are each examples of psychological barriers against breakup.

ATTRACTIONS

A person's attraction to membership in a relationship is directly associated with its perceived rewards and inversely with its perceived costs (Thibaut and Kelley, 1959). At any given moment, each reward or cost is weighted by its respective subjective probability.

Rewards are derived from positive outcomes associated with membership in the relationship. They include the receipt of resources such as love, status, information, goods, services, or money—as conceived in Foa's (1971) scheme of interpersonal resources. The relationship may also bring one support, security, and consensual validation. Costs of membership may include one's time and energy and the various other expenditures demanded from staying in a relationship.

Subjective probability refers to a person's anticipation of how likely it is that a reward will be obtained or a cost incurred. The higher the subjective probability of a reward or cost, the more it is perceived to affect attractiveness. For instance, a man may fancy great pleasure from associating with a wonderful woman he has met but see a low probability of developing the relationship; if he also sees a high probability of receiving a painful rejection, his effective attraction to the woman will be small.

The dissolution of intimate relationships is often marked by a drastic shift in perceived rewards or costs. When relationships are on the upswing, mutual rewards are believed to be highly probable and thoughts of costs are suppressed; later, during disenchantment, one or both partners find the old rewards less probable, and unanticipated costs are now discovered. In some cases, the eventual costs existed from the beginning but neither partner had wanted to see them; in other instances, the components of attraction change markedly over the course of time.

BARRIERS

Discussions of cohesiveness have usually ignored the existence of restraining forces. As originally proposed by Lewin (1951, p. 259), a restraining force affects a person only when he approaches the boundary of a psychological region; he is not restrained unless and until he attempts to cross the boundary. Restraining forces that derive from barriers between people act to keep them apart; barriers around relationships act to keep people together.

Barriers are important for keeping long-term relationships intact. An example is the partnership contract, legitimated by the norms of society. Barriers lessen the effect of temporary fluctuations in interpersonal attraction; even if attraction becomes negative, barriers act to continue the relationship.

If there is little delight in a relationship, however, the existence of strong barriers creates a prison. Such a marital relationship has been called an "empty shell" marriage:

The atmosphere is without laughter or fun, and a sullen gloom pervades the household. Members do not discuss their problems or experiences with each other, and communication is kept to a minimum. . . . Their rationalization for avoiding a divorce is, on the part of one or both, sacrifice for the children, neighborhood respectability, and a religious conviction that divorce is morally wrong. . . . The hostility in such a home is great, but arguments focus on the small issues, not the large ones. Facing the latter would, of course, lead directly to separation or divorce, but the couple has decided that staying together overrides other values, including each other's happiness and the psychological health of their children. [Goode, 1961, pp. 441–442]

The metaphor of an empty shell marriage evokes contrasting images of "full shell" and "no shell" pairs. A "full shell" marriage would be one in which not only the boundaries but also both partners' attractions are strong.

The left column of Figure 3-2 shows two distinct instances of "no shell" relationships which differ in their attractiveness. The top left corner refers to premarital or nonmarital relationships between partners who care deeply for one another, but who have not formalized any commitment. The bottom cell refers to partners who are estranged; divorced pairs are significant instances. Figure 3-2, then, describes a range of instances along two important interpersonal continua: fullness-emptiness of attraction and strength-weakness of boundaries.

ALTERNATIVE ATTRACTIONS

In almost every marriage, each spouse has numerous relationships with alternative role partners—family, friends, or fellow employees. Each such alternative relationship is the source of its own attractions and constraints; such alternative forces may compete with forces from inside the marriage relationship. Although ties to third parties often enrich the life of the couple, they also demand time and energy and can draw affect away from the pair itself. Images of "open marriage" to the contrary, an extreme commitment to such a relationship can do more to weaken rather than to strengthen marital attractions.

If one partner becomes immersed in relations that consciously exclude

		BARRIERS: None (or weak)	BARRIERS: Strong
ATTRACTIONS	Highly Positive	premarital pairs; uncommitted lovers	attracted and mutually committed marriages
ATTRACTIONS	Low or Negative	strangers; pairs that are now divorced	"empty shell" marriages; apathetic and dulled dyads

FIGURE 3-2

Varying Patterns of Pair Attractions and Barriers

the other, the fullness of marital interaction may be threatened—depending, of course, on how the other spouse interprets the action. A jealous partner can perceive even a mild detachment as threatening. Some spouses may not be at all disturbed by their partner's withdrawal or alternate affairs, but such extreme tolerance is rare. A key question is whether the externally involved spouse will eventually prefer the alternative enough to desire a rupture of the present relationship.

One member's withdrawal, if it proceeds, may indeed lead to the rejection of the entire relationship. Persistent exploration of alternatives is likely to build up a person's "comparison level for alternatives" (Thibaut and Kelley, 1959): The more one samples alternative relations, the more likely one is to find outcomes that appear to exceed those currently obtainable, even if one's present mate is very attractive.

Furthermore, the partner with the wider field of alternatives usually has greater power than the less extended spouse (Waller, 1938). Traditionally, the male partner has had wider latitude than the female, and the female has suffered from a power disadvantage. The woman has stayed home, deepening existing family relationships, while the man is away. Whether as a corporation executive on a trip, a soldier off to the wars, or a cave man searching for better hunting grounds, the husband traditionally has extended his opportunity to compare alternatives without a parallel extension of the wife's opportunities.

RECAPITULATION

Essentially, pair cohesiveness pertains to the net sum of the attractions and barriers inside a relationship minus the net attractions to and barriers around the most salient outside alternative. Let us note several cautions, though, before applying this concept to the empirical literature.

First, this conceptual lens focuses mainly on the dyad and its members. It does not itself suggest a theory of what environmental factors promote or destroy good feeling, facilitate or interfere with relational obligation.

Second, two partners' feelings toward their relationship (or its alternatives) are likely to differ. Cohesiveness—here distinguished from "individual connectedness" to the group (Levinger, 1967)—is a group-level concept which neglects differences among individual members. In a marriage, for example, one spouse may be so highly attracted as to ignore all thoughts of alternatives or barriers to breakup, while the other's continued membership depends mainly on existing barriers.

Third, it is far harder to ascertain whether a pair's cohesiveness is high than whether it is low. Outsiders to an intimate relationship do not readily discover how truly happy it is or how bound the partners currently feel. Even insiders, the partners themselves, are not fully aware of all their feelings.

after the advent of urbanization (Goode, 1962). Some time during the early part of the twentieth century, the association between divorce rate and income level became inverted. Attractions within the average marriage had probably been lowest among the poorest members of society even in previous centuries. With a reduction of legal obstacles and economic costs and an increase of alternatives through improved welfare programs, divorce became far more frequent among low-income couples (Levinger, 1965).

When wide ranges of income are considered, as in census studies of the entire U.S. population, there has been a clear inverse correlation between income and divorce or separated status. Cutright's (1971) analysis of 1959–1960 census data showed that family income was a far more important correlate of divorce than any other available census variable. With income controlled, neither education nor occupation appeared to predict the incidence of marital separation. Whether a couple's high income acted mainly as an attraction by increasing marital satisfaction or whether it acted more as a barrier against breakup by making spouses reluctant to break up their joint financial assets was uncertain (Cutright, 1971).

My research on the fate of marriages after application for divorce has shown that husband income has an inverse correlation with divorce proneness, but that the amount of wife income is positively correlated (Levinger, chapter 8). Wives with incomes independent of their husbands' earnings are likely to be less tied to their marriage (see also Norton and Glick, chapter 1).

One should not assume that divorce is inversely correlated with income at all levels of family income or that an inverse correlation will persist indefinitely into the future. Couples with extremely high incomes are often not the most durable. Although income "adequate for the needs of the family" (Locke, 1951) appears vital, increases in income beyond that point may be accompanied by massive increases in external organizational involvements. Dizard (1968) found that large increases in income were often accompanied by lowered marital satisfaction, and that drops in income were often associated with greater reported happiness if the husband involved himself more within his family.

Home ownership. Income is essential, and so is shelter. Home owners have been found to have proportionately fewer divorces than do nonowners (Levinger, 1965). This may be due to the owners' higher income and length of marriage (Levinger, chapter 8), but it makes sense that joint home ownership stabilizes the marriage tie. (If home ownership is an index of joint commitment, it can also be classified as a barrier to breakup.)

Other couple property, if it represents a truly joint investment, may add to the stability of the relationship. To the extent that partners have consulted mutually in acquiring the property and that it symbolizes what they both treasure, joint property would be a strength rather than a weakness of their relationship. Nevertheless, joint ownership also leads to maintenance problems and disputes about usage. Altogether, then, it is hard to specify how joint ownership is a significant source of interpersonal attraction.

SYMBOLIC REWARDS

Status in one's community would seem to be an important source of reward. A husband's educational or occupational rank has traditionally determined his family's place in society, and today the husband's socioeconomic characteristics still do contribute more than the wife's to a couple's social rank (Rossi, Sampson, Bose, Jasso, and Passel, 1974).

Educational status. Durable marriages have exceeded dissolved marriages in their mean level of husband's education (Levinger, 1965). The wife's attraction to her husband may be positively related to his education for reasons of social status, or perhaps high education encourages better marital communication and a higher value for marital companionship (Blood and Wolfe, 1960; Komarovsky, 1964). Even more likely, the husband's education is positively related to his financial income and therefore to the couple's living standard.

Cutright (1971) recently demonstrated that the association between high husband education and low divorce proneness could be mostly accounted for by variations of husband income. After controlling for husband's income level, Cutright found no overall association between husband's education and marital durability in the population represented by the 1960 U.S. census. Further examination of Cutright's analysis suggests a qualification. In his lowest 1959 income group, the higher the education, the lower the durability; in his middle income interval ($3000–$6999) there was no association at all; in his highest income category ($7000 or more) there was a definite association between increasing education and increasing marital durability. A theory of status congruence would suggest that either low-income husbands with high education or high-income husbands with low education suffer distress from status inconsistency. High income alone may not be enough; commensurately high education may still contribute to high marital durability.

What remains to be asked is what is the content of the "education"? Education may spread norms that counter the traditional valuation of marital stability and weaken the barriers of long-term commitment. Although data from a 1972 survey of 2500 college students showed over 95 percent looking for a permanent marriage in their future (Rubin, 1973), it is hard to project future trends.

Occupational status. Divorce proneness has also been considered an inverse correlate of occupational rank. A variety of studies have reported that couples where the husband's occupation ranks high have had less divorce proneness than those where it ranks low (Goode, 1956; Kephart, 1955; Monahan, 1955; Weeks, 1943). However, Cutright's (1971) analysis indicates strongly that, in 1960, occupational differences in divorce proneness almost disappear when differences in income are removed; high status alone did not reduce proneness to divorce.

Occupational differences may covary with divorce proneness, however, in ways that Cutright's census tabulations could not reveal. Occupations vary greatly in the stability of their work hours, the degree to which they interfere with family life, and the extent to which the employee has contact with alternative partners of the other sex.

There exist insufficient data for verifying hypotheses about occupational differences; furthermore, such differences vary by time and place. For example, while Monahan (1955) reported that in 1953 Iowa physicians had a higher divorce rate than dentists, Rosow and Rose's (1972) study of 1968 filings for divorce and annulment in California reported no difference between physicians' and dentists' rates (16.4 vs. 16.5 "complaints" per 1000 marriages). To the extent that occupational differences are associated with the instability of one's home life, with nonfamilistic norms, or to one's exposure to alternate attractions, it seems that they would be associated with differences in divorce proneness. But those separate factors currently defy neat summation.

Social similarity. Another potential source of symbolic reward is the partners' ability to communicate. Marriage partners are generally more similar than are random pairs. People marry homogamously not only because they encounter more similar than dissimilar others, but also because they prefer to be with socially similar others (Kerckhoff, 1974). Thus many studies have shown a positive correlation between spouses' race, their educational and socioeconomic backgrounds, their religion, and their age. Despite that evidence, it is not clear under what conditions heterogamous marriages are less successful or durable than homogamous ones. For one thing, heterogamous partners who brave significant dissimilarity on one or more social characteristics are likely to have taken more time or care in getting married (Golden, 1954; Smith, 1966). To the extent that they free themselves from the disjunctive forces of their social backgrounds, dissimilar partners may well develop an enduring cohesiveness.

Religious similarity has frequently been linked to marital durability (Levinger, 1965). In their careful analysis of a national probability sample, Bumpass and Sweet (1972) recently reported further confirmation of that linkage, but the similarity of *no* religious preference at all has been found to be even more related to divorce proneness than a mixed-faith preference (Landis, 1963). However, most divorces for which there are published data on religion are many years old. Today, particularly among college students, religious similarity seems to play a less important role. Recent research on the fate of "seriously attached" couples on Massachusetts and Colorado university campuses (Levinger, 1972; Levinger, Senn, and Jorgensen, 1970) found no correlation between religious similarity and the durability of those unmarried relationships. That finding is confirmed in the recent study of dating couples in the Boston area (Hill, Rubin, and Peplau, chapter 4); however, different-religion pairs were more similar than same-religion pairs on characteristics unrelated to religion, such as their educational plans.[1]

Similarity in educational background also has been found associated with marital durability, but many of the data are of borderline significance (Bumpass and Sweet, 1972). From a social psychological standpoint, one would hypothesize that educational similarity facilitates belief and attitude convergence; in turn, perceived agreement in attitudes furthers interpersonal attraction (Byrne, 1971).

Age similarity is a third frequently considered aspect of homogamy, but evidence on its effects is modest. Its effects appear contingent on other variables such as similarity in interests or in physical health. Perhaps the soundest evidence was found in the survey data analyzed by Bumpass and Sweet (1972). They reported higher than expected instability when age differences between spouses are large and when wives are older than their husbands. An analysis of 1954 Australian census data (Day, 1964) yielded parallel findings: The lowest divorce rates occurred among couples whose ages fell within the same 5-year category; if the spouses' ages differed by more than five years, the divorce rates were higher when the wife was older than the husband—a condition less in keeping with the social norm.

In general, social similarity enhances interpersonal attraction to the extent that it pertains to salient matters. Such similarity facilitates adherence to the same social norms—whether the partners are married or not—and helps avoid friction.

AFFECTIONAL REWARDS

Enjoyment of the spouse is obviously part of one's attraction. It can manifest itself in the spouses' high value for marital companionship, high esteem, and mutual sexual enjoyment.

Companionship and esteem. Desire for companionship is unrelated to marital durability in many non-Western cultures, and also in various Western subcultures (Bott, 1971). Particularly in Asia, husband-wife companionship has remained subordinated to the child rearing and lineage preserving functions of marriage (Mace and Mace, 1960), but mutual affection probably becomes more important with the advent of industrialization and loosened kinship ties (Goode, 1963). In American marriages, satisfaction with companionship has been found strongly

1. Rubin, Z. Personal communication, May 1975.

related to indices of marital adjustment (Blood and Wolfe, 1960; Kirk-patrick, 1937).

Esteem for the spouse, as manifested in giving good reports about the partner, has been found related to reported placidity (Locke, 1951; Kelly, 1941); voicing complaints has been linked to poor marital adjustment (Goode, 1956; Harmsworth and Minnis, 1955; Locke, 1951).

Sexual enjoyment. Sexual enjoyment has generally been found associated with marital satisfaction (Levinger, 1966b; Wallin and Clark, 1958), but its absence has not been clearly linked to marital instability. Concern with sex has been more typical of middle-class than of lower-class American spouses. For example, "sexual incompatibility" is a more common complaint among divorce applicants in the higher than in the lower social strata (Kephart, 1955; Levinger, 1966a).

FURTHER THOUGHTS ABOUT "ATTRACTIONS"

Attraction to the spouse is a function of the rewards and costs perceived obtainable from him or her. Many rewards and costs other than those reviewed above can play a part in marital attraction, but such factors are not well discussed in the literature.

The most parsimonious model of the determinants of attraction in marriage has been proposed by James G. March.[2] March's model of marital satisfaction hinges on two elementary assumptions: (a) that a husband desires the most attractive looking female for his consort, and (b) that a wife desires the best possible income producer for her mate. His proposal is reminiscent of Ogden Nash's suggestion that a husband and wife are incompatible "if he has no income and she isn't patible" (see Levinger, 1964). Although March derived a number of established findings from those two assumptions, many determinants obviously fall outside his simplistic duality.

A different attempt to develop theory about marital dissolution was reported by Nye, Frideres, and White (1968). Their principal proposition for explaining dissolution uses the concept of role competence: "The less competent the role performance of the spouses, the more likely the marital dissolution" (Nye et al., 1968). Since their paper specifies neither the ingredients of competent role performance nor the standards by which spouses judge it, however, as stated their proposition is impossible to disconfirm.

Sources of attraction (or repulsion) are likely to differ at different times in a relationship. An early attraction founded on the physical may subsequently be sustained by growing mutual interests, and still later a completely new set of joint interests may emerge from joint endeavors. Or, conversely, minor irritants that are ignored during the unfolding of

2. March, J. G. Personal communication, April 2, 1973.

a relationship can subsequently be inflated into major sources of stress. Such changes are rarely accessible to research.

One final point is worth noting when we consider sources of attraction and repulsion. People are not only affected by a particular partner, but also by their married status itself. For the large majority of adults in most societies, the mere fact of "being married" has been a mark of adulthood and a symbol of kinship (Lévi-Strauss, 1969). Others, the unconventional minority, may feel repelled by the status of being married; even if they are deeply attracted to a partner, they refuse to formalize their tie. Regardless of person-to-person attraction, then, one's internalized standards govern attraction to the status of marriage itself.

Sources of Barriers

Partnership has its costs, but so does the dissolution of partnership. The middle column of Table 3-1 lists costs associated with the termination of a marital relationship. Available findings are subsumed under the headings of material, symbolic, and affectional costs of termination.

MATERIAL COSTS

Divorce or separation is expensive. Two places of residence are less economical than one. And if there are children, complications in seeing them or providing for them usually require additional time and money.

Both high- and low-income partners who separate will have added financial cost. Fixed costs, such as for filing a divorce application or for legal services, affect the poor relatively more than the rich. Sliding costs, especially those for separate maintenance of wife and children, affect the rich more than the poor; a high-income husband is likely to pay proportionately more.

In some societies, divorce rates vary inversely with the size of the dowry, which the husband must return to the ex-wife (Goode, 1964). In matrilineal societies where an ex-husband must leave his children and property if he returns to his own kin, the divorce rate is rather low (Swift, 1958). The desire not to break up family financial assets becomes a significant restraint against marital dissolution when those assets are sufficiently large. Furthermore, the wife of a well-to-do husband who herself has little independent income tends to suffer a significant reduction of financial support; in contrast, if a husband's current support is already low, there is no such deprivation.

SYMBOLIC COSTS

Marriage is important not only as an arrangement of property, but also as a symbolic acknowledgment of one's place in a culture and in a kin network. This latter meaning of marriage—so important among tribal cultures—seems to have changed most during the past century. Symbols taken for granted in other cultures and at earlier times have changed.

> In the past hundred years, Americans have redefined the nature of marriage . . . as an arrangement of mutual gratification. Once this redefinition is made, it becomes impossible to marshall social pressure against divorce. Conditions are provided which allow couples to see divorce as a natural solution for marital difficulty. [Udry, 1974, p. 404]

Obligation toward marital bond. A firmly committed spouse does not yearn for separation and may never even think of divorce. Other spouses feel less obligation toward keeping their marriage intact. It is difficult to obtain direct measures of such feelings, but contributing factors may be posited.

Length of acquaintance before marriage has frequently been found to be a significant correlate of its durability (Goode, 1956). Partners who wait long before making a formal commitment probably take it more seriously and later feel more invested in it than those who wait little time. Quickie marriages of convenience or necessity, particularly those with a premarital adolescent pregnancy (Furstenberg, chapter 5), are especially divorce-prone. Furthermore, the longer an existing marriage has lasted, the less likely it is to dissolve (Jacobson, 1959). Here too the strength of spouses' mutual obligations is pertinent.

The probability of divorce is heightened by either spouse's experience of divorce in a previous marriage (Goode, 1956; Monahan, 1952). Previously divorced persons appear more prone than persons in their first marriage to consider divorce as a solution to conflict, or to be members of groups that find it acceptable.

Finally, a history of divorce between the parents of either spouse appears to contribute to divorce proneness (Goode, 1956; Landis, 1949; Pope and Mueller, chapter 6). A person's continued tolerance for his or her own marital difficulty would be lower if he or she previously experienced mutual intolerance in the parental family.

Religious constraints. The wedding ceremony and the marriage covenant are in many cultures tied to deep-seated religious beliefs. Nevertheless, both cultures and religions vary greatly in how much they constrain the perpetuity of the marriage tie.

Intrafaith marriages have had lower rates of marital separation than interfaith marriages, yet among intrafaith marriages there tend to be differences across religious denominations. Jewish couples have been found to have the least instability, Protestants the highest, with Catholics in between (Bumpass and Sweet, 1972). Further, couples married at a religious ceremony have been found less likely to get divorced than those joined by a civil ceremony (Christensen and Meissner, 1953).

Like-faith couples who attend church regularly have been found less likely to break up their marriage than those who do not (Chesser, 1957; Goode, 1956; Locke, 1951). Aside from their joint adherence to a general moral standard, such couples are members of a network of connected affiliations; membership in such a network is itself a source of cohesive pressure. At a time of weakened religious orthodoxy, however, today other sources of social integration are coming to exert more powerful effects on marital durability.

Effects of differing religious affiliation. If partners differ in their religious affiliation, new forces seem to emerge. Religious dissimilarity is not only the source of attitudinal dissimilarity, but it also can have disjunctive effects on either spouse's obligation toward his or her own nuclear family and parental kin. And religious faiths differ in the strength of their prescriptive pressures.

Landis's (1949) study of divorce rates in Catholic-Protestant marriages showed that mixed-faith unions were less durable than same-faith marriages. Furthermore, Catholic-Protestant marriages were three times as likely to break up when the wife was Protestant than when the husband was Protestant. Given that wives are the plaintiffs in about three quarters of all divorce filings, the simplest explanation for Landis's finding is that Catholic wives in mixed-faith unions were less likely to ask for a divorce than were Protestant wives.[3]

A parallel finding to Landis's is reported by Boekestijn (1963) in his comparison of 1951–1955 divorce rates among same- and mixed-faith couples in Holland. Mixed-faith marriages showed divorce rates that were four to five times higher than those of same-faith marriages. Within the same-faith sample, the more "relevant" the religion, the lower the rate. The lowest divorce rates were found for marriages in which both partners were Calvinists, next lowest were for both Catholics, next were both Dutch Reform, and highest was the rate among both "no church." Most interesting was the finding in the mixed-faith sample that, in each of six independent comparisons, marriages where the wife rather than the husband belonged to the more "relevant" of the two religions showed significantly lower divorce rates. Boekestijn's Dutch data thus support Landis's earlier United States findings.

3. A more complicated explanation (Levinger, 1965) assumes that women's identifications with their religion are generally stronger than men's, that mothers have greater responsibility for child-rearing than do fathers, and that parents in Catholic-Protestant marriages have generally felt obligated to raise their children as Catholics. The Protestant mother in such a marriage would feel greater conflict about religion than would a Protestant father.

Pressures from primary groups. Violation of the standards of church or other communal institutions is merely one potential source of termination costs. Affiliation with kinfolk seems more important, though less measurable.

Ackerman (1963) hypothesized that divorce rates vary across different cultures to the extent that cultures encourage conjunctive rather than disjunctive affiliation with kin. In the conjunctive case, husband and wife share a common network of kinfolk and friends; in the disjunctive case, the spouses' loyalties go in different directions. Ackerman did indeed find that cultures encouraging competing primary group affiliations showed more divorce proneness than those discouraging such competing affiliations.

Other social anthropologists have also noted the importance of connected kinship and friendship networks for stabilizing a pair relationship even in the absence of strong intrapair affection (Bott, 1971). On the other hand, in such tightly knit networks the more that close kinfolk or friends express disapproval of the marriage, the greater is the likelihood of divorce (Goode, 1964; Locke, 1951).

Pressure from the community. Another source of termination costs derives from community disapproval. Communal pressures are linked to a couple's social visibility; they are usually greater in small communities than in large ones, in rural areas than in urban ones. Thus it is reasonable that rural divorce rates are substantially lower than urban ones (Carter and Plateris, 1963). But this rural-urban difference holds only for settled farmers and farm managers; farm laborers and migrants have among the highest rates of marital separation (Cutright, 1971).

Adherence to conventional social norms does not, of course, necessarily create a barrier against divorce. If a society should publicly encourage marital breakup, then adherence to prevailing norms would raise rather than lower divorce proneness. Instances of that occur in some sub-Saharan tribes (Goode, 1963) and are reported anecdotally for some California suburbs and in some communes (Jaffe and Kanter, chapter 7).

AFFECTIONAL COSTS

The divorce of a childless couple is considered largely the couple's own private affair. For couples with dependent children, there is greater reluctance to sanction divorce. And husbands and wives with minor offspring themselves feel more restraint against breakup than those with no offspring. Findings from various sources do show that, with length of marriage controlled, childless couples have generally had higher separation rates than child-rearing couples, although the differences have decreased during recent decades (Carter and Plateris, 1963; Jacobson, 1959; Monahan, 1955).

One recent study reports that unsatisfied married couples usually mentioned "children" as their greatest or only marital satisfaction, while satisfied couples reported many other sources of gratification (Luckey and Bain, 1970). For unsatisfied pairs, children seem to have provided the major reason to remain together.

Even if marriages with and marriages without children had identical separation rates, one still could argue that the presence of dependent children exerts a significant barrier force. That is because American couples with children in the home tend to have lower marital satisfaction than those without children (Burr, 1970; Campbell, 1975). They have greater financial burdens and more interpersonal stress. On the basis of his recent national probability survey, Campbell writes: "Almost as soon as a couple has kids, their happy bubble bursts. For both men and women, reports of happiness and satisfaction drop . . . , not to rise again until their children are grown and about to leave the nest" (1975, p. 39).

The crucial question is what obligation or affection do the parents in an unsatisfying marriage feel toward their children? And to what extent do they feel that a divorce would hurt them? If parents believe the damage to their children will be substantially greater than that from continuing their conflicted relationship, then the existence of children is indeed a psychological source of restraint; if not, such restraint may be negligible. The youth (or dependency) of the children is inversely related to the parents' length of marriage, however, and it is exceedingly difficult to disentangle these opposing influences on cohesiveness (Jacobson, 1959, pp. 132–135). Thus it is hard to generalize about the effect of children on the durability of marriage (see also Bane, chapter 16; Furstenberg, chapter 5).

Alternative Attractions

Even if internal attractions are low and barriers offer minimal restraint, a relationship will not be terminated unless an alternative seems more attractive. Consciously or not, each individual is aware of his possible alternative outcomes (Thibaut and Kelley, 1959). Popular stereotype to the contrary, the alternative situation is not necessarily another woman or another man. It is logically necessary, though, that the individual who decides on marital separation expects a more pleasant existence outside the marital bond, whether in a new interpersonal relationship or in living alone.

Wives' alternative attractions are particularly important to consider, for they are plaintiffs in the large majority of American divorce actions. The percentage of female plaintiffs generally exceeds 70 percent (Goode, 1956; Jacobson, 1959; Levinger, chapter 8). Although the husband's actions often precipitate the break, the end of the wife's continuing tolerance appears to be the key factor in the application for divorce (Goode, 1956).

MATERIAL REWARDS

It is usually more expensive for a couple to live separately than together (Ross and Sawhill, 1975), but the ex-spouse may improve his or her financial well-being. For example, if a wife feels exploited by her husband, she will feel financially better off earning her living outside the marriage. Furthermore, under societal welfare programs such as Aid to Families with Dependent Children, the separated or unmarried mother can receive financial subsidies that are unobtainable while remaining inside the marriage (Moles, chapter 10).

Wife's independent social and economic status. In societies where an ex-husband returns to his former home without wife, children, or property, his diminished social status renders the male's divorced status unattractive. In Western societies, diminution of status has affected ex-wives far more than ex-husbands. Not only are women's opportunities on the remarriage market significantly smaller than men's, but their ex-married status is often surrounded with difficulty. In Ireland, for example, many traditional communities have not permitted divorced women to hold jobs.[4]

The cross-cultural evidence demonstrates, however, that divorce rates vary directly with the status of the divorcée (Goody, 1962). A wife can break her marriage tie more readily if she can support herself outside the relationship. Where differences between the husband's and the wife's potential income are small, an ex-wife can earn substantially what she would receive from staying married, and without the economic dependency. In the higher economic strata, where earning potentials between husband and wife differ widely, her alternative status is financially unattractive for her (Goode, 1962). In the lower economic strata, wives have materially less to lose and more to gain from a divorce.

SYMBOLIC REWARDS

Independence and self-actualization. The status of being divorced has often been a source of stigma or despair, but it can also symbolize free-

4. Aas, B. Personal communication, November 1972.

dom and new opportunity. Despite the distress associated with getting separated (Weiss, chapter 12), divorce also has positive aspects (Kohen, Brown, and Feldberg, chapter 14). What was previously a sticky interdependency dominated by the spouse's demands can now be considered totally one's own life and one's own territory.

Bernard (1972), for example, has pointed to the personally debilitating correlates of marriage for women. After citing statistics on the comparative mental and physical health of married and unmarried women, she concludes that being a housewife literally makes a woman sick (1972, p. 53). To the extent that they embrace the advice of liberationists, wives may come to feel that as divorcées they can achieve greater control over their lives than can the "stably married" woman.

Recent national survey results, however, do not support a belief that women generally find great emotional benefits from divorce. In a massive 1971–1973 field test of a "depression" scale developed at the NIMH Center for Epidemiological Studies, it was found that divorced or separated white women had significantly higher depression scores than did married, single, or widowed women (Radloff, 1975). Those were cross-sectional data, however, which could not reveal the direction of causes and effects. To understand the changes in feelings from before to after separation, longitudinal assessments conducted at related time points are required.

AFFECTIONAL REWARDS

Presumably, a divorcing spouse expects to find greater affection from persons other than the present partner. Two different sorts of alternate attachments can be considered: alternate sex partners and disjunctive kin affiliations.

Preferred alternate sex partner. Until recently in the United States, it was common to accuse the defendant in a legal divorce complaint of adultery or other sexual offense. Legal fiction aside, sexual incompatibility and infidelity do appear to play a part in a substantial minority of all divorce actions; the reported proportion varies between 15 and 35 percent across a number of published studies (Goode, 1956; Harmsworth and Minnis, 1955; Kephart, 1955; Levinger, 1966a; Locke, 1951). The attractiveness of remarriage and alternate sexual liaisons may help account for the fact that divorce is more common among younger couples and among persons married at an early age. One careful analysis found that remarriage probabilities of females varied from about 97 percent for 20-year-olds to 80 percent for 30-year-olds, down to 50 percent for 40-year-olds (Jacobson, 1959). Male remarriage probabilities also were found to decline with age, though less steeply. Early age at marriage not only implies a less mature commitment (Furstenberg, chapter 5), but young spouses have more years than older spouses to be exposed to alternate partners. Occupational differences also account for varying exposure to alternate partners.

Disjunctive kin affiliations. Other targets of competing affections are one's kin or friends. If feelings toward them conflict with one's attachment to the spouse, they promote strain in the marriage. It is not surprising therefore that disjunctive kin affiliations have been linked to divorce proneness (Ackerman, 1963). Conversely, it is reasonable that acknowledging "a little" conflict with parents or other kin—as reported by many of Locke's (1951) "happy" couples—would be conducive to intramarriage unity and identity. In fact, a recent investigation of the "Romeo and Juliet effect" among premarital couples found that intense conflict with parents appeared to drive premarital partners closer together than did the absence of such conflict (Driscoll, Davis, and Lipetz, 1972). Finally, there is fragmentary evidence that a heterogamous married couple with antagonistic in-laws strengthens its own relationship when it moves away from either parents' community of residence. The effects of disjunctive affiliations are hard to assess precisely, but they appear to have a significant impact on events in the couple system.

Conclusion

Marital dissolution constitutes a special case of relational dissolution. While breakups of less established pairs go unrecorded and often unrecognized, marital breakups have a public status. There are few data about the dissolution of friendships or acquaintanceships, but there is a large literature on marital separation. This review cites only a small portion of that literature. Nonetheless, it considers most of the documented determinants of divorce, organized according to a framework derived from Lewin's (1951) field theory and building on an earlier version of my framework (Levinger, 1965).

The conceptual framework is simple, too simple to account for all the complexities. It is based on the assumption that people stay in relationships because they are attracted to them and/or they are barred from leaving them, and that, consciously or not, people compare their current relationships with alternative ones. If internal attraction and barrier forces become distinctly weaker than those from a viable alternative, the consequence is breakup. Our social psychological perspective translates the effects of external events, pressures, or shocks into psychological forces experienced inside the pair.[5]

Although it spotlights the dyad, this perspective does not intend that the pair be seen as a closed system. Both cultural norms and social networks have important effects, which can be translated into forces of attraction and restraint.

Two conceptual problems bear mention. The construct "group cohesiveness," which stimulated the present formulation, poses difficulties. For instance, there is a difference between the cohesiveness of the total group and the connectedness experienced by its separate members; group members rarely have identical involvement in the group. Theoretical issues surrounding the term cohesiveness have not been analyzed here.

Another conceptual problem pertains to the distinctiveness of the three components: attraction, barrier, and alternative attraction. During the empirical review, interpretations were not repeatedly qualified; it is often possible, however, to interpret the same empirical variable (e.g., home ownership or religious precept) as a source both of attraction and of barrier forces. Such hypothetical constructs lose their purity in application; the road between abstract theory and natural phenomena is often muddy.

A final observation is historical. When I wrote my earlier review in 1963, divorce rates were near their post-World War II low (Norton and Glick, chapter 1). Durability of a marriage was then popularly con-

5. My conceptual framework has been used here primarily as an analytic device for integrating a large variety of findings about marital cohesion and separation. It has not been used to consider the subjective feelings that either spouses or ex-spouses have about their marriage. One may wonder, therefore, whether they themselves would consider their own marriage in terms of its "attractions" or its "barriers."

An exploratory study pertinent to that question was recently done by myself and several students. We interviewed fifteen married couples who believed their relationship to be fairly successful. During the course of a structured interview with each individual partner, we asked about the influences that tended either to keep the marriage together or to disrupt it. Although our respondents did not themselves use these terms, many of their responses could be coded under the category of attractions and some under barriers. Regarding *attractions*, the most frequent reasons given for staying together—or for enjoying their marriage—were as follows: having common interests, activities, ideas, goals; enjoying companionship, liking spouse; enjoying family or children, etc.; having shared experiences or projects; trusting or respecting the spouse. The average respondent mentioned each of these five items three or more times during the course of the interview.

As hypothesized in our study, *barrier* items were mentioned much less often by these rather satisfied spouses. Nonetheless, each of the following was mentioned by one or more of the respondents: our children would be hurt by a divorce; my family would object to a divorce; I'd be less sure of myself alone; my religion forbids divorce; it's morally wrong to divorce; or divorce is emotionally devastating. In other words, these spouses' expressions about their marriage can indeed be translated into the conceptual framework employed in this chapter.

sidered as an indicator of marital success. Fifteen years later that tendency is less common; success of a marriage is now often viewed less in terms of its perpetuity than its furtherment of both spouses' personal potential. Furthermore, in the early 1960s and before, marriage researchers tended to suggest that a wife's status is entirely determined by her husband's education and occupation; today this assumption is less acceptable. Temporal changes affect the external validity of social science generalizations across different cohorts of persons. Reviewing the divorce literature at different time points, one becomes very aware of historical relativity (see also Scanzoni, chapter 2).

These qualifications need not deter us from applying general conceptualizations to the understanding of the often inconsistent literature. It is hoped that the present framework draws attention to gaps in our knowledge and avenues for further investigation.

PART II

Social and Psychological Determinants of Breakup

Any ENCOUNTER with marital separation produces the question, "Why did it happen?" And any encounter with our increasing divorce rate produces the question, "What is responsible?" The issues are too complex to permit simple answers. There are many subtle social and psychological determinants of breakup, some of which are taken up in Part II; economic determinants will be considered in Part III.

One way to begin to look at marital separation is, paradoxically, to ask which couples survive the vicissitudes of courtship to go on to marriage (see chapter 4). For there is premarital breakup as well as postmarital. And we see in the premarital breakup the winnowing out of couples who, if they had gotten married, would be likely to swell the ranks of the divorced. Indeed, we may think of couples who separate soon after marriage as having failed to break up quickly enough. Among those who fail to break up before marriage, despite the difficulties, are couples to whom a pregnancy has occurred (chapter 5). The new baby becomes a deterrent to a breakup during courtship, but burdens the new marriage with early responsibility.

Even when courtship and early marriage have gone smoothly, some individuals may be more prone to produce marriages that hover on the borderline of separation. One possibility is that individuals whose own parents separated and divorced are themselves more separation-prone (chapter 6). Although this is only one among many individual characteristics possibly associated with the forming of unstable marriages, it is one worth investigating. Furthermore, the context of the marriage exerts strong influences on marital dissolution. As an instance of this, we will consider what may happen to marriages in a context that is often thought to pose unusual challenges—the communal household (chapter 7).

In the first selection, Charles Hill, Zick Rubin, and Letitia Anne Peplau suggest that breakups before marriage play an important role in the larger system of mate selection, and they provide a revealing comparison against which to view marital dissolution. From that viewpoint, they examine the process of breaking up in a sample of college dating couples followed over time, and they analyze the differences between couples who terminated their relationship and those still together after two years.

The degree of similarity between partners seemed to have only a minor part in determining which couples broke up and which ones stayed together. But pairs who later broke up were initially less invested in the relationship and their degree of involvement tended to be less equal. The timing of couples' breakups was significantly affected by external structural factors, especially by the school calendar. The partners' desires for a breakup were seldom mutual; the woman was more likely to notice problems in the relationship and somewhat more likely to be the one to precipitate a rupture. Each of these findings is discussed from a social psychological standpoint, with reference to general processes of social exchange and mate selection.

The next chapter, by Frank Furstenberg, considers the effects of one particular event that may immediately precede a marriage—premarital pregnancy. Using data from his five-year longitudinal study on the social consequences of unplanned parenthood among economically disadvantaged women, Furstenberg compares the marital careers of 203 teenagers who became premaritally pregnant with those of 90 of their high school classmates who did not.

Furstenberg finds almost twice as many breakups in the premaritally pregnant group as in the comparable group of women. When alternative explanations are examined, the data lend support to two: The disruption of the young couple's courtship process and the limitation of the couple's wage earning opportunities. Both explanations can be understood by noting that premature parents suffer from disruptive events in their family life cycle, events that may long put them "out of phase" with each other and with their external environment.

Earlier life experiences may also be associated with marital breakup. Chapter 6, by Hallowell Pope and Charles Mueller, examines the likelihood that marital instability in one generation is passed on to the next generation. Five probability surveys, four of them on national samples, provide their data.

Pope and Mueller show that respondents whose parents' marriages were disrupted by death or divorce during their childhood had somewhat higher rates of marital separation during their own marriage. Among white respondents, a greater transmission effect was found among offspring from homes disrupted by divorce than by death; and children who grew up with neither parent were more likely later to experience divorce than those who grew up with one natural parent. These findings support an interpretation that parents' marriages serve as a "role model" for those of their children. Other findings, including some data from black respondents, are not consistent with a role model rationale. Whatever the explanatory model, the findings do indicate that the parental marriage is likely to affect their children's later marital relationship.

Marriages are also affected by pressures exerted from other persons in the settings where the spouses live. A source of particular pressures is the nearby presence of other intimates, who may either support or threaten the ongoing primary relationship. Marriages in one such setting, the urban commune, are considered in the final chapter of Part II. Dennis Jaffe and Rosabeth Moss Kanter interpret findings concerning 29 married couples who were living in 17 urban communal households. Their interviews uncovered a variety of influences that appeared to affect pair cohesion and dissolution. The communal environment was in many ways supportive, but more supportive of individual members than of pairs. Married couples particularly seemed to be affected by their lack of territorial sovereignty and by the continuing presence of others in their intimate space—others who were likely to exacerbate whatever tensions or disagreements that were expressed by either spouse.

Jaffe and Kanter propose a general four-factor model to help account for the influences that encouraged couple separation. Their four factors include "contextual conduciveness," which emanates from the structure of a couple's immediate environment; "systemic strain," as experienced within the marital system's own incongruent meanings, discrepant needs, and malcoordinated roles; "generalized beliefs" of household members that are unsupportive of couple, as opposed to communal relationships; and later "precipitating events" that include specific instances of friction, arguments, violations of trust, or the spouses' trial separation.

Each of these diverse glimpses adds to our picture of the complexity of the determinants and precipitants of couple breakup. Another portion of the determinants—the economic context—will be considered in Part III.

Breakups Before Marriage:
The End of 103 Affairs

For all the concern with the high incidence of divorce in contemporary America, marital separation accounts for only a small proportion of the breakups of intimate male-female relationships among American couples. For every recorded instance of the ending of a marriage, there are many instances, typically unrecorded, of the ending of a relationship among partners who were dating or "going together." Such breakups before marriage are of fundamental importance to an understanding of marital separation for two major reasons.

First and foremost, breakups before marriage play a central role in the larger system of mate selection. In an ideal mate selection system, all breakups of intimate male-female relationships might take place before marriage. Boyfriends and girlfriends who are not well-suited for each other would discover this in the course of dating and would eventually break up. In practice, however, the system does not achieve this ideal. Many couples who subsequently prove to be poorly suited for marrying each other do not discover this until after they are married. In many other instances, couples may be aware of serious strains in their relationship but nevertheless find themselves unable or unwilling to break up before marriage. Many future sources of marital strain may be totally unpredictable at the time that a couple decides to get married; individuals' needs and values may change over the course of time in ways that could not have been anticipated initially. Nevertheless, it is possible that the selection system could be made to operate more efficiently than

This research was supported by National Science Foundation grant GS-27422 to Zick Rubin.

This chapter appeared in a slightly different form in *Journal of Social Issues*, 1976, 32 (1).

it currently does. Although the psychic cost of a premarital breakup is often substantial, by breaking up before marriage couples might spare themselves the much greater costs of breaking up afterward.

Second, breakup before marriage may provide a revealing comparison against which to view marital breakup. Many of the psychological bonds of unmarried couples resemble those of married couples. Thus the requirements and difficulties of "uncoupling" in the two cases may show similarities (see Davis, 1973). On the other hand, breakup before marriage takes place in a very different social context from that of divorce. The ending of a dating relationship is relatively unaffected by factors that play central roles in divorces—for example, changes in residence, economic arrangements, child custody, legal battles, and stigmatization by kin and community. Thus the examination of breakups before marriage may be helpful in untangling the complex of psychological and social factors that influence divorce and its aftermath.

Breakups before marriage have remained largely unexplored by social scientists. Although there has been a great deal of research and speculation about mate selection (Rubin, 1973), this work has rather thoroughly ignored the process of breaking up. One major investigation of breaking up before marriage is the study of broken engagements conducted in the 1930s and 1940s by Burgess and Wallin (1953) as part of their larger study of engagement and marriage.

In this paper, we report on breakups before marriage among a large sample of dating couples in the 1970s. Our data are primarily descriptive: How were those couples who broke up over a two-year period different from those who stayed together? What were the reasons for the breakups, as perceived by the former partners themselves? What were the central features of the breaking-up process: its precipitating factors, its timing, and its aftermath? We pay special attention to the two-sidedness of breaking up: the frequent differences in the two partners' perceptions of what is taking place and why, the pervasive role differentiation of breaker-upper and broken-up-with, and the possibility that there are important differences between men's and women's characteristic orientations toward breaking up before marriage.

The Research Context

In the spring of 1972, for a longitudinal study of dating relationships (Rubin, Peplau, and Hill, unpublished), we sent a letter to a random sample of 5000 sophomores and juniors, 2500 men and 2500 women, at four colleges in the Boston area. The colleges, chosen with a view toward diversity, included a large private university (2000 letters) and a small private college, a Catholic university, and a state college for commuter students (1000 letters per school). Each student was sent a two-page questionnaire which asked if he or she would be interested in participating in a study of "college students and their opposite-sex relationships." A total of 2520 students (57 percent of the women and 44 percent of the men) returned this questionnaire. Of these, 62 percent of the women and 54 percent of the men indicated that they were currently "going with" someone. Those who said that they and their partner might be interested in participating in a study were invited to attend a questionnaire session—with their boyfriend or girlfriend—either at their own school or at Harvard University, where we conducted the project.

The 202 couples who responded to our invitation, plus an additional 29 couples who were recruited by advertising at one of the four schools, constitute our sample (Hill, Rubin, and Willard, 1972). At the time of the initial questionnaire, almost all participants (95 percent) were—or had been—college students. The modal couple consisted of a sophomore woman dating a junior man. About half of the participants' fathers had graduated from college and about one-fourth of the fathers held graduate degrees. About 44 percent of the respondents were Catholic, 26 percent were Protestant, and 25 percent were Jewish, reflecting the religious composition of colleges in the Boston area. Virtually all of the participants (97 percent) were white; about 25 percent lived at home with their parents, another 35 percent lived in apartments or houses by themselves or with roommates, and 38 percent lived in college dormitories. Almost all of the participants—97 percent of the women and 96 percent of the men—thought that they would eventually get married, although not necessarily to their current dating partner.

At the beginning of the study, the couples had been dating for a median period of about eight months—a third for 5 months or less, a third between 5 and 10 months, and a third for longer than that. In three-fourths of the couples both persons were dating their partner exclusively, but only 10 percent of the couples were engaged and relatively few had concrete plans for marriage. Four-fifths of the couples had had sexual intercourse, and one-fifth were living together "all or most of the time." Sixty percent were seeing one another every day.

DATA COLLECTION

In addition to the initial questionnaire, a follow-up questionnaire was administered in person or by mail six months, one year, and two years after the initial session. At all points response rates were good. For example, in the one-year follow-up, two-thirds of the initial participants attended questionnaire sessions and another 14 percent returned short questionnaires in the mail. Four-fifths of the original participants returned the two-year mail questionnaire. To categorize a relationship as intact or broken after two years, we have reports from at least one member of all but 10 of the 231 couples. In all cases, boyfriends and girlfriends were asked to fill out the questionnaire individually. They were assured that their responses would be kept in strict confidence, and would never be revealed to their partners. They were each paid $1.50 for the initial one-hour questionnaire session and $3.00 for a somewhat longer session one year later. To supplement these data, a smaller number of individuals and couples were interviewed intensively. Of particular relevance to this paper is a series of interviews conducted in the fall of 1972 with 18 people whose relationships ended after they began their participation in the study.[1]

Which Couples Broke Up?

By the end of the two-year study period, 103 couples (45 percent of the total sample) had broken up. (Of the remaining couples, 65 were dating, 9 were engaged, 43 were married, 10 had an unknown status, and one partner had died.) The length of time that breakup couples had been dating before ending their relationship ranged from 1 month to 5 years; the median was 16 months. On the basis of data obtained in the initial questionnaire, could these breakups have been predicted in advance?

MEASURES OF INTIMACY

Burgess and Wallin (1953) list "slight emotional attachment" as a major factor associated with the endings of premarital relationships. Our data indicate that in general those couples who were less intimate or less attached to one another when the study began were more likely to break up (Table 4-1). On the initial questionnaire, compared to couples who stayed together, couples who were subsequently to break up reported that they felt less close and saw less likelihood of marrying each other; they were less likely to be "in love" or dating exclusively, and tended to have been dating for a shorter period of time. The data also indicate, however, that many relationships which were quite "in-

1. We are grateful to Claire Engers and Sherry Morgan, who conducted most of these interviews.

timate" in 1972 did not survive beyond 1974. For example, over half of the partners in breakup couples felt that they were both in love at the time of the initial questionnaire. Whereas some of the couples who were to break up apparently never developed much intimacy in the first place, others had a high degree of intimacy that they were unable or unwilling to sustain.

The various measures of intimacy listed in Table 4-1 tend to be correlated with one another, and therefore are not independent predictors; however, some measures predicted survival (or breakup) better than others. The partners' "love" was a better predictor of the couple's survival than their "liking" for one another, as measured by scales previously developed by Rubin (1970, 1973). This distinction is in accord with the conceptual meaning of the two scales, with love including elements of attachment and intimacy, while liking refers to favorable evaluations that do not necessarily reflect such intimacy. In addition, the women's love for their boyfriends tended to be a better predictor of dating status (point-biserial $r = .32$) than the men's love for their girlfriends ($r = .18$). Thus the woman's feelings toward her dating partner may have a more powerful effect on a relationship and/or provide a more sensitive barometer of its viability than do the man's.

Finally, two important measures of couple intimacy were totally unrelated to breaking up: having had sexual intercourse or having lived

TABLE 4-1

Initial Intimacy Ratings by Status Two Years Later

	Women's Reports		Men's Reports	
	Together	Breakup	Together	Breakup
Mean Ratings				
Self-report of closeness (9-pt. scale)	7.9	7.3**	8.0	7.2**
Estimate of marriage probability				
(as percentage)	65.4	46.4**	63.1	42.7**
Love scale (max = 100)	81.2	70.2**	77.8	71.5**
Liking scale (max = 100)	78.5	74.0*	73.2	69.6
Number of months dated	13.1	9.9*	12.7	9.9*
Percentages				
Couple is "in love"	80.0	55.3**	81.2	58.0**
Dating exclusively	92.3	68.0**	92.2	77.5**
Seeing partner daily	67.5	52.0	60.7	53.4
Had sexual intercourse	79.6	78.6	80.6	78.6
Living together	24.8	20.4	23.1	20.4

Note. $N = 117$ together, 103 breakup for both men and women. Significance by t tests or chi-square for together-breakup differences.
*$p < .05$.
**$p < .01$.

together. These behaviors apparently reflect a couple's social values at least as much as the depth of their attachment to one another. Having sex or living together may bring a couple closer, but they may also give rise to additional problems such as coordinating sexual desires or agreeing on the division of household tasks.

RELATIVE DEGREE OF INVOLVEMENT

In addition to "slight emotional attachment," Burgess and Wallin (1953) list "unequal attachment" as a factor underlying breakups. The hypothesis that equal involvement facilitates the development of a relationship was spelled out by Blau:

Commitments must stay abreast for a love relationship to develop into a lasting mutual attachment. . . . Only when two lovers' affection for and commitment to one another expand at roughly the same pace do they tend mutually to reinforce their love. [1964, p. 84]

Our data provide strong support for Blau's hypothesis. Of the couples in which both members reported that they were equally involved in the relationship in 1972, only 23 percent broke up; in contrast, 54 percent of those couples in which at least one member reported that they were unequally involved subsequently broke up. It should be noted, however, that there was a significant association between reporting high intimacy on a variety of measures (e.g., those in Table 4-1) and reporting equal involvement.

SIMILARITY AND MATCHING

Probably the best documented finding in the research literature on interpersonal attraction and mate selection is the "birds-of-a-feather principle"—people tend to be most attracted to one another if they are similar or equally matched on a variety of social, physical, and intellectual characteristics and attitudes (Rubin, 1973). Evidence for such matching was found among the couples in our study. The significant correlations in the left-hand column of Table 4-2 make it clear that the partners were matched to some degree on a wide variety of characteristics, especially in the domain of social attitudes and values.

Although there is less empirical support for it, some researchers have put forth "sequential filtering" models of mate selection which propose that social and psychological similarities or dissimilarities are recognized and responded to in particular sequences. For example, Kerckhoff and Davis (1962) and Murstein (1971) propose that filtering (i.e., the elimination of mismatches) takes place first with respect to social background, physical, and other external or stimulus factors, and later with respect to important attitudes and values (Udry, 1971).

We looked for evidence of sequential filtering by comparing the intra-couple correlations of the breakup and the together groups in our sample (right-hand columns of Table 4-2). Methodological problems, most notably involving the effects of varying ranges of scores on the correlations that may be obtained within subgroups, dictate caution in making such comparisons. But there appeared to be no evidence that couples who were better matched on attitudes were more likely to stay together over the period of the study than were couples who were less well matched—suggesting that if there was any filtering on attitudes it was before the time of our initial questionnaire. There was some suggestion that couples who stayed together tended to be more similar with respect to age, educational plans, intelligence (measured by self-reported SAT scores), and physical attractiveness (measured by judges' ratings of individual color photographs)—although the difference between together and breakup correlations was significant only for age. Hence it is at least

TABLE 4-2

Couple Similarity by Status Two Years Later

Correlation of Partners	All Couples (N = 231)	Together Couples (N = 117)	Breakup Couples (N = 103)
Characteristics			
Age	.19**	.38**	.13
Highest degree planned	.28**	.31**	.17
SAT, math	.22**	.31**	.11
SAT, verbal	.24**	.33**	.15
Physical attractiveness	.24**	.32**	.16
Father's educational level	.11	.12	.12
Height	.21**	.22*	.22*
Religion (% same)	51%**	51%**	52%**
Attitudes			
Sex-role traditionalism (10-item scale)	.47**	.50**	.41**
Favorability toward women's liberation	.38**	.36**	.43**
Approval of sex among "acquaintances"	.25**	.27**	.21*
Romanticism (6-item scale)	.20*	.21*	.15
Self-report of religiosity	.37**	.39**	.37**
Number of children wanted	.51**	.43**	.57**

Note. Total N for SAT scores = 187, for physical attractiveness = 174. Physical attractiveness based on ratings of color photographs by 4 judges. Religion categorized as Catholic, Protestant, or Jewish; random pairing would have yielded 41% same religion.

Probability of difference between Together and Breakup correlations (one-tailed) for age is $p < .05$, for SAT math and SAT verbal is $.05 < p < .10$, for highest degree planned and for physical attractiveness is $.10 < p < .15$.

Significance levels indicated in the table are for chance probabilities.

*$p < .05$.

**$p < .01$.

possible that social and stimulus factors may continue to have some effect *after* attitudinal and value filtering have occurred. In general, however, the evidence for any kind of filtering during the period of the study is weak. Thus our data lend support to the existence of matching in mate selection, but lead us to question the value of simple fixed-sequence theories of filtering (see also Levinger, Senn, and Jorgensen, 1970; Rubin and Levinger, 1974).

The Process of Breaking Up

Brief synopses of two breakups, taken from among the sample we interviewed, may help to illustrate the process of breaking up. Neither of these cases is presented as typical, but the two illustrate several features that are characteristic of the aggregate findings.

Kathy and Joe had been going together during the school year when she was a sophomore and he was a junior. Both of them agree that Kathy was the one who wanted to break up. She felt they were too tied down to one another, that Joe was too dependent and demanded her exclusive attention—even in groups of friends he would draw her aside. As early as the spring Joe came to feel that Kathy was no longer as much in love as he, but it took him a long time to reconcile himself to the notion that things were ending. They gradually saw each other less and less over the summer months, until finally she began to date someone else. The first time that the two were together after the start of the next school year Kathy was in a bad mood, but wouldn't talk to Joe about it. The following morning Joe told Kathy, "I guess things are over with." Later when they were able to talk further, he found out that she was already dating someone else. Kathy's reaction to the breakup was mainly a feeling of release—both from Joe and from the guilt she felt when she was secretly dating someone else. But Joe had deep regrets about the relationship. For at least some months afterward he regretted that they didn't give the relationship one more chance—he thought they might have been able to make it work. He said that he learned something from the relationship, but hoped he hadn't become jaded by it. "If I fall in love again," he said, "it might be with the reservation that I'm going to keep awake this time. I don't know if you can keep an innocent attitude toward relationships and keep watch at the same time, but I hope so." Meanwhile, however, he had not begun to make any new social contacts, and instead seemed focused on working through the old relationship, and, since Kathy and he sometimes see each other at school, in learning to be comfortable in her presence.

David and Ruth had gone together off-and-on for several years. David was less involved in the relationship than Ruth was, but it is clear that Ruth was the one who precipitated the final breakup. According to Ruth, David was spending more and more time with his own group of friends, and this bothered her. She recalled one night in particular when "they were showing *The Last Picture Show* in one of the dorms, and we went to see it. I was sitting next to him, but it was as if he wasn't really there. He was running around talking to all these people and I was following him around and I felt like his kid sister. So I knew I wasn't going to put up with that much longer." When she talked to him about this and other problems, he said "I'm sorry"—but did not change. Shortly thereafter Ruth wanted to see a movie in Cambridge and asked David if he would go with her. He replied, "No, there's something going on in the dorm!" This was the last straw for Ruth, and she told him she would not go out with him anymore. David started to cry, as if the relationship had really meant something to him—but at that point it was too late. At the time we talked to her, Ruth had not found another boyfriend, but she said she had no regrets about the relationship or about its ending. "It's probably the most worthwhile thing that's ever happened to me in my 21 years, so I don't regret having the experience at all. But after being in the supportive role, *I* want a little support now. That's the main thing I look for." She added that "I don't think I ever felt romantic [about David]—I felt practical. I had the feeling that I'd better make the most of it because it won't last that long."

THE TIMING OF BREAKUPS

If dating relationships were unaffected by their social context, it seems likely that they could end at most any time of the year. But the relationships of the couples in our sample were most likely to break up at key turning points of the school year—in the months of May-June, September, and December-January rather than at other times. This tendency, found for the 103 breakups, is illustrated most dramatically in reports of the ending of all respondents' previous relationships, for which there were more than 400 cases (Figure 4-1).

This pattern of breakups suggests that factors external to a relationship (leaving for vacations, arriving at school, graduation, etc.) may interact with internal factors (such as conflicting values or goals) to cause relationships to end at particular times. For example, changes in living arrangements and schedules at the beginning or end of a semester may make it easier to meet new dating partners (e.g., in a new class) or make it more difficult to maintain previous ties (e.g., when schedules conflict or one moves away). Such changes may raise issues concerning the future of a relationship: Should we get an apartment together? Should we spend our vacation apart? Should I accept a job out of state? Should we get together after vacation? If one has already been considering terminating a relationship, such changes may make it easier to call the relationship off. For example, it is probably easier to say, "While we're apart we ought to date others" than it is to say, "I've grown tired of you and would rather not date you any more." If one is able to attribute the impending breakup to external circumstances, one may be able to avoid some of the ambivalence, embarrassment, and guilt that may be associated with calling a relationship off.

FIGURE 4-1

*Months of the Year in Which Respondents' Previous Relationships
Ended. "Previous Relationship" Refers to the Relationship
Each Participant Had with the Person Dated Most Intensively
During the Two Years Before Dating the Current Partner (Hill, 1974)*

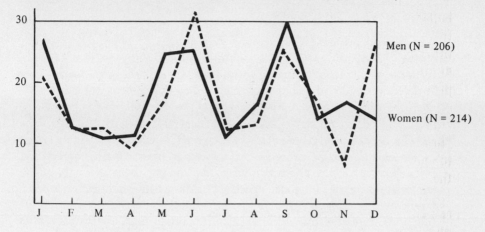

The structuring of breakups by the calendar year was also related to another aspect of the breakup process. In the majority of breakups, like the case of Kathy and Joe, the ending was desired more by the partner who was less involved in the relationship (in this instance, Kathy). In a significant minority of cases, however, the breakup was desired more by the more-involved partner (like Ruth), who finally decides that the costs of remaining in the relationship are higher than he or she can bear. We found a strong tendency for the breakups desired by the less-involved partner to take place near the end or beginning of the school year or during the intervening summer months—71.1 percent April–September vs. 28.9 percent October–March. The breakups desired by the more-involved partner, in contrast, were relatively more likely to take place during the school year—59.1 percent October–March vs. 40.9 percent April–September ($X^2 = 5.68$, $p < .02$). The summer months are, of course, times when college student couples are most likely to be separated because of external factors—for example, returning to homes or jobs in different areas. It seems plausible that less-involved partners would be likely to let their remaining interest in the relationship wane during such periods of separation. Summer separations may also provide a good excuse for the less-involved partner to say good-bye. For the more-involved partner, on the other hand, the period of separation may, if anything, intensify interest in the relationship—"Absence extinguishes small passions and increases great ones" (La Rochefoucauld, quoted in

Heider, 1958). The more-involved partner may be most likely to end the relationship in response to continuing pain and frustration. As in the case of Ruth, the final break may be precipitated by some "last straw" that occurs while the two partners are still together.

THE TWO SIDES OF BREAKING UP

The central principle that *there are two sides to every breakup* has both substantive and methodological implications. Very few breakups are truly mutual, with both parties deciding at more or less the same time that they would like to discontinue the relationship. In the present study, 85 percent of the women and 87 percent of the men reported that one person wanted to end the relationship at least somewhat more than the other. Thus in the large majority of cases there are two distinct roles: "breaker-upper" (to be more literary about it, the rejecting lover) and "broken-up-with" (the rejected lover). Identifying these roles is crucial to understanding anything else about a breakup—its underlying reasons, the termination process itself, or its aftermath.

The impact of this role differentiation emerged particularly clearly in self-reports of the emotional aftermath of breaking up (reports available on one-year follow-up for 31 women, 36 men). Both women and men felt considerably less depressed, less lonely, freer, happier, but more guilty when they were the breaker-uppers than when they were the broken-up-with (for most differences, $p < .01$). For example, whereas Kathy reacted to her breakup with relief, Joe felt deep regret. Indeed, there was a general tendency for the two partners' reactions to a breakup to be inversely related. The freer one partner reported feeling after the break-up, the less free the other partner reported feeling ($r = -.57$, $p < .05$; $N = 15$ cases with both reports). Similar inverse correlations—but of lesser magnitude—characterized the former partners' self-reports of depression, loneliness, and happiness.

A second sense in which there are two sides to every breakup is in the perceptions of the participants; the experience of breaking up is different for each of the two parties involved. For example, although members of couples agreed almost completely on the month in which their relationship finally ended ($r = .98$, $N = 77$), there was only slight agreement on the more subjective question of how gradually or abruptly the ending came about ($r = .24$, $N = 77$). When the former partners were asked to provide their attributions of the causes of the breakup, there was moderate to high agreement on the contribution of nondyadic factors but little or no agreement on factors characterizing the dyad (Table 4-3).

One systematic way in which partners' reports disagree concerns who wanted to break up. Although there is a high correlation between men's and women's reports of who wanted the relationship to end ($r = .85$, $N = 76$), there was a systematic self-bias in the reports. There seems

TABLE 4-3

Factors Contributing to the Ending of a Relationship
(Percentage Reporting)

	Women's Reports	Men's Reports	Partner Correlation
Dyadic Factors			
Becoming bored with the relationship	76.7	76.7	.23*
Differences in interests	72.8	61.1	.04
Differences in backgrounds	44.2	46.8	.05
Differences in intelligence	19.5	10.4	.17
Conflicting sexual attitudes	48.1	42.9	.33**
Conflicting marriage ideas	43.4	28.9	.25*
Nondyadic Factors			
Woman's desire to be independent	73.7	50.0	.57**
Man's desire to be independent	46.8	61.1	.55**
Woman's interest in someone else	40.3	31.2	.56**
Man's interest in someone else	18.2	28.6	.60**
Living too far apart	28.2	41.0	.57**
Pressure from woman's parents	18.2	13.0	.33**
Pressure from man's parents	10.4	9.1	.58**

Note. Data for those couples for which both man's and woman's reports were available ($N = 77$). Factors labelled "man's" and "woman's" above were labelled as "my" or "partner's" in the questionnaires. Percentages are those citing factor as "a contributing factor" or as "one of the most important factors." Correlations are based on 3-point scales.
   *$p < .05$.
   **$p < .01$.

to be a general tendency for respondents to say that they themselves, rather than their partners, were the ones who wanted to break up— 51.3 percent "I," 35.5 percent "partner," 13.0 percent mutual in the women's reports; 46.1 percent "I," 39.5 percent "partner," 15.0 percent mutual in the men's reports ($N = 76$). Apparently it is easier to accept and cope with a breakup if one views it as a desired outcome (as precipitated by oneself or as mutual) than as an outcome imposed against one's will. A similar self-bias appeared in ratings of factors contributing to the breakup—both men and women cited "my" desire to be independent as more important than "partner's" desire to be independent.

For some purposes, therefore, it is difficult to speak confidently about *the* breakup, as if it refers to a single, objective set of events. Instead it seems necessary to attend separately to "his breakup" and to "her breakup," in each instance looking at the matter from the respective partner's point of view—see Bernard's (1972) discussion of "his marriage" and "her marriage." This distinction seems particularly necessary since our data suggest that there may be some systematic differences between men and women in their orientations toward breaking up.

mutual (71 percent), than when the woman precipitated it (46 percent) ($X^2 = 5.83, p < .06$).

EMOTIONAL AFTERMATH

Our generalization would also suggest that breaking up would be a more traumatic experience for men than for women. Unfortunately, the data available to test this proposition are limited to the 15 couples in which we obtained reports of emotional reactions from both partners on the one-year follow-up. These data suggest that men were hit harder than women by the breakup. Men tended more than women to report that in the wake of the breakup they felt depressed, lonely, less happy, less free, and less guilty. Goethals (1973) presents a clinical discussion of sex differences in reactions to breaking up that seems consistent with these data. In our interviews, we were struck by a particular reaction that appeared among several of the men but not among the women. Some men found it extremely difficult to reconcile themselves to the fact that they were no longer loved and that the relationship was over (Jim, in the first of the cases reported above, is illustrative). Women who are rejected may also react with considerable grief and despair, but they seem less likely to retain the hope that their rejectors "really love them after all."

TWO INTERPRETATIONS

The evidence provides converging support for the notion that women tend to fall out of love more readily than men, just as men may tend to fall in love more readily than women (Rubin, 1975). Needless to say, these generalizations are offered as actuarial propositions; they take on importance to the extent that they are informative about aspects of the socialization of the two sexes for close relationships in contemporary America. Two aspects of sex-roles may help account for these tendencies.

Simple economics. Contrary to prevailing stereotypes about romantic and sentimental women, women may be more practical than men about mate selection for simple economic reasons. In most marriages, the wife's status, income, and life chances are far more dependent upon her husband's than vice versa. For this reason, parents in almost all societies have been more concerned with finding appropriate mates for their daughters than for their sons. In "free choice" systems of mate selection like our own, the woman must be especially discriminating. She cannot allow herself to fall in love too quickly, nor can she afford to stay in love too long with the wrong person (Goode, 1959). Men, on the other hand, can afford the luxury of being romantic. The fact that a woman's years of marriageability tend to be more limited than a man's also contributes to her greater need to be selective. Waller (1938) put the matter most bluntly when he wrote:

There is this difference between the man and the woman in the pattern of bourgeois family life: a man, when he marries, chooses a companion and perhaps a helpmate, but a woman chooses a companion and at the same time a standard of living. It is necessary for a woman to be mercenary. [p. 243]

Interpersonal sensitivity. Women are traditionally the social-emotional specialists in most societies, including our own, while men are the traditional task specialists (Parsons and Bales, 1955). The emphasis upon social-emotional matters in women's socialization may lead women to be more sensitive than men to the quality of their interpersonal relationships, both in the present and projecting into the future. One possible reflection of women's greater interpersonal sensitivity is the finding, replicated in the present study, that women distinguish more sharply than men between "liking" and "loving" components of interpersonal sentiments (Rubin, 1970). Because of greater interpersonal sensitivity and discrimination, it may also be more important for women than for men that the quality of a relationship remain high. Thus women's criteria for falling in love—and for staying in love—may be higher than men's, and they may reevaluate their relationships more carefully.

Breakups Before and After Marriage

We have suggested that breakups before marriage are relevant to an understanding of marital breakup in two different ways. First, breakups before marriage provide an interesting comparison against which to view marital disruption. Second, breakups before marriage can serve to prevent marriages that would otherwise be likely to end in divorce. We will briefly consider our results from each of these two perspectives.

COMPARISONS WITH MARITAL BREAKUPS

There are profound differences between the process of breaking up before marriage and the process of breaking up afterward. Some of the breakups of couples in this study took place quite casually—boyfriends and girlfriends went home at the end of the school year and simply never got back together again. Marriages seldom end so casually. Our interview data also made it clear that the experience of breaking up before marriage is generally less stressful than the experience of marital disruption (cf. Weiss, 1976). Such differences reflect fundamental differences between the social-psychological contexts of premarital breakups and divorce. Breakups before marriage take place in the context of a dating system in which coupling, uncoupling, and recoupling are approved and accepted elements. In this context it may be relatively easy for a person who has ended an old relationship to replace it with a new one. Marital disruption, on the other hand, remains a counter-normative phenomenon which is often stigmatized by kin and community. A marriage is typically ended only with considerable effort and stress, and the process of getting back into circulation and replacing a lost partner is likely to be much more difficult for both parties.

Comparing breakups before and after marriage allows us to focus also on commonalities—features that may be intrinsic to the process of ending close relationships (Davis, 1973). One such similarity may be the two-sidedness of breaking up; although there are exceptions, it is probably rare for any sort of breakup to be entirely mutual. As a relationship weakens or deteriorates, the balance of attraction of the two partners is likely to become increasingly unequal. We have found that whereas equal involvement tends to be associated with the growth of a relationship, unequal involvement is associated with its decay. In this asymmetrical context, one party is likely to be the breaker-upper, the other to be the broken-up-with. In addition, the finding that former partners often have very different perceptions of their breakup is probably true in the case of marital breakup as well. Given the fundamental asymmetries that characterize a weakening relationship, it may be inevitable for each party to see events differently, from his or her point of view. This difference in perspective leads to the recommendation that students of marital separation make every effort to obtain reports from both partners. Although this leads to complications in the interpretation of data, they are complications that seem to be an intrinsic part of the phenomenon being studied.

Another similarity between premarital breakup and divorce may be the possibility of sex differences in orientations towards breaking up. Just as we found that women cited more reasons for their breakups than did men, Levinger (1966) found that women cited more marital complaints than men in interviews of applicants for divorce. It is possible, however, that different processes underlie these findings since the kinds of problems cited were not the same. Just as we found some evidence that more women than men wanted to end their dating relationships, Goode (1956) found that women were more likely than men to first suggest getting a divorce. Although Goode hypothesized that the men were really the ones more interested in ending the marriage and that they drove their wives to seek a divorce, since he only obtained reports from the women, it was not possible to check that hypothesis.

BREAKUPS AS PREVENTORS OF DIVORCE

Breakups before marriage are highly relevant to divorce; as someone's grandfather used to say, "The best divorce is the one you get before you get married." A good deal of filtering takes place in the mate-selection process—although, as we have noted, the process is probably more complicated than that suggested by fixed-sequence filter theories. A central question for students of divorce, however, is what prevents still further filtering of the sort that would prevent marriages that result in divorce.

For some (e.g., DeRougemont, 1949), "romantic love" is seen as the culprit, blinding lovers to all practical considerations. But although a large proportion of the couples in our sample felt that they were "in love" (Table 4-1), many nevertheless managed to seek out partners who were similar to themselves with respect to such factors as age, education, intelligence, and, especially, social attitudes and values (Table 4-2). Moreover, many of the couples who were "in love" subsequently decided to break up. The central obstacle is not, in our view, the overwhelming power of romantic love.

Two obstacles which seem to have greater importance are the difficulty one may have in terminating a relationship without access to appropriate facilitating factors (e.g., external excuses) and the difficulty some people —especially men—have in withdrawing from a relationship in which their commitment is not reciprocated. External factors, such as separations that are orchestrated by the school calendar (Figure 4-1), seemed to be helpful in facilitating breakups, both because they encouraged comparisons between the relationship and alternatives and because they helped to provide easier verbal formulas for breaking up. As Albert and Kessler (1976) have remarked, special rituals and formulas are often necessary to facilitate the ending of brief encounters between friends or acquaintances in such a way as to keep intact the esteem of both parties. The availability of such formulas—for example, the ability to say, "I'll see you in the fall" (even when the nature of the relationship may shift in the interim) rather than "I don't want to see you any more"—seems even more necessary to facilitate the ending of close relationships.

This dependence on facilitating circumstances suggests that it may be useful for couples to consider and to create their own occasions for redefining and discussing their relationships. One way in which a couple may be able to do this is by participating in a study such as the present one—which, we have discovered, had the effect of doubling as "couples counseling" (Rubin and Mitchell, 1976). Taking part in the study had the effects of clarifying participants' definitions of their relationships and of facilitating disclosure of feelings, issues, and concerns. Other attempts to facilitate such self-examination and confrontation, whether through college courses, counseling programs, or the mass media, are of potentially great value.

An unwillingness to disengage oneself from a relationship in which one has invested heavily is probably a general human tendency. As Becker (1960) has noted, the investing of time and energy and the foregoing of alternative relationships commit one to remain in a relationship even if it turns out to be a painful one. Our comparison of men's and women's orientations toward loving and leaving suggests that this unwillingness to withdraw may be especially characteristic of men. More generally, the fact that one partner (regardless of sex) typically carries most of the burdens of breaking up makes the process especially difficult. The roles of breaker-upper and broken-up-with are probably common to all sorts of breakup, but this may not be an inevitable differentiation. Ideally, the two partners would be able to discuss and "have out" their differences, and to decide mutually to break up at some point before marriage if they anticipate severe strains or irreconcilable differences. How this ideal might be achieved is, of course, a difficult challenge. It is hoped, however, that continued research into the phenomenon of breaking up before marriage—and the dissemination of this research to young couples—may help to provide the sort of enlightenment that will ease the process for all.

Premarital Pregnancy and Marital Instability

In demographic and sociological studies, the concept of life cycle has become a useful device for summarizing a complex set of human events which tend to follow an orderly and sequential pattern. Events such as birth, marriage, family dissolution, and death can be conveniently arranged along a temporal dimension, facilitating comparisons of family careers within and between societies (Glick, 1957).

For a time investigators were content to use the family life cycle primarily as a descriptive device, but recently there have been attempts to expand the notion to make it more theoretically and analytically powerful (Clausen, 1972; Rodgers, 1973). Most of this work has taken primarily one direction, that of exploring cultural, social, and economic determinants which shape life-cycle patterns or bring about changes in the life course over time. However, it is no less important to ask how shifts in the staging of particular family events impose constraints on the operation of other related social institutions. Or, in focusing on the family itself, another question involves how certain arrangements of the life course affect the character of family relations.

Rather than accounting for the typical life cycle, attention needs to be directed at the consequences of variant or irregular careers for the individual, the family, and society. There is good reason to suspect that unscheduled departures from the typical life course may be socially stressful (Neugarten, 1968; Elder, 1974). While deviations of this nature

This study was supported by Grant MC-R-420117-05-0 from the Public Health Service.

This chapter appeared in a slightly different form in *Journal of Social Issues*, 1976, 32 (1).

frequently give rise to problems in role performance for individuals who pursue unconventional career routes, they do not invariably produce personal disadvantage. Individuals sometimes respond to and benefit from unanticipated opportunities occasioned by disruptions in the normatively prescribed schedule (Riley, Johnson, and Foner, 1972; Elder, 1977).

CONSEQUENCES OF PREMARITAL PREGNANCY

This paper examines one instance of life schedule disorder, premarital pregnancy, tracing its impact on conjugal stability and exploring how and why marital relations are affected by pregnancy before wedlock. Textbooks on marriage and the family tend to portray the courtship system as a well-ordered market where individuals carefully negotiate for their advantage, guided both by self-interest and romantic love. It is clear, however, that a large proportion of marriages take place because a premarital pregnancy has occurred. Figures derived from census data and social surveys reveal that approximately one American bride in four is pregnant at the time of her wedding (Hetzel and Capetta, 1973). Prenuptial conceptions commonly occur within all socioeconomic, racial, and religious groupings (Kantner and Zelnik, 1973).

Beginning with Christensen's (1953, 1960, 1963) pioneering examination of how the timing of first births affects the stability of subsequent marriages, a series of studies have shown that premarital pregnancy greatly increases the probability of eventual marital dissolution (Monahan, 1960; Lowrie, 1965). By linking records of marriages, births, and divorces, Christensen was able to show that couples who had experienced a premarital conception were more than twice as likely to divorce within the first five years of marriage. In a more recent longitudinal study of marital dissolution, Coombs and Zumeta (1970) also discovered a strong association between the occurrence of a premarital pregnancy and marital breakup. Of the couples who had conceived premaritally, 41 percent were no longer together five years later, compared to 18 percent of those who had not conceived prior to marriage. Several studies focusing on the consequences of illegitimate births for subsequent marital stability also report a high incidence of dissolution. Sarrel (1967), in a small retrospective study of black adolescents who became pregnant before wedlock, reported that within a five-year period three-fourths of the marriages were no longer intact. In a larger study with a more diverse sample, Sauber and Corrigan (1970) traced marriage careers of unwed mothers in New York. One-half of those who married during the study period no longer lived with their husbands at the time of the five-year followup.

A number of different reasons why a pregnancy before marriage might adversely affect the prospect of a stable union have been suggested. First, some investigators have assumed that one reason for the association is that individuals who become premaritally pregnant are different either in their personality and/or cultural values (Vincent, 1961; Paulker, 1969). The same set of personal or cultural factors which may predispose women to become premaritally pregnant are also thought to reduce their chances of making a stable marriage. In other words, marriages preceded by a pregnancy do not survive because individuals entering such unions are less capable of or committed to creating a viable union (Chilman, 1966).

Second, it has been hypothesized that a premarital pregnancy may cut short the process of preparing for married life. Christensen (1960) speculates that such marriages often occur "without adequate preparation, or in the absence of love, or in the face of ill-matched personalities" (p. 38). Couples who marry precipitately may not be ready to settle down, may have reservations about the suitability of their mates, and may be unwilling or unable to assume the responsibilities of married life (Havighurst, 1961). Compounding their own uncertainty are doubts voiced by their families. If the spouses do not encounter outright opposition, they often lack the kinship support generally provided at the time of marriage (Winch and Greer, 1964), and may lose out on the assistance provided by kin if they had remained single (Stack, 1974).

A third explanation considers the economic costs resulting from a premature marriage. Marriage often begins without the benefit of accumulated savings, and, since the partners are typically young, the problems of making an adequate livelihood are severe. Not only is the male restricted in his occupational opportunities, but the female is often unable to contribute to the family income because child care responsibilities are immediately thrust upon her. Moreover, the income required is greater than is usual for a newly married couple because of the presence of the child. This places an added burden on the wage earner (Schorr, 1965; Coombs and Freedman, 1970). It might also be expected that early marriage would restrict the occupational mobility of both parents, since they often must begin employment before completing educational or vocational training which might otherwise have enhanced their job opportunities (Rapoport, 1964). Further, their ability to change employment is limited by the greater family responsibilities they must assume in the early years of marriage.

Finally, another potential source of strain on conjugal relations is the accelerated family building which accompanies a marriage preceded by a pregnancy. It has been suggested that the abrupt introduction of the child into the family constellation can prevent the solidarity between partners that might otherwise develop during the early years of marriage (Pohlman, 1969). Relations may be further complicated by a rapid succession of additional pregnancies. The husband, particularly, may begin to feel trapped by the accumulating economic and emotional responsibilities. On her part, the wife may resent the heavy burdens of caring for several young children and have little emotional energy to invest in the marriage relationship.

Clearly, none of these four conditions—personal instability, lack of preparation for marriage, insufficiency of economic resources, and pressures from rapid family building—is unique to those who enter marriage as a result of pregnancy. All are common problems in blue collar marriages (Komarovsky, 1964; Chilman, 1966) and probably for many middle-class marriages as well. It might also be said, however, that the occurrence of premarital pregnancy at an early age would aggravate each of these problems and thus compound the probability of marital difficulty. Although this expectation is plausible enough, it has received remarkably little empirical support.

Method

As a part of a larger study of the consequences of unplanned pregnancy (Furstenberg, 1976), longitudinal data were collected on the occupational, marital, and fertility careers of a sample of 404 women who became pregnant during adolescence in 1966–1968 and of a sample of 269 of their former classmates. Although I will here make some use of data based on this larger sample, most of the findings refer primarily to the experiences of a subgroup of 203 adolescent mothers who married after becoming pregnant and who participated in the five-year followup interview.

Adolescent mothers (AMs) were contacted as soon as they registered for prenatal care at the obstetric clinic of a large private hospital in Baltimore. Each expectant mother was interviewed during pregnancy and in three subsequent followups—at one, three, and five years after the birth of her child. Each interview ran approximately an hour and contained both structured and unstructured questions on the educational, occupational, marital, and fertility experiences and plans of the respondents. All the fieldwork was done by trained interviewers who were closely supervised by a field director. The initial interview occurred in the hospital; thereafter, interviews generally took place in the home.

Throughout the study, cooperation was excellent. At one year, 95 percent of the respondents were located and reinterviewed; at three years, 90 percent; and at the final followup, 80 percent (323) remained in the study. Classmates of the young mothers were first contacted at the time of the three-year followup and 82 percent were interviewed again during the final stage of the study in 1972. Attrition was almost invariably due to difficulty in locating the respondents; the refusal rate was under 5 percent.

The two samples were well matched in background characteristics. Both were predominantly black (approximately 90 percent of each), and from working- and lower-class families—typically the head of the household was employed at an unskilled or semiskilled job and had not graduated from high school. A substantial minority (about 40 percent) of the women's families was headed by a single parent.

It is important to acknowledge that the sample includes a small percentage of whites—27 of the 203 AM subgroup—yet racial status is not here treated as an independent variable. There are so few whites in the sample that race could not have a sizable impact on our results even if patterns of marital experience differed substantially among blacks and whites. Even so, it is interesting to note that in our study racial status is not substantially related to marital stability. Apart from the fact that whites more often marry and marry sooner after becoming pregnant, their experience in wedlock is similar to that of nonwhites. About the same proportion of black and white marriages dissolved during the course of the study. While these findings may only reflect the selective characteristics of the white women in the study, they may conceivably suggest that, if we control for the risk of premarital pregnancy, the differences in marital stability between blacks and whites so commonly reported in the literature may be significantly reduced (Rainwater, 1966).

PATTERNS OF MARRIAGE

At the five-year followup, 323 young mothers and 221 of their classmates were interviewed. Nearly a fifth of the mothers had already wed before their first visit to the prenatal clinic, and by the time their babies were delivered more than one in four had married (all but a few of these women married the father of the child). These figures include a few cases of women who claimed to have married just prior to becoming pregnant, but the accuracy of their reports may be questionable, judging from the timing of the subsequent birth.

Deferred or postnatal marriage was an even more common pattern. The rate of marriage was nearly as great in the two years following delivery as in the twelve months preceding the birth of the child. Thereafter, the proportion of those marrying dropped off. These figures are subject to a certain amount of error because one-fifth of the sample was lost to followup. Also, it was not possible to reinterview respondents exactly five years after delivery, making it difficult to compute the precise percentage who had married at specific durations after the birth of their first child. These deficiencies can be corrected for by using a life table procedure which estimates the probability of a marriage occurring at the end of each year, measured from the point of delivery (Furstenberg,

Masnick, and Ricketts, 1972). The estimated marriage proportions deviate only slightly from the percentages cited above.

EXPERIENCE AFTER MARRIAGE

Since marriages occurred at different points in the period from 1966 to 1972, the proportion of marriages that were still intact at the final followup is not a very useful figure, for it does not take into account the fact that risk of separation varies with the length of exposure to marriage. It would therefore be fallacious to compare the proportion of unstable marriages among the AMs who wed after becoming pregnant to their classmates who married prior to pregnancy, since the latter had on the average married two or three years later. A life table analysis makes adjustments for these limitations by calculating the probability of separation at standard intervals from the point at which the marriage began.

Table 5-1 shows the mortality of marriages among the sample of AMs and their classmates. Marriages contracted during the study had less than an even chance of surviving beyond the first few years of wedlock. Based on probability figures, about one-fifth of the marriages broke up in one year, and nearly one-third were dissolved by two years. By the fourth anniversary of the marriage, less than one-half of the couples were still together. The rate of separation slows down thereafter; though the numbers on which the estimates are based are so small that the figures become less reliable, three out of five marriages break up within six years. By any standard, these rates of breakup are extremely high. Carter and Glick (1970) report from census data that, among non-

TABLE 5-1

Cumulative Probability of Separation by Timing of Marriage among Adolescent Mothers and Their Classmates

Months from Marriage Date	Adolescent Mothers (203)	Classmates (87)	Classmates Premaritally Pregnant (40)	Classmates Not Premaritally Pregnant (40)
12	.21	.10	.13	.08
24	.33	.18	.23	.16
36	.46	.26	.30	.24
48	.52	.31	–	–
60	.57	–	–	–
72	.61	–	–	–

Note. No probability reported when $N < 10$. Of 90 classmates, 3 did not provide marital data and 7 gave no childbearing histories.

white women married at least ten years before 1960, 28 percent were no longer living with their spouses. Even after twenty-five years of marriage, the nonwhite women in the census do not begin to approach the proportion of marital instability experienced by the young mothers in our study.

Although the rate of marital breakup during the first three and one-half years of marriage among the classmates is also not low, it is still only half that of the AMs' rate. When the cases of the classmates who married after conception are removed, the differences are even more striking. Among the women who had not experienced a premarital pregnancy, the probability of the marriage breaking up within the two years was one-half of the rate calculated for the AMs (Table 5-1). The figures for these women are similar to the rates cited earlier from census data for black women in the general population. The patterns of marital instability of the classmates who married after becoming pregnant are noticeably higher, though still less than the rate for the AMs. Apparently, the young mothers were particularly disadvantaged in marriage because their pregnancies occurred earlier in adolescence than those of the classmates.

Sources of Marital Instability

Our introduction briefly reviewed four alternative ways of explaining why premaritally pregnant couples may experience high rates of marital instability. How well each accounts for the high rate of marital instability among the women who married after becoming pregnant can now be examined.

INDIVIDUAL PREDISPOSITION

The first explanation holds that individuals who become pregnant before they wed have greater difficulty staying married because personal or cultural standards that make persons prone to prenuptial pregnancy may also make them prone to marital instability. The data do not permit us to rule out this interpretation completely; nevertheless, they provide no support for it.

Many of the young mothers in our sample were from broken families and therefore presumably more prone to separation and divorce. Two recent studies (Heiss, 1972; Duncan and Duncan, 1969) failed to find an intergenerational correlation of marital instability, though the findings of Pope and Mueller (chapter 6) suggest that the question is still un-

settled. Our data reveal no tendency for marital instability to be "heredi-
tary." AMs from broken families were not more likely to separate during
the duration of the study than those from intact families. The possibility
that a history of illegitimacy in the family created a predisposition toward
marital instability, by weakening the AMs' commitment to marriage, was
also examined. The probability of separation was almost the same for
AMs who did and those who did not have a family history of illegitimacy.
Finally, several indicators of the socioeconomic status of the AMs' family
of origin were found unrelated to durability of marriage, suggesting that
women from especially impoverished backgrounds were no less equipped
to assume the responsibilities of marriage. Thus, it would seem that the
high propensity toward conjugal dissolution cannot be explained by the
fact that many AMs grew up in families that were structurally variant
or economically disadvantaged.

If the predisposition for marital instability were transmitted culturally,
then women whose marriages break up should be found to hold distinctive standards and expectations regarding matrimony. At the five-year
followup the separated women did indeed express slightly less confidence
in the viability of marriage, but this sentiment seems to be a consequence
rather than a cause of marital unhappiness. Those women in marriages
that broke up were no less likely to have voiced confidence in the institution of marriage at the time of the first interview, and were equally
inclined to state their desire and intention to marry at that time. Moreover, in the final interview there was no difference between the married
and separated women in their responses to questions about the sources
of marital strain, the proper division of labor within the family, or
decision-making authority of husband and wife. Even after their marital
dissolution, the separated women maintained similar attitudes about
matrimony to those of their married counterparts (Furstenberg, 1976).

Examination of results collected from the classmates on the same set
of questions further confirms the conclusion that the separated women
do not hold a deviant set of sentiments about marriage. The classmates'
responses to the various attitudinal measures mentioned above closely
resemble the positions taken by both the separated and the married AMs.
No sizeable differences appeared between the subgroups. It thus seems
implausible that the greater marital instability among the AMs was a
consequence of a different cultural code.

PREPARATION FOR MARRIAGE

A consideration of the situation of the young couple at the time they
married seems to offer a more promising direction for understanding the
sources of marital instability. Previous studies have shown that age at
marriage is a powerful determinant of the stability of the union (Burchinal, 1965; Lowrie, 1965; Bumpass and Sweet, 1972). In contrast, in this

study age at marriage was itself not consistently related to stability. The association between age at marriage and conjugal stability was actually curvilinear; the oldest age group (18 and over) achieved even less success in marriage than the girls who were 16 or younger when they married. Introducing the marriage age of the male does not help; if the effects of both partners' marriage ages are examined simultaneously, no consistent patterns appear.

This unexpected finding may be due in part to the characteristics of the women in this sample. Perhaps differences by age of marriage would have been more apparent had a greater number of couples waited until their early twenties to wed. Yet there is reason to doubt this interpretation; couples in the sample who waited several years before marrying were less rather than more successful in maintaining their marriages. Moreover, data from census records indicate that marriage age has a different effect on stability for nonwhites than for whites. Marital stability is consistently lower for white women who marry before the age of 18, but this is not so for nonwhites. Regardless of age at marriage, nonwhite females have about the same chance of experiencing a divorce (Carter and Glick, 1970). One reason may be that younger black couples tend to marry only when their economic prospects are reasonably bright. Bearing this out, age is not an accurate indicator in our study of how adequately prepared couples were to assume the economic responsibilities of setting up a household.

A different and perhaps more direct sign of readiness for marriage is courtship experience. Textbooks on marriage suggest that the courtship period provides both a filtering procedure and an opportunity for the couple to explore future patterns of marital interaction (Burgess and Wallin, 1953; Winch, 1971). Ambivalence and uncertainty, while not completely eliminated, usually are lessened by sustained premarital contact. Consistent with this inference, previous studies have demonstrated that brief courtships are associated with higher conjugal instability (Burchinal, 1960). A premarital pregnancy generally cuts short preparation for marriage, adding to the difficulty of postmarital adjustment.

Several findings suggest that certain couples in the sample were indeed psychologically unprepared for marriage and therefore experienced marital problems. An index developed to measure the couple's relationship prior to marriage included items estimating the amount of time the partners had known one another before marriage, how frequently they had been going out together, and whether the AM had been seeing other men in addition to her husband.

A brief duration of contact between the partners prior to marriage was clearly associated with marital instability (Table 5-2). Women who reported frequent and intensive contact with their husbands for at least a year before marriage had half as much separation as those who had spent less time with their mates during courtship. In addition, AMs who

TABLE 5-2

*Probability of Separation by Length of Relationship
Prior to Marriage*

Months from Marriage Date	Brief Duration Prior to Marriage (43)	Extensive Duration Prior to Marriage (138)
12	.30	.17
24	.51	.29
36	.51	.43

Note. Brief duration is defined as under two years. Data
collected at third interview, at which time 22 married AMs
were not included.

reported sexual relations with more than one partner during the period
just prior to becoming pregnant were not as likely to achieve stable
unions as were those AMs who had exclusive sexual relationships with
their future husbands (Table 5-3).

These findings appear to be part of a larger configuration of results
having to do with the strength of the prenuptial bond. Women who wed
the father of their first child generally achieved more stable unions; their
rate of marital breakup was about 50 percent less than women who
married another man. These parents generally had a much stronger premarital tie than couples in which the husband was not the child's father.
The relationships could be termed "developed," because almost without
exception the marital partners had been involved in a long-standing and
exclusive alliance. By contrast some women formed "extemporaneous"
unions with other men, based on relationships which were hastily impro-
vised after the child was born. Some commenced shortly after the AM

TABLE 5-3

Probability of Separation by Sexual History Prior to Marriage

Months from Marriage Date	Infrequent Relations: One Male (77)	Frequent Relations: One Male (46)	Infrequent Relations: Several Males (14)	Frequent Relations: Several Males (16)
12	.16	.25	.38	.42
24	.28	.39	–	–
36	.43	.64	–	–

Note. No probability reported when $N < 8$. Data collected at first interview.
Women already married (50 cases) were not asked this information.

broke up with the father and are similar in some respects to the "rebound relationship" experienced by young divorcées (Hunt, 1966).

Having a child takes on a very different meaning in these two types of unions. Among couples with a developed relationship, the child reinforces the conjugal bond, serving as a common interest and focus of attention. The effect of the child could be just the opposite within the extemporaneous union, where he serves as a divisive intrusion, an ever-present reminder of the origin of the relationship. In a certain sense, these extemporaneous marital dyads really are triads consisting of husband, wife, and father of the child.

Although the history of the relationship has a definite impact on its outcome, by itself it is not sufficient to account for the high rates of marital instability within the sample of young mothers. Brief courtship was more the exception than the rule. Most relationships had all the features of a developed courtship—long-standing, exclusive, and intimate. Most couples were not completely emotionally unprepared for marriage, a finding which helps to elucidate why age was not strongly related to marital success. Those younger couples who married were especially likely to have relationships that were developed rather than extemporaneous.

Another reason to doubt that courtship relations can entirely explain the high rate of conjugal instability is the fact that the courtship histories of the classmates closely resembled those of the adolescent mothers. Since the classmates achieved a much higher record of marital stability, it does not seem likely that the courtship pattern alone could account for the differences between the two samples.

ECONOMIC RESOURCES AND MARITAL STABILITY

Although researchers disagree about why it is so, almost all existing studies show that economic resources are strongly linked to marital stability (Scanzoni, 1970; Cutright, 1971; Furstenberg, 1974). Economic resources matter even more for blacks than for whites. Not only do black males face limited employment opportunities, restricted occupational mobility, and unfair rates of compensation, but they are sometimes confronted with the fact that their wives are relatively more employable than they are. This situation results in a double strain on black marriages. At the same time that the husband feels that his role as provider is being undercut, his wife is likely to resent his inability to support the family (Rainwater, 1970).

There is every reason to suspect that this situation was common within our sample. Most husbands possessed none of the qualities that might overcome the considerable obstacles black men face in finding a decent job. The married males tended to be young, inexperienced, and unskilled.

Accordingly, economic difficulties were high on the list of reasons offered by the AMs for why their marriages did not work out. More than one out of every four wives explicitly attributed the failure of the marriage to their husbands' inability to support them and their children. Although it is difficult to calculate the precise number, it is also clear that an additional number of women appeared to redefine economic problems as shortcomings in the personality of the men they had married.

The impact of economic insufficiency on the viability of the marriage can be examined directly by considering the association between a male's earning capacity and the chances that his marriage will survive. As a rough measure of their earning potential, husbands were divided into two status categories: "low" if they had not completed high school and held an unskilled job, "high" if they were high school graduates and/or skilled workers. This admittedly crude index is the best single predictor of marital stability. Among the lower-status males, the probability of separation within two years after the wedding date was .45; for higher-status, it was only .19. This relative difference between the two status groups is maintained through the entire study period.

Thus one connecting link in the chain between premarital pregnancy and later marital termination is the weak economic position of the father of the out-of-wedlock child. Most of these men have little earning potential prior to marriage; an ill-timed marriage forces them to terminate school and to enter the labor force under unfavorable circumstances. Such a father is hard pressed to find stable and remunerative employment. How much he would have profited if he had been able to postpone the pregnancy and ensuing marriage is not easily answered by the data on hand. One study of white couples has shown that early parenthood has an adverse effect on a man's earning capacity over an extended period (Coombs and Freedman, 1970). One might expect that the effect of a premarital pregnancy would be even more severe for black men who have less opportunity to recover from a severe financial handicap at the outset of marriage.

One way of putting this speculation to the test is to examine the economic status of the men who married the classmates, comparing them to the spouses of the young mothers. There is a noticeable difference in the status level of the two groups of men, especially after we distinguish the couples among the classmates who married after a premarital pregnancy. Half of the husbands of AMs were in the higher SES category. In contrast, three-fifths of the premaritally pregnant classmates and 85 percent of the classmates who married before becoming pregnant married males who were (relatively speaking) of higher status.

Many of the young mothers shared responsibility for supporting their families, and it is therefore important to consider the impact of their status on the stability of the marriage. With the same status index of earning capacity, marriages of higher-status women, like the marriages of higher-status males, tended to be more stable. However, much of this association could be accounted for by the fact that individuals of higher status tend to marry one another. A simultaneous examination of the status of the husband and wife revealed that marital cohesion was more strongly related to the economic position of the male than the female, though both contributed to conjugal stability (Table 5-4).

The marital situation of the couple is based on a complex matrix of socioeconomic factors which shifts with the economic fortunes of each partner. Stress on the marriage fluctuates in response to both the accumulation and distribution of economic resources. Clearly, other factors also enter into the decision to remain together. Most AMs reported that personal incompatibility was the major reason why their marriages broke up. However, personal differences are necessarily evaluated with less tolerance when economic resources are low. There is simply less reason to maintain a problematic relationship when the female is not dependent on the male for support (Levinger, 1965). This is why unions in which the women's earning capacity was greater than their husbands' had such low rates of survival.

In a previous paper (Furstenberg, 1974), I showed that holders of lower-status jobs, or what some economists refer to as "secondary positions," command less marital loyalty primarily because they offer less long-term security. Not only is the current economic contribution of the secondary worker unacceptably low, but his prospects for improvement in the future are poor if not nonexistent (Gordon, 1972). In his own eyes and the eyes of his spouse, the lower-class male is a poor investment. Although this study provides only a brief time span in which to trace patterns of social mobility, there is more than a strong hint that marital stability is tied to economic advancement. The few men who improved their economic status during the course of the study had noticeably higher marital stability than those men whose status declined or re-

TABLE 5-4

Probability of Separation by Economic Status of Husband and Wife

Months from Marriage Date	Both Low (68)	High Wife, Low Husband (28)	Low Wife, High Husband (44)	Both High (54)
12	.28	.18	.14	.12
24	.50	.36	.22	.16
36	.60	.55	.31	.28
48	.67	–	.39	.40

Note. No probability reported when $N < 10$. Data collected at final interview; no information available for nine cases.

mained low during the period between followups (65 percent vs. 40 percent).

Apart from the impact that an unplanned pregnancy has on the male's earning prospects, it also contributes to the economic strain on the family in other ways. Although there is not complete agreement in the literature, a number of studies have claimed that rapid and frequent childbearing is related to marital instability (Coombs and Zumeta, 1970; Hurley and Palonen, 1967; Pohlman, 1969; Rainwater, 1966). It is not surprising that this should be so. Accelerated family building means that greater economic resources will be required to support the family within a short period of time. At the same time, the contribution that the wife can make in sharing the economic burden is severely restricted if she is pregnant frequently and must remain at home to care for the children. To the extent that this pressure is a divisive factor, the timing of the first birth (and of subsequent births) may be a source of marital dissolution.

The relatively brief span of this study precludes a definite answer to the question of how marital stability is affected by patterns of family building over the long term. This analysis produced no consistent evidence that repeated conceptions early in marriage have an adverse effect on the rate of stability. Multigravidous women were actually more likely to remain married than primagravidas, perhaps because marital difficulties may have dissuaded some couples from having additional children. Whatever the reason, low fertility does not forecast marital success within this population.

It is possible that spacing of births has a more significant impact on marital harmony than the number of births. At the time of the first interview virtually none of the AMs wanted to become pregnant again for at least two years; marital strain, therefore, should have been greater when subsequent conception occurred during this period. Again, the evidence for this expectation was equivocal at best. The marital stability of women who had repeated pregnancies (in less than 18 months) was contrasted with those who deferred additional childbearing. This comparison revealed no differences, suggesting that child spacing is not an important determinant of conjugal stability at least in the short term.

There may be a number of reasons why the data failed to show a connection between high fertility and marital instability. First, only a small proportion of women showed extremely high fertility within the limited duration of the study—only 28 married women had borne three or more children by the five-year followup. Second, mothers with several children were just as likely to be married to higher status husbands as were mothers with fewer children. It is possible that the number of children was more a response to than a determinant of economic status.

In other words it might have been too early to assess the extent to which children create an economic strain on the family, because most couples had not had sufficient time to build large families, and many of the large families had occurred among couples who were better able to afford them.

Also, the presence of children might temporarily have a cohesive effect in marriage. Particularly if the husband has participated actively in the decision to have children, he could be more reluctant to abandon his family. Similarly, the wife who has several children in the early years of marriage is rather dependent on her husband and hence may be disinclined to precipitate a marital breakup if the marriage is not going well (Figley, 1973).

Finally, the connection between fertility and instability is confounded in another respect. Couples whose marriages are going well may desire additional children. Moreover, we know that couples who stay together have a better chance of producing children. Consequently, it is difficult to test the effect of accelerated family building on marital instability, especially in the short run.

Conclusion

Of four different explanations of why marriages preceded by a pregnancy suffer high rates of disintegration, two were supported by the data and two were not. There was no confirmation for the premise that marital breakdown is the product of a distinctive set of cultural standards held by females who become premaritally pregnant. Also disconfirmed was the expectation that rapid family building would increase the probability of marital instability. While these two unsupported hypotheses cannot be completely ruled out due to limitations of the data, the results at least call into question their usefulness in explaining the link between premarital pregnancy and marital instability among women like those in our sample.

Our results provided more support for the argument that premarital pregnancy disrupts the courtship process and cuts short a necessary stage in preparation for marriage. Unions were unlikely to survive unless the couple had a long-standing and exclusive relationship prior to pregnancy. The marriages which had the best chance of lasting occurred among women who married the father of their child soon after conception.

The hypothesis supported most strongly by the data was the economic one. Regardless of their initial stake in the relationship, marriages fre-

quently floundered because the husband who married a premaritally
pregnant woman was unable to support a family. Even in instances where
the scheduling of family formation is ideal, many black couples—and
our sample was 90 percent black—are at a disadvantage due to racial
and economic discrimination. When pregnancy forces a revision of that
schedule, the effects on marital unions can be devastating.

These results support the general assumption that certain predictable
costs arise when individuals diverge from customary career routes. Persons who are "out of phase," that is, premature in their movements to a
new role, may be both reluctant to relinquish familiar positions and
poorly equipped to assume new ones. Even if they are adequately prepared, others on whom they depend for support may not be. Ill-timed
transitions may remove them from customary sources of social support
while denying them the necessary resources to function effectively in
their new positions. These reasons help to explain why the occurrence
of a premarital pregnancy augurs so poorly for a couple's prospects of
marital success.

The Intergenerational Transmission of Marital Instability: Comparisons by Race and Sex

Marital dissolution in the United States is primarily the consequence of the social organization of American society, which is highly differentiated and in which each societal unit has a specialized function. The family is focused on exchanges of affection; productive, recreational, educational, protective, and religious functions are largely accomplished outside of the family unit. Because women, as well as men, have access to employment, the economic deterrents to divorce are limited. Further, attitudes toward divorce are permissive; the marriage institution is not viewed religiously or morally but instrumentally. Marriage is considered a relationship within which to seek mutual gratification. If this gratification is not forthcoming, divorce and remarriage (or even singlehood) are considered an acceptable course of action (Nye and Berardo, 1973).

American marriages may also result in disruption because broken parental marriages make their children's marriages more susceptible to basic disrupting influences. Thus divorce may be viewed as the consequence of the above basic causes as well as of children's being made more susceptible to these basic causes as the result of their parents'

We express our appreciation to Larry L. Bumpass, David L. Featherman, Robert M. Hauser, and James A. Sweet for supplying some of the data sets used in this research. The 1970 National Fertility Survey data used in this publication were collected pursuant to Contract #PH-43-65-1048 with the National Institutes of Health, Public Health Service, Department of Health, Education and Welfare. Edward J. Lawler, David A. Parton, and Stephen G. Wieting provided thoughtful comments on draft versions of this paper.

This chapter appeared in a slightly different form in *Journal of Social Issues*, 1976, 32 (1).

marital problems. This may be referred to as the "transmission cause" of divorce. The paper presents descriptive data on the transmission hypothesis and discusses the correspondence between available data and one suggested explanation.

Herzog and Sudia (1973) note in their review that "despite the common assumption that growing up in a broken home is related to later marital disruption, evidence is relatively limited." Studies reporting data relevant for the transmission hypothesis have yielded inconsistent results. Duncan and Duncan (1969), with a national nonfarm sample coded for other purposes, indicate no transmission for blacks or whites. Bumpass and Sweet (1972) find that white women whose parents were divorced or separated are more likely to have their own marriages dissolved than are women from intact homes. Heiss (1972) reports that the transmission of marital instability is "quite small" among metropolitan blacks in the North. The inconsistency of reported results is due in part to differences in coding and analysis procedures across investigators. Our collection of available data sets with information on marital history in two generations, insofar as possible using parallel definitions and procedures, permits the most thorough test of the intergenerational transmission hypothesis to date.

Conceptual Background

In this article *marital instability* will refer to marriage with a high risk of being voluntarily dissolved (through separation or divorce), *marital dissolution* to voluntary dissolution only (and the adjective may be omitted when the context makes the meaning clear), and *marital disruption* to both voluntary dissolution and involuntary dissolution (through the death of either spouse).

Numerous rationales have been offered in support of the "transmission of marital instability" hypothesis, but there exists no systematic explication of their major premises. We will fully develop the "role model" rationale, both because our data allow testing of several of its implications and because it is the rationale most heavily relied on by sociologists and social psychologists. First, however, we will briefly identify four other possible explanatory schema.

The "personality" rationale argues that parental personality characteristics cause both the parents' marital problems and certain personality characteristics in the child, which in turn create the child's marital adjustment problems (Nye and Berardo, 1973; Dager, 1964). The "economic" rationale argues that the sudden and perhaps permanent reduction in economic resources caused by death or divorce in a family lowers the life chances of children from such a family (Brandwein, Brown, and Fox, 1974); the broken family's downward economic mobility lowers the child's chances for a high-status marriage and makes him and his marriage partner subject to the stresses that produce a higher marital dissolution rate for lower-class persons. The "social control" rationale argues that family members provide social control over a child (Hirschi, 1969); they discipline a child for bad behavior, control peer contacts, influence the choice of mate, and support any marriage contracted. A break in the nuclear family reduces the size and integration of a child's kin network and reduces its effectiveness as a social-control mechanism (Mueller and Pope, 1977). The "permissive attitudes" rationale is the simplest, asserting that parents who are tolerant of divorce will divorce as a response to marital problems, will transmit tolerant attitudes to their children, and will produce children who readily dissolve their own marriages. These four rationales should not be considered mutually exclusive; in fact, it is quite possible that they could be synthesized to arrive at a more complete theory of the transmission of marital instability. Nevertheless, we prefer to view them as distinct alternatives since the focus as to the primary cause(s) is clearly different.

The most common rationale given by social psychologists and sociologists in support of the transmission hypothesis is a role model rationale. Being able to generate "profit" for oneself in a marital relationship and to provide profit for the spouse depends on being aware of the normative structure defining the marital relationship (Nye and Berardo, 1973; Heiss, 1972). The relevance of family life for a child's role performance in later life is that the family is a major source of learning the content of social roles, particularly familial ones. Social learning theorists note that children learn roles by direct instruction from parents, by interacting with them, and by observing them, particularly in interaction with each other (Bandura, 1969; Kohlberg, 1969; Mischel, 1970; Mussen, 1969). The central idea in the role model rationale is that the appropriateness of the sex and marital roles learned in the family by the child determines his or her marital success; the child in an unhappy or broken home will not learn marital roles as appropriately as one in an intact happy home.

This rationale can also be used to account for results from four other comparisons, for each of which higher voluntary dissolution rates are predicted for the persons mentioned first: (a) persons who come from homes broken by divorce versus those broken by death, (b) persons who lived with neither natural parent versus those who lived with one natural parent after the break, (c) persons who lived with a single parent versus those who lived with a parent and stepparent, and (d) persons who lived with an opposite- versus those who lived with a same-sex natural parent.

Parents heading toward divorce present culturally inappropriate marital- and sex-role content to a child, and if a home is tension filled, parents are not as effective in transmitting role content to a child (Hill and Aldous, 1969). After disruption in a parental home has occurred, role theory suggests that continuing to live with one parent is important for role learning by the child. If the child remains with either his mother or father, emotional support and similarity in role demands and modeling would be provided for the child. However, in comparison to two-parent families, single-parent families are handicapped in presenting sex-role content because of the missing parent, even though the limited content presented may be appropriate and may even include content appropriate to the role of the missing parent. Children in single-parent families can obtain exposure to appropriate sex-role content through verbal instruction, observation of characters in the mass media, and through observation and contact with siblings and persons such as teachers and adult friends (Bell, 1971; Herzog and Sudia, 1973; Kohlberg, 1966). Even so, well-integrated complete families have an advantage over partial families in transmitting role behaviors. However, there is the additional question of whether the parent in the single-parent home is of the same or different sex than that of the child. It is sometimes argued that a child living with only an opposite-sex parent will have predominantly the content of the inappropriate sex role presented to him (Dager, 1964). This has been the assumption of some arguing that the female-headed black family is not successfully transmitting the masculine role to black boys (Moynihan, 1965).

Data Sources and Analysis Procedures

Because single data sets, especially those of small size, are subject to sampling error which can produce anomalous findings, we obtained and analyzed all available and relevant data sets. We utilized the following criteria in our search: (a) the data set must allow a reasonable test of the transmission hypothesis, and (b) it must be of sufficient size and scope to allow generalization about either male-female or black-white differences. The five sources of data used in our analysis are summarized in Table 6-1 and briefly described below.

OCG. The Occupational Changes in a Generation survey was conducted in conjunction with a March 1962 Current Population Survey;

TABLE 6-1

Data Sets

Name and Population Represented	Sample Size		Measure of Stability and Reason for Disruption	Post-Disruption Household Composition Given?	Measure of Respondent's Marital Stability
OCG: Male noninstitutional civilian labor force, aged 25-64 in 1962, native born.	Black: White:	1171 14752	With both parents most of the time up to age 16? Reason not given.	Minimally	Ever-disrupted for any reason.
Crain-NORC: Northern metropolitan black residents, aged 21-45 in 1966, native born.	Female: Male:	786 610	With both parents at age 16? Reason given.	Yes	First marriage disrupted by divorce, separation, or desertion.
Parnes: Noninstitutional females, aged 30-44 in 1967, native born.	Black: White:	1269 3230	With whom at age 15? Reason not given.	Yes	First marriage disrupted by divorce or separation.
Fertility: Noninstitutional females, aged under 45 in 1970, native born.	Black: White:	1150 5257	With both parents at age 14? Reason given.	No	First marriage disrupted by divorce or separation.
NORC: Noninstitutional population, aged 18-75 in 1972-1973-1974, native born.	Females Black: White: Males Black: White:	284 1693 209 1500	With whom at around age 16? Reason not available for all.	Yes	Ever-disrupted by divorce or separation.

Note. Actual sample sizes are indicated; however, for all but the NORC data set weighted data are used in the analysis. Also, for the NORC data set information on reasons is available only in the 1973 and 1974 samples.

it was designed to provide detailed information on the extent, form and determinants of occupational mobility in the United States (Blau and Duncan, 1967).

Crain-NORC. These data come from a 1966 study conducted by Robert L. Crain and others at the National Opinion Research Center (Crain and Weisman, 1972). The purpose was to study northern blacks and determine the effects of attending integrated versus segregated schools. These data are the only set used here that do not comprise a national sample.

Parnes. The 1967 National Longitudinal Survey of Work Experience of Women was part of a large-scale longitudinal research endeavor designed to measure numerous economic, sociological, and psychological variables important for understanding labor force behavior and work attitudes (Parnes, Shea, Spitz, and Zeller, 1970).

Fertility. The 1970 National Fertility Survey is one of a series of periodic surveys designed to gain fertility and contraceptive information from women of childbearing age in the United States to measure demographic trends, assess the demographic effects of recent historical events, and continue the development of theory and methodology in demography (Ryder and Westoff, 1971).

NORC. The National Opinion Research Center General Social Surveys represent three data sets for the years 1972, 1973, and 1974. These surveys were initiated to replicate findings from prior national surveys and to provide contemporary data useful to social science researchers.

In each survey respondents were asked to recount whether they had lived with both parents at some particular age (either 14, 15, or 16), and if not, why not. In addition, the living arrangement subsequent to the parents' death or divorce was ascertained and the respondent's own marital history obtained. As indicated in Table 6-1, some of the samples were limited to blacks, males, or females; consequently, the number of possible cross-sample comparisons is limited. Furthermore, certain information is missing from some data sets, thus limiting our analysis.

The statistic of interest is termed the "dissolution difference." This is the difference between two percentage figures: the percentage of voluntarily dissolved marriages for respondents from disrupted families *minus* the percentage of dissolved marriages for respondents from intact families. If the dissolution difference is positive, intergenerational transmission of marital instability is indicated—a higher proportion of marital dissolution in the child generation occurred among those from parental marriages that were disrupted. We consider that the marital dissolutions among children from intact families result from general social influences; any positive dissolution difference is considered to be the consequence of transmission effects. Disruption of a parental marriage by death is included as a possible reason for increasing the likelihood a child from such a marriage will experience marital dissolution; whether disruption by death has the same impact as disruption by divorce-separation can be estimated with our data.

We used dummy variable multiple regression analysis with marital dissolution (a dichotomous variable) for the child generation as the dependent variable, intact vs. disrupted parental families as the independent (dummy) variable, and a set of dummy variables which represent the difference between age at time of the interview and age at first marriage as the control. This procedure makes those from intact and those from disrupted families statistically equivalent on length of time since first marriage. This adjustment for time married rarely affected the interpretation of the results. Note also that no dissolution differences are reported where any proportion was based on fewer than 25 cases.

Results

Table 6-2 presents data from each of the five surveys and provides a basic test of the transmission hypothesis for race and sex subpopulations. Across subpopulations and data sets, in 11 of 12 comparisons between the amount of voluntary marital dissolution for children from intact versus disrupted families, there was more marital dissolution among children from disrupted families. These "transmission effects" range from 5 to 12 percentage points; they are not attributable to differences in length of exposure to marital dissolution (compare the unadjusted and adjusted dissolution differences). Data for females of both races show marked consistency; the variation of unadjusted dissolution differences is approximately three percentage points across the several female samples.

Dissolution differences vary far more across the five male samples. The only anomaly occurs for black males in the OCG sample where greater marital instability is found among sons from intact rather than from disrupted homes. More detailed analysis (Mueller and Pope, 1974) has shown that this negative transmission pattern holds only for those OCG blacks with nonfarm backgrounds; black males in the OCG sample from farm backgrounds show the usual transmission pattern.

Since the divorce rate varies inversely with socioeconomic status and is higher among persons of urban residence, these two variables might produce differential divorce rates in both the parent and child generations, thus making the transmission effect we have detected spurious. Therefore we controlled by regression analysis for socioeconomic status, measured by education of the natural father (or when not available, the

TABLE 6-2

Voluntary Marital Dissolution and Parents' Marital Stability

Race and Sex of Respondent	Parents' Marriage (Percentages)		Dissolution Difference[a]	Adjusted Difference[b]	Adjusted Difference with Control for Education of Father	Adjusted Difference with Control for Rural Origin
	Disrupted	Intact				
BLACK						
Females						
Crain-NORC	41.5	35.6	5.9	5.4	5.2	6.6
Parnes	42.4	33.7	8.7	8.3	9.2	7.1
Fertility	39.1	32.2	6.9	6.1	–	5.9
NORC	49.1	40.1	9.0	9.2	9.6	9.5
Males						
OCG	28.4	33.2	-4.8	-5.0	-7.3	-9.4
Crain-NORC	33.2	24.0	9.2	9.5	10.5	10.6
NORC	40.6	28.1	12.5	10.7	9.3	10.5
WHITE						
Females						
Parnes	24.5	15.1	9.4	8.6	8.8	8.5
Fertility	20.8	14.4	6.4	6.1	–	6.0
NORC	24.9	17.7	7.2	7.2	7.2	7.0
Males						
OCG	20.2	14.9	5.3	5.1	5.0	5.0
NORC	26.4	16.2	10.2	10.0	10.0	10.0

[a]The percentage of voluntarily dissolved marriages for respondents from disrupted families minus the percentage of voluntarily dissolved marriages for respondents from intact families.
[b]Adjusted for years since marriage.

natural mother). We also controlled for rural-urban origin, measured by the place of residence of the respondent at age 14–16. The resulting dissolution differences (Table 6-2) indicate that the effect we have observed is not spurious due to either of these factors.

THE EFFECT OF INVOLUNTARY PARENTAL DISRUPTION

Table 6-3 compares dissolution differences for children from families broken involuntarily by death and those voluntarily dissolved. We will focus on the dissolution differences adjusted for years since marriage.

For whites the data suggest that parental divorce or separation resulted in more transmission than did death. In the three comparisons possible, the dissolution differences are at least 5 percentage points higher for children from parental marriages that were voluntarily dissolved. For blacks the picture is more complex. Three studies on black females allowed the voluntary-involuntary comparisons: One shows no difference, whereas the other two indicate more transmission from voluntarily disrupted parental families. However, the one study with data for black males shows substantially more dissolution among sons from death-disrupted families.

The weight of the evidence for whites of both sexes and for black females supports the argument that the transmission effect is larger for

TABLE 6-3

Dissolution Differences by Reason for Disruption
(Percentage Differences)

Race and Sex of Respondent	Death-Disrupted		Voluntarily Dissolved	
	Unadj.	Adj.	Unadj.	Adj.
BLACK				
Females				
Crain-NORC	9.9	5.1	4.0	5.8
Fertility	2.9	0.1	9.6	10.0
NORC	6.3	1.3	19.2	17.4
Males				
Crain-NORC	15.7	16.2	4.3	4.9
WHITE				
Females				
Fertility	1.1	−0.1	10.6	10.9
NORC	6.2	6.2	13.4	15.2
Males				
NORC	8.6	7.5	11.5	12.7

Note. See notes to Table 6-2 for explanation. For NORC, only 1973 and 1974 data are used and N for black males is too small for reliable estimates.

children from voluntarily-disrupted as compared to death-disrupted families.

POSTDISRUPTION HOUSEHOLD COMPOSITION

Table 6-4 presents adjusted dissolution differences separately by household composition after the marital disruption. For blacks, inconsistencies among studies of females and lack of sufficient data for males make conclusions impossible as to the impact of living with neither parent.

For white respondents, the results are less equivocal. In all but one comparison (NORC females), the amount of transmission was highest for respondents living with neither parent. However, only for males in the NORC study were the differences very large. The adjusted dissolution difference for sons who lived with neither parent was 25 percent, whereas the next highest dissolution difference was 11 percent (for sons who lived with their mothers).

For the comparison between children who lived with a single or a remarried parent the picture for blacks is confused because of lack of

TABLE 6-4

Adjusted Differences by Household Composition
Following Parental Disruption
(Percentage Differences)

Race and Sex of Respondent	Single Parent		Remarried Parent		
	Mother	Father	Mother & Stepfather	Father & Stepmother	Neither Parent
BLACK					
Females					
Crain-NORC	1.2	11.5	17.1	–	6.8
Parnes	15.5	–12.6	–1.5	12.5	5.7
NORC	7.7	–	–	–	7.8
Males					
OCG	–	–	–	–	–4.6
Crain-NORC	13.4	–3.8			7.6
NORC	23.2				
WHITE					
Females					
Parnes	7.2	–2.9	13.5	8.2	13.9
NORC	6.5	–0.7	13.8	5.6	8.8
Males					
OCG	–	–	–	–	6.7
NORC	11.1	–1.3	–0.7	–3.3	24.7

Note. See notes to Table 6-2 for explanation. Empty cells reflect insufficient information or *N*s too small for reliable estimates.

information and because of inconsistency between studies. Nevertheless, the transmission of marital instability is not clearly greater among those children who lived with single parents.

The two studies on white females present a consistent pattern. If we compare those mothers who remarried with those who did not and do the same for the fathers, the children who lived with the single parent were less likely to have their first marriages end in divorce or separation. The differences for these four comparisons (two for each of two studies) range between 6 and 11 percentage points. The results for white males are different. Boys who lived with a mother who remained single had a greater chance of marital dissolution; the dissolution differences for boys living with a father are approximately the same whether he was remarried or not.

The third and final comparison is between the children who lived with the same-sex as compared with the opposite-sex parent, holding the marital status of the parent constant. Again, we could not interpret the data for blacks because of the inconsistencies and lack of data. For whites it is strikingly evident that, for both males and females, there was more transmission of marital instability for children who lived with their mothers rather than with their fathers. The average difference for the six possible comparisons is 7.6 percentage points. This result is interesting and warrants more scrutiny.

Discussion and Conclusions

The present evidence indicates a real, although small, amount of intergenerational transmission of marital instability. For whites, the pattern is consistent among studies and between sexes. For blacks, the four studies of females and two of the three for males indicate higher marital dissolution rates among children from disrupted homes. The consistency of these results leads us to minimize the single negative finding in one sample of black males, particularly because detailed analysis (Mueller and Pope, 1974) indicates that the transmission effect is present in at least one significant subpopulation, farm origin sons.

Although convinced by the data pattern, we are not surprised that the transmission effects detected are small. In addition to the variations and deficiencies in information noted, it should be remembered that parental family disruption is only a rough indicator for the theoretically meaningful categories in the role model rationale, as well as in alternative rationales. Each suggests a particular link, an intervening variable, between the parent and child generations that operates to produce marital instability in the latter generation (i.e., to "transmit" it). The personality rationale posits "deficient" personality characteristics; the economic, reduced household income and downward social mobility; social control, reduced control over the child on the part of family and kin network; permissive attitudes, tolerant attitudes toward divorce learned by the child; and role model, inappropriateness of sex-role learning.

We predict that further research will almost certainly show two things. First, there is no direct causal effect of parental disruption on the child's marital stability—all of the effect is mediated or transmitted through the intervening factors identified for each of these rationales. Second, no single intervening factor will be found to be *the* transmitter, although certain factors may have varying impact among blacks or whites, males or females. Unfortunately, we are in no position yet to test these hypotheses empirically.

THE ROLE MODEL RATIONALE

As indicated, the role model rationale implies higher rates of marital instability for: (a) children from homes broken by divorce or separation rather than by death; (b) children who, after a break in their parents' home, lived with neither rather than one natural parent; (c) children who lived with a single rather than a remarried natural parent; and (d) children who lived with a parent of the opposite rather than the same sex. Because of some differences in the findings across racial groups, we will discuss these hypotheses separately for whites and blacks.

Effects for whites. The data for whites show fairly consistently that children from voluntarily dissolved marriages and children living with neither parent have higher transmission rates as hypothesized.

The results are less supportive of the third and fourth hypotheses. The most apparent discrepancies are for women where the transmission effect is greatest when they, as girls, lived with a remarried rather than a single natural parent (whether natural mother or father) and with the same-sex rather than the opposite-sex natural parent (whether the parent was married or not). Because these patterns are consistent for two studies and the percentage-point differences relatively substantial, we accept them as clearly contrary to the role model rationale. We can offer no interpretation that successfully accounts for these results within the role model rationale without, at the same time, modifying it to make the rationale incapable of explaining other results now compatible with it.

The data patterns for white males are consistent with hypotheses *c* and *d* but for three of the four column categories in Table 6-4, variation in the dissolution differences is too small to allow interpretation (range of 2.6 percentage points). Because both men and women who lived with their mothers after a break in their parents' marriage have higher dissolution rates, the role model rationale is a dubious explanation. This particular result seems more easily interpretable using the economic rationale: Female-headed families are financially disadvantaged and therefore hurt their children's life chances. But speculations here merely highlight the need for better theorizing and more informed data collection.

Effects for blacks. The data pattern for blacks is neither totally consistent across studies nor between the sexes. The inconsistency across studies is sometimes surprising. As an example, the proportion of voluntary dissolutions among black males is 11 percentage points higher among those coming from death-disrupted, as compared with voluntarily dissolved, parental marriages (Table 6-3). This is one of the larger differences present in the data and is the only one of seven comparisons, considering both blacks and whites, males and females, in which dissolutions in the child generation are higher among children from death-disrupted families.

We should note two further points regarding the results for blacks. First, the anomalous findings are not all from one study; if this were so, the study itself could be questioned. Second, the variability of the results for blacks is undoubtedly in part due to sampling error. Only three of the seven black samples for a given sex are more than 1000 in size, whereas all white samples are larger than this. We did not utilize proportions based on fewer than 25 (unweighted) cases, but some of the figures are based on relatively few cases.

The data at hand for blacks must be considered inconclusive with respect to the patterns of the transmission of marital instability and therefore also with respect to the reasons for it. Not until more data on blacks become available can we safely use empirical results to test theoretical statements.

Overall, the findings weaken our confidence in the role model rationale, and we think this conclusion alone has justified this secondary analysis of survey-research data. Thorough analysis of fairly crude data can indicate the weaknesses in existing theories and can demonstrate that they are in need of refinement before more elegant tests are designed and conducted. This is exactly what the data and analysis at hand indicate to us.

THEORETICAL QUESTIONS REGARDING THE ROLE MODEL RATIONALE

The most useful development in the role model rationale would be specification of the general determinants regarding which adults will be utilized as role models by children. The following kinds of questions about how children learn social roles (sex roles and marital roles particularly) have occurred to us.

Does conflict between spouses interfere with their ability to act as effective role models for their children? Under conditions of mutual respect between spouses, we would expect each child to be reinforced by both partners for behaviors imitative of the appropriate-sex parent. Under conditions of pervasive marital conflict, however, children may be less often reinforced by their parents for appropriate sex-role behaviors because the partners will not wish to reward a child for behaviors imitative of a disliked spouse. If conflict between spouses inhibits sex-role learning, we would expect divorce-bound parents to be less effective role models, but would also expect all families in which there was lack of love and respect between the parents to be less effective in socializing their children.

For the child, what is the relative effectiveness of the following experiences for developing appropriate sex-role and marital-role behaviors: (a) interacting with a parent of the same sex; (b) interacting with a parent of the opposite sex; (c) observing interaction between parents; (d) being verbally instructed regarding sex-role behaviors by a parent; and (e) having all of the preceding experiences with a natural parent, a stepparent, or an adult who is not related to the child?

After a child has developed certain cognitive skills, it is likely he can learn sex-role behaviors through observation of others and by being instructed by an adult. To the extent this is true, complete families would be unnecessary to teach the child sex-role behaviors. However, it is also likely that practice in utilizing interaction skills improves these skills, and it may be essential that the child interact with a parent of the opposite sex to gain skill in those sex-role behaviors most relevant for marriage. It would be desirable to know exactly what kind of practice is most useful, what is the sequence of cognitive development in children relevant for role learning, and what are the determinants of role learning when the child is young and its cognitive skills less well developed (see Goslin, 1969; Macoby and Jacklin, 1974.)

We also need to consider the role of kinship as a determinant of whom the child takes as a role model. Americans have a strong belief in the permanence of the natural parent-child bond (Schneider, 1968), even if the child is not living with the parent. We suggest that this belief makes it difficult for a stepparent or other adults to become substitute role models for the absent natural parent, particularly if he or she maintains contact with the child (e.g., through exercising visitation rights after a divorce). This may be one reason death-disrupted families show less of a transmission effect than divorce-disrupted families; the dead ex-parent is a less effective competing role model for a child than a living one. We need systematic consideration of how our family and kinship structure determines the adults to whom children pay attention in choosing appropriate behavior, i.e., which adults become their normative reference persons. This needs to be done, not only for model family situations, but also for the various kinds of broken families which increasing numbers of children experience.

What part do extra-familial role models play in socializing children, particularly those that the child is exposed to through television and other mass media? Children may be able to learn sex-role behaviors by watching TV shows or by having a single-parent reinforce the sex-role behavior he or she wishes in a child by pointing them out in TV characters. Role models are also available elsewhere outside the home, such as neighbors or kin. Almost all of the literature we have reviewed emphasizes the family as the locus of socialization. This is why so much concern is expressed over the broken family. But if we studied the possibility of extra-familial socialization supports, especially in the case of broken families, we might find that resourceful single parents have an entire array of socialization aids available to them, which they are successfully using (Brandwein et al., 1974). Our results regarding transmission of marital instability give support to the contention that certain single-parent families, in comparison to reconstituted and even intact families, can successfully socialize their children—at least for stable marriages (see Table 6-4). The process through which this is accomplished awaits serious systematic study.

What is the effect on sex-role learning if the adult composition of a child's household changes, as when a child's natural mother divorces and then remarries? Researchers have focused on single- vs. two-parent families and have failed to recognize that many single-parent families were once two-parent families and will become two-parent families again. Our literature search uncovered no systematic discussion of the impact of remarriage on the role learning of children. The role model rationale is ambiguous with regard to the effects of remarriage and the place of the stepparent in role learning. On the one hand, the reconstituted family has the same social positions as the child's original family; on the other hand, the emotional relationships in the original and in the reconstituted family will be different. There is also the unknown impact of a shift from one adult role model in the household to another (potential) role model. The role model rationale suggests that a remarriage can facilitate appropriate role learning if the child accepts the stepparent as a role model and if this new role model is consistent in behavior and expectations with both the natural parents. There is limited knowledge of the process by which a shift in models might take place, the differences in the process by age, etc. Another interesting question posed by remarriage concerns the conditions that facilitate a child's taking two adults as important role models (for example, a stepparent and a natural parent).

This paper has raised more questions than it has answered. Nevertheless, we believe it has served to verify the presence of some amount of intergenerational transmission of marital instability. The research gates remain open, however, to attempts at identifying and validating the mechanisms responsible for this transmission.

Couple Strains in Communal Households: A Four-Factor Model of the Separation Process

This paper has a dual purpose: to examine some of the ways in which communal living tests the strength and durability of couple relationships, and to propose a model of the separation process based on these experiences. Couple separation can be viewed as a form of personal protest culminating in disengagement from an institutional relationship; it is analogous on the micro-level to social protest—a form of disengagement from institutionalized relations—on the societal or collective level. It is not enough to explain separation and divorce solely as functions of deprivation, dissatisfaction, or conflict, any more than the selective occurrence of social movements can be explained on these grounds. Instead, models are required that can take into account the differential existence of strain and the translation of strain into action.

Communal living makes visible a large number of forces that affect couple cohesion or dissolution. The operation of a joint household over which the couple does not have complete sovereignty, plus the presence of others in the immediate intimate realm, presents the couple with the necessity for making choices and intentional decisions about matters that could more easily be taken for granted or derived from tradition in a single-family household—e.g., when to be alone together, when and how

Portions of the research reported here were funded by a grant from the National Institute of Mental Health, Department of Health, Education and Welfare, No. MH-23030, to Rosabeth Kanter, and an NIMH traineeship, No. 5 T01 MH 13124 to Dennis Jaffe. This support is gratefully acknowledged.

This chapter appeared in a slightly different form in *Journal of Social Issues*, 1976, 32 (1).

to include or exclude others, how to divide chores, what territory to carve out as the couple's own domain. When couples live in single-family households, for example, they are naturally and automatically alone unless they choose to be with others; in communal households couples must make more deliberate choices to be alone or to define their own relationship boundaries. Secondly, the presence of any others (older children, relatives, friends, boarders) with a stake in the relationship territory —physical or symbolic—is likely to place added strain on the couple relationship; a classic example are in-law problems, particularly in working-class families in which a young couple may live with parents (Blood and Wolfe, 1960; Ryder, Kafka, and Olson, 1971; Komarovsky, 1964). Finally, any change in a couple's life circumstances (having children, changing residences) is likely to exaggerate tensions and disagreements; one indication of this is the finding by Blood and Wolfe (1960) that a large proportion of permanently childless couples—those whose relationship patterns had never been interrupted or disrupted—reported no disagreements. When a couple makes a change, as from a single-family to a communal household, they may encounter stress and unanticipated areas of disagreement. In all of these ways, then, the strength of a couple relationship is especially tested in the communal environment.

But not all communal couples separate. What distinguishes those who break up from those who do not? We propose that four factors combine to account for the separation process: (a) contextual conduciveness—structural effects of the couple's environment, the conduciveness of the couple's context to the weakening of their bond; (b) systemic strain—the experience of strains in the couple system from incongruent meanings, needs, or role orientations; (c) generalized beliefs—the existence of beliefs or values that interpret strain as a relationship problem and that legitimate separation as a solution; and (d) precipitating events—the occurrence of events that create friction, protest, and eventually separation. These factors are adapted by Kanter (1973a) from Smelser's (1962) general model of collective behavior.

The first three factors represent the general likelihood that a couple will separate, based on the structure of the couple's environment, the state of the couple as a system, and the norms and values to which the partners adhere. The fourth factor is the trigger which changes potentiality into actuality. Couples to whom the very same event occurs (e.g., an extramarital affair or a financial crisis) may not respond in the same way; we predict separation only for those for whom there is contextual conduciveness, systemic strain, and generalized belief that supports breakup.

Couples who separate in communal households experience a daily context in which couple ties are weakened: through the presence of others, reduced couple dependency, an absence of joint sovereignty, and the viable possibility of single status. But they tend also to be couples who already manifest systemic strain: incongruent definitions of marital reality, double standards, incongruent male-female needs and affiliations, and traditions incompatible with communal styles. Furthermore, they tend to share antifamilist beliefs which interpret strain as a problem that legitimates separation. Finally, events such as the formation of new sexual relationships and group intervention into couple conflicts tend to precipitate separation.

The Research Setting

Communal households are groups of four or more unrelated adults, living together, with or without children, with some intention to create collective or family-like bonds and to operate the household jointly. While it is difficult to estimate the number of such households in the United States, our research located nearly 300 self-identified "communes," "collectives," or artificial "extended families" in the Boston area alone. It is likely that many more joint households exist without such formalized labels.

Our research focused on 35 urban and suburban communal households in the Boston and New Haven areas from 1972 to 1974. The culture of the households tended to be avant-garde middle class rather than hippie or student. They were generally located in large old houses in middle-class or working-class areas. Economic support was derived from a typical range of urban jobs, from marginal to professional, with educational and social service jobs predominating. Mean household size was 9.6 persons.

CASES AND PROCEDURES

In-depth information about the impact of communalism on couple relationships was gathered on 29 couples from 17 households, who had lived alone in nuclear households for at least six months before living communally as a couple. These were all the couples living communally in New Haven who agreed to participate in the study, representing over three-fourths of the total communal couple population of the area. Twenty-five of the 29 couples were married; 20 had children. Their ages ranged from 23 to 57, with a mean age of 32.

Thirteen of the married couples and one unmarried couple, eight of them with children, separated after living communally. All but one of the 14 separating couples separated in their first or second year of communal living. Before splitting, they lived an average of six months in the communal household, suggesting that separation (but not necessarily leaving the group) tends to happen early in the communal experience, if it happens at all. Separated people were interviewed within the year following the split, about half of them after they had left the communal situation. Two- to three-hour unstructured interviews were conducted (by Jaffe) with each individual in both separated and nonseparated couples, followed by a long questionnaire covering their history as a couple, the decision to live communally, feelings about the household, conflicts both before and after the communal experience, ways the couple had altered, and present relationships and living arrangements (Jaffe, 1975).

COUPLES CHOOSING COMMUNALISM

Couples choosing to live communally generally talked about their decision in ways that reflect a concern with change. Slater (1970) and others have suggested that stability and permanence are being replaced for couples and families by greater emphasis on the quality of personal expression and growth, on intimacy, quality, negotiated roles, and the desire for expanded opportunities. In this view, the traditional family is too limited in the eyes of couples who join communes, while the collective household represents a viable alternative. Many couples who enter such households may be unstable because their relationships are already in transition. The communal situation may be used to help them explore, clarify, and alter their behavior. They thus trade flexibility for stability; during their period of personal transition, they expect conflict and uncertainty. Like the first year of marriage, only involving more people, the first year of a couple in a commune is experienced as an emotional pressure cooker; most changes in the couple occur quite soon after moving in. The second year or the second communal household is usually less stressful and more harmonious.

Despite sharing a number of still unconventional ideas, the communal couples reported conventional beginnings. The background of the couples who separated offers little that would have predicted either their interest in communal living or their subsequent separation. Just prior to entering the communal house, many of the couples had a year or two of conflict and role change, but only two couples report entertaining the possibility that their couple might not survive the commune. Only two persons had parents who were divorced.

Separating Couples and Their Communal Experience

CASE I: RICHARD AND RENEE

Richard and Renee married after college. She supported him through graduate school and then took care of their two children while he worked. She saw herself as a "goody-goody, anxious to please him, his parents, society, and everyone." They heard about communal living at a time when she was wanting to change their relationship, thinking about going back to school to become a teacher. At that time he took a new job and they moved. Looking for a place to live, they saw a sign asking for people to share a house with a single mother. Renee wanted to seize this opportunity, and Richard went along for economic reasons.

The household did not fit their high expectations. The others were not willing to deal with their conflict over sex roles, and the other women told Renee to go more slowly. The other house members supported Richard's feeling of being deserted, leading Renee to feel more alone than ever. She began to look for support outside the house. She became involved in the local women's center, and in consciousness-raising and encounter groups, at which she developed other close relationships, some sexual. She had been in therapy intermittently during their marriage, but the therapist had always said in so many words, "Go home and do your housework and don't be so angry." Now she had her feelings validated and found that the changes she demanded were reasonable. She said:

"I felt that my depth was not recognized by Richard or the others in the house, and their not wanting to talk about my feelings and changes and struggle forced me to go outside. Richard found this very threatening, and I had to spend much time calming him down about it. He was angry at my other relationships, threatening violence, and I finally got tired of it and left."

She defines her current relationship with a new man as an open couple— equal, nonpossessive, nonmonogamous—and the two of them are trying to find others who share their values to form a new communal group. They want a commune where the relationship to the house will be primary, not subservient to a couple or to a career. She is growing sexually, having experienced orgasm for the first time with her new partner. She works part-time in a free school. Richard still lives in the old house, and she feels he still does not understand why she had to leave. There is tension when they try to share childcare decisions, which they now share equally. Like others who initiate separations, Renee left a relationship which she felt did not enable her to grow, and she is experimenting with more open and flexible relationships. Like other partners left behind, Richard has changed somewhat adjusting to the new situation, but he still retains traditional views of what a couple and family ought to be.

CASE II: THE JS AND THE DS

John and Jill J. and Dave and Debby D. were friends with common interests in service professions, the Js with two children, the Ds with an infant. The Ds both worked, sharing housework, childcare, and decision making; the Js had a more traditional relationship—he worked long hours while she took care of the house and kids. After talking together for several months, they decided to buy a house together. They were joined by a single woman who never became very involved in the house. Dave and Debby were looking for more closeness and for help in sharing childcare. John wanted a communal situation because it would enable them to live in a nice house and it was handy to be near friends, while Jill was looking for support from Debby to pressure John to change his role. While John mentioned the possibility of sexual relationships forming among them before they moved in, Dave was strongly against it, and all of them felt it was unlikely.

They went through several stages. Within three months they got over their initial anxiety and began to move out of their separate family apartments to become more collective and spend more time together. They took full advantage of shared childcare and housework. They then had a party for all their friends and coworkers, "acknowledging our existence to the world." They had weekly "family" meetings, at which they discussed deep personal issues, ranging from John's difficulty in becoming fully involved with his kids, to problems in sharing the housework. At one meeting:

"We began to acknowledge how close we did feel. We discussed how we expressed physical affection to the kids but rarely touched each other. We decided to be open to developing relationships to each other. There was then a kind of permission, but no idea of what we felt comfortable doing."

There was a high energy period where each person courted their opposite-sex counterpart.

"We began to wonder then if we were so close what would it mean if we slept together. We talked of the pros and cons and all of us decided we would do that."

There were problems. Dave and Jill became very close, while John felt pressured into a relationship with Debby and their sexual relationship did not work out well. Jill, finding support from Dave and Debby, demanded that John work less and spend more time with the kids. He did and liked the change. John and Dave were in a men's group, but they felt uncomfortable, John feeling jealous and angry at Dave, until Dave finally quit the group. They never became very close. Both couples had problems meeting their mate's needs and with their changing expectations of the mate. As Dave and Jill grew closer, they compared their new relationship—which they experienced as supportive, open, energizing, and confronting—with their struggling marriages.

Since John was unsatisfied with all three of his relationships in the house, he began to look outside. The others opposed this, wanting him to be more involved in the household. Finally, as a flight from the intensity of the situation, each person began outside sexual relationships. There was also pressure on Dave and Jill to withdraw from their mutual relationship and work on the conflicts in their own marriage. Both couples began marriage therapy. They continued to unravel their relationships by taking separate bedrooms, separating finances, and generally leading independent lives. After a period of "trying to keep the house together," with each person living there though not in couples, both couples began to argue about which pair would move out. Currently, John and Debby (not as a couple) share the house with new people, Jill lives with some other women and her children, and Dave lives alone. All feel that their basic marital strains would have eventually surfaced without the commune, but the complexities of multiple sexual involvements speeded up the process of separation.

CASE III: ELLIE AND ED

Ed is several years older than Ellie. They married just after she finished high school, so that she did not go away to college. For three years they lived in suburbia. At first Ed worked long hours while Ellie took art courses and did volunteer work in a museum, but after one year they had a son, and Ed began to "reevaluate his priorities," cutting down on work and spending most of his time at home. Being a parent was a strain for Ellie, so Ed took over major responsibilities. At first, they tried to combine apartments with another family in their building into one collective household. Then, largely at Ellie's insistence, they moved into a large house with a number of younger, mainly single, people. She had felt increasingly lonely and isolated in the suburbs. They had been monogamous, largely due to Ellie's jealously and uncertainty, but she began to get close to another man in the house. She and Ed talked, and agreed that she should "go with her feelings" in the relationship. When Ed was away, Ellie slept with the other man. Ed responded ambivalently.

Although Ed and Ellie remained close, with intense highs and lows, in their next year and a half they went through a process of decoupling. Ed became involved in work for the alternate community service; Ellie took a paid full-time job for the first time and also began to grow and learn about herself in other relationships. Ed had been very controlling of their relationship, and as Ellie related to younger men she experienced her own power. The next summer she spent in Mexico with a lover, while Ed became involved with Sue, a friend of both, who moved into the house in the fall. Ed reported of his relationship with the two women:

> "It was difficult to manage. Politically, there wasn't anything to work out since all of our positions were in favor of it. Also, Ellie liked Sue and didn't resent her; she just didn't like the situation and didn't like herself for it. She finally met a guy and moved in with him. She wanted me to move into an apartment alone with her as a way of preserving the marriage but I wasn't willing. I said, 'Figure out what you want to do. I'm here, this is the way I want to live and deal with my life, and I would love to have you here living with me.' "

Ellie lived with the new man for the next year, but she and Ed remain close and open to the possibility of living together again. Both have changed. Ellie reports that she has learned about herself as "an important person, not as an appendage to a couple." Ed has begun to explore "non-couple relationships, primary friendships, where two people are independent and function on the basis of love, caring, respect but not ownership of each other." He is coming to grips with his penchant for controlling others and his sexual desires. He feels that "if you can deal with sexuality and power in your life, then you can deal with anything."

Four-Factor Model of the Separation Process

Separating couples much more often than nonseparating couples face the issues of incongruent expectations, sex-role conflicts, and outside sexual involvements that eventually become more important than the couple's mutual relationship. Each of these factors may be both a reflection and a cause of conflict; the communal household plays a role in bringing it to a head. Communal households can be structurally conducive contexts for the weakening of couple bonds because they may remove potential sources of couple cohesion, weaken barriers to separation, and provide alternate sources of attraction—the three elements Levinger (1965) identified in his model of marital dissolution. Data on the 14 separating couples compared with the 15 nonseparating couples enable the identification of the particular kinds of contextual conduciveness, systemic strain, generalized beliefs, and precipitating events affecting communal couples.

FACTOR I: CONTEXTUAL CONDUCIVENESS

There is some evidence that, statistically speaking, the risk of couple separation is greater in a communal living situation, perhaps because those couples who eventually split may have moved into a collective household in order to withdraw from a difficult relationship or revitalize a sagging one. Zablocki's (1973) study of over a hundred West Coast communes found that 70 percent of the married couples in the sample split, while only 30 percent of the unmarried couples did. Ramey (1972) suggests that in those more unusual collective households defining themselves as "group marriages" (where all members consider themselves married to and sexually involved with all other-sex members) the risks of breakup may be even greater. An intensive study of 11 group marriages found them to be notably short-lived, 56 percent dissolving after one year and 73 percent after three years, with ten of the 24 couples in these 11 groups separating after the experience (Constantine and Constantine, 1973).

Effects of the presence of others. Communal households increase the pressures for autonomy and individuation of couple members and for egalitarian roles; they decrease the couple's sovereignty over the household and control over one another; and they offer a set of others as potential audiences, intervenors, and allies (Kanter, Jaffe, and Weisberg, 1975).

The presence of others, first, provides alternatives: Almost every couple interviewed, including those who did not separate, remarked that they learned that if and when their mate could not meet a particular need, others were present who could do so. Relationships that cannot stand comparison are unlikely to survive a communal experience. Second, other household members are available to actively intervene in couple conflicts or to form supportive coalitions with one member of the couple; in either case there is opportunity and pressure for couple members to express conflict. Couples who previously had buried conflict thus experienced pressure to open it up, as one woman reported:

When there are other people around, you can express that conflict, your difficulty. When there are just the two of you, you have these old patterns— like you get angry and it doesn't affect anyone else, you're just angry for a couple of days, and the other person learns to ignore it. You don't talk about it or try to realize what's making you angry. When you're living with other people, they are affected by it, so you have to be more critical about what's happening to you emotionally and the effects of your behavior on other people.

Furthermore, the circumstances of communal living tend to defuse couple identity, providing a measure of autonomy and independent status for couple members. Communal households reinforce individuation by making membership and citizenship available only to individuals; couple members are expected to act separately and form individual relationships, rather than operating as a unit within the household. Couple members for example reported that when they behaved in traditional ways that accented their coupled status—sitting together at meals, performing house duties for each other, always agreeing, or immediately going to the mate when they arrived home—they were apt to be confronted by others for their exclusiveness or to themselves feel uncomfortable at their closed boundaries and excluding behavior. The household structure itself encourages couple members to think of themselves as individuals first, and part of the couple unit second.

Reduced couple dependency. The accessibility of resources other than the partner and the household's enlarged division of labor tend to remove a number of sources of couple dependency and interdependency. The division of labor in a traditional couple, with each depending on each other for particular activities and supports, and the desire for companionship both loom large in Levinger's (1965) list of sources of couple attraction promoting marital cohesiveness; if these dependencies are removed and affection for the spouse is not strong, conditions are ripe for separation. One woman in a nonseparated couple recalled her initial fear when she and her husband moved into a communal house that he would not need her any more because she was no longer *the* person making a home for him; she discovered, however, that their relationship was based on the pleasure they took in each other's company rather than a division of labor and, indeed, that their relationship flourished when mutual obligations were reduced. For other couples, the removal of dependencies leaves a gap not replaced by esteem and companionship. In those cases in which sexual enjoyment is extended beyond the couple, another source of couple cohesiveness disappears.

Absence of joint sovereignty. In communal households couples also lose a major source of "joining influences": sovereignty over the household. Because territory is more widely shared and decision making is a collective process, in weekly or biweekly meetings of the entire household membership the couple must share its domain with others. Couples no longer automatically exercise joint control and have an investment in maintenance of the joint interest; children remain one of the few areas of joint decision making, and even then some decisions about children are made collectively. Thus, there are fewer joint and exclusive couple interests and fewer joint issues forcing couple interaction.

Strong nonseparating couples tend to define a clear territory, either by taking on the greatest ownership of the house—in actual financial terms, through decision-making influence, or symbolically—or by making their couple quarters into a mini-household within the commune. (One nonseparating couple in a rather small house made their single room into the equivalent of an entire apartment by adding a refrigerator and a hot plate, building a loft bed with living room space underneath, converting one closet into desk space and another into a baby's room.) At the other extreme, however, are separating couples who maintain no common investments or joint territories once they enter the communal house: each contributing to household expenses separately and each entitled to a room of his or her own. Several of the people who became intimately involved with other household members, for example, recalled the process as part of a slow unraveling, a destructuring of their couple into two autonomous people with no obligations to each other. If both partners have alternative sexual relationships with housemates and no mutual financial obligations, there is little, except for children, to indicate which is their primary relationship.

Single status as a viable option. Finally, the very collective nature of the communal household is conducive to couple separation. Living with single people legitimates and supports the alternative of being single. (In the 17 groups studied in depth, single people outnumbered couple members by a ratio of three to two, with a majority of the singles being female, including single mothers.) If other couples split up or have outside relationships, those options receive added legitimacy. In seven of the ten groups in which couples separated, at least one other couple also split.

Furthermore, if others are part of the "family," the household can be maintained while couple members separate, even to the extent of both individuals remaining in the house after separating (in six cases) and even forming new couples, an unstable and stressful situation but one we encountered with three of the couples. The dissolution of a couple is not equivalent to dissolution of the household; the remaining persons are neither abandoned nor alone. Thus, several sources of guilt and pressure for staying together are removed.

FACTOR II: SYSTEMIC STRAIN

Systemic strain is a function of two kinds of incongruences found in separating couples: between each member's definition of the relationship and his or her perceived needs; and between incompatible systems, communal versus traditional role relations. These structural issues, rather than the appearance of conflict per se in the relationship, appear to distinguish separating from cohesive couples.

Incongruent marital realities. Incongruent definitions of marital reality reflected strain in those separating couples in which one member had felt the relationship was good while the other did not, or if couple members felt they had decided to live communally for quite different reasons and had made incorrect assumptions about what their partners wanted or intended. Living communally often made visible latent incongruent meaning attributions. The occasion of change—the move into a communal situation—gave couple members an opportunity to ask new things from the relationship and from their life situations. (Women, for example, often expected a change in role demands and task allocation—that they would have less to do around the house—while men did not necessarily anticipate such sharing.) Furthermore, since the basic norms and agreements of the relationships were not established in a communal context, the new situation confronted couples with a new set of issues about which they might not share assumptions. Since the community itself tended to push for differentiation rather than for automatic couple unity, couples often found themselves on different sides of an issue. The availability of others as supporters should a couple member disagree with his or her mate increased the expression of differences. A common characteristic of separating couples was their feeling that they could no longer agree on how they defined or evaluated their relationship.

Double standards. Incongruent definitions as a source of structural strain also emerged in instances of double standards: behavior acceptable for one member but not for the other. For example, men in general move more freely into additional sexual involvements inside and outside the group; women tend to do this only with sanction, usually after a joint agreement with the mate that they both have outside sexual relationships, often with both members of another couple. In the one case where a wife had a relationship with a male member of the group while her husband had no extramarital relation, he ordered her to stop and she did; a year later this couple's split was precipitated by his developing a relationship with a female newcomer over the objection of his wife.

Double standards alone do not lead to interpersonal protest any more than do societal inequities unless there is an expectation of equity. In communal couples, however, there is a norm of equity along with rising expectations: an assumption by women that communal living will involve sex-role liberation. Such ideas make vestigial double standards potent sources of strain.

Incongruent male-female needs and affiliations. There is indirect but suggestive evidence of incongruent needs or change agendas between members of separating couples. From our interview data we have the impression that women of separating couples seek primarily individuation or freedom from relationship obligations, while men seek more relationship options. According to Bernard (1972), sexual varietism and increased sexual options are primarily male-initiated fantasies; women seek rather a situation in which they can better mold their identity.

Indeed, men and women may enter communal situations at cross-purposes, leading to some of the preseparation strain. Men seemed to enter the household with fantasies of altering their couple toward greater sexual and personal freedom without guilt or fear; women seemed more concerned with developing a sense of self and autonomy, release from the burden of an isolated existence in a private household. Among the separating couples, a much higher proportion of men than women had outside sexual relationships, reflecting these differential agendas. The current living situations of former couple members reveal a similar trend toward male relationship-seeking and female autonomy-seeking: Nine men and four women currently live communally, while five men and ten women live in apartments. Six women but only two men live alone, and another three women in apartments live only with other women—suggesting that women wish to create a space alone after separation, while men prefer to remain part of a household. Similarly, more men than women are currently in couples.

Traditional role systems. The households we studied encouraged an egalitarian division of labor with minimal sex-role differentiation (Kanter and Halter, 1975), along with opportunity for individuation. Couples whose precommunal system differed from this orientation were much more likely to break up than those who had already established an egalitarian or two-career role pattern. About half of the couples in this study could be considered traditional, half innovative. Ten of the traditionals separated, but only four of the innovatives. We would propose, then, that the farther a relationship must move to accommodate the communal style, the greater the likelihood of separation.

FACTOR III: GENERALIZED BELIEFS

Belief systems play an important role in legitimizing disengagement from an institutionalized relationship; ideologies help people make sense out of their situation and move the dissatisfied to action. They thus translate strain into understandable concepts, locate it in terms of a coherent world view. Beliefs and values can also be impediments to change; Levinger (1965) includes feelings of obligation to marriage and family, and moral proscriptions among the barriers to marital breakup. In contemporary nonreligious communal households, however, the predominant beliefs are more likely to aid dissolution than cohesion. Some of these beliefs are structurally and ideologically connected with the very forming of communal households, e.g., a negative value on private, exclusive relationships; others are historically connected with the particular cultural milieux in which contemporary communalism operates, e.g., feminism. Communal couples, then, are unlikely to face traditional proscriptions against separating; often they face just the opposite: ideological encouragement to split. Encouragement comes from two major sets of ideas and values.

Feminism. For all but two couples, separation came after a long period of trying to alter their relationship toward the ideals of the women's movement. For six couples, interest in women's issues preceded entrance into the commune; for the other eight, it came during the experience of communal living. In three couples interest in the women's movement was initiated by the husbands, who wished a change in their wives' dependency and an increase in their own freedom. These couples were struggling with issues such as male participation in childcare, providing equal emotional (and often sexual) support, and each individual's autonomy, rather than issues of sharing housework or women's freedom to work and share economic decisions. Communalism was seen as one way of making significant sex-role changes. It was believed that with more people there would be less work and lower costs, as well as others to help with children, mediate disputes, provide companionship, and meet needs which one's mate might not satisfy.

Splitting couples often attribute their separation to unresolved sex-role conflicts. Feminist identification sometimes encouraged the woman to initiate separation. In nine couples the woman initiated the break, as opposed to four by men (two in couples where the man showed the initial interest in women's liberation) and one jointly. Support for the separation often came from a formal or informal same-sex group, sometimes within the commune and sometimes outside. Indeed, feminist values induced some women deliberately to seek communalism and to sacrifice their marriages. These women mentioned that they wanted to live communally because they felt they could get certain kinds of emotional support only from other women; some said that they wanted to identify with their own sex rather than with their husband or their couple. Eight women and six men were in male or female consciousness raising groups during their couple crises; these groups offered them overt support for the belief that they had to leave the relationship.

Downgrading familism. A second set of communal household beliefs minimized the importance placed on the nuclear family or on the marriage relationship (Kanter, 1972a, 1972b, 1973b; Kanter et al., 1975; Jaffe, 1975). In strong form, this is an anti-nuclear-family ideology in which private, exclusive relationships are negatively valued, and couples are encouraged to play down any special relationship. In some cases, the ideology around which communal households coalesced included convictions that the nuclear family was responsible for many of the psychic afflictions of society and that the commune represented an alternative. In other cases, the ideology was weaker; it was expressed as lack of support for couple maintenance and an emphasis on the importance of separate growth.

FACTOR IV: PRECIPITATING EVENTS

Precipitating events serve as the final prod. They give concrete substance to the general interpretations of stress provided by the belief systems, and they exacerbate the strains. Either suddenly or gradually, these occurrences force a choice. Following a precipitating event, one or both couple members can no longer avoid making a decision about the relationship's future. For one communal couple, the event that finally pushed them to separate was the man's offer of a good job in another city; his wife refused to move with him. She later reported that, without the job offer, their relationship could have "limped along forever," but the potential move crystallized and focused her discontent.

Depending on the couple's circumstances, many different events can trigger protest and disengagement. In the households we studied, two kinds of events were most likely to provoke the final decision to separate: new sexual relations and group involvement in couple crisis. The first not only reinforces tension, but it provides a comparison to the partner as well as an alternative. In most of the couples studied, intense extra-couple sexual relations generally followed rather than preceded couple strain, and served primarily to crystallize discontent.

The second kind of event, group involvement in couple crisis, precipitates separation in several ways. The support of others for either couple member generates coalitions that may push the couple further apart. The reflection of its conflict through the eyes of other people labels the couple's strains and makes them more difficult to avoid. Public acknowledgment of crisis eliminates a major barrier to separation (preservation of the couple image) and symbolically reinforces a public commitment to change, which the others encourage so as to reduce the couple's and the household's tensions. Once intimate others have intervened, it may also become harder for couple members to back down or to bury their conflict.

We are adding an important qualification, then, to the idea (noted in Blood and Wolfe, 1960) that the visibility of a relationship to others is an integrating force, preventing transgressions such as divorce. Others' observation of a relationship can be either a separating or a joining influence (Ryder et al., 1971), depending on the norms and belief systems of the situation.

Alternative sexual relationships. Extracouple sexual relationships caused the most conflict for communal couples and preceded most of the breakups. Couple members often entered communal houses expecting to get closer to other people, who then might take some of the pressure off each member to meet the mate's needs. But the diffusion of intimacy to include the formation of alternative sexual bonds generally led to difficulty for the group as well as the individual.

Zablocki (1971) has compared the sexual pair bond and the generalized closeness of community members to the ancient distinction between eros and agape. In the large, enduring, stable, and loving community he studied, solidarity was maintained by the buildup of community ties of an intimate but nonsexual nature. Because of the difficulties of managing multiple sexual relationships and their emotionally charged nature, communal history records very few successful groups built around them. Oneida was a striking exception, but its "complex marriage" was highly controlled, disciplined, and informed by strong religious norms (Kanter, 1972a). In general, then, multiple sexual relationships have been unconducive to the stability of either the couple or the collective unit.

Multiple relationships require a tremendous infusion of energy. People have described living a year in a house with such sexual involvements as "like a ten-year marriage." Under such circumstances they reported many more psychologically significant events per unit of time, including both moments of intimacy and fusion as well as intense struggle, uncertainty, and doubt. Members who have lived through the conflict caused by multiple involvements have subsequently, or in their next group, instituted a house "incest taboo," citing the need for stability and the difficulty of dealing with the conflicts which such relationships engender. All but two of the people who separated said they would like to live communally some time in the future, but would seek such an incest taboo.

In twelve of the 14 separating couples, one or both members had an extracouple sexual relationship (not necessarily inside the commune) after they moved into the household; only four of these couples reported that such relationships had occurred prior to the commune. Both people in seven couples had an outside relationship, including two cases where couple members had sexual relationships with their counterpart in another communal couple. Most of the outside relationships were intense and ongoing, rather than episodic affairs. In contrast, only five of the

15 nonseparating couples reported outside sexual relationships while living communally, and three of these were once-only episodes.

Outside sexual experiments represented a transition stage for most of the couples. Several of the people who entered sexual relationships with other commune members recalled the process as part of a slow unravelling, a destructuring of their couple into two autonomous people. In the cases where continuing the marriage becomes problematic, where couples experience conflict or stagnation, the experience of a new primary bond often helps one to make the decision to separate; the experience of satisfaction in a new relationship is a potent alternative to the old one. Among the separating communal couples, in most cases the alternative relationship immediately precipitated the separation decision.

Group intervention and public disclosure of strain. Group intervention also helped precipitate separation. In a nuclear household, an impending split need not involve any but carefully chosen others; in a communal house, a couple's crisis usually becomes a public event.

Almost all of the households studied encouraged public expression of conflict, and members of couples shared their struggle with other house members or asked individuals or the whole house to mediate. Communal norms legitimate involvement in a family crisis; the marital crisis becomes a group issue because it affects everyone. To the degree that other house members have feelings about what is happening, they need a forum for expressing them; the feelings of others also bring new information to the couple.

All the communes had meetings, usually weekly, at which such issues could be discussed. While the depth of sharing varied, most houses, particularly when a member or couple was in a personal crisis, would share their feelings. However, due to anticouple ideology, only two couples felt that they received pressure to stay together, and two men and one woman felt the other house members sided against them. One interesting tendency is that men reported seeking out the entire house group, either for help in understanding how their mate is changing or as a court of last resort for what they feel are unfair demands on them to change, while women usually turned to one close female friend or to a women's group.

During the crisis before a split there was a tendency, even for couples who had disclosed little of their relationship, to seek out others. It often began with one person, usually the woman, discussing her problem privately with another woman. For example, in one couple a crisis began after the man became sexually involved with a female colleague. He then promised his wife that he would not communicate with this woman again; but later proceeded to do so, arousing his wife's anger and distrust. She sought support from female housemates. As the couple struggled with their feelings, everyone else became involved. The house met every night for two weeks. It became apparent that the man would refuse to accommodate to his wife's feelings; other house members mentioned that he was exercising oppressive dominance. House members increasingly supported the wife, and she finally asked him to leave the house, which he did. According to this wife, the support of other women enabled her to realize her own power and find the strength to break off the relationship. In this case, group intervention directly precipitated separation.

In other situations, the couple in crisis would ask another house member to talk with them, to function as a mediator or clarifier in much the same way as a therapist. Comments by house members were particularly difficult to deny because the housemates, unlike a therapist, could observe the couple's daily behavior, which they could draw on to confront contradictions. Thus, public disclosure of conflict to housemates often called forth further evidence of couple strain. One husband was not able to understand his wife's feeling that he dominated her covertly, but was able to understand when another husband shared how he had worked on a similar issue with his wife. In another house, an ostensibly feminist woman was confronted by other women on the way in which she used "helpless female" ploys to get things. This frustrated her husband but she would not hear such feedback from him. Thus, during their crises, couple members have several support systems (same-sex friends, consciousness raising groups, and housemates) available, as well as pressures to publicly acknowledge the rift in the couple.[1]

After the Separation

Communal couples face different circumstances after their decision to separate than do couples in isolated households. After the separation, group intervention and group support may continue. In five cases, house

---

1. They also utilize a third, traditional support system—psychotherapy. In 11 of the couples who separated at least one member was in individual therapy at some time during their communal experience. Four couples utilized conjoint therapy during their crisis, although they said they found it less helpful than the interventions of other members or same-sex support groups. They suggested that this may be due to a therapist's focus on individual psychodynamics, rather than on sexism, sex roles, and feelings about autonomy and outside relationships. Some mentioned that the therapist's bias toward maintaining the couple or inability to understand their lifestyle, expressed as the suggestion that they should simplify their situation by leaving the house, inhibited its effectiveness. It is interesting that the therapists' interventions would have preserved the couple rather than the commune, while the groups' interventions were oriented in the reverse direction.

members urged the male to move out; in one, the female; in three cases, both people; and in the remaining five, neither. (Four of the men and one woman who received pressure to move out were the only people who reported negative feelings about the separation process.) In six cases the female left the commune; in five, the male; and in three cases both moved out. However, both members of one separated couple remained in their commune for nearly a year; in three other couples both members remained for several months following separation. The possibility that both members of the separated couple can remain part of the household during the difficult transition period is in striking contrast to separations in single-family households. In two cases, both members became part of new couples. The support of a household and friends appears important for reducing the pain of separation (Miller, 1970). Communal households are particularly suited to acting as a halfway house for people moving from couple to single status.

Since the eight couples with children were all experimenting with shared childcare, it is not surprising that six of them arranged for joint custody, each parent taking the children half the time. This suggests that the effects of communes on children include greater involvement of both parents, even after separation. The children of these six ex-couples see themselves as having two homes (one of which is communal), usually spending half a week in each. Some of the couples took pains to minimize trauma for the children, trying to spend time together in front of them and making joint decisions around childcare, education, and life style. Informal custody agreements were arrived at in all but three cases.

Nine men and four women currently live communally; the rest live in apartments, alone or with roommates. Four men and three women are now in couples not living together, and nine men and three women live as part of a couple, eight of them communal. Everyone now has a new sexual relationship. Few of the couples have gone through legal divorce, except in cases with children; none have remarried, although one person plans to do so.

Both men and women reported that they have sought more open, flexible, and ambiguous relationships since separating. Many feel that they learned enough about their needs and responses to others in their former couples to be able now to manage the open, communal, non-possessive, noninstitutionalized relationships they aimed at in their marriages; they noted that they have started new relationships without the traditional expectations of fidelity and enforced togetherness. Only two people of the 28 formerly coupled see their future relationships as including conventional families or couples, although several have settled into sexually exclusive couples, living alone together.

Conclusions and Implications

The issues raised here can be read neither as a lesson against innovative settings for couples nor as a success story for communalism. They indicate rather that entrance into a collective household represents both a risk to a couple—as structurally conducive to autonomy and perhaps separation—and an opportunity for learning and the development of more egalitarian, flexible styles of couple relationship. Communal settings may provide just the place for couples in transition to change their relationships or end those whose limits are finally acknowledged publicly. If communal environments are associated with more risk (perhaps because couples attracted to them already seek change), they also appear associated with less lonely, less stigmatized, and less traumatic separation. This, of course, removes a traditional barrier to divorce. The processes described here also contain provocative information about how couples in crisis can find support for change, about alternatives to couple living, and about the kind of household that might be provided for people in transition, for the separating or the newly separated.

It should be mentioned that the fragility of some couple relationships in the households in our study is more than matched by the fragility of the communal groups themselves: Generally they are short term, with minimal shared ideology or shared functions beyond the running of a household. Most belief systems in these contexts tend to support change and individuation. In other kinds of communal ventures, such as the Kibbutzim or the Hutterite communities who share more stability and tradition, community pressure tends to support the maintenance of established couple relations; yet these groups too may discourage the privatization of coupling. In the more than 100 Hutterite communal colonies, for example, nearly every adult marries and divorce is practically unknown (Hostetler, 1974; Zablocki, 1971). While a number of traditional utopian communities have handled the tensions between communalism and familism by choosing the extremes of either communal sex or celibacy with parent-child separation and collective childrearing (Kanter, 1972a; 1973a), other spiritually oriented communal groups maintain strict and traditional monogamous marriage but reduce its erotic nature or importance for the life of the individual. The major difference between urban groups and traditional communes, whether spiritual or missionary, lies in the purpose of their couple norms. In the traditional groups, sexual practices, whatever their nature, are ultimately oriented toward group survival and collective commitment; in urban communes, sexual practices reflect the personal growth orientation of members (Kanter, 1972a).

Thus, it is not communalism per se that causes couples to separate, nor strains in the couple alone, but the complex interaction of a number of factors. At each point in the model, it is possible to consider differences between relationships that remain cohesive and those which dissolve. Nonseparating couples were likely to respond to the communal environment differently, maintaining joint obligations and joint territory. They were likely to have more congruent definitions of their couple reality, and they were more likely to enter with nontraditional couple norms compatible with communalism. They are unlikely to share extreme forms of anticouple beliefs that place responsibility for couple difficulties on the inherent evil of traditional coupling. They were less likely to have intense extracouple sexual attachments or to make their conflicts public and subject to group pressure.

Hypotheses presented in this four-factor model can be tested empirically. Furthermore, the general model is applicable to the process of couple separation in any context, to protest against and to disengagement from any kind of institutionalized relationship. Any couple's context, the style of household or community in which it exists, is either more or less conducive to its continuing solidarity.

PART III

Economic Determinants of Breakup

CAN THERE BE a stable relationship with little money? A solid marriage without a stable job? Each chapter in Part III is concerned with some aspect of family income. Despite a popular impression that high income is associated with a high divorce probability, there has for at least the past half century been strong evidence of the opposite tendency (Goode, 1956; Levinger, 1965; Norton and Glick, chapter 1). We have known for years that couples from lower socioeconomic strata are more likely to separate and to divorce than those from higher socioeconomic strata. More recently we have learned that income is a stronger influence than either occupation or education (Cutright, 1971).

Less clear has been the meaning of the income-breakup connection. Does breakup depend more on the family's income or on that of the individual spouse? Is it the amount or the stability of the husband's income that counts more? What impact does the wife's income have? How do alternative sources of income, such as public welfare, make their mark: Do they offer incentives for marital dissolution? Such questions are addressed in the three following chapters, which draw on various kinds of data.

Chapter 8 presents George Levinger's exploration of a neglected question concerning the components of marital cohesiveness. He asks why some couples who apply for divorce later dismiss their suits. What "attractions" or "barriers" or "alternative attractions" (see chapter 3) help to explain their decision to dismiss or not to dismiss?

Relying on data obtained by conciliation counselors at a large divorce court, Levinger compares 300 dismissed cases with 300 divorced ones. The divorce applicants' income was a significant determinant of finalizing the divorce. Both husband's and wife's income level had an effect on dismissal, while other variables—e.g., their occupation, education, or length of marriage—had no such effect. High husband income—interpreted as an "attraction" to the marriage—led to dismissal; independent wife income—an "alternative attraction" for her—encouraged divorce. The other important determinant of divorce was the applicants' current physical separation—interpreted as a break in the "barriers" around the marriage.

In chapter 9, Andrew Cherlin focuses on the instability of the husband's employment and income, and also on the comparative wages of the husband and wife. His data derive from a national longitudinal survey of women aged 30 to 44. All of them were married in 1967, but during the next four years 4.4 percent became separated or divorced.

Cherlin's multivariate analysis detects significant effects on marital dissolution from both husband's and wife's regularity of employment and their relative earnings. Family savings and the wife's attitude toward work also played a part. He discusses the findings in relation to historical changes and the contemporary economic roles of husbands and wives.

While public welfare payments had a minor role in Cherlin's analysis, they are the central focus of Oliver Moles' investigation (chapter 10). He examines the frequently posed hypothesis—that public assistance payments provide an incentive for mothers with minor children to separate from or to divorce their husbands. Moles reviews a series of empirical studies conducted in the 1970s. Some based on census data, he concludes, have serious limitations; another more adequate set utilizing national longitudinal surveys presents conflicting findings.

While it seems possible that public welfare payments have some effect on marital dissolution, Moles indicates how better designed studies might lead to firmer conclusions. Finally, he considers implications of such findings for the present public assistance program and the effects on family stability of other possible income maintenance programs.

These three chapters help us better understand the significance of family income for marital dissolution. It appears that a husband's sporadic employment and low wages, relative to his wife's employment and wages, are pivotal determinants of marital instability. His job instability undercuts his status in the community and his attractiveness to his wife; it also seems to promote husband uncommunicativeness and even aggression, while accentuating wife dissatisfaction (Cutright, 1971; Levinger, 1966a). The effects of public assistance are less clearly evident, and better data are needed. Whether or not public assistance payments encourage initial separation, they do seem to retard the remarriage of the already separated. While the aspects of family income and employment that contribute to separation and divorce are now more understandable, sophisticated conceptualization and research are needed to unravel the effects of other sources of income.

Marital Cohesiveness at the Brink:
The Fate of Applications for Divorce

If we consider a marriage relationship at any point in its existence, we may ask what are the forces that continue to hold it together? And what are the forces that encourage its breakup? Elsewhere I have considered these questions from a theoretical viewpoint (Levinger, 1965; chapter 3). I have proposed that the psychological forces which promote continued cohesiveness stem from two sources: (a) each partner's net "attraction" to the marriage, and (b) each partner's "barriers" or felt restraints against terminating it. Counter to these forces are others that stem from comparable attractions and barriers regarding one or more alternatives to the ongoing marriage. This attraction-barrier schema has been fitted to a variety of previous research findings on marital dissolution. But these concepts have been applied in retrospect and not to actual couples whose decision to remain together or to divorce hangs in the balance.

The aim of the present study was to examine such hypothetical forces among married pairs who had arrived at precisely such a decision point. They were married pairs who had all applied for divorce, but who still had the option of dismissing their case rather than finalizing the separa-

This study was done with the assistance of many people, including staff members of the Court of Common Pleas in Cuyahoga County, Ohio, research students at Western Reserve University, and colleagues who reacted to earlier drafts of this paper. I appreciate the initial invitation from Judge Perry Jackson to do a study, and the generous help of Mandel Rubin, Richard Johnson, and Mary Gardiner of the Conciliation Department at the Court. I am indebted to Rowell Huesmann for his great help in the statistical analysis so that these data, collected in the early 1960s, could finally be given their proper interpretation. Andrew Cherlin, Phillips Cutright, Alice Eagly, Oliver Moles, and Marylyn Rands made useful comments on a previous draft. The work was supported by grants from the Cleveland Foundation and the National Science Foundation.

tion. In Cleveland, Ohio, when this study was conducted, more than 20 percent of all divorce applications were subsequently dismissed by the applicants—a proportion that has changed little over the years. Dismissal versus divorce, then, seemed to be an important indicator of couple cohesiveness for marriages at the brink of breakup.

To predict dismissal from a social psychological perspective, one would attempt to obtain data concerning the remaining attractiveness of the relationship—the remnants of material, symbolic, or affectional rewards (Levinger, chapter 3)—and the strength of the barriers to dissolving it. Such cohesive factors could be compared to the spouses' possible alternate attractions—the benefits of some state other than their present married one. Ideally, one would obtain such data directly from the couples; in actuality, we have found that divorce applicants avoid opportunities to discuss their current painful situation with social researchers. A substitute for direct interview data, though, was the availability of records from conciliation interviews at a divorce court.

This study, then, was concerned with the relative importance of a range of variables for influencing divorce applicants' decision. How were couples who dismissed their divorce case different from those who finalized the divorce? What sorts of attractions, barriers, or alternative attractions would make the most difference? And would that framework help us understand the factors that influence such a complex decision?

Method

AVAILABILITY OF DATA

In 1959, the Court of Common Pleas in Cleveland, Ohio, instituted a statutory procedure whereby all divorce applicants with children under the age of fourteen had to come in for a mandatory "marriage conciliation" interview. The court staff was interested in the usefulness of the new conciliation procedure, and the presiding judge agreed to ask a marriage researcher to study the process. That invitation was issued to me in December 1961.

Although my explorations with judges and other staff showed that collecting new data on the conciliation process was not feasible, my visits did lead me to discover a large file of records of interviews with divorce applicants in the Marriage Conciliation Department.

Records of couples participating in conciliation interviews. Each year in the early 1960s, more than 4000 couples filed for divorce or legal separation in Cuyahoga County (greater Cleveland). Almost half of those couples had children under fourteen and were subject to the compulsory interview. Beginning in May 1959, after the Court statute had taken effect, trained counselors in the newly instituted Marriage Conciliation Department started to interview all such couples. The mandatory rule was not enforced totally; occasionally one member or, more rarely, both members of an applicant couple failed to keep their appointment. In the large majority of cases, though, both partners did come for a joint interview with a counselor in the department.

Since its inception in May 1959, the department kept records of all interviews (about 2000 cases per year) on a standard record form. During subsequent administrative checks, the department discovered that a sizeable fraction of the interviewees—between 20 percent and 30 percent annually—*dismissed their suit* and presumably went back to live together.

SAMPLES

The major findings of this study derive from two contrasting sets of couples: a sample of 300 couples who later dismissed their divorce suit and a sample of 300 couples who finalized their break. We shall also consider parallel data from two additional samples, each of 100 couples, for purposes of cross-validation. All couples were seen jointly at the Conciliation Department by one of three regular counselors, who asked a standard set of questions during the course of the 90-minute long interview. All sampling was done by a member of our research team with the collaboration of the Director of the Conciliation Department.[1]

The Dismissed sample. The 300 Dismissed cases were selected as follows. Beginning with cases seen in May 1959, 60 cases were chosen from all couples interviewed jointly in 1959, 120 cases from 1960, and 120 cases were selected from couples seen in 1961, spread across each year by selecting approximately ten cases per month. All 300 cases were drawn from the case load of the three counselors who had the biggest case loads and were still in the department at the time of our study; the same limitation applied to the sample of Divorced cases. For purposes of cross-validation, an additional 100 Dismissed cases were later selected from applicants seen in the first ten months of 1962.

The cohesiveness of couples following dismissal. Did couples who dismissed their divorce proceedings show reasonably high cohesiveness after dismissal? In other words, did they live together satisfactorily?

To answer this question the department counselors did a confidential

1. Throughout, Dr. Mandel Rubin facilitated this research. He is the person who also was largely responsible for setting up the record form which counselors in his department were encouraged to complete for all interviews.

mail and telephone check on 50 of the original 300 Dismissed cases. They found that 48 of these 50 couples were still living together six to eighteen months after the date of their dismissal, and that 88 percent of the respondents reported themselves as getting along fairly well. On the basis of that information, we shall assume that the dismissing couples went back to a reasonably cohesive marriage—while the divorcing couples, of course, did not.

Divorced cases. To obtain the 300 cases in the Divorced sample, every eighth case was listed from the department's appointment book, from May 1959 to December 1961. After constructing that long list, the following sorts of cases were eliminated: (1) couples who had not yet received a formal divorce decree, so that their application outcome remained indefinite; (2) couples where only one partner had come to the appointment; and (3) couples interviewed by someone other than one of the three counselors. An additional 100 cross-validation Divorced cases were subsequently obtained by a similar method from 1962 conciliation interviews.

CODING PROCEDURE AND CATEGORIES

Variables. Although 113 items were provided for on the department's interview record form, less than half were either relevant or codable for all couples.[2] (Nevertheless, codes were constructed for many variables describing the couple's current or past situation and the partners' individual backgrounds.) Variables that were actually coded included items pertaining to the couple's current marital situation or complaints, their marital history, their sexual relationship, each partner's personal background, their income and occupational data, and to their children. Coding reliability was high, ranging from 85 percent to 100 percent.

Differences across counselors' records. Each of the three counselors whose records were used had seen about one-third of the clients in the sample. There was no significant difference in the proportion of dismissals versus divorces across counselors.

Furthermore, a comparison of counselor reports across variables revealed considerable consistency in their recording practices, particularly on the variables that dealt with objective information, such as age, education, frequency of separation, or income—the variables later found to distinguish between the two samples.

2. Most of the coding for the original sample was done by research practicum students at the School of Applied Social Sciences at Western Reserve University. Linda Robinson ably selected the samples, masking all names so that they would be anonymous for the coders. The coding for the cross-validation sample was done by Richard Johnson of the Conciliation Department staff.

Results

To begin with, we shall examine the association between marital cohesiveness and its potential antecedents by looking at a list of univariate correlations. Following that, results of multivariate analyses are presented —results of several discriminant analyses and of a multivariate analysis of variance. Since a couple's separation at time of application was also an index of low cohesiveness, some of the analyses consider the correlates of separation.

UNIVARIATE ANALYSES

What characteristics would differentiate between the 300 divorcing and the 300 dismissing couples, or between the separated and the unseparated pairs? Usable predictors were limited to the data codable from the records of the Conciliation Department. A list of these variables is contained in Table 8-1.

The variables are ordered roughly with regard to their indication of hypothetical attractions and barriers. The first eleven variables seem most pertinent to the attractiveness of a marriage—its felt rewardingness (#1–9) or its costliness (#10–11). The next three variables (#12–14) appear indicative of possible alternative attractions, in that the wife's income or either partner's youth would enable them to better exist outside of the relationship. The remaining variables (#15–23) seem most indicative of potential barriers against breakup.

The simplest analysis was to relate each possible predictor singly to the final divorce outcome. This was done both by correlation and by t-test. The correlations shown in Table 8-1 indicate that few of the available predictors were significantly associated with divorce versus dismissal, but somewhat more were significantly related to separation at application. (Parallel t-test analyses of mean differences between the Divorced and Dismissed groups confirmed the statistical significance of the correlational results.) Essentially, column 1 of Table 8-1 shows that the only clear correlates of *divorce* were separation at time of application and the two spouses' income. Separated couples and those where the wife had some income were more likely to go through with the divorce, while those where the husband had a high income were less likely to do so. The couple's frequency of sexual intercourse and their home ownership showed a lower association with the outcome, but none of the remaining variables were significantly related to divorce. (When the effect of prior separation was removed through partial correlation, husband's income, wife's income, and frequency of intercourse remained

TABLE 8-1

*Listing of Available Variables and Their Correlation
with Later Divorce and Current Marital Separation*

	Correlation[a] with	
Available Variables	Divorce	Separation
1. Husband's Income	−.14**	−.19**
2. Home Ownership	−.08*	−.23**
3. Husband's Socioeconomic Status	−.04	−.07
4. Husband's Education	−.02	−.05
5. Wife's Education	−.06	−.04
6. Couple's Similarity in Education	−.03	.01
7. Couple's Similarity in Age	−.07	−.08
8. Couple's Ethnic Similarity	−.01	−.08
9. Frequency of Sexual Intercourse	−.10*	−.02
10. Number of Wife's Complaints	−.05	−.04
11. Number of Husband's Complaints	.02	−.04
12. Wife's Income	.16**	.02
13. Wife's Age	−.08	−.30**
14. Husband's Age	−.08	−.32**
15. Current Separation	.28**	−
16. Length of Marriage	.04	−.25**
17. Previous Divorce (either spouse)	−.04	−.08
18. Wife's Parents' Divorce	.03	.09*
19. Husband's Parents' Divorce	.00	.01
20. Number of Children	−.04	−.16**
21. Age of Youngest Child	−.00	−.17**
22. Frequency of Church Attendance	−.04	.01
23. Catholic (vs. non-Catholic)	−.04	.05

[a]In computing these correlations, divorce and separation were each
assigned a score of *1*, while dismissal and togetherness at application
were assigned a score of *0*. (In view of the rounding to two decimals,
the same numerical coefficients here are not necessarily equal in statistical significance.)

*$p < .05$.

**$p < .01$.

significant correlates of divorce, but the independent effect of home
ownership was eliminated.)

What variables were significantly associated with these couples'
separation at application time? Column 2 of Table 8-1 suggests that
these correlates were rather different from those for divorce. Although
husband income and home ownership were significant, wife income
appeared irrelevant. Meanwhile, a new cluster of variables emerged
which were connected to the spouses' age and the length of their
marriage. The older a couple, the longer their marriage, the more children
they had, and the older their youngest dependent child, the more likely
the spouses were to remain together while applying for divorce.

DISCRIMINANT ANALYSES FOR PREDICTING DIVORCE

Simple correlational analysis is susceptible to various sorts of confounding. The correlations in Table 8-1 are useful for obtaining a preliminary idea about the possible influences on divorce and separation, but discriminant analysis is a better technique for determining the unique contribution of each variable in a prediction equation. The discriminant analysis in Table 8-2 not only shows whether there was a significant overall difference between the means of the Divorced and the Dismissed, but it also indicates the relative importance of each variable for discriminating between the two groups.[3]

The choice of the variables in Table 8-2 is based on their significant univariate correlation with either divorce or separation, as shown earlier in Table 8-1. The highly significant Hotelling T^2 (Morrison, 1967) in the first column reflects the significant differences in the means of five of the twelve variables chosen for the analysis. The discriminant equation for the separated couples was of borderline significance and that for the unseparated was unreliable.

The analysis reveals that, in column 1, separation was clearly the most important variable determining the divorce outcome. Next most important was the wife's income; the income of wives in the Divorced group was significantly higher than of those in the Dismissed group, and its large discriminant coefficient indicates that this effect operated independently of other variables. Income of divorcing husbands was found to be significantly lower than that of dismissing husbands, as was the reported frequency of sexual intercourse. None of the other variables made any significant contribution, a finding which corresponded to those from the correlational analysis in Table 8-1.

The discriminant function for all couples can be compared with the functions for the separated and unseparated subsamples in the second and third columns. This comparison shows no crucial contradictions, although only high wife income remains a significant predictor of divorce.

---

3. A discriminant function is a set of coefficients for multiplying the dependent variable under study. These coefficients are selected so that the mean composite score for group I (i.e., $w_1\bar{X}_{1I} + w_2\bar{X}_{2I} + \ldots + w_p\bar{X}_{pI}$) is as discrepant as possible from the mean composite score for group II (i.e., $w_1\bar{X}_{1II} + w_2\bar{X}_{2II} + \ldots + w_p\bar{X}_{pII}$). The T^2 statistic (see Table 8-2) indicates the overall significance of the difference between all means of group I versus those of group II; only if T^2 is significant does one pay much attention to the results of the discriminant equation.

One other important point should be noted: There is no one-to-one correspondence between the size of discriminant function coefficients and their statistical significance (by t-test or otherwise). For instance, in Table 8-2 there are several rather high discriminants which are not statistically reliable (e.g., Number of Children in the second and third columns), and one coefficient which is significant by univariate t-test, but makes almost no independent contribution to the discriminant equation (Home Ownership in the first column).

TABLE 8-2

Discriminant Analysis for Predicting Divorce

Predictor Variables	All Couples		Separated Couples		Unseparated Couples	
	Divorced (N = 300) versus Dismissed (N = 300)		Divorced (N = 222) versus Dismissed (N = 141)		Divorced (N = 78) versus Dismissed (N = 159)	
	Standardized Discriminant Function Coefficient	Significance of Difference Between Group Means (univariate t-test)	Standardized Discriminant Function Coefficient	Significance of Difference Between Group Means (univariate t-test)	Standardized Discriminant Function Coefficient	Significance of Difference Between Group Means (univariate t-test)
Separation	.767[a]	$p < .001$	—	—	—	—
Husband's Income	−.251	$p < .001$	−.227	—	−.523	—
Home Ownership	−.003	—	−.034	—	.019	—
Ethnic Similarity	−.063	—	−.263	—	.159	—
Frequency of Intercourse	−.309	$p < .02$	−.531	—	−.397	—
Wife's Income	.415	$p < .001$	.722	$p < .005$	.424	$p < .03$
Wife's Age	−.191	—	−.240	—	−.116	—
Husband's Age	−.024	—	.020	—	−.193	—
Length of Marriage	.137	—	−.117	—	.456	—
Wife's Parents' Divorce	.032	—	.194	—	−.153	—
Number of Children	.088	—	.507	—	−.310	—
Age of Youngest Child	.130	—	.171	—	.203	—
Overall T² Test	T² = 78.09	$p < .001$	T² = 20.47	$p < .05$	T² = 12.78	$p < .35$

[a] A positive coefficient means that the *higher* a couple's score on that variable, the more likely they were to become divorced; a negative coefficient means the opposite. The relative magnitude of a coefficient indicates the importance of that variable in predicting divorce independently of other variables.

Multivariate analysis of variance. The fact that some variables had coefficients of opposite signs between the separated and the unseparated groups, in Table 8-2, suggested the possibility of interactive associations between separation and divorce. To test for such statistical interaction, a two-way multivariate analysis of variance was done. This analysis showed, however, that separation and divorce did not interact significantly on any of the eleven variables; in other words, none of these variables had markedly different effects on the separated and the still together pairs (data not shown here).

DISCRIMINANT ANALYSES FOR PREDICTING SEPARATION

A second set of discriminant functions was calculated for the dependent variable of separation. Table 8-3 shows that the overall function was highly significant, reflecting significant differences on eight of the eleven variables in the equation. Compared to the unseparated, members of separated pairs were significantly younger and had been married a shorter time. They had fewer children and the age of their youngest child was somewhat older. They were also less likely to own a home and reported a lower husband income than did unseparated divorce appli-

TABLE 8-3

Discriminant Analysis for Predicting Separation

Predictor Variables	Separated (N = 363) versus Unseparated (N = 237)	
	Standardized Discriminant Function Coefficient	Significance of Difference Between Group Means (univariate t-test)
Husband's Income	$-.327^a$	$p < .001$
Home Ownership	$-.253$	$p < .001$
Ethnic Similarity	$-.085$	$-$
Frequency of Sexual Intercourse	$-.178$	$-$
Wife's Income	$-.010$	$-$
Wife's Age	$-.139$	$p < .001$
Husband's Age	$-.648$	$p < .001$
Length of Marriage	$-.075$	$p < .001$
Wife's Parents' Divorce	$.234$	$p < .03$
Number of Children	$-.167$	$p < .001$
Age of Youngest Child	$.066$	$p < .001$
Overall T^2 Test	T^2 = 101.43	$p < .001$

[a]A positive coefficient means that the *higher* a couple's score on the variable, the more likely they were to be separated, and a negative coefficient means the opposite.

cants. As Table 8-2 shows, however, *within* the separated and unseparated groups none of these variables had any further effect on a couple's divorce proneness. And, as shown in Table 8-1, none of these variables (except husband income and home ownership) had a significant univariate correlation with the divorce outcome.

A CROSS-VALIDATION ANALYSIS

The results of any single discriminant analysis are limited to the particular sample and circumstances from which the data are obtained. In the present research it was possible to test the generality of the original findings by doing a parallel analysis for 200 additional cases sampled from the 1962 court records. Again, half the cases had been dismissed and in the other half the divorce action had been finalized.

In this cross-validation study, the discriminant function for the separated versus the together applicants was almost the same as for the 1959–1961 pairs (in Table 8-3); all discriminant coefficients predicted in the same direction as before, and significantly so for six out of the eight previously significant coefficients (data not shown).

The discriminant function for the divorced versus the dismissed, however, showed only borderline statistical significance. The magnitude and sign of the coefficient for separation was similar to that in the original sample, but the coefficients for the income- and age-related variables were not. A subsequent check revealed that the couples in the cross-validation sample were younger and had had shorter marriages than those in the original sample.

Discussion

Our analysis of records from the mandatory interviews at the Conciliation Department showed that several variables were significantly related to whether or not an applicant couple dismissed its divorce suit. First, a final divorce was much less likely if the spouses were unseparated while they were applying for divorce. Second, the chances of final divorce depended on the husband and wife's income distribution. Separation itself, at time of application, was related to additional noneconomic variables; it was inversely related to the spouses' ages and length of their marriage, to the number of their children, and to the husband's economic stability.

In discussing those findings, we begin by looking at the significant predictors and then consider their relation to other literature on the determinants of divorce. Finally, the findings will be assessed in regard to the determinants of marital cohesiveness.

PREDICTORS OF DIVORCE

Separation. Whether an applicant couple was separated or still living together was the strongest predictor of its final breakup. This finding was strong both in the initial sample and in a smaller cross-validation sample.

Divorce applicants who continue to share the same residence probably continue to communicate more than those who live apart, and continue to share resources of bed and board. Thus they may well feel less negative about one another and may notice more deterrents against finalizing their rupture—such as merely having to find and pay for a new home for one spouse. Conversely, separated applicants have already grown farther apart, have faced their feelings of uncertainty and loneliness, and have explored the alternatives to their marriage.

I could locate only one comparable report on the connection between informal separation and formal divorce, a report by a New York State legislative commission (1971) on cases in one large court district. In that district, only one percent of the divorce applicants who had lived separately for over a year were reconciled, while more than 7 percent of all "other cases" were rejoined. Unfortunately, the category of "other cases" was not further elaborated.

Few research data would help us decide between the opposing proverbs: "out of sight, out of mind" versus "absence makes the heart grow fonder." The present finding supports the first proverb more than the second. In these marriages at the edge of final breakup, separation appears to have diminished the probability of later reconciliation. Nonetheless, our data do not speak quite clearly on the issue, for the separated and the unseparated also differed on a variety of other variables before they came to apply for the divorce. The implications of trial separation versus continuing togetherness ought therefore to be studied in prospective research especially designed for that purpose.

Income distribution. In the original sample of 600 couples, husband and wife income was the second determinant of dismissal versus divorce. Couples with relatively high husband income and no wife income were significantly more likely to dismiss their application; the two income variables exercised a stronger effect jointly than did either spouse's income singly. Although these results were not cross-validated in a smaller second sample consisting of shorter marriages than the first sample, independent evidence to be discussed below supports the idea that lack of wife income together with a reasonable husband income tends to keep long-term marriages together.

Variables that failed to discriminate. It is also important to note the variables which failed to discriminate between dismissal and divorce. One such variable was length of marriage; neither in the separated nor in the unseparated group did the length of a couple's marriage by itself predict whether they would dismiss their divorce action. Length of marriage affected divorce probability only indirectly, in that spouses with a longer marriage and of an older age were less likely to be *separated* at the time of their divorce application.

Other non-discriminating variables included the spouses' religion and their church attendance; at this point in the breakup process, such variables had no noticeable impact. The decision to dismiss was also not found to be constrained by the number of a couple's children or the age of their youngest child, nor by their own or their parents' history of previous marriage durability. Nor was it associated with the number of their complaints to the counselor.

A final set of variables which failed to discriminate pertained to socioeconomic status. It might be supposed that higher status couples would differ from lower status couples, but neither the husband's occupation nor either spouse's education had any bearing on the outcome of the divorce application. This finding parallels independent findings of Cutright (1971). Let us now turn to Cutright's and other investigators' findings on the connection between divorce and socioeconomic status.

INCOME AND MARITAL DURABILITY: FINDINGS FROM OTHER RESEARCH

How do the findings from this special group of divorce applicants in Cleveland, Ohio, correspond to findings about divorcing persons generally in other areas of the United States? Until recently there have been few relevant findings, but now a number of studies regarding the connection between income and marital separation have been published.

Evidence from U.S. Census data assembled by Cutright (1971) confirms the broader significance of income as a determinant of marital stability; it also suggests that level of occupation and education did not in themselves contribute to variations in divorce. Using census data on 1959 husband income, occupation, education, and the respondents' 1960 marital status, Cutright found a strong association between income and marital stability, even when he controlled for all effects of occupation and education. In contrast, he found little positive effect of either occupation or education when he removed the effects of income on stability. Although Cutright did not distinguish between total family income and the separate husband and wife incomes, his findings lend support to ours.

The effects of wife income were indeed considered in analyses of marital dissolution by Ross and Sawhill (1975) performed on longitudinal data obtained by the Michigan Panel Study of Income Dynamics. They show that the amount of husband earnings was positively associated with marital stability insofar as such income was fairly stable. Furthermore, among white wives, the wife's annual income was directly related to a higher probability of subsequent separation.

Also relevant is Cherlin's reanalysis of another set of national income and employment data (in chapter 9). Using data from a 1967–1971 national longitudinal survey, Cherlin concludes that high stability of the husband's employment and security of family income lowered the likelihood of divorce, while attractive labor market alternatives open to wives increased the probability of marital separation.

While it is valuable to compare our Cleveland data with those from the national samples of Cherlin, Cutright, or Ross and Sawhill, it must be noted that those samples contained only a very small proportion of divorced or divorcing respondents. (For example, only 4.4 percent of Cherlin's sample of women were separated or received a divorce during the four years of his survey.) In the present study, all sampled persons were divorce applicants, whose decisions either to dismiss or to finalize their divorce were all of focal interest.

HOW IS MARITAL COHESIVENESS RELATED TO ATTRACTIONS AND BARRIERS?

In looking back, what general observations can be made about the complex determinants of marital dissolution? We may draw inferences from this study, but it is important to remember that these married pairs were very unusual; they were certainly not representative of marriages in general. All these people had recently applied for divorce, all had at least one child under fourteen, all had come in jointly to see a counselor for a mandatory conciliation interview, and more than 80 percent were of lower socioeconomic status—Class IV or V on Hollingshead's (1957) five-class Index of Social Position. Their environment was that of metropolitan Ohio in 1959–1962.

Let us reexamine the initial question about what would be the key attractions and barriers affecting a couple's divorce decision. How can the present findings be coordinated to a field theoretical conception of marital cohesiveness? While the results seem interpretable in terms of attraction and barrier forces operating on these divorce applicants, the available variables were only indirect measures of such psychological forces. In this study, the only statistically significant attractions pertained to income, and the only significant barrier consisted of still remaining together at the time of the divorce application.

Consider first the effects of attractions or benefits of a marriage. The present findings—together with those of Cherlin (chapter 9), Cutright (1971), Ross and Sawhill (1975), and those reviewed earlier in chapter 3 —emphasize the importance of income and employment as determinants of marital cohesiveness. They suggest that the wife, the plaintiff in over four-fifths of the Cleveland cases, made an economic comparison between her marriage's net internal attractions (husband income and job security) and her independent external attractions (wife earnings and employment opportunities).

According to that interpretation, which is similar to Scanzoni's in chapter 2, the wife actively compared her net benefits from staying in the marriage relationship with those from leaving it.

Consider next the effects of barriers or constraints, which are usually ignored in social exchange interpretations of interaction in ongoing pairs. In the present study, a mixture of variables—such as length of marriage, number of children, and whether or not one's own parents had themselves been divorced—could be considered indicators of one's feelings of constraint against breakup. These variables were not found to affect the divorce decision directly; but they did appear to affect it indirectly through the intermediary decision of a couple either to remain together or to separate before applying for divorce and the fact that unseparated pairs were more likely than separated ones to dismiss their divorce action.

The separation variable itself suggests the important influence of barriers. Couples who were still together not only faced the difficulty of having to relocate residentially if they divorced, but they also possessed little concrete information about how each family member would weather the necessary readjustment. Both of these costs of termination had already been borne by the separated pairs who had broken through the barrier of a joint residence and explored alternatives; they had already tried out a life apart and had been able to attempt an adjustment to a different lifestyle (see Spanier and Casto, chapter 13). Furthermore, the separated pairs had in many cases probably passed the early stages of separation distress (Weiss, chapter 12). While plausible, this interpretation ought to be tested directly in future studies of separated and unseparated divorce applicants whose subjective experience can be more fully explored. Whatever the ambiguities of the present findings, they underscore the desirability of better research on the divorce experience— performed with the collaboration of divorce courts and divorce counselors concerned with generalizing from the immediate experience of people facing the divorce decision.

Work Life and Marital Dissolution

Our work lives affect our family lives. A growing body of evidence suggests that whether and when we marry, how many children we have, and whether we end a marriage in divorce are all determined, in part, by employment and income. Of course, noneconomic considerations—such as social norms, past experiences, and personal preferences—also have strong influences on family events. But other things being equal, our work lives make a difference. And it is this difference which a growing number of social scientists—economists, psychologists, and sociologists—have been examining recently. In this chapter, I will discuss some of their theories and findings and present new evidence on an increasingly common family event: marital dissolution. (By "dissolution" I mean divorce or separation.) My findings are derived from a national sample of women aged 30 to 44 who were interviewed in 1967 and reinterviewed in 1969 and 1971.

For a long time, we have known that husbands who earn the least amount of money are the most likely to become divorced (Goode, 1956; Cutright, 1971; Glick and Norton, 1971; Udry, 1967). Although this statistical association is well-documented, its explanation has been unclear. Most sociologists have accepted it at face value, either offering no explanation or assuming that lack of money ruins marriages. As a

This research was supported by a Graduate Student Fellowship from the Russell Sage Foundation and by Employment and Training Administration grant number 91-06-76-01. An earlier version of this paper was presented at the Secretary of Labor's Invitational Conference on the National Longitudinal Surveys of Mature Women, Washington, January, 1978. I thank the following people for helpful comments: Dorothy Burlage, Rosabeth Moss Kanter, Gay Kitson, George Levinger, Oliver Moles, Valerie Oppenheimer, and Finis Welch.

result, most sociological research on economics and family life has begun and ended with the measurement of the husband's earnings.

But it is possible that some other problem which is correlated with low earnings is a more fundamental cause of marital dissolution among poor couples. I will argue that one such problem, the stability of the husband's employment, is as important in determining marital dissolution as the level of his earnings. Although employment stability and earnings are related variables, they are nevertheless distinct. One person may hold a steady, low-paying job while another has a series of intermittent, higher-paying jobs which yield the same total earnings. This difference between steady and unsteady work and between stable and fluctuating earnings can be important to the successful functioning of families.

In fact, sociologists writing during the Depression emphasized the importance of employment stability for marital stability. Mirra Komarovsky (1940), in interviews with 59 families in which the husband had been unemployed for at least one year, found numerous examples of what she called the "breakdown of the husband's status" in the family. This breakdown, she wrote, was due most frequently to the loss of earning power: "loss of earning ability has lowered the prestige of the man in the eyes of his wife" (p. 42). The basic threat to family stability, Komarovsky found, was not lack of money, although that obviously was a severe problem, but rather the failure of the father to fulfill the expectations of his family. Other researchers also noted the importance of stable employment. Burgess and Cottrell (1939) analyzed marital adjustment scores for husbands with different occupations and concluded that "there is some evidence in the distribution to indicate that it is not the amount of income but its degree of certainty which is related to marital happiness" (p. 143). And they reported higher adjustment scores for couples who had some bank savings.

The connection between marital dissolution and the instability of the husband's employment and income makes good sociological sense. Of all the social roles which a married man must perform, the role of "bread-winner" is perhaps the most important. Husbands are supposed to provide for their families by bringing home a regular income, even if their wives also work outside the home. It may be that the regularity with which a husband fulfills this expectation is as important to his family as the level of his income. A husband with steady employment and some savings is dependable; his family faces little uncertainty about his financial contribution, and they know what to expect in the near future. I hypothesized, consequently, that when a husband experiences greater instability of employment and income (as measured below by weeks worked in the previous year and amount of savings), the probability of marital dissolution in subsequent years will be higher, independent of the husband's income level.

Yet the husband is often not the only employed family member, especially in low-income families. The earnings of the wife also can contribute to the stability of the marriage, or to its dissolution. Although most sociologists have ignored women's economic contribution to the family until recently, economists and a few sociologists have provided a framework for including wives' earnings and employment in the study of marital dissolution (see Becker, 1973; Ross and Sawhill, 1975).

The earnings of a wife can have two effects on the marriage. On the one hand, her earnings increase the total income of the family, which should decrease the probability of dissolution because higher-income families are less likely to divorce (Bernard, 1966). On the other hand, her job represents a source of income which is independent of her husband. If the marriage is troubled, a woman with an independent income may be more likely to separate—or her husband may be less reluctant to leave. Following others (Ross and Sawhill, 1975; Hannan, Tuma, and Groeneveld, 1977), I will label these two effects as the income and the independence effects, respectively, of wives' earnings.

The independence effect depends on the husband's earnings level as well as the wife's earnings level. This is so because a wife capable of earning $2.00 per hour should be more likely to dissolve her marriage if her husband earns $2.30 per hour than if he earns $5.00 per hour, other things being equal. In other words, when the wife's earnings are higher relative to her husband's, she has less to lose by separating. And wives in low-income families—which, as I have noted, have the highest dissolution rates—tend to have higher relative earnings levels.

Different economists have formalized these ideas in several ways, but almost all see the economic gains of marriage as rooted in the complementarity of the skills of the husband and wife, especially in their skills at labor market work and housework. The independence effect, in particular, usually is viewed as depending on the ratio of the wife's labor market productivity to the husband's labor market productivity (where market productivity frequently is measured by wages). When this ratio is higher, the wife gains relatively less by trading housework for the husband's market wages, assuming that both are equally productive in the home. But regardless of how we formalize the independence effect, we still can hypothesize that the greater the wife's actual or potential wage relative to the husband's wage, the more likely is marital dissolution.

We have, then, two main hypotheses: one concerning the instability of the husband's employment and income, and the other concerning the relative levels of the husband's wage and the wife's wage. There is evidence from other studies to support these hypotheses. Among married couples in the Michigan Panel Study of Income Dynamics, according to Ross and Sawhill (1975), a history of unemployment for the husband increased the probability of dissolution in the next four years, as did a lower than usual family income in the year prior to the first interview.

But once employment and income stability were considered, the level of annual earnings of the husband at the start of the panel had no effect on the subsequent probability of dissolution.[1] The lack of effect of husband's total earnings or total family income surprised the authors:

> . . . the level of family income is not predictive of greater marital stability. This last finding is somewhat surprising in view of past research on this subject, but it is a result which has held up throughout our work on this data base. [pp. 38–39]

They also reported that wives with higher annual earnings at the start of the Michigan panel were more likely to separate or divorce during the panel. And in a study of 600 couples who filed divorce suits in Cleveland, Levinger (see chapter 8) found that couples were more likely to dismiss the suit (and, presumably, to reconcile) when the wife had a lower income and the husband had a higher income.

These findings are consistent with the hypotheses advanced here. The Michigan Panel Study, a longitudinal survey (that is, a survey in which the same people are reinterviewed at regular intervals) of 5,000 families, is the only adequate source of longitudinal data on marital dissolution to have been fully analyzed, other than the data to be presented in this chapter. But Ross and Sawhill's findings were somewhat unexpected. The analysis presented here, consequently, will help us to determine whether their findings can be generalized, or whether they merely reflect peculiarities of the Michigan panel or methodological artifacts. Moreover, Ross and Sawhill had no usable measures of wives' attitudes toward employment outside the home. For these reasons, the present analysis should add to our knowledge about the relationship of employment and income to marital dissolution.

In addition, there are other sources of income available to wives who divorce or separate, such as Aid to Families with Dependent Children (AFDC). The common opinion is that the current AFDC system encourages fathers to leave their families so that wives and children will be eligible for AFDC. Moles (see chapter 10) reports that higher state AFDC payments were associated with greater proportions of separated women (excluding divorced women) for blacks in 1960 and blacks and whites in 1970. But as Moles notes, this may be true because high AFDC payments encourage the postponement of remarriage among those already separated, rather than because AFDC encourages separation. An analysis of the effects of AFDC payment levels will be presented below, although shortcomings in the data limit the conclusions that can be drawn.

In addition, we must consider the influence on wives of prevailing

---

1. An exception was poor and near-poor blacks, for whom husband's income did make a difference in the expected direction.

norms about whether women should work outside the home. It may be that some wives feel more constrained to conform to the traditional role of housewife than do others, due to internalized norms or to pressures from the community. Women who feel less comfortable with a role which includes market work should be less likely to separate or divorce, regardless of their opportunities in the labor market. I will therefore examine a set of attitude questions which provide evidence of the effect that attitudes toward market work have on the probability of dissolution.

Data and Methods

The study of the determinants of marital dissolution has been hampered by the lack of adequate, large-scale statistical data (see Carter and Glick, 1976; Hauser, 1975). Most available information is from either state divorce records or Bureau of the Census surveys. These data are all cross-sectional; that is, they measure the characteristic of individuals at one point in time—and they all present problems to the social researcher.

The Bureau of the Census tabulates the number of people who are divorced, separated, married, single, or widowed at the time of a census survey. It is possible to compare the divorced and separated respondents with others on a number of social and economic characteristics, but it is not possible to determine what the characteristics of respondents were when they separated. In fact, it usually is not possible to determine the date of divorce or separation. These restrictions make it very difficult to sort out causes from effects when investigating the determinants of marital dissolution using census data or any other cross-sectional data.

In addition, the snapshot of the nation offered by the census suffers from the fact that some people, such as those with lower incomes, tend to stay divorced longer than others (see Norton and Glick, chapter 1). Because of these differences in remarriage rates, the characteristics of the group of people who report themselves as divorced at any one time do not adequately reflect the characteristics of people who obtain divorces. The census sample of divorced people will contain an overabundance of people with low remarriage rates.

For all these reasons, census information is of limited use in the study of the determinants of marital dissolution. State divorce records, on the other hand, do present information on all people who have ever obtained divorces, rather than on just people who are currently divorced. State records, however, are notoriously incomplete from a social scientist's point of view (Carter and Glick, 1976; Hauser, 1975). Many states collect only a minimum of information on the characteristics of applicants for divorce. Other states have cooperated in filing more complete divorce information with a central government statistical center; but the number of states comprising the so-called "Divorce Registration Area" stood at only 26 in 1971 (Hauser, 1975), with such populous states as New York, Texas, Florida, and Massachusetts excluded.

THE NLS DATA

In this report I present an analysis of data from the first four years of the National Longitudinal Survey of Labor Market Experience in Women Aged 30 to 44, a national probability sample referred to as the "NLS." The survey includes personal interviews with a panel of 5,083 women who were interviewed in 1967 and reinterviewed in 1969 and 1971.

This paper is based on information from the 2,126 white, non-farm women who reported themselves as married with husband present in 1967, who remained in the panel at least two years, and who had no missing information on the variables in this analysis.[2] The sample has been described in detail elsewhere (see Parnes, Shea, Spitz, and Zeller, 1970; Kim Roderick, and Shea, 1972). The level of attrition was relatively low; 7 percent of the women left the panel before the end of two years, and a total of 9 percent left before four years. The women who left the panel did not differ significantly from those who remained with respect to age, race, duration of current marriage, and labor force status.

During the four-year period, 4.4 percent of the white, non-farm women reported that they had become divorced or separated. This relatively low dissolution rate was a result of the selection of women in the 30 to 44 age group. We must bear in mind that the choice of this age group means that we will be examining "older" dissolutions, which usually account for only a portion of the dissolutions reported in census or state data. The results presented here may partly reflect age-specific effects. This longitudinal data set, nevertheless, represents a great improvement over cross-sectional data. And the age range allows us to examine the economic potential of wives who were old enough to have finished all schooling and initial job training.

PROCEDURE

A binary (two-valued) variable was created which took the value of zero if the woman remained with her husband from 1967 on and the value of one if the woman separated or divorced during the course of the

2. The data for a smaller number of blacks, which were analyzed separately, resulted in regression estimates which were largely nonsignificant.

study. A series of ordinary least squares regression estimates were calculated with this as the dependent variable and various characteristics of the woman and her husband in 1967 as independent variables.[3] To test the hypothesis concerning the relative wages of husband and wife, I needed measures of the actual or potential wage for each wife and her husband. For husbands and wives in the labor force, I used the 1967 hourly wage rates which they reported. However, 52 percent of the non-farm women who were married with husband present in 1967 had not worked for pay during this period. Since these women probably would have expected to earn some money in the event of a dissolution, I estimated a potential wage for them by comparing their measured characteristics with the characteristics of men and women who did report a wage. More formally, I estimated a wage equation for working women by ordinary least squares, and then I used the parameters of this equation to predict a wage for nonworking women. The results of this procedure compared favorably with similar attempts by others to predict wages for women in this panel (Mincer and Polachek, 1974; Sandell and Shapiro, 1975). A description of this procedure and the estimated wage equations are presented in Cherlin (1976). The key variable for the relative wage hypothesis, then, was constructed as follows. The numerator was the actual hourly wage of the wife, if she had worked at least two weeks between the beginning of 1966 and May 1967, or the expected wage outlined above if she had not worked during this period. The denominator was the actual or expected hourly wage of the husband.

Results

Table 9-1 displays the estimated coefficients for the set of economic variables from a regression of the probability of marital dissolution between 1967 and 1971[4] for non-farm white women aged 30 to 44 who were married with husband present in 1967. Several demographic variables also were included in this specification, but an adequate dis-

3. The dependent variable can be viewed as the probability of dissolution during the four years for a woman. There are some statistical difficulties with ordinary least squares estimates when the dependent variable is two-valued, notably heteroskedasticity (Goldberger, 1964). When I repeated the data analysis using an alternative procedure (a logistic model estimated by maximum likelihood methods), the results were very similar (see Cherlin, 1976). Consequently, I will present only ordinary least squares estimates in this chapter.

4. For the 88 white women who left the sample after 1969 and whose records had no missing data, the interval from 1967 to 1969 was used.

TABLE 9-1

Regression Estimates of Four-Year Dissolution Probabilities
on Selected Economic Variables, for White Nonfarm Women
Aged 30 to 44 with Husband Present in 1967

(Net effects shown; other variables were included in the equation. See text.)

Dependent Variable: Unity, if the woman separated from or divorced her husband between 1967 and 1971; zero, otherwise.

Independent Variables	Estimate	t-Statistic
Ratio of the wife's actual or expected 1967 wage to the husband's actual or expected 1967 wage.	.0239	2.38*
Savings:		
$1 to $999 in Savings in 1967.	−.00986	0.87
$1000 or more in Savings in 1967.	−.0253	2.12*
Work Attitude Scale, 1967.	.00613	3.37*
Average AFDC Payment Per Recipient Per Month in Region of Residence of Respondent in January, 1967	.00002	0.03
Weeks worked by Husband, 1966	−.00127	2.23*
Weeks worked by Wife, 1966	.000012	0.55

*Significant at the 5% level.
R^2 (including other independent variables): .072
F: 7.03
n: 2,126

cussion of their impact on marital dissolution is not possible within the space limitations of this paper. Here they will be treated as controls. They include duration of marriage, age at marriage, current ages of husband and wife, number and ages of children, educational attainment of wife, whether in a first marriage or remarriage, whether the wife gave birth before the marriage, and the population size of the place of residence. The complete estimated equation is presented in Cherlin (1976, 1977). Readers who are unfamiliar with regression equations may prefer to examine the adjusted probabilities of dissolution in Table 9-2, which will be discussed in more detail below.

WAGES

The wage ratio variable was statistically significant at the 5 percent level. In this subsample, the greater the ratio of the wife's to the husband's actual or expected wage in 1967, the greater the probability of dissolution by 1971. Consequently, we see that the independence effect of the wife's relative wage on marital dissolution was noticeable in the NLS sample. No additional measure of family earnings was statistically significant in several other regression equations I estimated. Although I have argued that it is the *ratio* of the wife's to husband's wages, rather than the absolute level of those wages, which is important for dissolution, the issue cannot be settled by this one study. The three variables (husband's wage, wife's wage, and wage ratio) could not all be entered into the equation at once without the statistical problem of multicollinearity becoming severe. In another specification (not reported here) I excluded the wage ratio variable and entered both the wife's and the husband's actual or expected wages as separate terms. In this specification, as I anticipated, the effect of the husband's actual or expected wage on dissolution was negative and significant at the 5 percent level, while the effect of the wife's actual or expected wage was positive and significant at the 10 percent level (the coefficients were −.0065 for husbands and .0157 for wives). The effects of employment stability of the husband, savings, AFDC payments, work orientations, interactions, and other variables all remained the same despite the changes.

EMPLOYMENT STABILITY

As predicted, women whose husbands worked more weeks in 1966 had a significantly lower dissolution probability between 1967 and 1971, independent of controls for wage levels, savings, and other economic and demographic variables. This finding of the importance of employment stability is consistent with the results from the Michigan panel study (Ross and Sawhill, 1975). The convergence of the findings from two national, longitudinal studies provides strong evidence that the employment stability of the husband is an important determinant of marital dissolution, independent of income levels.

WELFARE

Although the Census Bureau, which conducted the interviews, did not identify the state of residence of each woman, the Bureau did classify the residence of each woman as located in one of nine regions of the country. It was possible to calculate the average monthly AFDC payment per recipient in each region in January 1967, and to append the appropriate average to each woman's data record.[5] As the estimates in Table

5. In an analysis of variance, I partitioned the variation among January 1967, state AFDC payment levels into inter-regional and intra-regional components. The regional averages, which must be used in this analysis, preserved 55 percent of the state-level variation in the AFDC levels. Thus, somewhat less than half the information about AFDC payment levels was lost by the need to use regional rather than state data. A good deal of variation remained, nevertheless, and it seemed appropriate to undertake the analysis using the regional data.

9-1 reveal, the AFDC variable had virtually no effect for whites. Since AFDC is an alternative only for low-income families, I constructed an additional regression term for women who had low actual or expected wages and who also lived in regions with high AFDC payment levels. Even when this interaction term was added to the analysis, there was virtually no AFDC effect. I concluded that for whites there was no evidence that regional differences in AFDC payment levels influenced the probability of dissolution. Within the limits of the NLS data, this finding is consistent with the contention of Sawhill, Peabody, Jones, and Caldwell (1975) and Bane (1975) that the effect of the AFDC program on the proportion of female-headed families is not primarily centered on the decision to separate but rather on the decision to marry or remarry. But the regional averages used here may not adequately reflect state-by-state differences. In chapter 10, Moles will present a more detailed discussion of the effects of the welfare system on marital dissolution.

SAVINGS

As discussed previously, I have used savings as an indicator of income stability and security. The panel was divided into three similar sized groups: those with no savings, those with savings of below $1,000, and those with savings of $1,000 or more. Binary variables were entered into the equation for each of the latter two categories, and the coefficients of both binary variables were negative. The presence of savings of $1,000 or more decreased the probability of dissolution by two and one-half percentage points, indicating that income security did lessen the probability of dissolution, independent of wage levels and employment stability.

WIVES' ATTITUDES TOWARD MARKET WORK

The 1967 interview contained three questions which allowed me to make some inferences concerning the consequences of the attitudes of wives on whether it is proper for women to work outside the home. The panel members were told the following:

. . . People have different ideas about whether married women should work. Here are three statements about a married woman with children between the ages of six and twelve (HAND CARD TO RESPONDENT). In each case, how do you feel about such a woman taking a full-time job outside the home?

1. If it is absolutely necessary to make ends meet.
2. If she wants to work and her husband agrees.
3. If she wants to work, even if her husband does not particularly like the idea.

The response categories and their coded scores were as follows: (1) definitely not all right, (2) probably not all right, (3) undecided, (4) probably all right, and (5) definitely all right. A three item scale was constructed by summing the three scores. As can be seen from Table 9-1, women who in 1967 approved of married women working were more likely to separate or divorce during the succeeding four years. So it appears that married women's attitudes about working outside the home influenced the chances that they would separate or divorce, independent of their actual or expected wage, their husband's wage, his employment stability, and their savings.

REMARRIAGE

So far, I have not distinguished between women in first marriages and women in remarriages. But it is possible that the relationship between work life and marital dissolution is different for women in remarriages than for women in first marriages. We know that women who have been previously divorced are likely to have lived alone or with relatives for a time and are likely to have faced the problem of supporting themselves and their children. Because of this experience, remarried women might be more concerned than women in first marriages with their family's economic position. If so, then the couple's economic situation would become a more important determinant of breakup for women in remarriages.

To test this notion, I added five terms to the regression equation which measured the additional effects for remarried women of five economic variables: the number of weeks in 1966 worked by the wife, the number of weeks in 1966 worked by the husband, the wage ratio, a binary variable representing family savings of $1 to $999, and a binary variable representing family savings of $1,000 or more. Adding these terms increased the amount of variance accounted for by the regression model, and the increase was statistically significant at the 5 percent level. (The estimates which included these interaction terms are not shown here— see Cherlin, 1976.) This result means that remarried women did differ from women in first marriages in how their economic situation affected their chances of divorcing or separating. In particular, the estimates suggested that the couple's savings and whether the wife worked made more of a difference for those in remarriages. Remarried wives, for example, who worked throughout 1966 were more likely to divorce or separate in the next four years than were wives in first marriages who also had worked throughout 1966.

HOW LARGE WERE THE EFFECTS?

So far I have concentrated on identifying those estimated regression coefficients which were statistically significant; that is, those estimates which were unlikely to have differed from zero due to chance variation alone. This is a fundamental statistical issue in a regression analysis. A second issue, which is perhaps more important, is the size of the estimated coefficients. A coefficient may be highly significant (that is, almost certainly nonzero) but very small in magnitude, with the implication that the independent variable in question has only a small effect on the dependent variable.[6]

In order to compare the magnitudes of the effects of the various independent variables, I have constructed adjusted probabilities of dissolution for categories of each variable, based on the regression estimates. The adjusted probabilities, which are presented in Table 9-2, express the effect on the probability of dissolution of an increase or decrease in one variable for a woman whose other characteristics were average in terms of the sample. Of course, no single woman had totally average characteristics, but this device is a useful way to compare the effects of increases or decreases in the value of one variable, net of the effects of other variables. For all variables except savings, the categories shown in Table 9-2 correspond to the mean and approximately one standard deviation above and below the mean. For the binary savings variables, adjusted probabilities are presented for each possible category.[7]

On examining Table 9-2, we see that most women were unlikely either to separate or to divorce, whatever their economic characteristics. The uniformly low adjusted probabilities are to be expected since divorce and separation are more likely among younger women than among those aged 30 to 44. But despite the low probabilities, certain variables do appear to have made a difference. Women with no family savings, for instance, had adjusted probabilities of dissolution nearly double those of women with family savings of $1,000 or more. In addition, the adjusted probability of dissolution increased by more than 50 percent as the wage ratio increased from about one standard deviation below the mean to one standard deviation above the mean. Also, women with a high score on the work attitude scale had an adjusted probability of dissolution that was twice that of women with a low score. And greater employment of the husband in 1966 led to a steady, if unspectacular, decrement. For those few wives with husbands who experienced prolonged unemployment in 1966, the adjusted probabilities of dissolution would have been much higher.

6. The reader may have noted that the squared multiple correlation of the regression estimate in Table 9-1 is small. In part, the size of the R^2 is a result of the highly skewed, binary nature of the dependent variable. Some statisticians believe that ordinary least squares estimates with a binary dependent variable have an upper bound on the magnitude of R^2 which is less than 1.0 (Morrison, 1972). It is possible, however, for individual independent variables to have large effects despite a small over-all "explained variance."

7. For a discussion of a closely related procedure, see Bowen and Finegan (1969).

TABLE 9-2

Adjusted Probabilities of Dissolution, 1967-1971, for White,
Nonfarm Women Aged 30 to 44 with Husband Present in 1967

Mean (Unadjusted) Probability of Dissolution: .044

Independent Variable	Value	Adjusted Probability of Dissolution
Weeks worked by husband, 1966	42.0	.054
	49.8	.044
	52.0	.041
Weeks worked by wife, 1966	0.0	.041
	18.4	.044
	40.0	.046
Wage Ratio	.35	.033
	.78	.044
	1.25	.055
Savings	No Savings	.056
	$1 to $999	.046
	$1,000 or more	.031
AFDC payment level	$28.00	.044
	$36.50	.044
	$45.00	.044
Work Attitude Scale	7.5	.029
	10.0	.044
	12.5	.059

Note. For all variables except savings, the categories shown here correspond to the mean and approximately one standard deviation above and below the mean. For the savings dummy variables, adjusted probabilities are presented for each possible category.

Whether one considers the effects in Table 9-2 large or small depends on one's point of view. In absolute terms, the effects are small. In relative terms, the effects are larger; large percentage increases or decreases in the probability of dissolution follow from differences in the value of any of several economic variables. And in combination, the effects appear rather pronounced. For example, let us compare two hypothetical women, *A* and *B*. Mrs. *A* worked all 52 weeks in 1966, earned the same wage as her husband, and believed strongly that it is proper for women to work (as evidenced by a score of 13 on the work attitude scale). Her husband had worked only 26 weeks in 1966, and the couple had no savings in the bank. Mrs. *B* did not work in 1966, had a potential wage only one-third as large as her husband's wage, and had reservations about whether women should work (as evidenced by a score of 8 on the work attitude scale). Her husband had worked 52 weeks in 1966, and the couple had $500 in savings. On all other characteristics, Mrs. *A* and Mrs. *B* had average values. The predicted probabilities of dissolution, from the estimates in Table 9-1, would be 0.12 for Mrs. *A* and 0.02 for Mrs. *B*. Thus, Mrs. *A* would have been six times more likely to separate or divorce between 1967 and 1971 than Mrs. *B*.

Discussion

We have seen that several aspects of a couple's economic situation influenced the probability of marital dissolution. Two influences seem to have the most substantive importance. First, greater stability of the husband's employment decreased the probability of dissolution, independent of income levels. It appears that, for marital stability, how regularly a husband brings home a paycheck may matter more than how much he makes. Second, wives whose potential wage compared favorably with the wage of their husbands had a greater probability of dissolution. Alternative sources of earnings, it seems, increased the independence of wives from their husbands. These findings are consistent with those from the Michigan Panel Study of Income Dynamics. That the evidence from these two national, longitudinal studies coincides should increase our confidence that these findings are indeed valid.

The evidence from these two studies suggests, above all, that the relationship between two married partners' work lives and their chances of divorcing or separating is more complex than earlier studies implied. Perhaps the most glaring weakness of older sociological research on work life and marital dissolution was its exclusive concentration on the husband, and especially on the husband's income level. But it is easy to understand why researchers working in the 1930s, such as Komarovsky (1940) and Burgess and Cottrell (1939), tended to ignore wives' economic contributions: at that time most married women worked at home. Although wives made important contributions to the economic well-being of their families through home work, their opportunities in the labor market were restricted. As a result, the high unemployment rates of the Depression had a more direct impact on husbands than on wives. These early researchers, nevertheless, noted that the stability and the security of the husband's employment might be more important than the level of the husband's income to the stability of his marriage.

But this distinction between employment stability and income level was lost in most of the studies that appeared in the 1960s (Bernard,

1966; Udry, 1967). These scholars used statistical techniques for analyzing the effects of economic variables on marital dissolution. Yet in order to do so, they relied on Bureau of the Census reports which typically had much better information on income levels than on unemployment. And other limitations of the existing census data forced them to ignore wives' incomes, although during this period the labor force participation of married women was increasing rapidly. Consequently, their economic analyses, while instructive, were largely limited to considering the impact of husbands' incomes on dissolution.

By the 1970s, however, the actual or potential wages of wives could no longer be ignored. Economists (Becker, 1973) took the lead in incorporating wives' earnings into models of marriage and divorce. And at the same time, better data sets became available. The inclusion of wives' earnings brought analyses of marital dissolution more in step with existing labor force trends. In recent years, a number of studies have noted the independence effect of wives' income (Ross and Sawhill, 1975; Hannan et al., 1977). But until very recently, the distinction between the husband's employment stability and his income level—which was prominent in the literature of the Depression Years—had not re-emerged. That it has now surfaced again is partly due to the availability of longitudinal surveys such as the NLS which allow for more comprehensive consideration of a couple's economic situation.

Whether the effects I have mentioned here will continue to influence marriages in the same way is difficult to predict. At this time, the labor force participation rate of wives is still rising, which suggests that the independence effect of wives' earnings may continue to be important for marital dissolution. But wives' earnings, as others have stated, also contribute to the family's total income, and a higher total income should lower the couple's chances of divorce or separation. At the moment, this income effect of wives' earnings seems weaker than the offsetting independence effect, but this balance could shift in the future.

And the effect of unstable employment for husbands also could change. The NLS results and the Ross and Sawhill (1975) study imply that family members still expect husbands to bring home a steady income. If husbands fail to do this, they fail to fulfill an important part of their family role. Yet if the earnings of most wives increase so that they earn a larger proportion of their family's total income, the social pressure on husbands may be eased. That is, if most husbands are no longer the sole or predominant source of their family's income, then the social consequences of the husband's unemployment might be less severe. In this case, unemployed husbands would not face the "breakdown" of status which Komarovsky observed in Depression families.

But regardless of whether these changes occur, it seems clear that future studies of marital dissolution must consider the economic situations of both husbands and wives. We can no longer ignore the wife's actual earnings, or her potential earnings if she is not in the labor market, or the unearned income—such as welfare payments—she may be able to collect after a separation. And we also must consider both the stability of the husband's employment and the size of his paycheck. This study and several others have shown that the work lives of husbands and wives can have significant effects on the chances that they will remain together.

Public Welfare Payments and Marital Dissolution: A Review of Recent Studies

The provision of financial assistance to needy persons by the government has been a subject of controversy for many years. The debate has largely focused on whether able-bodied but often unskilled adults, including mothers without husbands, should be expected to support themselves. In recent years the debate has centered on the joint federal-state program of Aid to Families with Dependent Children (AFDC). This is the largest and perhaps the best known public assistance program in the country. In 1974, AFDC recipients numbered over 3.2 million families, over 85 percent of them headed by women (National Center for Social Statistics, 1974a, 1974b).

When this program began in the 1930s most recipients were widows, but in recent years the caseload composition has shifted markedly toward including more mothers made destitute by the voluntary withdrawal of husbands from the household. The economic repercussions of separation and divorce on women are severe indeed. In chapter 16, Bane documents the reduction in their family income. She notes that in 1974 over half (51.5 percent) of the children under 18 in female-headed families fell below the poverty level. And in chapter 14, Kohen, Brown, and Feldberg describe in detail the financial problems of the divorced women in their sample. But the husbands' low economic status also appears to contribute to marital dissolution, as chapters 1, 5, 8, and 9 indicate.

The views expressed in this chapter are those of the author; they do not represent the position or policies of the National Institute of Education. The author wishes to thank Andrew Cherlin, George Levinger, and Kristin Moore for their helpful comments on an earlier version of this paper, and to thank Kristin Moore for making available preliminary findings from her study being supported by the Center for Population Research of the National Institutes of Health.

One frequently heard contention is that AFDC encourages low-income and unemployed fathers to leave home in order that their wives and children may become eligible for the program. Some may remain nearby, seeing and supporting their families covertly. Another contention is that low-income mothers push out or leave their husbands when AFDC is a more profitable and dependable source of income. For whatever reasons, separated and divorced women accounted for 50 percent of all family heads receiving AFDC in 1973 (NCSS, 1974a).

The claim that the AFDC program as a whole contributes to marital dissolution would be hard to test. All states have operated some sort of program in conjunction with the federal government since the 1930s. Nonrecipients similar to recipients in income and location are difficult if not impossible to find, because eligible persons have enrolled in increasing numbers. It has been estimated that by 1971 some 94 percent of all eligible persons participated in the program, up from 63 percent in 1967 (Boland, 1973). However, states vary a good deal in program characteristics such as rates of accepting AFDC applicants, amounts of payment, and requirements that adult recipients work—factors which might affect the propensity for parents to separate and for mothers to apply for AFDC.

This paper will examine the hypothesis that a major characteristic of state programs, the size of average payments per recipient, contributes to separation and divorce. Effects of payments on voluntary marital dissolution in recent years will be examined by reviewing a set of studies conducted over the last ten years.

Other AFDC program characteristics could contribute to marital breakups, but seem unlikely to do so. One such factor, for example, is each state's rate of accepting AFDC applicants which in the past was affected by the length of residence in the state among the pool of applicants. However, by 1970, state duration-of-residence requirements had been invalidated by the Supreme Court. In addition, the high overall rate of enrollment among eligible persons noted above (Boland, 1973) leaves little room for variation in acceptance rates or the likelihood that such variation plays any large role in the decision to separate.

Another aspect of the AFDC program, aid to families headed by unemployed parents (mostly fathers), covered only 85,000 families in the 25 states with such a program (NCSS, 1974b), too small a number to have broad impact on marital dissolution. A third factor, the requirement in some states that recipients accept available jobs, was found in a previous analysis (Moles, 1976) to be associated with *higher* ratios of separated to married women in both 1960 and 1970 regardless of race or place of residence. These findings argue against the idea that work requirements on the books are a deterrent to separation, although the enforcement of work requirements may vary and was not determined in the Moles (1976) study.

If the prospect of receiving welfare benefits is an incentive to marital dissolution, it follows that women living in states with higher AFDC payment levels would be more likely to separate and divorce. Such a connection would not prove that welfare benefits "cause" marital dissolution since various explanations of the relationship are possible, but covariation is a necessary condition though not sufficient to prove causation.

In the sections to follow, different kinds of studies bearing on the welfare payments–marital dissolution hypothesis will be reviewed. First, studies using census data will be described, followed by a discussion of their limitations. Then findings drawing on large-scale longitudinal data sets will be portrayed; suggestions will be offered toward reconciling the differences among the best designed studies. Finally, some policy considerations based on the observed findings will be discussed.

Studies Using Census Data

Only quite recently have the effects on family life of the AFDC program been studied with much breadth and precision. The availability of decennial census data and special purpose census surveys, the desire to subject the welfare-dissolution hypothesis to an empirical test, and the growing use of multivariate statistical techniques combined to make possible a series of sophisticated census based studies in the early and mid-seventies.

Honig (1973) performed an important early analysis. She examined the impact of state welfare payment levels on variations across states for two variables: proportion of females heading families with children under 18, and numbers of AFDC cases in relation to adult females. Eighteen is the upper age limit for children to be supported by AFDC in most circumstances. Using census data on 44 of the largest Standard Metropolitan Statistical Areas (SMSAs) which are scattered among a number of states, Honig held constant the effects of male and female wages, female unemployment rates, and several AFDC eligibility factors. She concluded that in 1960, and less strongly in 1970, higher welfare payments contributed to husbandless families and induced mothers without husbands to become welfare recipients. In both years the amount of the AFDC stipend predicted the proportion of female-headed families among nonwhites, but in 1970 the association was not statistically significant for whites.

A study by Cutright and Scanzoni (1973) also related AFDC payments in 1960 and 1970 to measures of family status among white and non-white children, but arrived at rather different conclusions. Using states rather than SMSAs as units, Cutright and Scanzoni found no effect of AFDC benefit levels on the proportion of white or black children living in two-parent families. They also showed no effect of benefit levels over the period 1950 to 1970 on changes in the percentage of white or non-white women in different age categories living with a husband. States with different payment levels had similar declines from 1950 to 1970 in the percentage of married women with a spouse present. Cutright and Scanzoni attributed this in large part to the increased proportion of women remaining single after 1960 in the younger age groups of 15–19 and 20–24.

A third study, by Ross and Sawhill (1975), focused on explaining the proportion of women aged 16 to 54 who headed families with children under eighteen. They used 1970 census data on low-income areas of 41 American cities. Predictors of female-headed families included several welfare benefit variables, women's earnings, and husband-wife family income. Welfare recipiency rates and the existence of a state AFDC program for unemployed parents did not affect the proportion; a third welfare variable combining the value of state AFDC benefits plus food stamps, as compared to male earnings, was associated with larger proportions of women heading families, but only among nonwhites.

None of these three studies was restricted to marital dissolution, as the term is used here, since widows and unmarried mothers were also counted among female heads of families. This is an important point, since widowhood is involuntary, and unwed motherhood too is subject to different forces than the decision of married couples to separate. In addition, both the Honig and the Ross and Sawhill studies examined data for less than 50 urban areas; it is an open question as to how well their findings would apply to smaller cities or to whole states. Their focus on female-headed families may also have ignored some mothers and children living with relatives or in other housing arrangements.

Two other recent studies have focused exclusively on marital dissolution in broadly representative samples. Public assistance and decennial census data from all 50 states and the District of Columbia were used by Moles (1976) to examine whether welfare payments provide an incentive for mothers with minor children to separate from their husbands. For each state, the number of women with children under 18 reported in the census of 1960 or 1970 as being separated was divided by the number married with children under 18 at the same time to form separation ratios. Separation rather than divorce was chosen, because separated females have lower incomes and represent a larger proportion of the AFDC caseload than the divorced.

In this state level analysis, higher AFDC payments were associated with higher separation ratios—for blacks in 1960, and for blacks and whites in 1970. A further analysis of separation ratios within regions showed higher ratios for whites in 1960 in groups of southern states with higher payments, and for whites and blacks in the North and the South in 1970. Larger payment increases from 1960 to 1970 were linked to greater increases in separation ratios among both races, urban and rural residents, and all mothers combined.

Bane (1975) has made a more sophisticated use of census data on two counts: more predictors and individual level analysis. She examined a large number of predictors of divorce for the 123 largest urban areas using data on individuals from the 1970 census. This permits generalizing to the behavior of individuals rather than only to state-wide relationships. In a regression analysis holding constant the other predictors, Bane found that the average amount of welfare payment per recipient in each urban area was unrelated to whether men or women ages 25–44 living there had ever been divorced. Higher payments were, however, associated with a lower probability for divorced or widowed men and women to remarry. The Bane study is illustrative of the best uses of census data and also of their shortcomings.

Limitations of Census Based Studies

Most analyses which rely on census data to study the welfare payments-marital dissolution hypothesis suffer from at least three drawbacks. First, they count the number of separated or divorced persons at one point in time. This does not take account of those who have already remarried, which over time is the majority of divorced persons. Thus an association between welfare payment levels and numbers separated and/or divorced will reflect differences in the probability of remarriage as well as differences in rates of dissolution. In chapter 1, Norton and Glick point out that blacks are less likely to remarry than whites. Bane's 1975 study points to the possibility that the welfare-dissolution link can be explained by the incentive AFDC offers to minimize remarriage rather than to break up existing marriages.

A second drawback of census based studies is their frequent inability to control over variables which may affect marital dissolution. Cherlin's chapter in this volume points to a set of relevant economic variables, and Norton and Glick's chapter cites demographic and other variables. In order to determine the unique contribution of AFDC payments, the effects of such other likely sources of breakups must be held constant. Unless one has access to special sets of data on samples of persons from the census, as Bane did, the only alternative is published census reports which generally cross-classify by only a small number of variables at a time. Even here variables important from a theoretical standpoint may not have been measured.

A third limitation of census based studies is that almost all information on independent variables of interest pertains to the same single point in time—e.g., 1960 or 1970, or whenever the study occurred. This makes it impossible to decide which events and conditions preceded marital dissolution, and therefore might have contributed to it, in contrast to those occurring simultaneously or after dissolution has occurred. This problem of deciding on causes and effects is common to cross-sectional studies, although retrospective questions can help to some extent. Such retrospective questions are not frequently utilized in the census, and they suffer from failures of accurate recollection. For the reasons mentioned, one must be very cautious in interpreting the results of census based studies of the welfare-dissolution hypothesis.

Evidence from Longitudinal Studies

The best alternative to cross-sectional studies is longitudinal studies which begin with broadly representative samples of two-parent families and follow them long enough to observe sufficient numbers of separations for a statistical analysis to be conducted. Following couples over time distinguishes the married from the remarried; and it clearly places possible causes of dissolution, including the level of AFDC payments, in their proper temporal order.

Two recent national longitudinal surveys fit this description; in addition they provide measures of other variables potentially relevant to the decision to break up a marriage. Findings from these surveys are reported below.

THE PANEL STUDY OF INCOME DYNAMICS

Begun in 1968, the University of Michigan's Panel Study of Income Dynamics (PSID) was designed to investigate factors that affect changes in the economic well-being of families over time (Duncan and Morgan, 1976). As the study discovered, decisions about marriage and other family composition changes seem to be the major decisions that affect one's economic status. The PSID has interviewed a national sample of about 5000 families repeatedly since 1968. Those who began as husband-wife couples have been the subject of several special studies which relate AFDC payments and other explanatory variables to subsequent separation and divorce.

A most comprehensive analysis performed by Sawhill and others (1975) also examined the welfare-dissolution hypothesis separately by race, and within each race among the poor and near-poor. In each case, a number of other possible predictors were included such as the presence of children under 18, husbands' and wives' earnings, unemployment, age at marriage, duration of marriage urban living, and region of residence. All were measured at the beginning of the study period.

These and an estimate of the 1968 average AFDC payment in each couple's state of residence were entered into a regression analysis which determines the unique contribution of each predictor variable. As shown in Table 10-1 there was no significant effect of state payment level on separation or divorce over the subsequent four years to 1972 either in the total sample or in any of the race and income subgroups. This is particularly striking because it is among the poor and near-poor that the incentive of AFDC payments should have its strongest effects. However, a similar study by Sawhill of the total sample using a different statistical technique (logit analysis) found a small though significant effect of AFDC payment levels on dissolution (see Bishop, 1977).

A second study using the Panel Study data traced the likelihood of separation or divorce over six years from 1968 to 1974. Hoffman and Holmes (1976) held constant a set of predictor variables similar to those utilized by Sawhill et al. (1975) and grouped states into high- or low-1969 AFDC payment levels. As described in Table 10-1, they came to a quite different conclusion: couples with low income relative to their needs were more likely to separate if they lived in a high-payment than a low-payment state. In fact, Hoffman and Holmes (1976) estimate that the availability of high welfare benefits decreased marital stability by 12 percent among families with low income in relation to their needs.

In preliminary findings from yet a third study of the PSID data, Moore and Waite (1978) found a statistically significant but very weak effect of 1972 AFDC benefits on marital dissolution over the 1972–1976 period (see Table 10-1). Their regression coefficients showed that $1,000 of additional AFDC benefits would only increase the dissolution rate by 0.3 percent.

Moore and Waite also held constant a number of other variables similar to those utilized in the two previous studies, and added several more. One of these, the AFDC acceptance rate in 1972, was unrelated to the probability of being divorced, but overall Moore and Waite's set of predictor variables explained considerably more of the variance in marital dissolution than did those of Sawhill et al. (1975) or of Hoffman and Holmes (1976).

TABLE 10-1

Evidence from National Longitudinal Studies Bearing on Welfare Payments and Marital Dissolution

Data Sources, Samples, and Investigators	Sample Size	Major Findings Holding Other Relevant Variables Constant
PSID:[a] Husband-wife couples in 1968 with head under age 54:		No relation of 1968 average state AFDC payment to separation or divorce by 1972 in total sample or any subgroup. A similar analysis on the total sample using logit analysis found a small effect of AFDC payment levels (Bishop, 1977).
white	1306	
white and poor or near-poor	538	
white and non-poor	768	
non-white	588	
non-white and poor or near-poor (Sawhill et al., 1975)	501	
PSID: Husband-wife couples in 1968 with head under age 55 (Hoffman and Holmes, 1976).	1732	Low income couples more likely to separate or divorce by 1974 in high than low AFDC payment states. Payments based on 1969 figures.
PSID: Husband-wife couples in 1972 with wife ages 18-48 (Moore and Waite, 1978).	1770	Weak but significant effect of AFDC benefits in 1972 on chance of being divorced or separated by 1976.
NLS:[b] White, nonfarm women aged 30-44 with husband present in 1967 (see chapter 9 by Cherlin).	2126	No relation of 1967 regional average payments to separation or divorce by 1971. No relation for low income women separately.
NLS: Black women aged 30-44 with husband present in 1967 (Cherlin, 1976).	770	1967 regional average AFDC payments related to separation or divorce by 1971, but payments highly correlated with region of residence making interpretation unclear.
NLS: White women aged 14-24 with husband present in 1968 (Cherlin, 1978).	848	1968 state average AFDC payment related to separation or divorce by 1972.
NLS: Women aged 14-24 with husband present in 1968 (Moore and Waite, 1978).	1277	No relation of 1968 regional average AFDC payments to separation or divorce by 1972. No relation among white or black segments of the sample.

[a] Data taken from the Panel Study of Income Dynamics (see text).

[b] ⎯⎯⎯⎯ from one of the National Longitudinal Surveys (see text).

Before attempting to resolve the discrepancies among these three studies, it will be useful to consider the findings from the only other major source of longitudinal data.

THE NATIONAL LONGITUDINAL SURVEYS

The National Longitudinal Surveys (NLS) were begun in the late 1960s to assess the labor market experience of a national probability sample of men and women over the subsequent years. Personal interviews were conducted with one panel of about 5000 women aged 30–44 in 1967 and again in 1969, in 1971, and in later years. A similar study was conducted among younger women aged 14–24. The samples are described elsewhere (Parnes et al., 1970; Kim et al., 1972).

An analysis of these data pertaining to the welfare-dissolution hypothesis is presented by Cherlin in chapter 9 in this volume. Focusing on white, non-farm women aged 30–44 with a husband present in 1967, he finds no effect of AFDC benefits on rates of marital dissolution in the subsequent four years after holding constant a set of family work life variables (see Table 10-1). And in a separate analysis, Cherlin detected no effect among the low-income segment of this NLS sample. These surveys do not identify the state of residence of respondents, so Cherlin's AFDC measure was the regional average payment in 1967. He notes that this aggregation preserved 55 percent of the state variation in welfare payment levels.

In a separate analysis of the black women aged 30–44, using a larger number of predictor variables, Cherlin (1976) did find a link between regional AFDC levels and separation rates over the same four-year period (see Table 10-1). However, he cautions that the high negative correlation of the AFDC variable with residence in the South ($r = -.92$) renders the finding inconclusive. When residence in the South was added to the regression equation, neither it nor the AFDC variable was statistically significant. Hence, it may be something about region of residence rather than state welfare payments that makes the difference.

The younger set of women aged 14–24 from the NLS has also been studied with regard to marital dissolution. Again conflicting findings occur, as shown in Table 10-1. Cherlin (1978) detected an effect of state AFDC payment levels on dissolution over the period 1968–72, whereas Moore and Waite (1978) using regional benefit levels did not.

Toward Resolving the Inconsistencies

The longitudinal study findings just presented defy simple conclusions. About the same number of studies affirm a link between the size of AFDC payments and marital dissolution as those that negate it, but adding the subgroup analyses done in some studies would tip the balance more against the welfare-dissolution hypothesis. Without equivalent subgroup analyses in all studies, however, it is difficult to render a complete accounting.

It seems unlikely that the magnitude of AFDC payments has a strong effect on marital dissolution, given the interplay of other variables. Only the Hoffman and Holmes (1976) study demonstrated a strong connection, but the several other studies which indicated weaker connections suggest that state AFDC levels may play some part in the decision to separate. Before a firm conclusion can be reached, however, certain conceptual and methodological refinements will be needed in future studies of longitudinal data.

Most important is the need to focus on those families that might be influenced the most by AFDC payments. In general these would be families with sporadic employment of parents, with incomes below welfare benefit levels, and with children under 18. More specifically, in such families where the wife is not working and has limited job skills, or earns less than AFDC would pay, public assistance might seem an attractive alternative. Economists refer to the independence effect of the wife's own income which makes her more willing to consider ending an unhappy marriage. Cherlin in Chapter 9 and Levinger in Chapter 8 have documented such a connection. But the *source* of AFDC income (not from earnings) and its *timing* (after dissolution only) suggest that welfare benefits exert another kind of independence effect on mothers of minor children.

Thus, a first requirement of better-designed studies is to include variables identifying the families most likely to be attracted by welfare benefits. None of the longitudinal studies reviewed here was designed primarily to test the AFDC-dissolution hypothesis; it was always tested in the context of interest in an array of social and economic variables which might influence marital dissolution.

Focusing on the AFDC variable's impact suggests another mode of controlling for other variables than regression analysis which was used in each of the longitudinal studies reviewed here. Regression analysis typically creates interaction terms called pattern variables to handle subgroups which are formed of two original variables such as families with low incomes who also have children under age. But the additional specification of the wife's economic status suggested above would require more than the typical two-variable interaction term. With more variables in an interaction term, its interpretation becomes difficult and the sample size in relevant categories becomes small.

Another strategy might be to include in the sample only those families most likely to be influenced by AFDC payments. This would, of course, reduce very substantially the size of each sample below the sample sizes listed in Table 10-1. Still, the 500 or more white and black poor and near-poor families in the PSID analyses described in Table 10-1 indicate that this might be possible. As the PSID and NLS accumulate more years of data, the number of couples who divorce or separate will also grow, providing more cases for a statistical analysis.

A second requirement toward resolving the inconsistencies is the need for clearer conceptualization of variables and a consideration of the role of intervening variables. Regression analysis by its structure cannot accommodate intervening variables. Path analysis may also need to be utilized because it can be used to test conceptual models that include different kinds of intervening linkages (see Duncan, 1975). The PSID and NLS contain relatively few perceptual, cognitive, and attitudinal variables. Nevertheless, intervening conditions such as knowledge of welfare benefits and stigmatization of those receiving benefits could very strongly affect the likelihood of applying for benefits. Such variables are not included in the PSID or NLS at present.

One reason for the different results from the longitudinal studies reviewed here may be that while generally they employed similar independent variables, there are some notable exceptions. For example, the number of independent variables ranges from six (Cherlin, chapter 9) to twenty-one (Hoffman and Holmes, 1976), but more rather than fewer variables is the rule. As more variables are controlled, effects tend to weaken.

Hoffman and Holmes (1976) employed a pattern variable for income in relation to needs, and grouped states into those having high- and low-payment levels. Ross and Sawhill (1975) created a ratio variable by comparing actual earnings of the husband to the earnings expected for men with similar characteristics. Neither variable was used by any other investigator, so these and other unique variables could account for some of the differences in findings.

Region of residence is an especially troublesome variable because, as Cherlin noted, it correlates so highly with regional AFDC payment levels. Hoffman and Holmes (1976) did not include region when they found strong welfare effects, whereas Sawhill et al. (1975) did when they found none. The high correlation of region with AFDC tends to wipe out any AFDC effect when the two are entered together in a regression equation.

While there are fairly strong regional differences in divorce rates, their meaning is not entirely clear. Does the fact that one region may be more rural, less wealthy, more conservative, or more populated by blacks influence the level of AFDC payments in that region? If this were the *sole* effect, region as a variable might be discounted because it only contributes to welfare benefit levels. And if regions merely differed in the racial composition of their population, race was almost always considered as a variable in the studies reviewed. But if region also affects other welfare rules, or the likelihood of applying, or other factors beyond the welfare system that independently influence marital dissolution, these should be conceptualized and measured as distinct variables separate from region. From such efforts will come more adequate conceptual models of the dissolution process which involve the public welfare system.

Some Policy Considerations

Firm conclusions cannot yet be drawn about the effects of welfare payments on marital dissolution. Some census based studies show a connection, while others do not. The same is true of recent longitudinal data analyses which avoid some of the serious methodological limitations of the census based studies.

Accepting for the moment the evidence of an effect found by Hoffman and Holmes (1976) and more weakly by others using longitudinal data, what implication would this have for the public welfare program? One answer might be to reduce AFDC payments to the point where they would no longer serve as an incentive to breakup. While appealing in its simplicity and cost savings, the amount of AFDC benefits would appear to be only one factor in the decision to break up a marriage. To hold separated and divorced mothers at the lowest subsistence level would seem an inhumane penalty for their decision to separate—or for the decision of their ex-spouses over which they may have had little influence. A larger proportion of formerly married women will become employed than go on welfare (Hoffman and Holmes, 1976); but for those on welfare who may have no one to care for young children, no strong job skills, or the misfortune of living in areas of high unemployment, society needs to provide a respectable alternative.

While the evidence for a welfare-dissolution link is tenuous, the evidence for a welfare-remarriage link is more consistent. Bane (1975) found that higher welfare payments were associated with divorced or widowed men and women being less likely to remarry. And Sawhill et al. (1975) report that after controlling for other likely influences on remarriage, only 5 percent of the mothers in the PSID who were welfare recipients remarried within four years, compared to 12 percent of other mothers. The availability of welfare payments may delay remarriage by providing financial support to the family. If this results in longer courtship before remarriage, the stability of the new marriage is likely to be increased (see chapter 5 by Furstenberg).

Another way of looking at the welfare payments–marital dissolution hypothesis is to consider those for whom welfare is likely to have the greatest utility; namely, low-income families where the wife can earn little. As noted previously, when husbands have a weak economic position, their marriages are especially vulnerable to dissolution. A direct income supplement might bolster such husbands' position sufficiently to make a difference, and thus reduce the attraction of welfare payments.

Since in most states AFDC supports families at a level below the poverty line, parents must have very sporadic or low-paying jobs for AFDC to be attractive. The small AFDC program for unemployed parents (AFDC-UP) might appear to offer enough support to two-parent families that the unemployed parent (usually the father) would remain. However, a recent study cited by Bishop (1977) found that 22 percent of the mothers in AFDC-UP families in 1972 in a California county moved into an AFDC program within a year, mainly because the father had left home. This is far above average dissolution rates for one year. If the welfare program is to have an effect, something more than AFDC-UP would appear to be needed.

Another way of bolstering the husband's economic position, as well as the wife's, has been explored in income maintenance programs originally designed as prototypes of a radically restructured welfare program. Their basic idea was to provide an income floor to each family member by simple government transfer payments which avoid the bureaucratic procedures and stigma of the welfare system. If husbands and wives were given an adequate income, perhaps they would display fewer income-related problems, the proponents reasoned. Income maintenance plans have been put into effect on a small scale in New Jersey, Seattle, Denver, and in other localities. Families have been randomly assigned to different payment levels or to control groups for three to five years, and interviewed every quarter.

Such an income maintenance experiment might be expected to enhance marital stability, but in New Jersey, and in Seattle and Denver, families receiving payments had higher rates of marital dissolution than did the controls (Bishop, 1977). However, the higher rates occurred only for those receiving payments close to AFDC levels. These were always less than the highest-payment level. Hannan, Tuma, and Groenvald (1977) have provided a test of one explanation. They argue that the independence effect for husbands and wives of receiving payments that were not contingent on staying together operated more strongly at low-payment levels, and that at higher levels the benefits of an increased income (the income effect) to the family as a whole became more powerful.

Whether this explanation will also fit the New Jersey experiment data remains to be seen. In any event, if an objective of an income maintenance program is to remain neutral with respect to influencing marital dissolution, one must ask whether the high-payment levels which make such neutrality possible could be afforded in a national program, since they are above present AFDC levels and would include many more families.

A jobs strategy is another direction that policy might take. Sawhill et al. (1975) have shown that, for individuals, periods of serious unemployment are strong predictors of dissolution. Hoffman and Holmes (1976) show that the husband's employment problems are a precursor of separation and divorce. In the same vein, Cherlin in chapter 9 has shown that when husbands worked fewer weeks in the previous year their marital dissolution rate was higher.

A jobs strategy might take the form of job training, creating jobs, or employment subsidies to mention a few options. This would assist the husband/father to be more effective in his role performance as breadwinner rather than simply as income provider. The former is much more acceptable as a traditional male role, and has the additional merit of producing goods and services for society. The current federal CETA program, named for the Comprehensive Employment Training Act, is a step in this direction which has created a large number of jobs in the public sector.

On the other hand, if American society is to be egalitarian with regard to job opportunities, then it follows that women should be given the same training and employment advantages as men. But as wives' income rises, so may their likelihood of separation and divorce (see chapters by Norton and Glick, by Levinger, and by Cherlin).

In the case of the welfare payments–marital dissolution hypothesis, the weak effect of payment levels demonstrated to date is a reminder that public welfare is only *one* source of support for families and only *one* of many factors that potentially contribute to separation and divorce. In assessing the public assistance program, policy makers and the public need to view the issues from as many sides as possible in deciding which strategies of public welfare to pursue—whether to keep or revise the present public assistance system, or to discard it in favor of other alternatives such as those discussed here. In the decision process, we would all do well to recognize as explicitly as possible which values and behaviors are likely to be affected by each strategy. Social scientists can help inform public decisions by providing evidence from well-designed studies.

PART IV

Consequences for the Ex-Spouses

IN HIS ANALYSIS of stresses associated with a divorce, Paul Bohannan (1970) identified six overlapping experiences faced by each spouse:

(1) the emotional divorce, which centers around the problem of the deteriorating marriage; (2) the legal divorce, based on grounds; (3) the economic divorce, which deals with money and property; (4) the coparental divorce, which deals with custody, single-parent homes, and visitation; (5) the community divorce, surrounding the changes of friends and community that every divorcee experiences; and (6) the psychic divorce, with the problem of regaining individual autonomy. [p. 34]

Each of those six experiences is touched on in some fashion in the chapters comprising Parts IV and V. Part IV is concerned mainly with the legal, emotional, psychic, and economic aspects of the divorce experience. Part V addresses itself primarily to the parental aspects of divorce, although economic and community aspects also enter that picture.

Each chapter in Part IV acknowledges that marital separation is stressful. The issue is in what ways stress occurs. What aspects of the separation impact are most deserving of our attention? Does it have important implications for the incidence of abnormality or psychological impairment? What seem to be normal, predictable emotional stresses faced by the readjusting ex-spouse? What psychic benefits may be counterposed to the various costs of divorce? And how do professional helpers view the divorcing process?

Chapter 11, by Bernard Bloom, Stephen White, and Shirley Asher, offers a broad review of the correlates and implicit consequences of marital disruption. Marital status—i.e., being single, married, widowed, or otherwise separated—is found to be associated with various aspects of personal well-being or distress: psychiatric hospital admissions, motor vehicle accidents, disease morbidity, and mortality from disease, suicide, and homicide. In almost every instance, the rates appear to be lowest for the married and highest for the divorced; those differences between the married and the divorced are especially large for men.

Bloom and his colleagues note "an unequivocal association" between marital disruption and both physical and mental disorder, but they consider it debatable whether such disruption precedes or is preceded by disease or disturbance. Two competing explanations are that (a) "marital disruption is the product of previously existing disabilities that serve to mediate entrance into or exit from various marital categories," and that (b) "various marital statuses or status changes may themselves produce enough stress to precipitate psychiatric or other disabilities." Despite the inconclusive meaning of its statistics—and its emphasis on only the gloomy consequences of marital disruption—this broad review is a useful preamble for the subsequent chapters which are based on interviews with smaller, intensively studied samples of the separated or divorced, and with groups of professional interveners.

In chapter 12, Robert Weiss takes a searching look at the emotional aftereffects of marital separation. From his extensive acquaintance with women and men whose marriages have disintegrated, he concludes that normal spouses are likely to suffer extreme emotional distress after separation, sometimes alternating with bouts of euphoria. Weiss believes that the marital attachment remains emotionally crucial long after even the most unsatisfactory marriage has ended; he believes such distress parallels that of children who lose an attachment figure. Separated individuals, he proposes, desire not only to rejoin their spouses, but to express anger toward them. The resulting ambivalence may be managed by suppression, by compartmentalization, or by the expression of alternating positive and negative feelings.

All of Weiss's data were derived from his Seminars for the Separated, where recently divorced persons came for an educational program of eight evening meetings; those volunteers probably were rather willing to reveal their feelings of distress. One wonders, therefore, how comparable are these people's expressions to those of other divorced persons. The two subsequent selections throw a somewhat different light on the experiences of the divorced.

Chapter 13, by Graham Spanier and Robert Casto, is based on lengthy interviews with 22 recently separated men and 28 recently separated women from a primarily rural county in central Pennsylvania. Respondents were interviewed with regard to their marital history, and their current situation and difficulties.

According to Spanier and Casto, "people who separate and divorce have to make two distinct but overlapping adjustments." One is to the dissolution of the marriage; it includes the business arrangement of the breakup as well as dealing with its emotional effects. The other adjustment pertains to setting up a new life style and establishing new relationships. Spanier and Casto believe that Weiss's findings require qualification; they contend that the average person's emotional reaction to a marital separation depends largely on how well he or she makes the adjustment to a new life style.

Chapter 14, by Janet Kohen, Carol Brown, and Roslyn Feldberg, emphasizes several positive aspects of divorce for the ex-wife. From their interviews with 30 Boston area divorced women, the authors analyze the contrasting costs and benefits of single motherhood.

These divorcées acknowledged difficulties regarding finances, the control and conduct of family life, and the stigma of being divorced. At least as notable, however, were these single mothers' new-found authority over finances and family management, their freer social life, and the augmentation of their formerly deflated self-concept. A clear majority of these women, who had each been divorced between one and five years, said that they preferred their present status to a return to married life.

During the divorce process, couples usually seek the advice of lawyers, and frequently also of psychotherapists and clergy. Chapter 15 presents an exploratory study of 59 such professional interveners by Kenneth Kressel and his three social psychological colleagues. They summarize and compare the views of the members of those groups regarding the divorce process, criteria for a constructive divorce, and the role of professional assistance.

Psychotherapists and clergy appear to take a similar stance in aiming to reduce emotional turmoil, and to build their clients' self-esteem and insight. Lawyers, in contrast, appear far less homogeneous in their views. The spectrum of opinion runs from a focus on "winning" cases, in a narrow materialistic sense, to a humane psychologically oriented concern with the client's and the family unit's emotional readjustment. Kressel and his colleagues suggest that the large differences among lawyers are attributable to the considerable role strain under which lawyers function; their position is much more problematic than that facing either therapists or clergy.

The chapter concludes with an analysis of a recently developed alternative to the lawyer-run adversary system: professional, nonadversarial divorce mediation. It discusses the potential benefits and difficulties of such an approach, and the need to further conceptualize and evaluate new modes of divorce settlement which recognize the differing characteristics of divorcing couples.

Each of these chapters illuminates different aspects of the immediate or eventual problems faced by separating persons. A better understanding of such problems can contribute to better coping, not only by divorcing persons, but also by society at large.

[11] *Bernard L. Bloom, Stephen W. White, and Shirley J. Asher*

Marital Disruption as a Stressful Life Event

In 1976, more than three million persons were directly involved in a dissolution of marriage in the United States. There were over one million divorces and in each divorce an average of 1.08 children. Thus, more than 2,000,000 adults and over 1,000,000 children were affected by divorce in a single year, representing, in one year alone, 1.5 percent of the total United States population (see National Center for Health Statistics, 1977a, 1977d). These figures might have little interest to any group other than to demographers were it not for a growing body of evidence supporting the fact that marital disruption (separation or divorce) constitutes a severe stress and that the consequences of that stress can be seen in a surprisingly wide variety of physical and emotional disorders.

Continuing interest in marital disruption as a specific stress parallels the increased general interest in those events that appear to precipitate physical and psychological disorders, an area which represents one of the most significant developments in the field of social epidemiological research in recent decades (see, for example, Reid, 1961; or, more recently, B.S. Dohrenwend and B.P. Dohrenwend, 1974; Zautra, Beier, and Cappel, 1977).

A longer version of this chapter appeared in the *Psychological Bulletin*, 1978, *85*, 867–894. Reprinted by permission of the American Psychological Association.

Correlates of Marital Disruption

PSYCHOPATHOLOGY

Of all the social variables relating to the distribution of psychopathology in the population, none has been more consistently found to be so crucial for the population than marital status. Persons who are divorced or separated have been repeatedly found to be overrepresented among psychiatric patients, while persons who are married and living with their spouses have been found to be underrepresented. In a recent review of eleven studies of marital status and the incidence of mental disorder reported during the past 35 years, Crago (1972) did not find a single exception to this summary statement: Admission rates into psychiatric facilities are lowest among the married, intermediate among widowed and never-married adults, and highest among the divorced and separated (see also Redick and Johnson, 1974). This differential appears to be stable across different age groups (Robertson, 1974), reasonably stable for each sex separately considered (Thomas and Locke, 1963), and as true for blacks as for whites (Malzberg, 1956).

Not only are the highest admission rates reported for persons with disrupted marriages, but the differential between these rates and similarly calculated rates among the married is very substantial. National data regarding admission rates into psychiatric facilities by sex and marital status have been available since 1969 for inpatient facilities and since 1961 for public psychiatric outpatient clinics. These data are presented in Table 11-1 for inpatient facilities and in Table 11-2 for outpatient facilities. As can be noted, the ratio of admission rates for divorced and separated persons to those for married persons into inpatient facilities varies from 7:1 to 22:1 for males and from 3:1 to 8:1 for females. In the case of admissions into public psychiatric outpatient clinics, admission rates are also substantially higher for persons with disrupted marriages than for married persons. Ratios of these admission rates vary from 4:1 to 9:1 for males and from 3:1 to 6:1 for females.

Another view of the magnitude of these admission rate differences can be seen from data collected between 1969 and 1971 in the city of Pueblo, Colorado (Bloom, 1975). In this study, data from public and private inpatient facilities are combined but are separately analyzed by sex; also according to whether the person has been admitted for the first time or has a prior history of inpatient psychiatric care. In all cases, admission rates are substantially higher for persons with disrupted marriages (divorced and separated patients combined) than for persons married and living with their spouses. Specifically, in the case of first admissions, admission rates for males with disrupted marriages are nine times

TABLE 11-1

Admission Rates Per 100,000 Population into Public or Private Psychiatric Hospitals in the United States by Year, Marital Status, and Sex

Year	Type of Hospital	Sex	Never Married	Marital Status			Total
				Married	Separated/Divorced	Widowed	
1969[a]	Public	Male	757.6	169.8	2012.6	1046.9	310.2
		Female	398.8	119.4	712.3	359.7	195.4
1970[b]	Public	Male	438.8	132.6	2975.9 2167.6	629.6	331.3
		Female	242.1	124.8	1065.5 758.6	249.2	212.2
1970-1971[c]	Private	Male	927.4	271.8	1904.9	416.1	422.5
		Female	524.6	300.8	907.6	543.1	357.7
1975[d]	Public	Male	501.1	122.1	1712.4	355.6	318.5
		Female	216.8	81.7	595.1	152.6	159.7

[a]Taube (1970a).
[b]Redick and Johnson (1974).
[c]Bachrach (1973).
[d]Bachrach, L.L. Personal communication, Feb. 17, 1977.

TABLE 11-2

Admission Rates Per 100,000 Population into Outpatient Psychiatric Clinics in the United States by Year, Marital Status, and Sex

Year	Sex	Never Married	Marital Status				Total
			Married	Separated/Divorced		Widowed	
1961[a]	Male	208.1	83.1	449.5	284.2	54.3	118.8
	Female	182.6	95.6	430.3	295.1	54.0	117.6
1969[b]	Male	770.9	374.2	1884.4		757.7	444.3
	Female	764.6	344.6	1701.0		945.4	542.3
1970[c]	Male	806.3	276.0	2653.8	1365.6	310.9	492.7
	Female	743.0	423.2	2834.5	1621.7	286.3	578.7

[a]Kramer (1966).
[b]Taube (1970b).
[c]Redick and Johnson (1974).

higher than for males with non-disrupted marriages (30.0 versus 3.3 per 1,000). For first admission females, the difference is on the order of three to one (10.7 versus 3.2 per 1,000).

For patients with histories of prior psychiatric care the differentials by marital status are greater for both sexes. Among males, the difference is about 16 to 1 (46.3 versus 2.8 per 1,000); among females, about 6 to 1 (12.9 versus 2.2 per 1,000). Just as for nationally collected public inpatient data previously reported (see Table 11-1), the differential admission rate for persons with disrupted marriages, when contrasted with persons with non-disrupted marriages, is far greater in the case of males than in that of females. Another way of viewing the Pueblo data is to note that while divorced and separated males constitute only 6.5 percent of ever-married males age 14 and above, they constitute 46 percent of ever-married patients in the same age span. Similarly, while divorced and separated females constitute only 8 percent of ever-married females age 14 and above, they constitute 32 percent of ever-married patients in the same age span. More than 7 percent of males with disrupted marriages are hospitalized annually because of a psychiatric condition.

In examining these local and national data the following facts stood out: first, regardless of type of facility or sex, admission rates are highest for those with disrupted marriages; second, males with disrupted marriages have substantially higher admission rates than females; and third, regardless of sex or type of facility, where rates are separately calculated, those for separated persons are notably higher than those for divorced persons.

Psychiatric facility utilization rate differences as a function of marital status have also been reported in Great Britain. In Scotland (Robertson, 1974), divorced males had the highest rate, almost twice as high as the group with the next highest rate, divorced females. Married men and women had the lowest first admission rate of all groups studied. In two communities in England, Grad and Sainsbury (1966) found referral rates to be very similar to those already reported for the United States, that is, highest rates for the separated and divorced and a ratio of those rates to the rates for married persons on the order of 10:1 for males and 4:1 for females.

Similar findings linking psychiatric status with marital disruption are derived from household survey studies. Srole, Langner, Michael, Opler, and Rennie (1962) in their Midtown Manhattan survey reported that "the Midtown divorced of both sexes have the highest mental morbidity rates of all four marital status categories" (p. 185). Their data show that among males, 19.3 percent of the married in contrast to 40.0 percent of the divorced are psychiatrically impaired. Among females, 19.9 percent of the married and 42.1 percent of the divorced are impaired. Similar results were most recently reported by Radloff (1975) in two communities in Missouri and Maryland, and Pearlin and Johnson (1977) in Chicago.

MOTOR VEHICLE ACCIDENTS

Two studies serve to demonstrate excess vulnerability to motor vehicle accidents among the divorced. The analysis of total U.S. mortality data published by the National Center for Health Statistics (1970a) shows that in both sexes and among both whites and non-whites, automobile fatality rates are higher among the divorced than among any other marital status group, averaging about three times as high as automobile fatality rates among the married. Secondly, a study by McMurray (1970), demonstrated that the accident rate of persons undergoing divorce doubled during the period of time between the six months before and the six months after the divorce date.

DISEASE MORBIDITY

A variety of studies have attempted to link stress experience to disease morbidity. Indeed, such linkages form the empirical basis of psychophysiological disease hypotheses. Holmes and Rahe (1967) have developed a measure of stressful life events based on the amount of readjustment required by each such event. Although the initial development of this scale was based on perceived rather than actual stress, a substantial amount of subsequent research utilizing actual life stresses has shown both prospectively and retrospectively that people experiencing more stress (including marital disruption) are more likely to become ill (Cline and Chosy, 1972; Holmes and Masuda, 1974).

In the first study conducted by the National Center for Health Statistics of differentials in health characteristics as a function of marital status (1976), residents of 88,000 households in the United States were surveyed during 1971–1972. Results are shown in Table 11-3 in which age-adjusted rates by marital status and sex are given. Generally, widowed, separated, and divorced persons had higher rates of illness and disability than married or never-married persons, with never-married persons having lowest rates. Females generally reported more illness and disability than males, regardless of marital status. Separated and divorced persons, particularly women, seem unusually vulnerable to acute conditions. When illness and disability rates are available for both separated and divorced persons, rates are usually higher for those persons who are separated. Similar findings were obtained in an earlier study of psychological distress (National Center for Health Statistics, 1970b).

Two recent studies have appeared which suggest that alcoholism (both acute and chronic) is more prevalent among the divorced than among the married, a finding which corroborates much earlier literature. Wechsler, Thum, Demone, and Dwinnell (1972) studied the blood alcohol level of over 6,000 eligible consecutive admissions to the emergency service of Massachusetts General Hospital. The authors found that "in both sexes,

TABLE 11-3

Age-Adjusted Rates of Selected Health Measures for Persons
Age 17 and Above by Marital Status and Sex

Selected Health Measure	Sex	Marital Status				
		Never Married	Married	Separated	Divorced	Widowed	Total
Restricted Activity Days Per Person Per Year	Male	17.0	16.2	27.3	25.6	26.2	16.9
	Female	17.2	18.9	33.3	26.6	28.7	20.4
Percent Limited in Activity Due to Chronic Conditions	Male	23.8	17.5	26.1	25.3	–	18.6
	Female	17.9	13.8	23.3	19.6	22.0	15.7
Incidence of Acute Conditions Per 100 Persons Per Year	Male	149.5	157.8	–	164.2	–	154.2
	Female	176.4	188.8	247.1	245.8	151.2	192.6
Physician Visits Per Person Per Year	Male	3.8	4.4	5.3	4.8	–	4.3
	Female	5.3	6.6	7.4	7.6	6.7	6.3

the divorced or separated had the highest proportion with positive Breathalyzer readings. . . . Divorced or separated men included 42 percent with positive alcohol readings" (p. 138). Widowers had the lowest proportion with positive readings (10 percent), and single (24 percent) and married men (19 percent) were intermediate. Rosenblatt, Gross, Malenowski, Broman, and Lewis (1971) contrasted first admissions with readmissions for alcoholism and concluded that their results "reveal a significant relationship between disrupted marriage and multiple hospitalizations for the acute alcoholic psychoses at ages below 45" (p. 1094).

The role of social and psychological factors in coronary artery disease is attracting an increasing amount of attention (Jenkins, 1976a; 1976b). While there do not appear to be remarkable differences in the incidence of coronary disease as a function of marital status, stress clearly increases the risk of the disease. Among such stressors, rejection by a loved one and family conflict have been specifically implicated. Lynch (1977) has reviewed numerous studies linking marital status with a variety of diseases as have Carter and Glick (1976, pp. 324–357). The latter have concluded that "a relatively large proportion of people who have serious trouble with their health are likely to have serious trouble in becoming married, maintaining a viable marriage, or becoming remarried" (1976, p. 324).

SUICIDE, HOMICIDE, AND DISEASE MORTALITY

Important sources of data serve to link marital disruption to deaths from suicide, homicide, and from specific diseases. The maritally disrupted are consistently found to be overrepresented among all three groups (Kitagawa and Hauser, 1973, pp. 108–112).

Shneidman and Farberow (1961) have compared some personal characteristics of attempted and committed suicides from the year 1957 in Los Angeles County. Thirteen percent of committed suicides were divorced and 3 percent were found to be separated. Both of these figures are more than double what would have been expected on the basis of the proportion of divorced and separated persons in the Los Angeles population. Furthermore, the divorced, separated, and widowed were significantly overrepresented among persons who committed suicide and significantly underrepresented among those who attempted it. Shneidman and Farberow suggest that "it seems probable that the losses and disturbances in dyadic relationships occurring among the older groups, where more divorced, separated, and widowed appear, are also more likely to result in more lethal suicidal behavior" (p. 30). In a related study, Litman and Farberow (1961) in proposing a strategy for emergency evaluation of self-destructive potentiality note that "many suicide attempts, especially in young persons, occur after the separation from a spouse or loved one. . . . When there has been a definite loss of a loved person, such as a spouse, parent, child, lover, or mistress, within the previous year (by death, divorce, or separation), the potentiality for self-destruction is increased" (p. 51).

Another source of data linking suicide with marital status comes from the continuing reports of the National Center for Health Statistics (1970a). With particular reference to deaths from suicide, among white females and both white and non-white males, the suicide rate is higher among the divorced than among people of any other marital status. In the case of non-white females, the suicide rate is highest in the widowed and second highest in the divorced, where the rate is still twice that of the married.

Gove (1972b), reviewing data on sex and marital status regarding suicide, found that these findings hold true not only for the United States but also for Switzerland, Canada, New Zealand—and, with respect to all marital status categories except the single, for Sweden as well.

In regard to deaths from homicide (National Center for Health Statistics, 1970a), the figures are even more striking. For both sexes and for both whites and non-whites, risk of death by homicide was far higher among the divorced than in any other marital status group. For white women, the risk was more than four times higher among the divorced than the married; and for white men, it was more than seven times higher. Among non-whites, the risk was twice as high for women and three times as high for men.

Important links between marital disruption and mortality rates from specific diseases can be found in the special studies of the National Center for Health Statistics (1970a). Both the widowed and the divorced had higher age-adjusted death rates for all causes combined than did married persons of equivalent age, sex, and race. With respect to specific diseases, death rates from tuberculosis and cirrhosis of the liver were consistently higher among the divorced than among the married. For white males and non-whites of both sexes, the death rate was higher among the divorced than among the married from malignant neoplasm of the respiratory system, and among non-white males the death rate was higher among the divorced than among the married for diabetes mellitus and arteriosclerotic heart disease (also see Kobrin and Hendershot, 1977).

In a review of the literature linking mortality, sex, and marital status, Gove (1973) reports that mortality rates are lower among the married than among the unmarried and that the differences in mortality rates between married persons and single, divorced, or widowed persons are larger among men than women. In addition, these differences are accentuated when considering mortality from causes potentially affected by social factors or by one's personal psychological state (e.g., suicide, homicide, and cirrhosis of the liver) while they are reduced for mortality rates from causes unaffected by social or personal psychological factors (e.g., leukemia).

Gove (1972a, 1973) has also proposed that the differences among marital statuses and between sexes in the prevalence of suicide, and in disease-specific death rates are due to the nature of marital roles occupied by men and women in Western society (see also Bernard, 1972). He argues that because of the advantages that marriage offers males, married males are less likely than the unmarried to feel the stresses that may result in suicidal behavior or the onset of certain diseases. More recent data, however, do not generally support Gove's hypothesis (Bloom, Asher, and White, 1978).

Problems Associated with Marital Disruption

Most of the literature on the problems faced by maritally disrupted persons focuses on divorced women. This attention appears to be a consequence of the belief that marital disruption is more stressful for women than men, and the fact that children of divorced parents are likely to live with their mothers. It also may reflect the rising interest in changing roles of women in all marital status groups. We have seen, however, that the link between marital disruption and a great variety of illnesses and disorders is stronger for men than for women. Until recently, the evidence has been rather unsystematic; it has ranged from autobiographical accounts (e.g., Baguedor, 1972) to clinical reports of persons seen in psychotherapy whose problems were judged to be precipitated by, exacerbated by, or associated with marital disruption (see, for example, Stewart, 1963). Recent studies have attempted to deal more systematically with the effects of marital disruption on parental and family functioning.

We have chosen to review most carefully the literature published since 1960 dealing with problems faced by persons undergoing marital disruption. Attitudes towards marriage and its termination have changed so dramatically in the past fifteen years that research studies published prior to 1960 seem to emerge from a different era, almost a different world (see Norton and Glick, chapter 1). Two studies are of special historical importance, however; the work of Goode (1949, 1956), who studied a sample of divorced mothers in Detroit; and of Locke (1951), who compared samples of divorced and happily married persons in an Indiana county and in the process developed a well-known scale for the measurement of marital adjustment.

Bohannan (1970) has suggested that divorce is a complex personal event involving at least six different experiences of separation. *Legal* divorce is but one of these, and does little more than create opportunities for remarriage. The other experiences of separation include: *emotional divorce*, which results from the loss of a love object; *economic* divorce whereby community property has to be divided; *coparental* divorce if children are involved; *community* divorce, involving the attitudes of, and relationships with friends and relatives; and *psychic* divorce, leading to the becoming of an autonomous individual. Each of these experiences must be dealt with, in one way or another, beginning before the point where a couple physically separate, a point that usually occurs long before the divorce is final.

PROBLEMS FACED BY THE INDIVIDUAL OR FAMILY

People appear to be differentially vulnerable to the stresses associated with marital disruption. Blair (1970) analyzed data collected from 65 white middle-class divorced women and concluded that post-divorce adjustment was most difficult for those divorcées who were older at the time of divorce, and those who had been married longer, had been divorced a shorter period of time, had low self-esteem or high anxiety, had obtained a divorce at the suggestion of their husbands, had family opposition to their marriage, and had inadequate economic status.

Myers (1976) interviewed 60 newly separated women who were divided into four groups defined by age or length of marriage, and by presence or absence of dependent children. She found that adjustment to separation was a function of age, presence of children, sex-role identification, and the process of initiation of the separation. She found, as did Blair and Goode, that adjustment was more satisfactory in the case of younger women. Age was, in turn, highly correlated with length of marriage. In addition, adjustment was easier for women without dependent children, women with nontraditional sex-role orientations, and women who had played an active role in the decision to separate.

Several researchers have attempted to identify the specific problems faced by separated and divorced women and men. Schlesinger (1969), after indicating that more than 90 percent of one-parent families are headed by the mother, lists problems faced by single-parent mothers: difficulties with children, the need to work, sexual problems, problems in reestablishing social relationships, financial difficulties, and the problems associated with feelings of failure and shame. Schwartz, commenting on the difficulties faced by divorced and remarried persons seen at a family agency, notes that "divorced persons . . . continue to be bound together . . . in ways that are destructive to themselves, the children, and their new family units" (1968, p. 214; see also Pearlin and Johnson, 1977).

Ilgenfritz (1961) reported on a group educational program for twelve single-parent women with children and attempted to identify the major problems that were discussed. These turned out to be fear of being alone, concern with the loss of self-esteem as a woman, hostility toward men, practical problems of living, specific concerns regarding child-rearing, and interest in the development of self-help strategies.

White and Asher (1976) interviewed 30 divorced men 6 to 12 months after they were divorced concerning their marital disturbances and post-separation adjustment. Few men experienced difficulties in the areas of employment, education, and income, or in managing cooking, cleaning, and other practical problems. Loneliness was a major emotional problem for 60 percent of the sample. In general, the men who made the most successful adjustment to the divorce were those who had not been totally dependent on their wives and had a social life independent of the marriage.

The economic problems faced by divorced persons, women in particular, have been extensively documented (Stein, 1970). Brandwein, Brown, and Fox (1974) cite economic discrimination against women as a major reason for the financial difficulties of divorced mothers. The median earnings of full-time, full-year employed women averaged 55 percent of men's earnings, even within the same occupational categories. Childcare and household responsibilities make it difficult for women to work full-time. While men complain about the economic strain of supporting two households, only one-third of husbands were found to be contributing to the financial support of their ex-wives and children (Brandwein et al., 1974). Rheinstein (1972) has noted that the divorce rates of countries having family allowances and other forms of family support have all been lower than that of the United States, even countries that are heavily industrialized. He suggested that research should be undertaken to determine whether the alleviation of economic tension in families might reduce the incidence of marital disruption.

Maritally disrupted persons, both men and women, are faced with maintaining a household; many, in addition, must provide childcare. Hetherington, Cox, and Cox (1977) found that the households of divorced mothers and fathers were more disorganized than those of intact families. The irregular eating habits and erratic sleep patterns exhibited in some of these families had the potential for exacerbating or precipitating mental health problems. Both Hetherington et al. and Brandwein et al. found that more men than women receive assistance from either female friends or an employed housekeeper. Brandwein et al. further noted that the Washington, D.C., welfare department has provided free homemaking services to single fathers, but not to single mothers unless they were mentally incompetent, chronically ill, or disabled.

Ferri (1973) noted that similar patterns of childcare exist in Great Britain. Her work on single-parent fathers is an outgrowth of a longitudinal study of all children born in England and Wales during a single week in 1958. At the time of her study, 237 of these children (1.7 percent) were living in families without their biological mother and 7.7 percent were living in families without their biological father. Single-parent fathers had an easier time finding substitute mothering for their children than mothers had in finding substitute fathering. Ferri stated, "These findings may reflect differences in social attitudes towards men and women as sole parents" (p. 93). Such attitudes seem to isolate women, make it difficult for them to find adequate childcare, and place the entire responsibility for raising the children on the mother.

Marital disruption can precipitate intense and complex emotional reactions. Hetherington et al. (1976, 1977) and Weiss (chapter 12) have examined such reactions. Hetherington et al. (1977) found that divorced parents felt more anxious, depressed, angry, rejected, and incompetent than married persons. Both divorced men and women experienced changes in self-concept. Men seemed to undergo greater initial changes because they were usually the ones to leave familiar surroundings. Fathers felt a lack of identity, rootlessness, and complained of a lack of structure in their lives. Men often engaged in a flurry of social activities as a way of resolving some of their identity problems. Familiar surroundings and the continued presence of their children provided divorced mothers with a sense of security. Their changes in self-concept evolved more slowly than those of their ex-husbands but the effects were longer lasting. Divorced women complained of feeling unattractive, helpless, and of having lost their identity as married women. The most important factor leading back toward a positive self-concept for men and women was the establishment of a satisfying heterosexual relationship.

Weiss (chapter 12) has analyzed stresses associated with marital disruption for about 150 men and women. Both men and women found marital separation distressing; being the spouse who initiated the separation helped only slightly in minimizing the distress. Weiss reported that even when positive feelings toward the ex-spouse had faded, feelings of strong attachment remained.

An extensive literature suggests to the negative consequences of marital disruption for children of the disrupted family. There is, however, recent evidence that the effect is not unidirectional, that children who are disturbed by parental separation may in turn be a source of stress for their parents. Hetherington et al. (1976, 1977) studied the families of 48 nursery-school-age boys and girls from divorced families and the same number of boys and girls from intact homes using a wide variety of measures. Divorced persons were found to have difficulty parenting, mothers having many problems with their sons. Divorced parents did not communicate well with their children, were not very affectionate, were inconsistent in disciplining the children, and lacked control over them in comparison to parents in intact families. Hetherington et al. suggested that children's behaviors, particularly those of boys, can cause emotional responses in mothers such as anxiety, feelings of helplessness, incompetence, and depression. Under such pressure, the mother becomes an ineffective parent and often provokes further negative and aversive behaviors in the child.

Children may also precipitate stressful interactions between estranged parents. Cline and Westman (1971) studied the incidence and characteristics of post-divorce turbulence by following 105 families in which the parents had recently obtained a divorce. In nearly one-third of the cases there were hostile interactions requiring court appearances. Five patterns of post-divorce turbulence were identified: (a) hostile interaction over parenting roles; (b) hostile conflict not involving the children; (c) perpetuation by the children of interaction between their divorced parents; (d) special alliances between one parent and the child or children against the other parent; and (e) continued tension between divorced partners perpetuated by the extended family.

These studies converge on identifying a small but important set of problems faced by persons undergoing marital disruption. Included in such a list would be a weakened social support system, a need to work through one's psychological reactions to the disruption, as well as a need for assistance with child rearing, resocialization, and with one's practical problems, such as finances, educational and employment planning, housing and homemaking, and protection of legal rights. Evidence indicates that the most critical time in the marital disruption process is around the time of separation.

Explanatory Hypotheses

It is now appropriate to examine hypotheses that have been advanced to account for the associations between marital disruption on the one hand, and various physical and emotional disorders on the other. Bachrach has noted that "there is far less certainty about the *reasons* for the statistical relationships between marital status and mental disorder than there is about the fact of such relationships" (1975, p. 5).

In her review of the hypotheses that have been advanced to account for the statistical associations found between marital status and mental disorder, Bachrach (1975) examines role theory, stress theory, and selectivity theory. Selectivity theory, which asserts that marital statuses may not all be equally accessible to persons who vary in psychological well-being, can help account for the fact that psychopathology among the never-married exceeds that typically found in the case of the married. Role theory, which asserts that roles played by persons in differing marital statuses may expose them differentially to disorder-producing risks, can help account for the fact that the married are at lower risk of disability than all the nonmarried (including the never-married, separated, divorced, and widowed). Stress theory, which asserts that the occurrence of a stressful event may precipitate the appearance of a disability, particularly when there is an already existing predisposition, can help account for the fact that disability rates are far higher in the case of the separated, divorced, and widowed than in the case of the married. These three theoretical perspectives are clearly not incompatible with each other.

If one takes the additional step of asserting that various marital statuses induce differing amounts of stress, then role theory and stress theory can be seen, in Bachrach's words, as "different facets of a single phenomenon" (1975, p. 13). The three perspectives then reduce to two hypotheses: first, that marital disruption is the product of previously existing disabilities that serve to mediate entrance into and exit from various marital status categories; and, second, that various marital statuses or marital status changes may produce enough stress to precipitate psychiatric or other disabilities.

Marital disruption and physical and emotional disorders are clearly interactive, in the sense that each has the potential to influence the other. These interactions have yet to be explored empirically, in part, no doubt, because of the complexity of the task (see B. P. Dohrenwend, 1975). One pertinent longitudinal project has been undertaken (see Myers, Lindenthal, and Pepper, 1971, 1974, 1975; Myers, Lindenthal, Pepper, and Ostrander, 1972). In this study, designed to delineate the connection between life events and psychiatric symptomatology, the authors conducted two sets of interviews, once in 1967 and again in 1969, obtaining each time an index of the respondent's mental status and the number of life crises occurring during the year prior to interview.

Their findings generally indicate "a substantial and positive relationship between psychological impairment and the experiencing of life events" (1971, p. 156). In analyzing the changes on the two measures between the first and second interviews, the authors found a strong, direct association, noting that "the sheer quantity of events alone seems to have a striking effect upon one's capacity to maintain a state of mental health" (1972, p. 404). In sum, "the greater the number of life events or the greater their increase over two years, the greater the number of on increase in psychiatric symptoms" (1975, pp. 424–425). Their findings were not affected by socio-demographic variables, including sex, race, age, religion, social class, and household size.

Myers et al. (1972) found that divorce was one of only 6 of the 62 individual events in which the predicted association was not found, that is, those who had experienced divorce recently (noted at the second, but not the first interview) did not exhibit a worsening of symptomatology.

This finding suggests that divorce is perhaps the *resolution* of a stressful situation and not a stressor per se, particularly in light of the finding that both separation and a "major change in relationship with spouse" were significantly associated with an increase in psychiatric symptomatology. Divorce significantly postdates the actual stressful experience of separation, underlining the necessity of distinguishing between divorce and the prior, perhaps far more stressful, separation.

In a careful retrospective study, Smith (1971) contrasted a sample of 880 mental health center patients with 2400 randomly selected adults, and found that 5 particular life events were reported significantly more often by mental patients than by the control group in the prior year— getting into trouble with the police, loss of employment, onset of a problem with one's own drinking, the beginning of a family member's heavy drinking, and divorce or separation. In a subsequent phase of the study, it was found that only marital disruption or onset of a family member's drinking tended to precede mental disorder. The findings of Myers et al. suggest that it would have been useful to have distinguished between the phenomena of divorce and of separation, although these findings clearly support those of the Myers et al. prospective investigation.

The most appropriate interpretation of the research and conceptualizations reviewed here is that an unequivocal association between marital disruption and physical and emotional disorder is demonstrated. Furthermore, this association suggests at least two interdependent components: first, illness (physical or emotional) can precede and can help precipitate marital disruption; and second, marital disruption can serve to precipitate physical and psychiatric difficulties in some persons who might otherwise not have developed such problems.

It is important to note that this literature review is limited to research published in the English language. It is true that the divorce rate is higher in the United States than in most other countries (United Nations, 1976, pp. 428–431), but the problem of divorce and separation is not unique to the United States and a large non-English language literature exists. There is also evidence that substantially different types of problems exist in different parts of the world. For example, we have said that the stresses associated with marital disruption are particularly severe at the time of separation. Yet this may be true only where there is no significant housing shortage. In Eastern Europe, where housing is often in short supply, it is not uncommon for divorce to occur without the possibility of separation. Under such circumstances, for example, different problems undoubtedly occur as a divorced couple (often with children) continue to share essentially indivisible and limited living space. This one example demonstrates the significant contribution that cross-national research would have for our understanding of the causes and consequences of marital disruption.

General Implications

Substantial federal resources are allocated for the continuing collection of information on marital status and on the utilization of psychiatric facilities. Such information is far from complete (Carter and Glick, 1976, pp. 384–386). Increased collaboration among appropriate data gathering agencies could significantly improve information, including data linking changes in marital history and marital status with a wide variety of measures of physical and psychological morbidity.

One particular impediment to the coordination of data is the absence of a standard measure for the most important indicators of marriage and divorce. Since it is usually desirable for rates to be interpretable as probability statements, most biostatisticians urge that in the calculation of rates, denominators include only persons at risk of being in the numerator (see, for example, Linder and Grove, 1943, pp. 28–39). It has become traditional to report marriage and divorce rates per 1000 total population. Consequently, it is not possible to make valid contrasts among the marriage rates of communities that differ in the proportion of their unmarried population, nor is it possible to contrast divorce rates among communities that differ in the proportion of the population that is married. It seems far better to describe marriage rate as a proportion of unmarried persons above a specified age; divorce rate as a proportion of married couples; and remarriage rate as a proportion of widowed and divorced persons as has been done by Glick and Norton (1977 and chapter 1).

Another problem in understanding the connection between marital disruption and psychopathology derives from the fact that statistics generally pertain to current marital status rather than marital history. Two persons may be currently married, but may have arrived at that status by far different pathways. For example, one may be married for the first time, while the other is in his third marriage following an earlier divorce from one spouse and the death of the second. Bloom attempted to collect marital history as well as marital status data from patients admitted into psychiatric inpatient facilities, and found that six patterns were sufficient to identify the marital histories of 93 percent of ever-married patients (1975, p. 223). He found that patients with prior histories of psychiatric care had more disrupted marital histories (more separations and more divorces independent of current marital status) than did first admission inpatients. If marital history information were collected as part of the U.S. Census, it would be possible to calculate morbidity rates for each of the various marital history (as contrasted with marital status) groups.

Johnson (1977) has suggested the establishment of a National Center for the Study of Divorce. Such a center might very well provide a most useful administrative structure for dealing with these and other substantive as well as methodological issues.

Concluding Comments

The principal objective of this chapter has been to assess the degree to which marital disruption can be considered a stressful life event. The evidence overwhelmingly supports the hypothesis that separation and divorce are stressors of the first magnitude. Any community interested in improving the well-being of its citizens would be advised to examine the social and psychological costs of marital disruption and to examine ways of reducing such costs.

The results of this review, however, must be seen in a broader perspective. First, most marriages do not end in separation and divorce. Second, most persons who go through a marital disruption do not appear to be at excess risk of developing illness or disability. Third, attitudes toward separation and divorce are undergoing a rapid transformation so that, within a foreseeable future, the more favorable public attitudes may lead to a reduction in their stressfulness. Finally, both the rapid rise in divorce rates and the gradual fall in marriage rates appear to be ending. To the extent that the stresses are a consequence of societal reactions and of the increase of divorce, we may therefore witness their decline.

For the present, though, it is clear that separation and divorce are difficult periods in many persons' lives. Terminating an unhappy marriage continues to be a decision not to be taken lightly. Community agencies that deal with the separated (e.g., the courts, attorneys, and social welfare agencies) would do well to become more aware of their potential role in mitigating stresses associated with marital disruption.

The Emotional Impact of
Marital Separation

In Goode's (1956) survey of divorced mothers, about two-thirds said that some level of trauma had been associated with the disruption of their marriage, for the most part occurring either at the time of final decision or at the time of actual separation. Goode's approach relied on survey interviews, in many cases held years after the point of separation. Insofar as retrospective reconstructions may be expected to err in the direction of minimization of distress, we might assume Goode's respondents to have understated the regularity with which marital separation gives rise to distress.

As yet there have been no survey studies comparable to Goode's in which men as well as women were interviewed. But on the basis of group discussions with separated men and women it appears that marital separation is as likely to be distressing for men as for women (Weiss, 1975).

Being the spouse who initiated the separation does not seem to be especially important in deciding whether the separation will be accompanied by distress. Goode's data suggest that it helps a bit to be the one who first suggested the divorce, but it does not help a great deal. Both those respondents who defined themselves as having been left by the spouse and those who defined themselves as having been the leavers appeared to be distressed by the end of the marriage.

A recent study of recovery from bereavement provides further evidence that marital disruption almost uniformly gives rise to distress, irrespective of the quality of the marriage. In this study 52 widows and 22 widowers were interviewed within the first three weeks after the death of their spouses, again a month later, and again about a year later

This chapter appeared in *Journal of Social Issues*, 1976, 32 (1).

(Glick, Weiss, and Parkes, 1974). These widows and widowers, all forty-five or younger, included all individuals bereaved within the study period in the age category of interest who lived in the Boston metropolitan region and were willing to cooperate with the study. Only three of these widows and widowers appeared not to have experienced marked grief. Only one seemed not to have suffered grief at all: a woman whose alcoholic husband had several times left her and had moved in with another woman at the time of his death.

Except for disproportionate representation of alcoholic husbands, the marriages dealt with in this study appear to have been the usual run, some very good, some adequate, and some unhappy. The near universality in this sample of distress on loss of the spouse suggests that within American society virtually all marriages, happy or unhappy, make an important contribution to the well-being of the partners.

This study found no simple association between the intensity of grief and the happiness attributed to the marriage. Grief appeared to be somewhat less intense than typical in instances where there had been estrangement between the spouses but also in instances where the marriage had been extremely close. Apart from minor variations, however, nearly disabling grief was the rule, even among individuals who could say about the preceding marriage, as one widow did, "Ours wasn't the best marriage in the world."

A Persistent Marital Bond

The Harvard Laboratory of Community Psychiatry, during the three years beginning in 1971, provided a program of eight educationally oriented meetings for recently separated individuals. This program, called "Seminars for the Separated" (Weiss, 1975), contained both a didactic component and an opportunity for group discussion. Participants included individuals of widely varying educational attainment, but were for the most part college-educated. About 150 recently separated individuals at some point participated in this program. The participants, although self-selected, did not differ from Goode's survey respondents in the kind of distress they reported, and their more detailed descriptions may provide a basis for better understanding of the nature of that distress.

Several participants in the seminars said that even though their marriage had become unhappy, contemplating its end had made them anxious, even terrified. A woman about 30 years of age reported:

When the idea occurred to me that I could live without Dave and be happier, my immediate next feeling was just gut fear. It's really hard to explain. It was just terror.

This suggests that even though a marriage may have become burdensome, it may nevertheless continue to provide security at least to the extent of fending off anxiety. Other participants in Seminars for the Separated reported that after their separation they now and again felt impelled by anxiety to reestablish contact with their spouse: to telephone or to see the spouse. In a few cases anxiety was reduced simply by driving by where the spouse now lived.

Some among the separated felt drawn to the spouse without being able to account for the feeling. One man whose wife worked in a bookstore repeatedly visited there, even though his wife was rude to him when he encountered her. Another man reported that although he was angry with his wife and resented what he felt to be mistreatment by her, he was disappointed if she was not at home when he visited his children. A woman who was exasperated by her continued yearning for her husband said:

It is like the battered child syndrome. You never find a battered child that does not want to be back with its parents, because they are the only parents it has. I just have very much this feeling.

Most among the separated continue to feel drawn to the spouse even when a new relationship is established which appears in many respects satisfactory. There may be exceptions to this generalization, especially among individuals who left their marriages for relationships that had already become emotionally important to them. But by and large another figure is not easily substitutable for the original partner, and individuals may continue to pine for the spouse even after they have established new relationships. A man whose wife had left him as the final scene in a stormy marriage and who thereupon traveled across the continent to see a former girl friend said:

Here I was, three days with someone of the opposite sex, trying to start rebuilding, and I just got overwhelmed with panic at being three thousand miles from Laura. And these waves built up until I was just white. It is an unbearable feeling.

The marital bond whose characteristics we are noting appears to be unrelated to liking, admiration, or respect. Some among the separated reported that they could continue to like their spouses, even though they or their spouses had decided that they would no longer live together. But even those who now disparaged their spouses felt drawn to them. One woman said of her ex-husband:

I don't like him. As a man I find him boring. If I met him at a party I'd talk with him for about two minutes and then I'd say, "I'll see you." But the emotional tug is still there. He is still attractive to me.

To summarize, there persists after the end of most marriages, whether the marriages have been happy or unhappy, whether their disruption has been sought or not, a sense of bonding to the spouse. Some feel anxious, fearful, or terrified both when contemplating a prospective separation from the spouse and when experiencing the spouse's absence. Others feel drawn to the spouse after separation, even though they may have decided against a continued relationship with the spouse. Pining for the spouse may continue despite the availability of alternative relationships and despite absence of liking, admiration, or respect. In all these ways this persisting bond to the spouse resembles the *attachment bond* of children to parents described by Bowlby (1969). Indeed, it seems reasonable to surmise that the bond we observe to persist in unhappy marriages is an adult development of childhood attachment. I will, in consequence, refer to it as attachment (Bowlby, 1969, 1973; Cohen, 1974).

An issue of some interest is the relationship between attachment and love. Most people would seem to think of love as a condition combining positive regard for another with urgent desire to maintain the other's accessibility. Rubin (1973) has shown that love is ordinarily a syndrome including a number of components such as trust, idealization, and liking which can exist independently of one another. Attachment would be one such component. It would appear that in unhappy marriages most of the components of love fade, sometimes to be replaced by their opposites. In this way trust may change to mistrust, idealization to disrespect, liking to disdain. Attachment, however, seems to persist. It appears that most components of love are modifiable by negative experience, but that attachment once developed can be sustained by proximity alone and fades only slowly in response to absence.

Data collected in a study of early marriage[1] suggest that a significant minority of marriages may be entered by individuals whose attachment to one another is not yet firm, who remain in some degree attached to a parent. Continued attachment to a parent is displayed by separation distress on contemplating departure from the parental home and homesickness while on the honeymoon. Yet it appears from our study of bereavement that loss of a spouse almost uniformly produces intense distress. It seems reasonable to conclude that the marital relationship sponsors attachment even in couples who were not attached to one another when they married. It might perhaps do so through the intensity of shared emotional experiences (which may facilitate the spouses be-

1. The study of early marriage was conducted at the Laboratory of Community Psychiatry by Rhona Rapoport.

coming emotionally charged for one another), through the nearly continuous intimate contact with one another required by marriage, and through
the barriers established by marriage to other intimate relationships.

Responses to Loss of Attachment

The disruption of attachment is a major source of emotional disturbance following separation, but it is far from the only such source. Marital
separation is an extensively disruptive event, not only ending the continued accessibility of the spouse but also producing fundamental changes
in an individual's social role and in his or her relationships with children,
kin, and friends. Reactions to the loss of the spouse as attachment figure
become intermeshed with reactions to these other disruptions.

The loss of attachment may, however, be seen as the primary cause
of the "separation distress" syndrome described by Parkes (1972). It
includes the organization of attention around the image of the lost figure,
an urge to make contact with the lost figure, anger toward the lost figure,
guilt for having produced the loss, and the presence of an "alarm reaction" (Parkes's term), including hyperalertness to indications of the lost
figure's return, great restlessness, and feelings of fear or panic. Difficulties
in sleeping and, to a lesser extent, loss of appetite are also expressions
of heightened vigilance.

The symptoms of separation distress in adults are very similar to
those exhibited by young children who have lost attachment figures. One
list of reactions among children to loss of a parent includes, among
others, rage and protest over desertion, maintenance of an intense fan-
tasy relationship with the lost parent, persistent efforts at reunion,
anxiety, and a strong sense of narcissistic injury (Crumley and Blumenthal, 1973; Bowlby, 1973). Some among the separated themselves recognize the similarities between their current experience of marital separation
and an earlier experience in which they were separated from parents.

When my husband left I had this panicky feeling which was out of proportion to what was really happening. I was afraid I was being abandoned. I
couldn't shake the feeling. I remembered later that the first time I had that
feeling was when I had pneumonia and my mother left me in the hospital, in a
private room, in the winter. And this picture came back of this hospital and
these old gray rooms, and it was winter and every night at five o'clock, when
the shadows would come across my bed, my mother would put on her coat and
say: "Goodbye, I will see you tomorrow." And I had such a feeling of panic
and fear at being left.

In what would at first appear to be a very different sort of reaction from this, some recently separated individuals are euphoric for varying intervals. They report not a diminution in self-confidence and self-esteem but rather its increase. They may insist that the separation was wholly for the best, that they feel that by separating they have opened the world for themselves, that their lives have suddenly become adventures in which they are totally engaged. Individuals experiencing this euphoric mood may be untroubled by minor reverses that would once have upset them: by a parking ticket, for example, or a missed appointment. They may become more active and outgoing than they had been previously.

It seemed unusual, at least among participants in Seminars for the Separated, for euphoria to be reported as a dominant mood throughout the period following separation. Much more often it alternated with separation distress or only briefly interrupted separation distress, a circumstance which suggests that it may be another approach to managing a loss of an attachment figure. The following excerpt from one man's diary suggests what may be the process involved:

I woke about four, thinking about [a further rejection by his wife]. I wondered what I might have done to provoke it. I couldn't get back to sleep. I got out of bed and made myself follow my morning routine . . . [Later] I got dressed and went out. It was still early so I started to walk, instead of taking the bus. It was a brisk, snowy morning, just after dawn. I suddenly felt happy. I had got myself through the night. I was going to see people during the day. I was all right. It was a fine world.

What we see in this quotation is a shift from the insecurity of separation distress to the self-confidence of euphoria. The early waking and the agitation indicated by "I couldn't get back to sleep" suggest tension stemming from rejection by the figure whose accessibility had been security-providing. But then the individual's recognition that he had been able to manage alone seems to have convinced him that he would be able to care for himself in the future. When he says "I had got myself through the night," he seems to be saying that he had provided himself with reassurance, just as, if things had been different, another person might have provided such reassurance. He felt that he could serve as the guarantor of his own security and in consequence needed no one else. My surmise is that the mechanism responsible for euphoria is the establishment of just such a narcissistic attachment.

Corroboration for this surmise is furnished by the observation that euphoria can be ended by a demonstration that the self is in some significant respect inadequate. Euphoria is likely to disappear suddenly should the individual suffer rejection or serious failure—should he or she, for example, be rejected by a potential date. The individual thereupon is likely not to feel only a bit sadder or to sustain only slightly reduced self-esteem, but rather to experience the full impact of unmitigated separation distress.

Separation distress, as a syndrome of symptoms one of which is continued pining for the spouse, seems to fade as time passes without contact with the spouse. However, those who do not form a new attachment-providing relationship are likely to discover, when separation distress fades, that its place is taken by loneliness. Loneliness too produces feelings of restlessness, vigilance, anxiety, even panic. But there is in loneliness no image of a particular figure whose accessibility would return the individual to security. Instead there is only a vaguely developed image of a satisfying relationship that would allay the loneliness—often together with the conviction that the world is barren of anyone with whom such a relationship could be established. Lonely individuals sometimes also feel a barrenness of internal community which they may describe by saying that they feel "hollow" or "empty" (Weiss, 1973). Loneliness of this sort can be characterized as "separation distress without an object."

Anger as a Response to Loss of Attachment

Since loss of attachment produces the intense discomfort of separation distress, it might be expected to give rise to anger. In bereavement there is ordinarily no clear object for anger, although anger is sometimes expressed toward medical personnel and more rarely toward the spouse or the self (Glick, Weiss, and Parkes, 1974). In marital separation, in contrast, the spouse is ordinarily seen as bearing responsibility for the separation. This attribution is particularly likely if the spouse has initiated the separation and refused pleas for reconciliation. But anger with the spouse may also be felt by individuals who themselves initiated the separation, since they may feel that they were forced to do so by the spouse's faults.

Separating spouses may be angry with each other not only because they blame each other for their distress but also because of genuine conflicts of interest. Such conflicts are most likely to occur in relation to property division, support payments, custody of the children, and visitation. Except in relation to visitation, resolutions of all these issues are zero-sum: What one spouse gets, the other loses. As a result, each spouse may be led to view the other as an antagonist in relation to issues of vital importance.

Anger toward the spouse can become intense. In some individuals the feeling is one they had never before experienced. One young woman said:

In separating from someone you discover in yourself things that you had never felt before in your life. That's one of the things that really freaks you out. I've always used my mind to keep down anything I didn't like. And now I discover, wow, I can hate!

Occasional individuals have murderous fantasies about their spouses. One man said that after reading a newspaper story about an estranged husband who had shot his wife with a rifle, he decided that he could do that too. Some feel their anger to be entirely justified and may be willing to act to hurt the spouse. But others feel their anger as alien from their genuine selves and wish to disown it. The latter development was illustrated by a young woman who said:

In many respects I really do hate my husband. But I don't want to think nothing but hate. You know, when I see him walking down the street, I don't want to think, "I hope when you step off the corner you get run over."

Yet even when an individual seems most enraged with his or her spouse, the suppression of positive feelings rarely seems complete. Often it is possible to discern within the expression of hostility an attempt to maintain proximity. One man telephoned his wife at two in the morning to tell her that he would kill her if she did not permit him to see his children. To be sure, he was terrorizing her; but he was also keeping in touch. Quarrels over property, money, and custody sometimes appear to have as one aim keeping the relationship alive through transfusions of hostility. An older woman said:

I call him up about everything—if the child is sick and I want him to pay for a doctor, or I need money for a baseball glove. I haven't money for taxes, for anything. He is purposely torturing me and making me do this. He wants me to call up. So he can hang up the receiver. Because that's what he does. He curses at me, he hangs up on me.

The Management of Ambivalence

Continued attachment produces both desire to rejoin the spouse and, because of the spouse's role in the production of separation distress, intense anger with the spouse. There are also likely to be additional motives for rejoining the spouse, such as shared responsibility for children, and, as has been noted, additional motives for anger.

Because they remain attached to each other and are simultaneously angry with each other, the relationship of separated spouses is intensely ambivalent. One of the problems the separated must deal with is the management of this ambivalence. Some suppress their positive feelings, some suppress their negative feelings, some manage by alternating the feelings they express or by compartmentalizing their discrepant feelings.

The suppression of either positive or negative feelings rarely seems complete. Desires for rejoining, as has been noted, often are discernible in the most hostile of actions. By the same token, rejoinings frequently are marred by the sudden eruption of anger. One young man reported:

There are some times when I sleep with her or I'm at her apartment and she does something that bothers me like it did when we were married, and I feel like yelling and doing a whole big thing again.

Some among the separated express positive feelings in one setting and negative feelings in another. It is not unusual for a couple to battle with one another through their lawyers, even to testify against one another in court, yet to see one another in the evening as friends or lovers (see Baguedor, 1972).

Couples who establish postmarital relationships in which their discrepant feelings are allocated to separate settings sometimes try to keep the positive aspects of their relationship secret from all but their most intimate friends. Having told their family and their lawyers how much they have suffered at each other's hands, a husband and wife can hardly admit that they now look forward to evenings together. As a result, some couples may temporarily adopt a bizarre variation of the marital practice of hiding fights from public view; now they may be estranged in public but affectionate in private.

Some couples find that a period apart permits them to be loving to one another, but after an interval of good feeling they again become hostile. In this way their positive and negative feelings seem to alternate. A man reported:

I was gone for a week and I came back. . . . And we had the most fantastic weekend, really. It was great, it was fantastic. And then things started up again. The bickering, the whole thing, started up Sunday.

Ambivalence makes separated individuals uncomfortable with any resolution of their separated state. Reconciliation may result not only in relief at the ending of separation distress, but also in dismay at the return to an unsatisfactory relationship. The decision to divorce may also have mixed implications: not only gratification that freedom appears within grasp but also sorrow that the spouse will be irretrievably lost. Lawyers who specialize in divorce work sometimes express their frustration with clients who do not seem to know their own minds (O'Gorman, 1963).

Maybe it is first love or whatever, but I'm still attracted to him. There is a basic something, and I can't seem to get rid of that. I do want a divorce and I don't want a divorce.

Conclusions

Emotional responses to marital separation frequently appear paradoxical, even to those experiencing them. Individuals who feel themselves to have been left may be desolate at the absence of a spouse they can no longer respect or trust. Individuals who have shared in the decision to separate may alternate between deep depression accompanied by lessened self-esteem and euphoria accompanied by heightened self-confidence, and in each state feel that the other state was a temporary mood. Individuals who urgently sought the separation may, after having obtained it, report as did one woman: "I wouldn't want to go back, but I hadn't expected to feel as bad as I do." No matter how decided the individual appears on a particular course of action, there is apt to be intense ambivalence regarding the spouse.

On the basis of these observations we might offer as counsel to the recently separated and to those who may interact with them that they attempt to tolerate the emotional upset that appears to be a nearly inevitable accompaniment to marital separation. And we might warn the separated that at least in the short run they may not be able to resolve their ambivalent feelings about their spouse. Whatever they decide—whether it is to reconcile or to continue their separation and, perhaps, move on to divorce—they will leave one set of feelings unsatisfied.

Adjustment to Separation and Divorce: A Qualitative Analysis

Separation and divorce are disruptive and traumatic for the adults involved. However, there have been relatively few systematic attempts to find out precisely what factors affect adjustment and what problems are most often encountered. With few exceptions (e.g., Goode, 1956), the data dealing with the problems spouses have in adjusting to separation and divorce are drawn from clinical case studies and research on persons who attend discussion or counseling programs (e.g., Weiss, 1975).

This chapter reports on the first phase of a study which was designed to test some of the hypotheses suggested by earlier studies, and to provide an analysis of adjustment during the post-separation period. Possible sources of adjustment problems that were examined include the legal system, lawyers, property settlements, children, economics, the respondent's social network, heterosexual relationships, and emotional adjustment. Four hypotheses were examined pertaining to the effects of lingering attachment to the former spouse, the degree of social interaction outside the home, the role of dating relationships, and the relative effects of sudden and unexpected separations.

This research was funded by grants from the National Institute of Mental Health (RO3 MH27706), the Institute for Life Insurance, and the College of Human Development of the Pennsylvania State University.

Method of the Study

The research was conducted during the fall of 1976. It consisted of 50 lengthy, unstructured interviews with individuals who had filed for divorce within the preceding two-year period. The interviews were guided only to the extent that we tried to get a general idea of the couple's premarital and marital history, a detailed picture of the determinants of the separation, and as much information as possible about its process and problems. We therefore tried to focus on the problems that the respondents felt were of primary importance.

SAMPLING

Respondents were recruited through public records available in Centre County, Pennsylvania. Three types of records were used as a basis for sampling: divorce decrees granted, divorce petitions filed, and child and spouse support agreements filed in conjunction with separation. In Pennsylvania, such records reveal all separated and divorced respondents except those who have separated informally, but have neither filed for divorce nor requested support. Potential respondents were individuals who had either filed for divorce or were divorced within the previous two years.

We eventually contacted, in person or by phone, 37 percent of the persons whose names we had obtained from the county records. The remainder were primarily people who were no longer residents of the county. Of the 37 percent we personally contacted, 61 percent agreed to be interviewed. The other 39 percent refused to participate in the study.

DATA COLLECTION

Interviews ranged from 1½ to 3½ hours, with a mean length of 2½ hours. The interviews were conducted by four graduate students trained in open-ended, unstructured interviewing techniques. Following each interview, the interviewers prepared field notes, as nearly verbatim as possible. The project director and the interviewers read each others' notes and met weekly to share ideas and to suggest topics or questions to be included in future interviews. Approximately 1000 pages of field notes provided the basis for the findings presented here.

CHARACTERISTICS OF THE RESPONDENTS

The respondents in this study were 28 females and 22 males, all Caucasian. They ranged in age from 21 to 65 years old, with a mean age of 36. The mean length of marriage was 12 years, with a range of one to 38 years. Thirty-two of the respondents were divorced at the time they were interviewed, while the remaining 18 were separated but not yet divorced.

The time since the couple last separated ranged from less than one month to 12 years, with a mean of 21 months and a median of 12 months. Only six respondents had been separated for more than three years.

Twenty-nine of the respondents were the plaintiffs in their divorce actions, while 21 were the defendants. Sixteen of the respondents were childless, while 34 cases involved a total of 82 children, including the adult children of older respondents. The respondents were fairly evenly distributed across the working, middle, and upper-middle classes.

Overview of Findings

In analyzing our field notes we concluded that people who separate and divorce have to make two distinct but overlapping adjustments. First is the adjustment to the dissolution of the marriage. This includes dealing with the legal process, working out a property settlement, and working out custody arrangements if children are involved. It also includes informing and otherwise dealing with persons in one's social network, such as family, friends, and business acquaintances. It involves coping with the emotional effects of the dissolution, including feelings about the (former) spouse, such as love, hate, bitterness, guilt, anger, envy, concern, and attachment; feelings about the marriage, such as regret, disappointment, bitterness, sadness, and failure; and more general feelings, such as failure, depression, euphoria, relief, guilt, lowered self-esteem, and lowered self-confidence.

The second adjustment is to the process of setting up a new life style, such as finding a new residence, living on less (or occasionally more) money, getting a job, or applying for welfare. If children are involved, it includes adjusting to single parenthood if one has custody, or adjusting to limited visits with the children if one does not. It also usually includes finding new friends and establishing new heterosexual relationships. Finally, the separated and divorced must adjust to feelings such as fear, frustration, loneliness, or inadequacy, as well as possible feelings of freedom, happiness, and heightened self-esteem if their adjustment is to be successful.

Adjustment to Dissolution of Marriage

LEGAL SYSTEM

Pennsylvania is one of only three states presently without any no-fault divorce provisions. Sixty-eight percent of those interviewed expressed strong dislike of the legal system. Most of these individuals expressed resentment at what they were forced to say about the partner under an adversary arrangement. Typical comments were: "It was just terrible, all the listings of indignities, and placing blame and fault," or "You have to make him look rotten. I didn't like making him look worse than he really was." For 20 percent of the respondents, the system presented additional major problems. Usually this occurred when there were property or child custody disagreements. Of the 16 respondents who did not specifically complain about the system, 12 had only minimal contact with it, being either the defendant in an uncontested divorce or someone who had barely begun the divorce process. Three of the remaining four cases were handled by Legal Aid.

Adversary divorce laws. There are two key questions about an adversary divorce procedure: (1) Do such procedures help to keep marriages intact? (2) What are the effects of the laws on the people who are going through the divorce process? Our study provides no insight as to whether the Pennsylvania adversary system initially discourages people from separation or divorce. We did, however, find evidence that once in the process, the system makes it very difficult for spouses to reconcile (see also Kressel et al., chapter 15). In response to a follow-up question about how the system was "forcing us further apart," one woman replied:

I think it could work out. Ours could. But to help myself, I have to go there and tell things that are husband and wife business, and he has to do the same. I don't want to hurt him. I want to be fair.

The legal system appears to encourage couples to become adversaries to a greater degree than they already are. It encourages them to lie about each other and to use "dirty tricks" to get the best of the other. Sixteen percent of those interviewed admitted lying to get their divorce. One woman said:

. . . we had to decide who would divorce who. I just couldn't do the lying, so he did. It really got to me—all the dirty little games you have to play. Having to tell all those twisted half-truths.

A few of the respondents stated that their lawyers "beefed up" the charges without consulting them until after the charges had been filed. Some expressed fears of being charged with perjury:

I really resented saying all those mean things. . . . I had to swear I was telling the truth and I had visions of being convicted of perjury.

Regarding the effects of the system on individuals who do get a divorce, we found that not only does it often aggravate relations with the spouse, but that it also upsets and humiliates people who must openly discuss their intimate marital problems. We found that the legal system offers little support for people going through a separation or divorce.

Attorneys. About a third of the respondents who dealt with attorneys found them understanding and helpful, while another third had negative feelings toward their lawyers. Many felt that they received no real support, and reported that the lawyers seemed in it only for the money.

One woman who had been involved in a long fight over both child custody and the property settlement, and who had consulted a total of four lawyers, stated:

I was beginning to feel bitter about the legal process. Most lawyers are just making money. They really take advantage of people when they are vulnerable.

A younger woman, who was pregnant and in need of welfare when she separated, presented the opposite viewpoint:

My lawyer is a doll. Really helped me out. Got me a doctor and mothers' assistance right away . . . he only charged me $90 for all the work that he did. He helped me get my name changed for free.

Several respondents felt their lawyers or their spouses' lawyers used delaying tactics and other "dirty tricks" to prolong the process and increase the fees. One man said that he thought it was all "a game to the lawyers" and gave a variety of anecdotes to illustrate his opinion. He claimed that, after months of costly fighting, the final settlement was essentially the same as he had first proposed and blamed his wife's attorney for having given her very unrealistic expectations in order to prolong the proceedings.

A number of women reported that they had suffered humiliation and emotional distress in the hands of their lawyers. One woman involved in a lengthy property dispute described the following tactics which were almost identical to those described by several other female respondents:

His lawyer tried to make me crack. I don't know how they live with their conscience. . . . [He] broke me down in stages. I just gave up for peace and serenity. After we started the court case he [husband] wouldn't let me charge anything and would let checks bounce that I wrote. We never finished the case. He told lies. I felt deflated. It was all part of his lawyer's tactics. They work. . . . He [attorney] knew it was tearing me up. I know [it was the lawyer] because other people who have used him told me.

In this case the interviewer knew from previous interviews who the lawyer was and could name him before the respondent did.

Property settlements. Two-thirds of those interviewed with property settlements, legally arranged or informally agreed upon, had few difficulties in this area and reported working out fair and equitable settlements. However, where there were problems, they usually became major points of contention. All of the cases where there were complaints about the attorney's tactics pertained to property settlements.

CHILDREN

In every marriage with dependent children, the children were the catalysts for some of the major adjustment problems. These problems included worrying about the effects of the separation on the children, deciding who should have custody, and, for those without custody, feelings of loneliness and/or guilt. Most of the parents interviewed seemed to be trying to work together to minimize the effects of the separation and to settle custody in the best interests of the children. One father's words seemed to represent the attitude of many of these parents:

We wanted there to be as little disruption as possible for the kids. Because both of the kids were loved very much by both of us and because of our agreement to share custody, I feel they suffered only minimally . . . now they don't have to compete with the other parent for attention and they don't have to live with constant quarreling.

In general the respondents said they were making an effort not to let their marital difficulties affect their child's relationship with the other parent. However, this is not always easy. As one mother put it after describing her anger against her husband,

It was so hard to tell them [the children] your daddy loves you when you want to say something so different.

Another mother said her daughter had told her she was "always accusing daddy with your tone of voice."

We did find three notable cases, however, where it seemed that children were used either to punish the other spouse or to get a better settlement. When we were told about the children being thus used, these tactics were attributed to the spouse not being interviewed. For example, a mother of three—with two girls from a previous marriage and a boy from the marriage in question—stated that the hardest part of the divorce is:

. . . the way he treats the boy. I have to really avoid him. [If I meet him around town] he's so bad he just ignores the boy and [son] will get so upset and cry for his daddy. . . . He [husband] takes it out on the little boy. He whips him for no reason when he has him . . . he comes and gets him once a week. That's what hurts. He'll tell [son] he doesn't love him, that he never did. And the poor boy gets so upset. . . . He told the girls he doesn't want them calling him daddy anymore and things like that. He's really turned them against him.

Two respondents, one male and one female, stated that their spouses continually threatened to cut them off from the children if they should contest either the divorce or any part of the settlement. Both respondents yielded because they said they could not take the chance of losing their children.

One mother later regretted trying to turn her children against their father:

The pain of the children being torn is the hardest. . . . I worry about my kids being alienated and about what I've said to them about their father. I stopped that. It was only when I was so angry. But I wonder what damage this has done.

SOCIAL NETWORK

Eighty-four percent of the interviewees stated that their friends, relatives, and other acquaintances were generally supportive during the separation process. In the few instances where friends or family were not supportive, however, this lack of support seemed to increase the overall difficulties in adjusting to the separation, especially the emotional adjustments.

In most of the cases where there was little or no support from family members, the families had strong feelings against divorce in general. Several respondents said that it was difficult for their parents to understand or accept the fact that they were divorcing. One woman had not told her mother she was getting a divorce even though she saw her several times a week, because "it would hurt her too much," and she couldn't help anyway because "she wouldn't understand how I could do it." The most severe case of parental conflict came, surprisingly, from a mother who was in favor of the divorce. However, she was pessimistic about her daughter surviving it on her own:

She just knows I'm not going to succeed at living alone. I'll show her I have to. . . . She thinks I have very weird ideas. Her idea of weird is anything she doesn't like. . . . When she's here she tries to tell the kids how bad their father was. I've tried to explain to her that that just makes it worse, but she doesn't stop . . . [now] she's telling the kids how bad they are. Finally she told them they were so rotten I should send them to their rotten father. I got really angry and she hasn't written to me since.

Only a few respondents had friends who were actively hostile after the separation, but these respondents felt very hurt:

The community attitude is hard to take. I've been isolated and ostracized by my former friends. Around here if your husband doesn't work at the university you're nowhere—nobody knows you. . . . I don't get invited any-where anymore. It's like I was just cut off. . . . My emotional feeling is like being an Eskimo stranded on an ice floe. I'd always felt like I belonged some-where, but not now. I've got nothing, no place.

Some respondents, on the other hand, who isolated themselves said that they did this because they didn't feel like being social: "Those that are happy, I don't want to go near. They make me feel terrible." Others felt like a third wheel or that their couple friends might consider them a "threat" now that they were single. Whatever the reason for isolation from friends or family, we found that those persons who did not make new friends had a very difficult adjustment.

EMOTIONAL FACTORS

The degree of initial emotional difficulties appeared to be related to how unexpected the separation was for the person interviewed, and whether the respondent was in favor of or opposed to the separation.

Nine of the eleven interviews in which the separation was described as sudden and unexpected were cases of wives leaving husbands. One husband, whose initial response was typical of this group, described it as follows:

I was at first extremely distraught. I think that I was in a suicidal state for a while. I contemplated suicide at one time. After this period I just kind of went into a state of shock that lasted [a couple of months]. After that I just felt hurt that all of it had happened.

A common factor in several of these cases was that the respondent did not know exactly what the situation was that led to the separation until somewhat later. Another man said:

The worst thing was . . . the period when I didn't know what was going on. I was depressed and confused and I just didn't know what I had done or what to do about it. . . . After I learned what the real story was [wife left him for another man], I was actually relieved. I wasn't happy about it or anything, but I was relieved because everything fell into place and started to make sense.

Statements such as the above led us to hypothesize that *the degree to which the separation is sudden and unexpected is positively related to the degree of initial emotional problems*. Respondents' initial emotional reactions to the separation were rated as mild (38 percent), moderate (36 percent), or severe (26 percent). Also, respondents were classified accord-ing to whether (a) they had initiated or expected the separation (78 percent) or (b) they had found it sudden and unexpected (22 percent).

Of those whose initial reaction was rated severe, 62 percent stated that their separation had been sudden and unexpected. Only 17 percent of those whose initial emotional reaction was rated moderate, and none of those with a mild reaction, stated that their separation had been unexpected. Thus, this hypothesis was confirmed ($X^2 = 17.5$, df $= 2$, $p < .001$).

While a sudden and unexpected separation produces strong initial distress (Weiss, 1975), the long-term effects are variable. Some of the respondents with unexpected separations took a long time to recover; for others the recovery was rapid. In the long run, the degree to which problems persist seems to depend on how well the individual makes an adjustment to a new life style.

Attachment. An important area of concern is the individual's feeling toward the (former) spouse. Weiss (chapter 12) suggests that continued feelings of attachment for the (former) spouse are nearly universal after marital dissolution and are a major cause of emotional problems that follow separation.

We also found evidence of continuing attachment. One man who had been separated for about a year described his continued attachment in the following way:

I think about her every day of my life. I wonder who she is with, if she's working, how she's treating my daughter, and lots of other things. I still love her quite a lot.

A young woman put it this way:

I still think about him. Knowing that he won't come home for dinner is sad. Dinner is the hardest time. We still talk and I wonder how he's doing . . . [there are other] memories, like him cooking breakfast on Sunday mornings. And the family at home at Christmas. It's hard seeing his car downtown and thinking about he and I apart.

In contrast to such statements, many respondents showed little or no evidence of attachment. When asked if he thought about his ex-wife or tried to find out about her life, one respondent replied:

No, I don't really care what she's doing. I don't think about her at all except in terms of the settlement.

Others stated that although they did not miss their spouses, they did miss some things about being married. One woman, asked if she missed her ex-husband, replied:

No. I miss having a primary relationship, I miss affection. I don't think I ever missed [husband]. But it was funny—I was surprised it took a long time to get used to sleeping alone.

Because of conflicting statements like those above, we had the impression that while feelings of attachment and difficulties due to the loss of a close relationship were very evident in some cases, there were many others in which these feelings were less evident or important. We therefore examined in more detail whether or not, following the separation, individuals reported continuing attachment, and what effect this had on their new adjustment.

As evidence of continued attachment, we looked for (1) specific expressions of love, affection, or stated attachment for the (former) spouse; (2) continuing thoughts about him or her, including negative ones; (3) efforts or desires to contact the spouse; and (4) efforts to learn about his or her activities. We excluded activities pertaining to the divorce proceedings, children, or support payments. On the basis of these criteria, we divided the respondents into three categories: (1) those with strong attachment (36 percent); (2) those with mild attachment (36 percent); and (3) those who showed no evidence of attachment (28 percent).

Although Weiss (chapter 12) found feelings of attachment and distress to be nearly universal among his respondents, he points out that Goode (1956) found evidence of separation distress in only two-thirds of his cases. Weiss attributes this discrepancy at least partially to the length of time between the separation and Goode's survey interview. Our findings were closer to Goode's (28 percent felt no attachment). Therefore, it is possible that there is a substantial minority of ex-spouses for whom attachment or its loss presents no major problem.

An equally important issue is the effect that feelings of attachment have on the overall adjustment to the separation. We hypothesized that *the greater the attachment to the (former) spouse, the more difficult will be the adjustment to the separation.* To rate the overall adjustment of the respondents in each of these groups, the respondents were divided into two categories: those who were judged by the authors to have serious problems in the majority of the areas we examined—i.e., legal, emotional, social, heterosexual, and economic (22 percent)—and those who were having only mild or no problems in these areas (78 percent).

Twenty-eight percent of those who still felt strong attachment were rated as having serious problems, while 22 percent with mild attachment and 14 percent with no attachment were in this category. The relative magnitudes of these percentages were as hypothesized, but did not differ significantly. Both the extent of reported attachment and its apparent impact on adjustment were considerably less than of the participants in Weiss's study (1975; chapter 12).

There are at least two possible explanations for the discrepancy between Weiss's findings and ours. One possibility is that his respondents all had sought professional help in adjusting to their separation. In contrast, our method of sampling reached respondents who ranged from those with severe adjustment difficulty to those reporting little difficulty; for such a range of persons, the continuing effects of attachment may be less important than suggested by Weiss. A different possibility is that because Weiss's interviews took place over several sessions, he elicited much deeper feelings from his respondents than we were able to elicit in our single interviews.

Adjustment to a New Life Style

ECONOMIC ADJUSTMENTS

Economic adjustment was the only area of adjustment in which we found significant sex differences. Only one of the 22 men reported major economic problems caused by the divorce. Most men held a full-time job before the separation and either continued in that job or obtained another good or better job. Twenty-three percent of the men reported that they were somewhat, but not substantially worse off economically since the separation. However, the large majority reported themselves at least as well off than before.

For women the opposite was true. Thirty-nine percent, primarily younger women and those married for a short period, reported that they were at least as well off economically as before the separation, but most said that they were substantially worse off (see also Bane, chapter 16 and Kohen et al., chapter 14). Many women not working before the separation, or only working part time, were finding it difficult to get a job. For many, economic problems affected their whole adjustment. One woman, who said she was "excited" when she first realized that she was getting a divorce and "viewed it as an adventure I was looking forward to," was very depressed at the time of our interview. She said:

Do you want me to characterize divorce in one sentence? It's hell, sheer hell. . . . The lack of financial stability is the worst part. It creates all sorts of fears and anxiety. The kids don't understand why. I'm still so messed up. . . . If only I could earn some money, maybe I could relax and pull myself together. Somehow I'm supposed to come out of this a whole human being, but I'm not sure how. . . . The worst part of the divorce has been the job problems and the financial insecurity.

Some women had been out of the labor market for a long time or had never been in it; many had few marketable skills. The presence of young children made it particularly hard to find work, and babysitters' wages often cut deeply into earnings.

Discrimination. Several women reported discrimination against separated and divorced women, in addition to discrimination against women in general. Some also reported discrimination in housing and credit because of their separations. Quite a few women, and some men also, objected to being asked to indicate "divorced" or "separated" on job applications. One young woman currently looking for a job said:

I was thinking about the social stigma. My friends and I were talking about filling out job applications, and about how I should fill out marital status. They were making me uneasy about it. I wish you didn't have to answer that on applications. I'm afraid it might hurt my chances.

A common area of concern reported by older women married for many years was being cut out of their husband's social security and insurance programs, even though most of his benefits had accumulated during their marriage. Even among older women with good jobs, there was much concern about what they would do after retirement.

CHILDREN

Whether or not they received child custody, all parents reported the necessity of major adjustments. Parents with principal custody as well as those without custody experienced adjustment problems related to their children. Fathers with custody reported the same problems as mothers with custody, and mothers without custody similar problems to fathers without custody (see also Gersick, chapter 18). The only sex difference we found was that mothers who did not get custody reported more public censure than did fathers without custody. One mother who had split the custody of their four children with the father reported:

Everybody seems horrified that we had split the children—like "How could you do such a thing?". . . . [my attorney] laid a real guilt trip on me about giving up the two children. He was always asking me, "Are you *sure* you want it this way? How could you?"

Parents with custody. The parent who receives principal custody now must fulfill alone roles previously performed jointly by two parents. It is hard to get time away from the children and this creates problems with work, dating, and social life in general. Parents with custody report feeling much more responsibility and a greater sense of being trapped by the children. One mother, thinking back about her major problem after an earlier divorce, stated:

[My major problem was] knowing I had four children on my *own* to be responsible for—trying to keep us together, raising two boys to be boys. That was hard.

Another mother described her current situation:

I hate feeling totally responsible for the kids. They're mine completely. At least when I was married, I could mentally not feel responsible at times. . . . It gets lonely with the kids in bed by 8:00. It's an ambiguous role. [I want to go out but] I don't want the kids to be stuck with a babysitter three or four nights a week.

One complaint many custodial parents have is that the other parent, who only sees the children occasionally, does not have to deal with discipline and, therefore, may be more attractive to the child. A father with principal custody put it this way:

One big problem that aggravates me a lot is that now my wife sees the kids during all the nice and fun times and I have to be the one who makes them clean their rooms and do their homework, etc. I have to be the disciplinarian. I know I can't let that alter the way I treat them because they do need discipline, but sometimes I don't think it's fair. . . . Too often when I say something they'll say, "but mother said the opposite."

While there are hardships in having principal custody, most who have custody are glad that they do. Many of them cited their children as a major source of support during their separation or divorce.

Parents without custody. Parents without custody must adjust to being with their children less often, which most see as a serious deprivation. They miss their children greatly and regret this lack. Several parents stated that the main thing, or in some cases the only thing, they regretted was losing the children.

Many parents report feeling guilty about "deserting" their children, and they are dissatisfied with the limitations of their relationship. The mother who had split the custody of her four children with her husband said:

I was feeling really sad about the two children who weren't with me. I felt I had nothing to give. The most I could do was be their friend, so I worked really hard at that. And I saved for Christmas because that has always been very important to me.

Another woman with a split custody arrangement worried about her son's care:

I worry he's not getting the attention he needs. They go out a lot and I think the children are neglected. But I don't know what to do about it. I feel so powerless. . . . My heart aches for them more than myself.

Parents without custody also tended to find their children to be sources of support through the divorce process. One father of three older children [one married, two living with mother] said:

One of the pluses of this experience has been my relationship with my children. Their behavior has been admirable. They have been available, supportive and caring towards both their mother and me without intruding in our marital problems and without being judgmental. Their adjustment and maturity in handling their own lives during this time have been very freeing for both of us.

SOCIAL ADJUSTMENTS

Although most respondents reported that their friends were supportive, about half also reported growing away from many of their close friends after the separation. This was especially true if the friends had been shared with their spouses and, particularly, if the friends were also couples. One man we interviewed said:

Mostly we had a group of friends in common. We ran around with a group of other married couples. . . . I think most of them knew it was coming. I still see some of them occasionally and we're friendly, but my main social group now is very different. I think it was mostly my idea and my doing to break up with the group. I used to get invitations and such from them but I wanted to end it. I was single and they were all married and I was sort of out of place. I didn't want to rock the boat by hanging around so I just stopped seeing them and built up another group of single friends.

His case was typical of people we interviewed. For the most part, when there was a growing apart from old friends, the separated individual was just as responsible, perhaps even more so, as the friends. Typically, the individuals felt that they were no longer part of the group. Occasionally they also reported feeling that they were a threat to married couples, either because they represented the possibility of marital failure or, more directly, because they might be considered a sexual threat.

Many of the interviewees had been quite successful at finding new friends, or had already developed their own circle even before the separation. When they did have an intact network of friends, their adjustment was much easier. For those who were losing old friends but were unable to find new ones (8 percent), and those with no real friends during or after the marriage (34 percent), the process of adjusting to separation was much more difficult.

Because social support and activity seem to be important factors in helping a person manage a separation, we examined more closely a hypothesis similar to one tested by Raschke (1974): *The more social interaction the separated individual has (with relatives, friends, and the community), the fewer will be the adjustment problems.* To test this hypothesis we related overall adjustment (using the same two categories as before) to level of social interaction. Respondents were classified as having either moderate to high social activity (52 percent) or low social activity (46 percent). Only eight percent of those with moderate to high social activity reported serious adjustment problems, while 39 percent of those with low social activity reported serious problems ($X^2 = 6.93$, $df = 1$, $p < .01$). Thus, this hypothesis was supported. It is reasonable to assume that social interaction may contribute positively to adjustment while reasonably successful adjustment will likewise be conducive to social interaction. Bi-directional influences undoubtedly exist in most heterosexual relationships.

HETEROSEXUAL RELATIONSHIPS

A related hypothesis was: *Separated individuals who participate in heterosexual dating or cohabitation relationships will have fewer adjustment problems than those who do not.* We found that of the 60 percent of the respondents who either were dating regularly, living with someone of the opposite sex, or were remarried, only 7 percent were having serious problems. In contrast, 45 percent of those with few or no heterosexual relationships (40 percent of the whole sample) were having major adjustment difficulties. Thus, the hypothesis was confirmed ($X^2 = 10.28$, $df = 1$, $p < .01$). Dating a variety of people even without close or steady relationships seemed to be about as helpful as having one very close relationship.

A number of respondents discussed how important heterosexual relationships were for their adjustment. A statement by a recently divorced male was typical:

Getting involved with a woman has helped me to realize I can now communicate intimately and establish a relationship with someone. This has been very helpful. It's made the adjustment much easier.

Another male talked about the effects of his ex-wife's new relationship:

I also think that forming another relationship helped my ex-wife. Shortly after the separation she got involved in another relationship and I noticed a real change after that. . . . The separation bothered her at first because of her insecurities, but after she formed a new relationship, then she adjusted rapidly and we became friends again. I think more than anything, that helped to ease things between us, so we stopped fighting.

Many of those not dating also corroborated our hypothesis by discussing how much they wanted to form new relationships. A common set of problems was where to meet others and how to start dating again after not dating for so long. Several women also said it was difficult to establish new relationships because "the only thing men want from a divorcée is sex."

Many ex-spouses who are now dating regularly are still fearful of being hurt again. As one woman explained:

I'm dating a man now who has a gentleness I never knew. He's older too. In the past couple of weeks I've had to cool it. I'm very much afraid to get too involved. I want a relationship, but I fear too much intimacy. I don't want to hurt him either. . . . I have sexual desires, but I have to have some feeling for someone before going to bed with them. . . . I want opportunities to meet the opposite sex without pressures for sex. But where and how? I have a great fear of loneliness. . . . I would like to remarry someday, but it scares me.

EMOTIONAL FACTORS

Individuals who have difficulties adjusting to a new life style report depression, loneliness, frustration, low self-esteem and self-confidence, as well as heightened negative feelings toward and regrets about their (former) spouse, marriage, and the separation. In contrast, those individuals who are successful in establishing a new life style are likely to feel that divorce is the right thing, to feel tolerant of their (former) spouse, and to report positive feelings such as freedom, relief, happiness, heightened self-esteem and self-confidence.

Discussion

Our findings suggest that, in the transition to separation, establishing a new life style is more problematic than adjusting to the dissolution of the marriage. Raschke (1974) also found that variables we have described as part of the adjustment to a new life style—high social interaction, economic success, and sexual involvement—are important to post-separation adjustment.

Creating a new life style appears to be more crucial to overall adjustment than successfully coping with the dissolution of the marriage. But more research is needed to understand fully the interconnection between these two processes. Our preliminary findings indicate that individuals who successfully launch a new life style have less difficulty dealing with problems related to dissolution of the marriage than do those who cannot or will not adopt new life styles. Other painful reactions to marital dissolution, such as feelings of regret, attachment, and bitterness towards the spouse actually may increase over time through failure to create new relationships. Some respondents who reported few problems immediately after separation and who, in some cases, reported that separation had made them feel free, excited, or eager about life for the first time in years, were at the time of the interview very despondent and showing signs of separation anxiety. In every instance, these respondents were having major economic or social difficulties.

While successful establishment of a new life style seems to aid in the adjustment to the breakup, it should not be assumed that the association between these two variables goes in only one direction. Adjustment to the separation tended to affect the establishment of the new life styles. For example, some respondents who were having legal difficulties had little energy left to deal with the demands of new relationships. Others stated they would not feel right dating until the divorce was final. Also, where the dissolution was particularly sudden, some respondents needed a recovery period before they desired social interaction; for others, a severe initial shock seemed to be an impetus for establishing new relationships.

Our qualitative analysis has suggested that adjustment to separation and divorce is a challenging task. The difficulties that individuals encounter vary greatly, depending on the circumstances surrounding the dissolution of their marriage, the support they receive as they make the transition, and the nature of the post-marriage life style. Children, parents, friends, the former spouse, representatives of the legal system, and dating partners all play important roles in the lives of the recently separated.

While one's ability to negotiate the transition depends on economic stability, custody arrangements, and social and sexual involvements, it remains hard to predict the exact nature of post-separation adjustment. However, we believe such prediction is a worthwhile goal. Knowledge about adjustment to marital separation will be useful not only for those who experience it, but also for the scientific understanding of interpersonal and family conflict and their aftermath.

Divorced Mothers:
The Costs and Benefits of
Female Family Control

Rarely is the concept put forward that the female-headed family is an acceptable family form or that, once divorced, it is all right for a mother to stay divorced. As the position of women relative to men has come under scrutiny, such presumptions in favor of the male-headed family have begun to be questioned (Gillespie, 1971; Bernard, 1972). The myth of the "happy homemaker" has been criticized as analysts have become more aware of both the disadvantages of marriage and the advantages of singlehood (Gove and Tudor, 1973; Rollins and Feldman, 1970). Yet, attitudes for or against a woman heading her family tend to be based on opinion rather than on examination of the lives of divorced mothers. Our study provides such an examination by investigating the lives of thirty divorced mothers as they were organized following the first year after divorce. We focus on the issues they must deal with and the costs and benefits that they experience in day-to-day life as family heads.

We expected to find both costs and benefits in being a divorced mother. Motherhood in most Western societies is normatively structured so as to be dependent on wifehood. The social resources made available to men—money, recognition, interpersonal power, social rights—enable them to head families. While lower-class men have fewer resources than upper-class women, each man gets some resources denied to women of his class. Since such resources are not equally and directly available to

This research was partially supported by the Russell Sage Foundation. We would like to thank George Levinger, Marylyn Rands, and Pat Thompson for reading and commenting on an earlier draft of this chapter.

A previous version of this chapter appeared under a different title in *Journal of Social Issues*, 1976, 32 (1).

women, most women must become dependent on husbands for the resources needed to be mothers. In return for a share of these resources, women must provide men with services and satisfactions.

If a couple divorces, the woman loses most of her right to the man's resources, but she also loses her personal dependence and obligations of service. She now stands in direct relationship to society as the head of her family. But male-dominated society neither recognizes a divorced woman's right to head a family nor makes available to her, as a woman, the necessary resources. The divorced mother has exchanged direct dependence on one man for general dependence on a male-dominated society. Employers, welfare officials, lawyers, judges, politicians, school authorities, doctors, even male relatives and neighbors, set the parameters of her ability to take on successfully the role of family head.

Nevertheless, being divorced does make a positive difference. Patriarchal authority is now outside the family, not inside, and the woman can choose to some extent the way in which she will relate to those authorities and the use she will make of whatever formal and informal resources are available.

What has she gained? What are the trade-offs? Are there advantages to divorced motherhood that compensate for the problems? Indeed, does anything change at all?

Method of the Study

From the above perspective and our earlier review of the literature (Brandwein, Brown, and Fox, 1974) we identified a number of dimensions of family life for our research such as economic factors, authority allocation, child care, household management, and social and psychological supports. Since earlier studies were not similarly oriented, we adopted the procedure of interviewing divorced mothers in depth, using general questions that permitted the women to discuss their situation with the broadest possible latitude. In each area of questions we probed for advantages as well as disadvantages of being divorced. For example, we asked, "What are some of the easy things in raising children alone?" "What are some of the problems?" When applicable, we asked interviewees to compare their current situation to their situation when married. We found that the women not only expressed problems we had anticipated, but they also articulated problems and benefits we had not expected.

THE SAMPLE

We interviewed 30 Boston-area mothers who had at least one child under 16 living with them and who had been divorced or separated from one to five years. This time span eliminated the crisis immediately following separation (e.g., Weiss, 1975) and restricted our sample to women for whom single parenthood had become a stable, but not necessarily permanent, situation. The interviews were conducted in the latter part of 1974.

Potential respondents were located through institutional sources such as youth agencies, health clinics, daycare centers, and organizations of single parents. Several respondents were students at a local college who were contacted through an author or colleague; a few were friends of friends of friends; others were friends of previous respondents. To assure their anonymity, no one with whom an author was well acquainted or who was known to more than one of the authors was interviewed. Quotas were imposed to assure that no group was overrepresented in relation to the Boston-area population. Selected background characteristics presented in Table 14-1 reveal the group's diversity and range.

In each case an institutional representative or individual who knew the woman contacted her to explain the study and ask if she would agree to be interviewed. If she agreed, her name was then given to us for formal contact. Interviews averaged 3½ hours and were conducted in the

TABLE 14-1

Background Characteristics of the Respondents

Religion		Race/Ethnicity	
Catholic	14	English, Dutch, Swedish	8
Protestant	11	Irish (all or part)	7
Jewish	5	Jewish	5
		Italian (all or part)	4
Age		Black	2
Under 25	2	Foreign-born (Scotch,	
25-29	9	Irish)	2
30-34	7	Greek	1
35-39	6	French-Canadian	1
40-44	4		
45 or over	2	Education	
		Less than H.S.	4
Monthly Cash Income		H.S. diploma	7
$ 0- 499	14	Some college	8
500- 899	8	Nurses' training	3
900-1199	6	College graduate	4
1200 and over	2	Graduate training	4

respondent's home with no other person present. (Babysitting money was provided to assure privacy and lack of interruption.)

The rapport was excellent, in part because all five interviewers were women in their late 20s and 30s who were familiar with problems of family life, and in part because the respondents had thought a lot about their situations and appreciated an opportunity to discuss them.

Our findings do not always agree with those of other researchers because we confined our research to the women's lives, and because we used open-ended interviews always probing for advantages as well as disadvantages of single parenthood as these mothers experienced it. In addition, we eliminated respondents who were still adjusting to the first year of single parenthood. However, in several major areas, such as changes in income, proportion wishing to remarry, and types of problems encountered, our findings are consistent with the patterns reported in earlier studies (Goode, 1956; Kreisberg, 1970; Marsden, 1969).

Marriage: the Wife-Mother Package

Most mothers are wife-mothers. Economic and social dependence on a husband is the normal condition of adult womanhood in our society. Most American women marry and 88 percent of married women are dependent on their husbands for at least half of the family's income (U.S. Department of Labor, 1976). All but seven of the mothers in our sample had been similarly economically dependent on their husbands during their motherhood. The exceptions were primarily among women married to low-earning husbands.

Such dependence is not necessarily anticipated by women. Only nine had expected, when they were teenagers, that they would become dependent wife-mothers as adults. Nine others had thought solely of work careers, and eight had expected to combine work and family. Four did not recall specific teenage plans for adulthood.

Whatever the reasons for marriage, husband and children became the package around which the wife/mother makes her life. This combination is seen not simply as a job, but as a way of life. As one mother said,

Based on *Ladies' Home Journal* and *Seventeen*, I was going to finish nursing school, marry, have kids, a white picket fence, and live in an upper middle-class neighborhood like the one I grew up in. I was certainly not going to be living in a city and *not* be divorced.

The distinct activities of the wife/mother (caring for husband and children, washing, cooking, maintaining a household) are transformed from a series of tasks into a personal commitment to her children and husband. No hours mark the boundaries of her involvement—at any time, for as many years as her spouse and children need her, she is expected to respond as wife and mother. Economic and social dependence make it possible for her to fulfill this commitment, but they also are the conditions which enable her husband to exercise the traditional power in the family. As a result, she often chafes at her subordination. One woman now living on child support payments and earnings from part-time domestic service said,

I think it's strange that men take so much for granted. I don't resent getting meals for kids, but I often resented getting meals for my husband—I couldn't just have a hodge-podge of a meal. My friends did all these things and were happy, but I was going stark raving mad.

Another mother, in a semiprofessional job, said:

I had to put his needs before myself and I felt resentful, overburdened by the responsibility of keeping his life stable and positive when my own seemed negative and unstable. I resented being a mother. Now at last I have the opportunity to develop myself without the hostility of a husband.

The woman's desire for freedom is not necessarily the reason for divorce. As we shall show later, it is often a benefit she realizes only *after* she becomes a single parent. Instead, the precipitating circumstances in 24 of the marital breakups in our survey were traditional—violence, alcoholism, infidelity, and willful non-support; the other 6 were "modern" divorces: the spouses simply felt incompatible. In 8 of the 30 marriages the man had wanted the breakup more than the woman; in 4 the feelings were mutual.

Women may opt out or be pushed out of wifehood, but rarely do they opt out of continuing motherhood. As recently as 1975, in 90 percent of U.S. divorces involving children, the children remain with the mother. Continuing motherhood may be socially prescribed or personally favored. Over 80 percent of the women in our sample said there was "no question" about who would take the children. "It was understood—he got the car, I got the child," said one. For some women, child custody was not voluntary—"I was left with them"—while for others, gaining complete custody of the children was a reason for divorce. Said one mother of five, "I and the kids wanted the breakup—he would have hung right in there. My three teenagers were going to run away—that clinched it. He'll never get the children—I put it in my will."

Transition to Divorced Motherhood

Women are no more prepared for divorced motherhood than they are for married motherhood. Indeed, they are less so. Cultural models for married motherhood are pervasive, but, as Goode analyzed it in 1956, the divorcée exists in a "social limbo," without an established "place" in the social structure. There are no socially recognized models of successful divorced motherhood to help her know what has to be done and how to do it. The popular wisdom tells her it cannot be done. On an issue so basic as money, 15 of our 30 respondents told us that at the time of their divorces they had no concrete plans for how to support themselves. They knew they must have money, but when they thought about it there were no ready-made answers.

Despite their lack of preparation, the women often felt relieved, if somewhat worried, to be on their own. Twelve reported their feelings about the marital breakup as happy or relieved, another six felt similarly but had some reservations, and 12 were unhappy. Said a mother with five children, "I don't believe in divorce . . . I only did it because I had to . . . it's peace of mind after seven years of hell."

Whether divorce brings relief or unhappiness, it is only the beginning of a new situation that has both problems and rewards. The problems are immediately obvious, for example, lack of money; the rewards may be noticeable only later. This is tied to the nature of change introduced by divorce. The change is not merely a legal or a personal one. It involves a shift from marriage to divorce, from a culturally supported life arrangement to a resource-deprived limbo.

They are non-wives. The lack of a new model to organize their lives around often creates initial problems of self-identity. Our respondents frequently spoke of the initial period as traumatic, frightening, or depressing. "It was like I was asleep for two years," said one. Said another, "Your whole life drops out." Eighteen respondents described such emotional upset during the initial period. Thus, added to the material crisis of breaking up, there is often a psychological crisis (Brown, 1976; Weiss, 1975).

After a while, however, many ex-wives do get back on their feet and the relative merits of the two ways of living can be evaluated. When we talked with them, at least a year after the breakup, we asked if things were easier now or when they were with their husbands. Seventeen women said "easier now," three said "things are harder," and ten said, "things are different," with both good and bad aspects. The drawbacks were primarily financial problems and a sense of overwhelming responsibility; the good things were control and emotional growth. In the following sections we will argue that, despite the drawbacks, their experiences of heading a family are often better for these women than were their marriages.

Problems of Divorce

FINANCES

The resources men bring to families are for the most part withdrawn following the divorce. The fact that female-headed families do not have access to comparable resources is the source of many of the problems divorced mothers face. Such resources include, but are not limited to, money. Only 16 husbands of our respondents provided any financial support to their ex-families and only 9 provided as much as 50 percent of the family's income at any period after the divorce. The woman's own paid work or welfare[1] had to become immediate substitutes. But wages for women workers (full-time, year round) are low: in 1974 they averaged 57 percent of men's wages, due to a combination of job segregation and sex discrimination (Stevenson, 1973; Sawhill, 1975). Welfare is also a minimal form of support, some argue, because of sex discrimination (Komisar, 1973).

From an average pre-divorce family income of $12,500, the women in our sample fell to a post-divorce average of $6,100, a drop of just over half. This overall average obscures an important class difference— the higher they start, the farther they fall. The 8 highest income families dropped 60 percent, the 8 lowest income families dropped only 19 percent. The less the husband had contributed, the less he could take away.[2]

Sixteen of the 30 women turned to AFDC either immediately or within a year. AFDC must be seen as an equivalent of unemployment insurance for mothers.

At the time of the interviews the sample's average income was $8,300,[3] an improvement of one-third over the post-divorce plunge, but still only

1. Welfare for these families is provided through Aid to Families with Dependent Children (AFDC).

2. This pattern is also discussed by Levinger (chapter 3) in this volume.

3. National statistics (Bane, chapter 16) show lower average incomes for female-headed families than in our sample. Included in national samples are unwed mothers, teenagers, and aged women, all of whom tend to have very low incomes, as well as female-headed families in low-income rural areas, in states with punitively low welfare payments and in locations in which there are poor job opportunities.

66 percent of their average marital income. The improvement had been least among the 8 highest income families and greatest among the 8 poorest. Twenty of the women had part- or full-time jobs; 15 were supported mainly by their jobs, 5 received primary support from their husbands, 2 received primary support from Social Security, and the remainder received the major portion of their family income from welfare.

Economically, a divorced mother may be forced to rely on her ex-husband or on social service agencies for subsidies, whether she is employed or not. The patterns of discrimination in employment and prejudices against the divorced mother can create a "Catch 22" situation. The mother fights for what is usually a low wage job while simultaneously incurring childcare expenses. The problems of one woman typify many:

> I was trying to get into the accounting field. . . . I started at the bottom at $90 a week and they promised I would move up. I got no promotions, a $2, $3 raise in pay. I couldn't get childcare until I had a job, and people at the job wanted me to have childcare before they would give me the job. They said I had no experience, asked about my marital status, did I have a boyfriend? They were worried about pregnancy. When I was unemployed I couldn't get a job because they said I was "over-experienced"—I had worked three years. At one place I said I'd work for less, but they wouldn't hire me. They had three openings.

If she is not employed, she generally must depend on welfare or on her ex-husband for income. But *help* is never free. These sources of income or service mean more strings, more constraints on her activities and choices. Having her life open to questioning and having rules imposed on her activities limit the woman's ability to determine her life. Said one about her husband, "I have the feeling I'm dependent on him still because of the alimony. He could move away and not send it, and that does affect the way I handle it. If I press too hard, he could take off." Another woman, receiving child support, reported that, "I was doing things to please my husband—he looked around to see if there were any flaws when he visited."

Current social arrangements make it difficult for the divorced mother to be economically responsible for her children, to provide adequate housing for them, to obtain credit or access to other resources necessary for an independent life. These structural arrangements encourage the dependence of women on men.

AUTHORITY OVER FAMILY LIFE

Male-dominated society provides power to men rather than to women. The divorced mother may legally be the head of her family, and therefore be legally entitled to make family decisions, to make demands on social institutions, or to protect the family from unwarranted intrusion, but she is not socially legitimated in this role. Time and again the women told us of intrusions that had not happened when their husbands were heads of the family—schools and hospitals ignoring their requests for their children, men attempting to break into the house, landlords refusing to rent to them, their own parents interfering in their lives. "The whole world thinks they can run your life better than you can," said one woman. A common refrain was "they didn't do that when my husband was here." In at least six cases, the ex-husband himself was the biggest offender against the family's privacy and, on occasion, against their safety by barging in, making demands, making sexual passes, or becoming violent.

Whereas a man is accorded the status of head of family automatically, a woman has to "earn" it, through the strength of her personality or her willingness to do battle (Marsden, 1969; Holmstrom, 1973). To constantly validate their claims to authority, women must expend time and energy that are unnecessary for a male head. Belligerence is a frequent tactic. "They wouldn't dare!" said one when questioned about school authorities ignoring what she wanted. Said another about her husband, "He may still have the money, but he knows I won't take it lying down." A third told us that, as a general principle, "It pays to be a bitch, especially when you're on your own."

FAMILY LIFE

The single mother's problems are not merely a function of her female status. She has the same difficulties that any family faces in meeting the day-to-day needs of its members. Despite the industrialization of many areas of family responsibility—such as growing food, making clothes, or educating children—those that are not easily routinized—such as the physical, social, and psychological care of children, housework, emotional support, and the tailoring of market products to meet individual tastes—remain family responsibilities. When marriages break up, these responsibilities are shifted from two parents to one. As one mother put it:

The hard part is having to make important decisions alone—not having anyone to share with, having the feeling of sole responsibility. There's the constancy of the burden—no one else to take over. A married mother doesn't feel so "on her own."

The personal characteristics of the divorced mother—her ability to manage, her competence, her emotional stability—are not the source of her day-to-day difficulties. As a single parent, she must spread her time to cover all of the family demands. Her personal needs and the individual concerns of family members are squeezed into the interstices of formal schedules. One mother described her day,

Everything is a trade-off, a continuing conflict. There is no one else to do anything—shopping, dentists, chores, everything has to be done in the evenings and weekends. I need my job, so I can't tell the boss to go to hell and take time off.

Another said,

The situation has real conflicts. I feel I should be in two places at the same time. After work I come home, fix dinner, shop. I don't have energy to do things. It's hard to do both job and family well. Everyone gets short-changed. It's full-time nothing.

Asked the difference between herself and a married mother, another commented, "I have to get up and lose sleep and still go to work the next day and there is no one else to take care of my child. I can't take a breather." Said another, "Life consists mostly of work and child-raising."

The difficulties in family life arise from the structure of our society, but they are viewed as private problems, not public issues (Mills, 1959). Some social policies can and do aid families, i.e., childcare assistance and welfare, but these are often publicly conceptualized as residual services, for people who cannot do what they ought to be doing for themselves.

Finding adequate childcare arrangements is a difficulty for divorced mothers as it is for other mothers. With licensed childcare available for only about 20 percent of the children who need it (Roby, 1973), women who would like to work or go to school may choose to stay at home because facilities are either unavailable or inadequate (Hedges and Barnett, 1972). "It was awful looking for babysitting—they all wanted high pay and no one was good. Having the daycare center has made all the difference—childcare was always a worry."

Housework, repairs, and maintenance must also be sandwiched into the single mother's schedule. Many women do their own repairs, such as fixing appliances or plastering walls, because they cannot afford repair services. Said one mother in our sample, "Who does the fixing? I do. Washing machine, painting, minor repairs, TV—I learned how to do lots of things." More difficult maintenance jobs go unattended—one woman has three broken TV sets because "I can't afford a service person and I can't do it myself." Another cannot get fire insurance on her house—the only item of value the family owns—because the outside staircase is broken and she cannot afford a carpenter. The problems are complex, as one mother explained:

Someone I wanted to have make repairs on the house, also a washing machine repairman, they won't come because of my being on AFDC. They won't wait to get paid, all they want is money. Same way with the doctor. He was rude to me, said he didn't have time to give my daughter a physical because AFDC takes such a long time to pay. You really do get shoved around, but it's AFDC, not just being divorced. I am ecstatic if anyone will fix anything. I try to fix things myself, if I can't, I call a service person. If someone offers, like this boyfriend . . . but I don't want to get into too much of that unless—you don't ask for favors, "'cause then you owe."

STIGMA

In addition to the problems discussed above, the divorced mother finds herself facing stigma as a result of her divorced status and facing discrimination as a female head of household. Treated as irresponsible financially, as "fair game" sexually, often as psychologically disabled, she must repeatedly fight these images in negotiations between herself and those people and bureaucracies around her. Yet she continues to be held primarily responsible for the children and the housework. The divorced father is often seen as doing something special and praiseworthy when he takes care of his children; the divorced mother is seen as just doing her job, even when she is employed full-time (George and Wilding, 1972).

This contradiction in attitudes is shown in the example of a woman with a handicapped child:

No one has felt any commitment to me as a result of my having to take care of Barbara alone—no one has offered any help. When she is with my husband, they get invited out all the time. When people come here, they take it for granted that I'll cook for them. But they'll take food all prepared out there [her husband's house].

The Benefits of Divorce

Costs are only one dimension of single motherhood. There are also concrete benefits experienced by women who manage their families alone. Married mothers must take their husbands into account in everything they do. Once divorced, mothers no longer have to consult or please them in their daily lives. They have the freedom to please themselves, and this freedom is the basis of definite benefits.

Their freedom is not, however, merely a psychological condition. Gaining control over their lives involves more than changing their own minds; it means a change in the circumstances of their lives. Although their responsibilities may be burdensome, divorced mothers gain control over the money, the children, the standards of housekeeping, and the daily routine which structures family life. Whatever resources they can muster on behalf of the family are under their own control. They may not have much, but whatever they have is theirs to use as they think best.

These benefits are not always apparent to women as they move from marriage to divorce. They have to become independent; they have no choice. But taking over provides an opportunity to learn that they may be better off when they have control, and they may come to enjoy the freedom which is part of independent responsibility.

FINANCES

Even with reduced resources, divorced mothers may feel "better off" and even be "better off" financially. The income a husband contributes to a family is an advantage to his wife only if she has use of it. But a man may consume more than he provides, or he may retain control over the money to the detriment of the needs of the mother and children.

The women with the lowest marital incomes in our sample actually experienced an increase in standard of living after divorce. One mother, employed full-time while her husband "didn't do much," told us what she had expected as a result of divorce: "I knew it would get better— one less to support, plus I'd get help from AFDC." Said another whose husband gambled, "I knew it would be better—he wouldn't be taking anything out of the till." For these women and several others, divorce meant an end to the husband's power to impoverish the family.

Above the lowest income level the standard of living did drop, but the women's greater control over family income sometimes meant an actual increase in cash at their disposal. Four women said that there would be more money in the family if their husbands were still there, but that they themselves would not be able to control its use. Said one mother of four, whose current income of $9,000 is half of the marital income: "I'd be even worse off because he spends it all. He wanted to go bankrupt. He rents now. He doesn't have a home. I just paid off the mortgage." She added that "It's less worrisome now. Living on AFDC I almost lost my health, but I didn't have to worry about his charge cards, his golf clubs, etcetera."

We do not wish to imply that divorce is financially beneficial for mothers. Most had lower family incomes *and* less cash at their disposal. But sixteen women who now had less income said they *felt* better off because they now decided where the money would go. Said a mother of four who is now on welfare, "I'm better off now. I'm getting less than I had but I'm doing more with it." Said another welfare mother, "I'm worse off now, but I feel better off because I have control of it."

Having control makes the budgeting process easier. "It's much better because I know how much money I have to live on and I just do." Said another about welfare, "It's steady. You know what you've got. You never know what you've got with a husband."

Not every woman felt better off, especially not those who had been married to affluent men. Said one about her reduced income, "I don't worry about what to do with it, just how to get more of it." For these women, problems from loss of income far outweighed the benefits of increased control.

AUTHORITY OVER FAMILY LIFE

Without a husband, the organization of life is often easier and the expenditure of energy less. One woman said about housekeeping:

Lots of women who are married say to me, "You don't know how well off you are," because they have to do all the work anyway.

Housework responsibilities were not reduced for all of the mothers. Some found more work as the children got older, or as roommates were added to relieve financial burdens. In other cases, they felt like doing more for their own satisfaction. "I do more housework now," said one woman. "I'm fussier. I don't have to please anyone, so I do it right." Regardless of its amount, almost two-thirds (19) of the women felt happier about doing it: "I had to keep the house spotless or there were arguments. Now I do it when I want to and I don't mind—I even enjoy it." Another said the best thing was that

I don't have to be on any schedules. Housework is my own business. I don't have to answer to anyone. I can be more relaxed. No one says, "You god-damn slob, why isn't the floor clean?" I can spend more time with the children, it's more relaxed. I can make my own time. I'm my own boss.

For these mothers, increased satisfaction followed from the end of supervision by their husbands and the obligation to meet their husbands' standards. The other eleven women either had not changed their attitudes about housework because they "always hated doing it," or they found it worse because they now had to fit it in between their new jobs and their family obligations.

Relationships with their children were another source of increased feelings of mastery. Most of the mothers in our sample felt they were doing a great job of raising their children, an appraisal certainly at variance with the attitudes of the society around them. One comment heard time and again when mothers described their current relationships with their children was "the peace" and the lack of conflict. One of the 18 who mentioned this said: "Easy things? I don't have to cope with or

straighten the children out from being with a person with a sick mind."
The same change occurred for an older mother who had put up with an
alcoholic husband for seven years. "I can spend more time with the
children because I don't have *him* to contend with. I don't have to share
myself—I'm mother *and* father. There is less problem with discipline,
because there's only one authority."

Despite the stereotype that a child will suffer from the absence of a
male model, only four mothers actually mentioned this as either an
existing problem or a potential problem. There are several reasons for
this unexpected finding. In 11 families, the fathers continue to provide
a male model through weekly contact with the children. In addition,
children in all 30 families have other male models—grandfathers, uncles,
neighbors, and mothers' boyfriends. It is commonly assumed that when
the father is present he will provide an adequate male model. Several
mothers in our sample pointed out that their children were better off
without the male image that the father had provided.

SOCIAL LIFE

The benefits of independence for the divorced mother in arranging her
family life—the finances, the housework, the children—were also evident
in her own social life. No longer "half a couple," she can make her own
decisions about the friendships she needs or wants. Asked if they had
lost any friends because of divorce, several answered as did this woman:
"Lose friends? No, because they weren't my friends, they were *his*. Now
my friends are different—more intelligent, active people who do things."

"Couple society" did give a predictable structure to social life. Moving
away from it was difficult, particularly for women who had been married
a long time or who lived in family-oriented neighborhoods. But they did
it. They found new friendships with divorced mothers, with married
women they saw in the daytime, and with boyfriends or dates they
included in their evening hours.

Gaining control over "social time" is like gaining control over money.
They may have less, but they can decide how to spend it (Stein, 1976).
Having choice over activities is a treasured commodity. "I'm in Parents
Without Partners, and in some historian groups about New England
history. I wouldn't have done it if I were married. I love to have freedom
to do things—I didn't when married."

Control over social life includes control over sex life. They can choose
to engage—or not to engage—in sexual relationships. When asked to
evaluate their current sex life, 19 women reported that it was better than
when married, largely because they had more to say about it. "I have
less sex now, and I might add a lot better than before." The other 11
women were less satisfied, either because they had less sex than they
wanted, because they found it difficult to have an unmarried sex life

while raising children, or because they would have preferred more stable sexual relations with fewer partners.

SELF-CONCEPT

Taking on new responsibilities and doing unfamiliar tasks with little social support are not easy, but the experience of making decisions and mastering tasks forms the basis of a new, more satisfactory self-concept. "I had to work to get back my sense of self-respect," said a mother of four. "On the whole, it is easier now—I can handle things. I don't have a club over my head. I have problems, but at least now I have a fighting chance. I have a mind of my own." Not only in the family but also in relation to outside agencies, women have stronger self-concepts. Says one mother who is doing more with less money, "I'm a fighter now." These changes in self-concept derive from a real increase in their personal power. The women offered a variety of examples of this: "It's easier making all the decisions—decisions are *faster*. All kinds of issues —moral, ethical. Examining values—lifestyle and God. There is no one to answer to but yourself. Your own schedule, own plans." "It's easier now. You can do so much when your mind is free and you don't have any aggravation. Nothing *is* easier, but it *feels* easier. I have to live up to my own expectations, no one else's."

Only seven of the 30 women we interviewed were seriously interested in remarriage. The rest were either ambivalent (10) or disinclined to remarry (13).[4] Opposition to remarriage is often linked to the satisfactions of independence: "I'm not looking for it—not interested. I want to lead my own life. I don't like to report to someone what I'm doing." "There are the horrors of loneliness—but the loneliness with him around was much more acute. I feel pride in making it on my own." "I'm more independent, more demanding than I used to be." "I would have to trust a man a lot to give up my job again—this is my security."

Independence was less clearly indicated by those ambivalent toward remarriage, although it is implied. "I haven't given up the idea, but it's not likely. Maybe someday, to take care of the loneliness in my old age."

Rejection of remarriage did not mean rejection of men or of long-term close relationships. Rather, these women rejected the traditional model of marriage as incompatible with their new identity. They had exchanged domination by, and direct dependence on, a particular man for domination by and dependence on a system. This exchange brought new difficulties into their lives, but it also gave them options that their marriages

---

4. Our finding that 43 percent of our sample opposed remarriage differs little from that of Kriesberg (1970) who found that 52 percent of husbandless mothers in his sample did not want to marry again. Goode combined love and marriage, thus obscuring the difference, yet still found that 30 percent of his sample of divorced mothers felt negatively toward both (1956).

had precluded. Most were unwilling to give up these options. Their response to this conflict was often to express a desire for alternative male relationships outside of the "marriage model." As one woman commented, "My attitude toward men is—they are nice for friends, they're fine for sex. A good man is a guy who has his own money and enjoys sex. I don't want to take anything from anybody." Yet another responded to our questions of her interest in remarriage with:

Yeech. Most men are basically childish. I'm not a very good ass-kisser. I don't know how I could readjust my whole life. But I get lonely, and I would like to have someone around, permanently. Now there are too many people walking into and out of our lives. I would like to have a long-term relationship, but maybe without material ties to bind me.

National statistics have shown that the majority of divorced mothers have remarried; this indicates that these women's current attitude is not necessarily a predictor of future behavior. Several women in our sample were aware of the disjuncture between desire to remain divorced and objective pressure toward remarriage. One woman now on welfare said:

I dislike the idea of remarriage. Ninety-seven percent of the time—no way. But an occasional time—mostly when I'm having financial difficulties, when problems are getting me down—I think, "that's what security is going to be."

Another agreed: "My mother said to me, 'The first time marry for love, the second time marry for security.' My biggest fear is that I might remarry for security, because with the other pressures I may need that security."

Recent statistics (Norton and Glick, chapter 1) indicate a drop in the remarriage rate. Perhaps women today are more willing or more able to act on their expressed desire to remain independent than they were in the past.

Policy Implications

How can the costs of divorced motherhood be reduced? There is no need for new policy proposals to answer that question. Those policy changes needed to make women autonomous have already been strongly advocated by women's groups and policy makers sympathetic to the situation of women, non-whites, and the poor. Time and again, such individuals and groups have argued that women should have access to the same resources available to men: jobs which pay something approximating a family wage, "automatic" social respect, and the resulting access to housing or credit without harassment. Insuring equal access—or as Rowbotham (1973) has said, "equal exploitation"—means providing equal education, in subject matter as well as in "quality." It means ending job-related discrimination at all levels—in training programs, in hiring, in on-the-job treatment and promotion, and, most essentially, in wages and benefits. It also means equalizing family costs off the job with children's allowances and freely available daycare.

But these or other policies are unlikely to be implemented for a number of reasons. First, government practices and business profits are geared to male-headed families. Keeping women dependent on men provides the conditions for a low-paid labor force as well as making domestic services and childcare a low-cost, wifely proposition. Second, all men have a partial interest in policies that maintain women's dependence. They receive direct personal benefits as the socially approved head of a family: better wages and job opportunities, personal services from women, and rights to make decisions. (We say only *partial* interest, because the high rate of marital dissolution suggests that many men may feel that the services and companionship of a wife and the joys of children are not worth the expense.) Third, these changes are expensive. Opposition to them would come both from business interests, whose profits might be taxed to implement them, and from middle- and lower-income families and individuals who, given the tax structure of the United States, pay a disproportionate share of taxes.

National and local government policy has been addressed more to issues of divorce law than to the needs of families. Some policy changes now under consideration or partially in force, such as no-fault divorce, divorce insurance, displaced homemaker protection, equalizing custody, and the use of HEW to track delinquent child support payments, do address the special situation of divorced mothers. However, they do not attack the underlying causes of their problems—that women get insufficient pay for their work and therefore must rely on husbands to provide the bulk of a family income. Nevertheless, the changes must be welcomed because they provide some immediate improvements, as well as a basis for more holistic changes in the future.

At the local level, divorced mothers themselves, the organized women's movement, and other sympathetic groups and individuals can respond to the needs of divorced mothers by providing services such as crisis intervention or information on locally available services and options. They are doing so in many cities and towns. Policy makers need to recognize that it is better to spend money to support and maintain locally organized services than to encourage expensive professionally organized demonstration projects, which end when the demonstration period ends.

As we said in the beginning of this section, we are not offering new policy proposals. Those that would improve the lives of divorced mothers have been made clearly and consistently in the past. What is needed is political commitment to make women equal members of this society. Ultimately the policy changes divorced mothers need await the time when women, including divorced mothers, have the power to implement the policies they know are needed.

[15]   *Kenneth Kressel, Martin Lopez-Morillas,*
Janet Weinglass, and Morton Deutsch

Professional Intervention in Divorce: The Views of Lawyers, Psychotherapists, and Clergy

In spite of the soaring divorce rate and the evidence that divorce is a trying legal, economic, and emotional occurrence, the roles of professionals in assisting individuals in the process of divorce have been studied very little. To our knowledge, only two studies of the role of the lawyer have been reported (O'Gorman, 1963; Cavanagh and Rhode, 1976). We are aware of no study which systematically describes the assistance of either psychotherapists or clergy. The present report summarizes a series of intensive interviews on the nature of the divorce experience and the role of the professional.[1]

The research reported in this chapter was supported by grants from the National Science Foundation (#BN74-02477 A02) and the Marshall Fund. The principal investigator was Morton Deutsch. Kenneth Kressel was project director.

This chapter appeared in the *Journal of Divorce*, 1978, 2 (2), 119–155. Reprinted by permission.

1. We are aware that terms like "professional" and "client" are not totally appropriate in the case of the clergy. We have used them throughout this report as a matter of convenience, since no other vocabulary is shared as well by all three groups.

Goals of the Study

Our aims were to identify the primary obstacles to a constructive divorcing process and to illuminate the psychological and interpersonal experience of those who divorce. We were particularly interested in the role of the professional in helping to produce a cooperative climate between divorcing spouses and an equitable and mutually acceptable separation or divorce agreement.

Separate accounts of each of the three professional groups with whom we spoke have been given elsewhere (Kressel and Deutsch, 1977; Weinglass, Kressel, and Deutsch, 1978; Lopez-Morillas, 1977). In this paper, we wish to highlight themes common to all these studies and to underscore certain issues unique to each group of respondents.

Method

THE INTERVIEWS

The investigation took the form of a series of lengthy, semistructured interviews. Each interview lasted an average of 1½ to 2 hours, and was tape-recorded.

The interview had two parts. The first part surveyed the respondent's views on the criteria of and obstacles to a constructive divorce, as well as the most effective strategies of intervention. The second part asked respondents to discuss in detail (but without any identifying information) a case in which they felt they had been particularly successful.

THE RESPONDENTS

Fifty-nine professionals, including psychotherapists, lawyers, and clergy, were interviewed. Since the study was exploratory, no effort was made at systematic sampling. Instead, highly expert practitioners were located through professional organizations, personal contacts, and referrals by previous respondents. Several of the respondents in each group had written articles and, in some instances, books on the subject of divorce. With rare exceptions, every individual contacted agreed to participate.

The respondents were all from the northeast United States, the majority from the New York metropolitan area. By the respondents' own characterizations, the population whom they serve consists of predominantly highly educated (75 percent with the BA or above), upper middle-class individuals (average annual income, $30,000), who have been married between eight to fifteen years; approximately 60 percent have dependent children. Salient characteristics of each of the three respondent groups follow:

Psychotherapists (n = 21: 11 men, 10 women). Average age, 52. By training, six were M.D. psychiatrists, eight Ph.D. psychologists, four Ed.D.'s, two MSW's, and one Master's in Psychology. Most characterized themselves as specialists in marital or family therapy. The average time spent specifically on divorce was 20 percent.

Clergy (n = 21: 18 men, 3 women). Average age, 52. The respondents included six Orthodox rabbis, six Episcopal ministers, one Episcopal deaconess, four Catholic priests, one Greek Orthodox priest, one Mormon brother, and two laywomen active in Catholic divorce adjustment groups. Close to half the respondents considered themselves specialists in the area of marriage and family problems, and all had a minimum of three years' experience in divorce work. Since the purpose was to examine the unique role of the clergy, individuals with extensive training in psychotherapy or pastoral counseling were intentionally excluded.

Lawyers (n = 17: 9 men, 8 women). Average age, 50. With one exception, all listed themselves as specialists in divorce work, and most were members of the American Association of Matrimonial Lawyers.

Our respondents constitute a unique, highly expert sample. Whether their views are representative of their respective professions we cannot say. Our goal, however, was the exploratory one of identifying underlying issues in the divorce process. Before proceeding to our findings, we briefly describe the context of professional intervention in divorce.

The Context of Intervention

PSYCHOTHERAPISTS AND CLERGY

There is much similarity in the roles which therapists and clergy assume in divorce. Two main issues tend to be the focus of intervention: giving help with the difficult decision of whether or not to divorce, and, less commonly, assistance with negotiating the terms of settlement.

The frequency with which psychotherapy is sought by divorcing individuals is largely undocumented, but appears to occur in perhaps 20–30 percent of all middle-class divorces, although the trend may be upward.

An unknown but considerable percentage of this help is strictly *pro forma*, deriving from either the need to assuage a guilty conscience on the part of one or both spouses, or a state regulation for mandatory conciliation counseling. Generally, serious counseling in divorce is arranged and conducted privately. All 21 therapists were engaged in private practice, of which divorce counseling was a part.[2]

When people seek help with a marital problem, they are more likely to consult a clergyman than a psychotherapist (Gurin, Veroff, and Feld, 1960). The clergy's work with the divorcing occurs in two primary contexts: as part of congregational responsibilities or in connection with religious courts of divorce or annulment. Thirteen of our respondents functioned at the congregational level. At this level, the clergyman's activities are akin to those of a psychotherapist in that they tend to be focused on reducing emotional turmoil, building self-confidence, and promoting insight. Eight of the respondents were also affiliated with religious courts. At this level the clergy's role tends to be more circumscribed and legalistic. Effectuating the religious divorce or annulment is the major, although not necessarily the only concern.

THE LAWYERS

Of the three groups, lawyers are most frequently consulted by the divorcing, since divorce represents the end of one legal contract and the beginning of a new one. Every divorce action must be formally filed with and approved by an appropriate court. The partners may need to reach agreement in five major areas: custody, visitation, child support, alimony, and division of property. In most divorces, settlement is reached by mutual consent (although frequently with considerable conflict). In only a small percentage of cases is there a contested issue which requires a court action and judicial intervention for resolution.

Formally, at least, the lawyer's role in divorce is far more clearly structured than that of either therapist or clergy. Allowing for individual

2. We know of no reliable estimates on the percentages of individuals who receive psychotherapy during the divorcing process. Goode (1956, p. 156) reported that 29 percent of his sample of divorced women (n = 425) said "yes" to the question, "Have you ever consulted a marriage counselor?" Goode noted, however, that the percentage receiving any real counseling was probably much smaller, since 14 percent of the total had their only counseling experience as part of a domestic relations court requirement. Gurin et al. (1960) report that in their national survey 40 percent of separated or divorced women and 22 percent of the divorced men had received therapy at some time. It is not possible to tell from their figures, however, what percentage of this help-seeking was precipitated by and addressed to the problems of marriage dissolution. More recently, Hetherington et al. (1976) report that roughly 15 percent of the divorced women and 8 percent of the husbands in their non-random sample had received therapy. Hunt and Hunt (1977) indicate that 60 percent of their respondents sought psychotherapy for specific help with marital distress; however, their sample was unsystematic and consisted primarily of members of Parents Without Partners.

differences in style and personality, the views of lawyers would therefore be expected to show far more consensus than those of the other two groups. In fact, just the opposite pattern was found. While therapists and clergy differed from their colleagues on important issues only occasionally, differences among the lawyers were common. What accounts for this pattern of responses? We believe that the answer is largely to be found in the high degree of strain that characterizes the role of the matrimonial lawyer.

The Lawyers: Stresses and Mechanisms of Professional Coping

THE STRESSES

Much more frequently than either therapists or clergy, the lawyers mentioned sources of stress inherent in the nature of their work. Formal codes of conduct and training provide little relief from these stresses; indeed, they appear to contribute to them. Let us set forth the major sources of role strain reflected in the lawyer interviews.

The adversary nature of the legal proceedings. Despite many changes in recent years, divorce remains largely an adversary process in the eyes of the law; one spouse is the "aggrieved" party or "plaintiff," and the other the "guilty" party or "defendant." Enlightened public and legal opinion is aware that this model of innocence and guilt is inappropriate to marital conflict. Nonetheless, the law's formal bias, the availability of legal threats and counter-threats, as well as the emotional agitation of clients, may push even the most cooperative of lawyers toward serious escalation of conflict. (No-fault divorce has not removed the problem; couples still file bitter suits and countersuits over who shall have custody, how much child support shall be paid, etc.)

The one-sidedness of the lawyer's view. The lawyer's objective appraisal of the marital situation is greatly limited by the professional injunction that lawyers deal with only one of the spouses. Our respondents referred frequently to the difficulty of ascertaining the true state of affairs from the perspective provided by their own clients. Hearing only one side, the lawyer is more easily led to overidentify with the client's point of view—and the client may have strong motives, conscious or unconscious, for wishing to use the adversary system as a vehicle for retribution.

The shortage of material resources. Since two households cannot be supported as cheaply as one, it is highly unlikely that both parties to a divorce will be happy with the terms of the economic settlement. The attorney, therefore, is often in the position of being the bearer of bad news:

There are the run-of-the-mill cases where the man makes $15,000 a year and there are three or four children and a non-working wife. There you have complete chaos. And anybody who tried to introduce so-called "equity" would be much better off introducing money, because it's the only thing that's going to solve this insoluble problem.

The position of either therapists or clergy is much more comfortable in this regard. Therapists can avoid the topic on the grounds that disputes over money are not a proper area of psychotherapeutic intervention (except insofar as unconscious, neurotic conflicts are concerned); clergy are more often willing to address financial matters, but their role is the positive one of trying to augment resources through congregational funds or by making a referral to a charitable agency. It is only the lawyer who, in the course of professional duties, is obligated to confront the client with unpleasant financial realities. We may also note that, unlike the therapist or clergyman, much of the lawyer's work is done in the client's absence. At a time when clients are experiencing the financial strains of divorce, there is thus a good possibility that the lawyer's bill will be seen as unreasonable and unwarranted.

The economics of the law office. "There are some lawyers who want to litigate, litigate, litigate. They get better fees that way—the taxicab with the meter running." How widespread this phenomenon is nobody knows. It represents nonetheless a serious potential conflict of interest between lawyer and client.

Another potential source of conflict stems from the fact that it is generally the husband who pays the wife's legal costs. The lawyer who represents the wife, therefore, is in the anomalous position of having his fee paid by the opposing side. Unconscious pressures may thus be created for a less than totally effective representation of the wife's interests. The wife herself may have doubts about the degree of allegiance which she can expect from the arrangement.

The non-legal nature of many of the issues. In major areas of their activity, lawyers are operating largely outside the domain of law or legal training. Relatively few of the issues that arise are strictly "issues of law." Moreover, even many legal and financial issues engage psychological judgment and expertise, or personal values (e.g., custody or visitation arrangements that would best meet the emotional needs of both children and parents). Unfortunately, the training of lawyers poorly equips them to understand or handle the psychological and interpersonal issues in divorce, even though such issues may be crucial for creating equitable and workable agreements.

The difficulties in the lawyer-lawyer relationship. Almost universally the lawyers noted that a crucial determinant of divorce outcomes is the relationship between the two opposing attorneys. Indeed, for some respondents a constructive divorce was defined as one in which the two attorneys "come to operate within each other's framework," as one respondent put it.

If you are lucky enough to have an adversary with whom you have had experience to know that the person has the same philosophy you have, then you have very few problems; you can work out something beautifully. You're lucky if you find one who is really in complete consonance and communication with you and understands the way you want to handle the divorce. That is very rare, I want to tell you.

In summary, the role of the matrimonial lawyer is in many ways unenviable: lawyers cannot hope to find much satisfaction in the adversary use of the law but can expect strong pressures to utilize the adversary system. In addition, their attempts to predict how the dynamics of the marital relationship will affect the proceedings will be hampered by the one-sided source of their information and their own lack of psychological training; their efforts are likely to be regarded with disappointment and mistrust by clients; and there is a good probability of being matched with an opposing counsel whose views are very different than their own and with whom it is difficult to work.

Consequently, each practitioner is obliged to solve the professional dilemmas of matrimonial practice as best he can. The solutions arrived at, however, are not entirely idiosyncratic. We refer to the systematic differences that arise as lawyer *stances*—or role definitions. The adoption of a stance provides lawyers with a buffer against the contradictory terms of their employment and a rationale for managing the client and the opposing attorney.

MECHANISMS OF PROFESSIONAL COPING:

VARIETIES OF LAWYER STANCES

There were three key areas of systematic difference in the lawyers' views: attitudes towards the client; the objectives of legal intervention; and the nature and value of collaboration with mental health professionals. A lawyer's view in one of these areas tended to be highly correlated with the views which he held in the other two. On the basis of these differences, we have outlined six distinctive stances with which different groups of lawyers view their work.

Given our small sample and the exploratory nature of this study, we are reluctant to claim more than a suggestive value for this typology. However, its claims to validity are supported by an earlier study by

O'Gorman (1963) which is remarkably parallel to our own with regard to the range and general nature of lawyer role definitions in divorce cases.

We have ordered the six stances that characterize the lawyers' views from those that involve a more narrow, legalistic rationale for intervention to those that are broader and marked more by social or psychological, rather than by legal concerns. (While stances are best conceived along a continuum, rather than as discretely defined categories, respondents each fell rather clearly into one or two adjacent classifications.)

1. *The Undertaker.* This metaphor (supplied, incidentally, by one of our respondents), rests on two assumptions: that the job is essentially thankless and messy; and that the clients are in a state of emotional "derangement." This stance is also characterized by a general cynicism about human nature and the doubt that good or constructive divorces are ever possible. It is the only lawyer stance, and the only instance within any of the three groups, in which, in its more extreme manifestations, there was a clear derogation of the client.

> I'm not interested in my client's personality; that's not my function. I knowingly represent psychotic people. All of my clients are neurotic, some of them actually psychotic. If mine aren't, the other side is.
> The ideal client would not be in a lawyer's office. In other words, the ideal client is somebody well-adjusted, able to cope with reality, cope with their problems, who can enter a relationship with a lawyer where they could be helpful. They're not the kind of people who get involved in divorces.

Not surprisingly, lawyers with an undertaker stance are not enthusiastic about the value of psychological counseling, even though they may refer clients to psychotherapists to satisfy "technical" requirements.

2. *The Mechanic.* This is a pragmatic, technically oriented stance. It assumes that clients are basically capable of knowing what they want. The lawyer's task primarily involves ascertaining the legal feasibility of doing what the client wants.

> If a husband says he wants to give $25,000 a year to his wife, I don't think it's the duty of the lawyer to say to him, "you're out of your mind." I think that if a lawyer is asked, "What risk do I run in the courts?" then he has a professional responsibility to give his opinion as to what the risk is.

Like the Undertaker, the Mechanic tends not to call into question the existing legal system. Unlike the former, however, he does not actively disparage the client, and also accepts the possibility of "good" outcomes. A good outcome lies in producing "results" for the client, "results" usually understood in financial terms.

Comments about other professionals centered around their usefulness in buttressing a case or corroborating evidence. Thus, if there are allegations that the client is alcoholic, the Mechanic might seek the testimony of a doctor or psychiatrist to disprove it.

3. *The Mediator.* This stance is oriented toward negotiated compromise and rational problem solving, with an emphasis on cooperation with the other side and, in particular, the other attorney. Generally, there is an appeal to the client's "better nature" and the view that what the client wants should be tempered with a sense of "what's fair." There may also be a posture of emotional neutrality or noninvolvement in response to emotional or conflicted clients. Unlike the Undertaker and Mechanic, but like the following three stances, the Mediator tends to downplay the adversary aspect of his role. Only when provoked by the other side does the Mediator like to fight:

If the man (the client's spouse) cuts off the telephone, if he changes the lock on the door, I don't talk; I get into court and get that remedied immediately. That doesn't preclude negotiations at a future date, provided it is understood that we're not going to enter into an agreement because of economic pressure.

For the Mediator a good outcome is a "fair" negotiated settlement that both parties can "live with" (a frequently used phrase). A primary motive in maintaining contact with other professionals is in using them as resources for de-escalating conflict.

4. *The Social Worker.* This stance centers around a concern for the client's post-divorce adjustment and overall social welfare. Regarding women clients in particular, there may be an emphasis on the client's "marketability."

The main thing is to fully explore her ability to contribute to her own support. I have had agreements where I have been able to get money for college or a business course—or, in one case, a course in cooking.

Even though the attorney represents only one of the parties, there may also be a tendency to consider the interests of the entire family:

I think the family unit should be treated as a unit that is having an illness or problem that can be solved by the separation of the spouses; and a whole solution be worked out that would be best for each of the family members, in a cooperative venture.

The lawyer with a Social Worker stance may also attend to long-range plans for the children (summer camp, higher education, and the like). This stance is also frequently associated with the view that, contrary to many clients' expectations, divorce is not usually an easy solution to marital unhappiness. The involvement of therapists or clergy is welcomed, either before entry of the lawyer (with a view to providing a troubled family with assistance) or after the divorce (to aid in post-divorce adjustment). As might be expected, a "good" outcome is perceived to be one in which the client achieves social reintegration.

5. *The Therapist.* This stance involves active acceptance of the fact that the client is in a state of emotional turmoil. There is a concomitant assumption that the legal aspects of a divorce situation can be adequately dealt with only if the emotional aspects are engaged by the lawyer. Correspondingly, there is an orientation toward trying to understand the client's motivations:

> I don't see that there's any difference in my work and the work of the psychiatrist or the psychologist. I have to understand the individual. When the individual comes in for an interview, I think the most important part of the case is right there in the first interview. If I know how to ferret out the motivations. If I know how to ferret out the interpersonal things that are happening.

This stance tends to be accompanied by a strongly expressed view that the legal system "isn't working" in terms of meeting people's real needs.

A "good" outcome is conceptualized more or less as it would be in a therapeutically oriented crisis-intervention situation: personal reintegration of the client after a trying, stressful period. Predictably enough, this is also a stance that welcomes involvement of psychotherapists and in which clients may be encouraged to seek such assistance.

6. *The Moral Agent.* In this final stance there is a more or less explicit rejection of neutrality; it is assumed that the lawyer should not hesitate to use his or her sense of "right" and "wrong." This stance appears to be particularly salient when the divorcing couple has children, with the lawyer attempting to serve as a kind of guardian and protector of the children's interests. One facet of this orientation is the use of child psychotherapy.

> I try, very desperately, to get the parents to put the children into professional hands, because I am thoroughly convinced that the average parent, because of the emotional reaction to the situation, doesn't even realize that he or she is using the children.

A constructive outcome is one in which the lawyer's sense of "what is right" is satisfied, not only in relation to the client, but to the other spouse and the children.

We have sought to explain this typology of lawyer stances largely as a product of the role strains characteristic of matrimonial practice. At this point we may note that lack of congruence between the stances of any two lawyers in a divorce may well be both an effect of role strain as well as one of its principal causes: the cross-pressures of professional practice produce alternative methods of professional coping in the form of differing stances; the differing stances further complicate the problems of professional practice by introducing a powerful new element of potential conflict and uncertainty. One may well imagine the results should an Undertaker and a Moral Agent meet across the bargaining table.

The Client: Stresses and Mechanisms of Coping

THE STRESSES

However difficult the divorce lawyer's position, the problems are minor compared to those experienced by the divorce client. Elsewhere in this volume the precise nature of the stress experienced by those undergoing a marriage breakup and the empirical evidence on the effects of this stress are described and evaluated (see chapters 11, 12, 13, 14, and 16). Here we may simply note some major sources of such difficulty.

Rapid, simultaneous changes in life circumstances. One obvious source of stress is that spouses need to adjust to new living arrangements, new jobs and financial burdens, new patterns of parenting, and new conditions of social and sexual life. The transition may be especially difficult for the wife, particularly since sole custody creates intense immediate pressures in nearly all spheres of activity.

Non-mutuality of the divorce decision. Our interviews with all the professionals suggest that non-mutuality is more the rule than the exception in divorce, certainly as far as clinical practice is concerned.[3] The precise effects of an unequal decision to divorce may be difficult to predict, but certain recurring patterns were noted, particularly by the therapists.

Frequently, the partner who wishes to end the marriage feels guilt at abandoning the spouse. Once the initiator finally broaches the topic of divorce, continued guilt, combined with the equally strong desire to leave, may produce a virulent form of the "settlement at any cost" mentality. At the same time, the spouse who wishes to keep the marriage may escalate demands, motivated by feelings of humiliation and anger, combined with the prospect of a bleak and unchosen future. Unreasonable demands may also be a means to prolong the marriage and ultimately prevent the marital breakup.

An opposite pattern was also noted by several of our respondents: guilt in the initiator may be expressed as anger directed at the non-initiator, in whom feelings of diminished self-worth may inhibit the ability to bargain constructively, or produce an abject acceptance of almost any terms. A settlement may thus be quickly arrived at whose inequitable and unworkable nature may not become apparent until several years and several court fights later.

Separation distress. The final and, in many ways, most profound source of psychological turmoil in divorce is what Weiss has aptly

3. There is little empirical research to help verify our respondents' impression. In Goode's (1956) classic but dated investigation, only 13 percent of the interviewed ex-wives reported that the initial decision to end the marriage was mutual. See also Hill et al. in this volume regarding the non-mutual nature of premarital breakups.

labelled "separation distress" (1975). Anxiety, irritability, anger, depression, and, above all, a heightened focusing in thought and deed on the soon-to-be divorced spouse are characteristic. These feelings are in addition to, although not easily distinguishable from, the other emotional upsets which may be occurring.

MECHANISMS OF COPING: THE PROCESS OF PSYCHIC DIVORCE

While every divorcing person's experience is unique, the interviews suggest that there does exist a general pattern of coping. The details of the process have been described, under the heading of psychic divorce, in our reports on therapists and clergy (Kressel and Deutsch, 1977; Weinglass, Kressel, and Deutsch, 1978). We will summarize only the most salient characteristics.

Within broad limits the process is unavoidable and unmodifiable (although self-awareness and/or professional intervention can mitigate its more extreme manifestations). Throughout, decision making and rational planning are impaired, at certain points markedly so. The process occurs in distinct stages that embody powerful swings in mood and in quality of marital interaction. On balance, the more painful moods and types of relating predominate.

The experience of the initiator, while basically similar to that of the noninitiator, is less difficult. The distinctiveness of the initiator's experience is related to the relatively earlier occurrence of some of the psychological stages and the relatively shorter time span of the entire process. Much of the difficulty in adjustment attributed to the noninitiator can be viewed as a consequence of a lack of psychological preparedness and intense feelings of diminished self-regard. Some respondents noted that the noninitiator could not be expected to recover for as long as three years or more.

Although the phenomenon of psychic divorce is inevitable, the successful completion of the process is not. Thus, legal divorce may, and frequently does, occur in the absence of psychic divorce. The worst examples of post-divorce legal battles, bitterness, and general mayhem may be most often ascribed to a failure of psychic divorce.

The implication of the psychic divorce process for the negotiation of the divorce settlement is that the potential for displaced and particularly intense conflict is high, and the prospects for enlightened and realistic negotiations (even in the absence of overt conflict) are low. The primary implication for the nonpsychological counselor—for the lawyer, accountant, real-estate agent—whom divorcing individuals are likely to consult, is that normal assumptions about what can be expected from a client are likely to be disappointed. It is more realistic to assume that divorcing clients will be slow to act, unable to comprehend or retain information, and changeable in their decisions.

It needs to be emphasized, however, that the process of psychic divorce represents a *normal* and *temporary* reaction to a stressful life experience. Divorcing individuals may give a misleading appearance of serious psychopathology, particularly to individuals who have contact with them only during the acute stages—such as lawyers, for example. Even trained psychological counselors need to be wary of diagnoses of the divorcing which suggest the need for long-term reconstructive treatment. Such diagnoses are likely to be unreliable for individuals in the acute stages of coping. Moreover, at least in our view, they are likely to detract from more immediate and useful interventions aimed at strengthening the client's temporarily impaired powers of judgment and planning, and assisting with regard to the complex substantive issues that require settlement.

Criteria of a Constructive Divorce

As we have already observed, the lawyers' views on a constructive divorce are an important component of role definition, and ranged from denying that a constructive outcome is possible to notions of psychological and social reintegration. The views of the therapists and clergy showed a much higher degree of consensus, with the exception that for the clergy, the best divorce is generally no divorce. This viewpoint is in keeping with the traditional religious orientation toward the sanctity of marriage and family life. Apart from this difference, however, the views of therapists and clergy on the goals to be accomplished in the event of divorce—all the clergy allowed for the inevitability and even desirability of divorce under certain circumstances—may be summarized together.

The self. At a minimum, the individual should experience a gradual diminution in feelings of guilt and failure; an absence of regret that the marriage has been ended; and a balanced and charitable view of the ex-spouse. Like any crisis, divorce can call forth new skills and unsuspected strengths, and compel a redefinition of values and goals. It should also produce a new level of self-understanding, particularly with regard to one's role in the marital breakup. The therapists, in particular, were inclined to the view that divorce is a function of the conflicts and behavior of both partners. To view oneself as innocent victim is thus to engage in a fundamental distortion, the consequence of which is a high probability for an equally bad remarriage. (There was no consensus on remarriage itself as a criterion of successful divorce. Therapists tended to speak more of the ability to form new intimate attachments, with or without marriage. Jewish and Protestant clergy favored remarriage, while Catholics tended to view singlehood as a viable alternative.)

Two areas where learning in the clients is desirable concern insight into unconscious dynamics (e.g., what psychological needs led to such a poor marital choice in the first place? what unconscious conflicts from childhood were being projected onto the spouse?), and an understanding of the dysfunctional patterns of marital interaction that characterized the marriage (e.g., what faulty modes of communication or conflict resolution were established?).[4]

The relationship between the ex-spouses. If there are children, an essential criterion of a constructive divorce is that there be a constructive co-parenting relationship; in particular, that visitation and child support agreements be kept and that unexpected contingencies concerning the children's welfare be handled with flexibility and good grace. With a few exceptions, respondents tended to distrust the ex-spouses' continuing involvement with each other as friends, business partners, or lovers — largely on the grounds that such attachments reflect separation distress rather than realistic caring, and that they drain energies that are more productively spent in forming new relationships. Most respondents felt that for childless couples the best policy is to sever all ties.

The children. Only rarely did a respondent speak of divorce as an opportunity for children's psychological "growth." The consensus was that psychological distress was inevitable for youngsters when parents divorce. First, for optimal psychological development, it is assumed that children need two parents to serve as appropriate sex-role models. Second, because they are immature in their cognitive and emotional development, children are considered poorly equipped to handle any significant estrangement in their relationship with parents. (For the more psychodynamically inclined respondents, the gratification of strong oedipal wishes was seen as another source of psychological distress for children.)

While parents should not necessarily stay together for the sake of the children, a central criterion of a constructive divorce is the degree to which it minimizes negative consequences for children. A cooperative co-parenting relationship is the surest means by which this can occur. Specifically, children should not get the feeling that it is somehow disloyal to love or to be with the other parent; they should not be cast in the role of informant on the other parent's activities and love relationships; and they should not become bargaining pawns or emotional footballs in a continuing parental war.

4. The view that divorce is a product of mutual, if covert, collaboration between spouses is an untested clinical hypothesis. The notion that divorce can be a result of outside forces or events over which neither party has much control or awareness may seem naïve, but not necessarily untrue. (Statistical evidence indicates that the divorce rate is affected by social and economic events in the external society; see Part III of this volume.) Indeed, it is a concept with which many of the clergy were comfortable, even if the therapists were generally not.

The nature of the divorcing process. The key words here are *mutual,* *active,* and *gradual.* Regardless of who initiated the idea, both partners should come to accept divorce as necessary and desirable; negotiation of terms should be conducted actively by both spouses, and in a self-interested but cooperative spirit. Failure of one or both partners to take an active negotiating stance suggests psychological non-acceptance of the divorce or guilt about it. The consequences of such passivity are that the final divorce settlement, arranged by lawyers or the courts, will not be based on a sense of psychological ownership and may not adequately reflect realistic needs or wishes. The entire process should be marked by an absence of precipitate decisions on major issues such as remarriage, relocation, or job change, since the stresses of the divorcing experience strongly, if temporarily, impair decision-making ability.

Strategies of Intervention

Four major strategic goals are shared by therapists, clergymen, and lawyers in their work with the divorcing: establishing a working alliance; diagnosis and information gathering; improving the emotional climate; and assisting in decision making and planning.[5]

ESTABLISHING A WORKING ALLIANCE

Creating a relationship based on trust, confidence, and fellow-feeling was the primary goal described by therapists, clergy, and lawyers alike. This is a difficult task for members of all three groups, albeit for different reasons. We have previously reviewed the problems often encountered by lawyers. In one important respect, the relationship between therapist or clergyman and client is even more problematical than that between lawyer and client: while lawyers are likely to be partisans in the marital conflict, therapists and clergy are likely to aspire to the role of mediator. The distinction is significant for establishing a working alliance, particularly with regard to confidentiality and impartiality.

Confidentiality. The traditional cornerstone of a trusting professional-client relationship is that of confidentiality. A central role of any media-

5. In this section we have largely treated lawyers as a homogeneous group rather than detailing specific strategies associated with the different stances described earlier. There was not sufficient material to make such an effort consistently feasible. The connection between lawyer stance and the preferred (and actual) behavior of lawyers is an important topic for future research.

tor, however, is to open lines of communication and reduce secretiveness. The preferred means to achieve this are alternate separate and joint meetings with the parties. From the perspective of the clients, however, what trust can be placed in a person who, in separate meetings with one's spouse, may reveal one's most secret plans and thoughts?

A solution to this dilemma appears to be the invocation by therapists and clergy of what might be called *conditional confidentiality*, in which clients are told that an important skill of the counselor is knowing what information needs to be relayed from one party to the other, and that the counselor will at all times be bound by the wishes of either party to be silent on issues they do not want discussed with their spouse. However strategic conditional confidentiality may be, it is clearly a position that makes much higher demands on the counselor's tact and diplomatic skills than does the lawyer's unequivocal confidentiality.

Impartiality. The lawyer's primary allegiance is to his client. For therapists and clergy, maintaining impartiality is the central task of establishing a working alliance. Impartiality is easier talked about, though, than achieved. Important aspects of the situation mitigate against its attainment, including the two parties' emotional turmoil, the conjoint counseling situation which may further heighten tensions, the strong counter-transference reactions that marital conflicts may trigger, and the activist stance favored by all the respondents. For the clergy, and for Catholic priests especially, impartiality is further complicated by their anti-divorce sentiments.

Respondents described a variety of tactics by which they endeavor to maintain their impartiality. Among the more prominent of these we may include: an explicit statement of their impartial role to the clients; inviting feedback from clients so that client misapprehensions of bias may be corrected; the use of co-therapists as a check on therapist perception of the conflict; and a thorough understanding of counter-transference phenomena and one's own motivations for intervention.

DIAGNOSIS

The preferred diagnostic strategies were tactful and imaginative questioning, patient listening, and consultation with the client's friends or relatives, or other professionals. The conjoint counseling situation favored by therapists and clergy is an important source of information about the couple's interaction. Clergy may also benefit from a prior relationship with the couple and their previous knowledge of the marital history (they may be handicapped, though, by their clerical status insofar as clients are inhibited from speaking about matters for which they anticipate censure).

One central diagnostic issue concerns all three groups equally: Is this marriage truly headed for divorce? The criteria that were mentioned as signs of imminent divorce included: high levels of physical and/or emotional abuse of spouse or children; mutual and repeated collusion of the spouses in sabotaging efforts at reconciliation; denial by one or both spouse that there are serious marital problems, in spite of obvious evidence to the contrary; a deeply neurotic, unrealistic basis for the initial marital attraction; and an unequivocal decision by one spouse to end the marriage (the diagnostic trick being in the determination of "unequivocal").

Diagnosing the fate of the marriage is not easy. The primary difficulty is the psychology of divorce which makes divorcing individuals extremely unreliable about the true state of the marriage and their own intentions. Moreover, for therapists and clergy the motivation to formulate and refine diagnostic criteria is low. For practical, ethical, and psychological reasons the decision must be made by the client, with a minimal amount of intrusion. In addition, clergy are fundamentally conservative on the entire topic of divorce. They are ready to assist if divorce is inevitable, but their primary allegiance is to marital stability.[6]

The lawyers' perspective on the diagnostic issue is another illustration of the role strain that generally characterizes their position. On the one hand, lawyers have a much higher stake in accurately determining whether the client is serious about divorce than do either therapists or clergy. Legal services, apart from an initial consultation, are only needed if the client requires a separation agreement or divorce. Further, the lawyer may feel a strong obligation to refrain from initiating a divorce action if reconciliation is at all possible. Finally, an ambivalent client is a poor risk to endure the rigors of hard bargaining that may be necessary in the event of divorce.

On the other hand, lawyers are in a much poorer position than either therapists or clergy to interest themselves or to thoroughly accomplish a diagnosis. First, their view of the marital situation is foreshortened in time, and by having access to only one spouse; second, psychological understanding is a time consuming job, for which they have no official role sanction and for which they are not being paid; and third, and most important, lawyers are poorly equipped by training, and often by personal inclination, to engage in such diagnosis.

The net result of these counter pressures is that different lawyers adopt very different views of their responsibilities toward assisting in diagnosing the fate of the marriage. The position taken is yet another facet of lawyer stance. None of these positions, however, appears based on any systematic or sophisticated notions of what to look for in a marriage on the brink of termination.

---

6. Formal psychometric approaches to marital and family dynamics are poorly developed. The most reliable and valid tests are global measures of marital adjustment based on self-reports. With one exception (Ravich, 1972) performance tests of divorce proneness are unknown to us.

Lawyers who gravitated toward the Undertaker, Mechanic, or Mediator stances generally indicated that they explored the possibilities for reconciliation in a rather perfunctory way, simply advising the client of the importance of being sure about wanting a divorce before starting proceedings. Some Mediators may advise speaking with a psychotherapist.

Attorneys with a Social Worker stance tended to initiate an exploration of reconciliation by injecting a note of caution that divorce is not a panacea for marital unhappiness. For lawyers with a Therapist stance, involvement in reconciliation seemed to be an aspect of the overall orientation toward trying to understand the client's motivation, while for Moral Agents it appeared to derive from a philosophy that the welfare of children is generally best served by marital stability.

IMPROVING THE EMOTIONAL CLIMATE

The emotionally volatile atmosphere of many divorces represents a major obstacle to effective intervention. The task of the professional is to channel this reactivity so that it does not disrupt the decision-making process or, indeed, the counseling relationship itself. Although guilt and depression can create problems, the respondents gave foremost attention to the need to contain excessive anger and revenge-seeking.

Shared tactics. Several tactics were common to therapists, clergy, and lawyers. Among the most important of these were explicit statements of norms of equity and fair play; appeals to self-interest (e.g., "in the long run a court fight will cost you more than a negotiated compromise"); reiteration of the potential harm that can be inflicted on children by endless legal and psychological warfare; introduction of a future oriented perspective for regarding present pain as temporary; and the countering of well-meaning, but destructive influences of relatives, lovers, and friends.

Tactics of lawyers. Common tactics notwithstanding, the interviews with lawyers reflect a somewhat narrower orientation to the goal of reducing tensions than those with therapists or clergy. Lawyers' preferred tactics include reminders that the lawyer's job is to be objective and rational, not to deal with emotional problems (the "I'm not a psychiatrist" disclaimer); disabusing inflamed clients of the notion that the law permits them to punish their spouses for real or imagined hurts; and stern warnings about the legal repercussions of threats, emotional abuse, or physical attacks on the spouses. As a last resort, the lawyer may simply threaten to withdraw from the case.

Tactics of therapists and clergy. Therapists and clergymen spoke of efforts to improve the climate by making suggestions to resolve seemingly superficial, but nonetheless irritating disagreements; applauding friendly gestures and intervening when such gestures are missed or misinterpreted; and shifting the focus from blaming the other to understanding the self. Perhaps nothing marks more distinctly the difference between lawyers, on the one hand, and therapists and clergy, on the other, than this commitment to self-understanding as an instrument of conflict resolution. For therapists in particular, anger was conceptualized as but a symptom of painful, if unacknowledged, feelings of loss, self-depreciation, and fear of the future. The most effective cure for such reactive anger is not exhortations to rationality and self-control, but the identification and examination of the underlying emotional issues.

Numerous structural tactics were also described by therapists, and, to a lesser degree, by the clergy. Among the interventions mentioned were creating "cooling off" distances between the parties by arranging separate counseling sessions or suggesting changed living arrangements; using co-therapy to foster effective male-female negotiating styles, or couples groups to socially inhibit the more extreme forms of name-calling; and even insisting on payment in advance as a means of insuring commitment to treatment.

The greater variety of tactics of therapists and clergy, as contrasted with lawyers, stems in part from differences in the nature of professional training (particularly between lawyers and therapists). Another basic force producing more diversified strategies of intervention among the therapists and clergy appears to be the structural and psychological opportunities of the mediator role as opposed to that of the advocate. As mediators, therapists and clergymen are more often at the center of the communications network connecting the spouses and thus are psychologically committed to serving both partners. The lawyer's role is structurally more peripheral—he has direct access to only one spouse—and his inclination to serve both sides would be seen as idiosyncratic and, in the eyes of his profession, an ethically questionable choice.

DECISION MAKING AND PLANNING

The establishment of a working alliance, diagnosis, and the reduction of emotional tensions are but preliminary to assistance in decision making and planning. It is in this area that the perspectives of therapists, clergy, and lawyers most clearly differed.

The therapists. As detailed by our respondents, therapeutic intervention has two distinct foci: to help the clients make the difficult decision to divorce or stay married, and to smooth the path of marital dissolution if the decision is to divorce.

Decision-making interventions were described as essentially educative. Education occurs in two areas: promoting understanding about current dysfunctional interaction and the role of each spouse in such exchanges; and explicating the historical roots of the marital difficulties in terms of each spouse's own psychological development. By making these matters conscious, the parties will be able to make an informed decision about the fate of the marriage. If they do decide to divorce, they will have learned lessons about themselves that will help them after the divorce. In particular, they will be less vulnerable to the "same mistake twice" syndrome—another unhappy marriage.

The strategy which most clearly differentiates divorce therapy from marital or family therapy is what we have labelled *orchestrating the motivation to divorce* (Kressel and Deutsch, 1977). This strategy rests on the fundamental assumption that a constructive divorce process is unlikely if both partners are not equally ready to end the marriage—and in our respondents' clinical practice non-mutual readiness to divorce is the common situation. Thus, once it becomes apparent to the therapist that one partner has made an irrevocable decision to divorce, the task becomes one of motivating the noninitiator to adopt a similar view and to stick to it whenever the stresses of separation threaten to produce unrealistic efforts at reconciliation.

The tactics for orchestrating the motivation to divorce are many and complex. They may include countering feelings of failure and self-disparagement; assisting in the development of skills needed in the post-divorce period; openly arguing for the advantages of the divorce as opposed to continuing marital unhappiness; enlisting family and friends as allies in providing emotional support; and suggesting "trial" physical separations to ease the transition into single life.

A critical area of disagreement among the therapists was whether or not they should play any significant role in assisting the parties with the negotiation of separation agreements or divorces. Five of the respondents ruled out such a function. The 15 remaining respondents, while stressing the psychodynamic aspects of their role, acknowledged that there is a place for helping couples negotiate terms of settlement. Only three of them, however, discussed such assistance in any detail or expressed any enthusiasm for the role.

The most frequently discussed tactics involving negotiations included reducing tensions to a level that permits rational discussion; suggesting an agenda; making suggestions for compromise; serving as a go-between in the client/lawyer relationship (e.g., by keeping the lawyer informed of the client's psychological conflicts or by building up clients' self-esteem so that they can better participate in negotiations), and finally making the parties "face reality." This latter tactic is central because of the emotional turmoil which temporarily distorts clients' objectivity, and also because the economic, psychological, and legal forces are of a complexity and novelty for which many divorcing couples are unpre-pared. As a corrective to wishful thinking, the therapist may remind the client of "realities" of such diverse kinds as the net assets available for division, the motives of the spouse, and the future needs of self and children.

The clergy. In many respects the interviews with clergy reveal a pattern of activities in decision making and planning very similar to that described by therapists. Three salient differences may be noted:

1. *An emphasis on the concrete and practical.* Perhaps as a reflection of the traditional paternal aspect of the clerical role, two clergymen emphasized the importance of providing immediate concrete assistance in the form of financial help (either through church funds or referral to social welfare agencies), referral to lawyers or psychotherapists, and a general effort to assist clients with the formulation of practical plans. For the most part, the clergy did not view long-term help in dealing with underlying psychological conflicts as part of their role.

2. *Accomplishing the religious divorce or annulment.* Judaism and Roman Catholicism are the two religions represented in our sample that have highly formalized divorce/annulment procedures. For the rabbis and the Catholic priests, involvement in such procedures is the most distinctive and difficult aspect of their role in divorce. The difficulties arise from several sources: the fact that initiative for the religious divorce generally comes from only one spouse; the emotional climate between the partners, which may have deteriorated as a consequence of the secular divorce settlement; and the absence of secularly enforceable sanctions for non-compliance with the religious procedures. Moreover, in the religious proceedings the clergyman functions more as an advocate of one or the other spouse, and hence may have lost to a considerable extent whatever strategic leverage the mediator role affords. (We have discussed elsewhere the somewhat different strategic problems facing priests and rabbis; Weinglass, Kressel, and Deutsch, 1978.)

3. *A heightened concern with post-divorce adjustment.* The most organized efforts to cope with the post-divorce period were described by priests and lay respondents working in centers for divorced Catholics. The services of such centers were viewed as a form of crisis intervention, similar to the model established by Alcoholics Anonymous. Parishioners undergoing a traumatic experience are provided with a reference group of similar others, frequent social contacts, and a religious community that accepts them. The services provided by the Center may include a limited amount of individual counseling, group activities for children, religious group rituals, and workshops on special problems (e.g., dating, sex, or relationships with family).

Because divorce is such a critical experience, an individual's religious affiliations are more likely to be maintained and even strengthened when the experience is conceptualized within a religious framework. Thus, clergy may reassure clients regarding their standing in the religious community and encourage them to maintain religious ties. At a deeper level, clients may be encouraged to see their emotional suffering and personal doubts as a potential source of religious and moral renewal.

The lawyers. A major task of the matrimonial lawyer is advice about the negotiation of substantive issues. Our respondents occasionally referred to such substantively oriented interventions as educating the client to the law and the philosophy of the courts; assistance in framing and narrowing the issues; eliciting information about the marital relationship and the material assets to be divided; and the importance of knowing the law thoroughly so that the most advantageous bargain may be struck. On the whole, however, they did not tell us much about this aspect of their work. This may be attributable to our own failure to probe in areas in which we were uninformed, combined with the respondents' implicit assumption that the technical side of the law would be of little interest to psychologists. It may also reflect the role strain issue and the respondents' corresponding desire to articulate matters of general orientation and philosophy rather than the more mundane aspects of working out a settlement.

Some Comments on the Present and Future of Professional Assistance to the Divorcing

It is a common theme both within and outside the legal profession that, in divorce, the adversary system creates more problems than it solves. This was the position of nearly all the therapists and clergy with whom we spoke and several of the lawyers as well. Our analysis of role strain among the lawyers suggests, however, that the problem goes beyond the adversary system per se. For one thing, we have argued that one product of role strain is the development of a variety of lawyer coping styles or stances. Consequently, in any given divorce there is a high probability that the defects of the adversary system will be exacerbated by the pairing of two attorneys with very different objectives.

Furthermore, the lawyer's role contains nearly as much potential for conflict between self and client as between self and the "opposing" side. Strains in the lawyer-client relationship derive from a variety of factors, including the lawyer's lack of psychological training and the economic circumstances in which the lawyer-client relationship is embedded, not the least of which is that the lawyer is the one who communicates the unhappy economic aspects of the divorce.

The available empirical evidence suggests that both the quality of divorce settlements and the degree to which spouses keep their agreements is low. (For empirical data on the mediocre quality of divorce settlements, see Cavanagh and Rhode, 1976; for evidence on how poorly visitation agreements are kept, see Hetherington, Cox, and Cox, 1977; for the extremely low compliance with child support agreements, Goode, 1956; Jones, Gordon, and Sawhill, 1976.) Clearly, there are numerous possible explanations for this unhappy state of affairs. Moreover, in spite of the weaknesses of the adversary system, there are no controlled studies which compare it with any alternative. Nonetheless, the data support the hypothesis that a primary contributor to post-divorce difficulties is the poor conditions under which divorce negotiations are conducted. In our view, the divorce lawyer is as much a victim of these conditions as their cause.

An Alternative: Divorce Mediation

If the lawyer-run adversary system is not working, though, what is to replace it? Perhaps the most likely alternative is some form of mediation, akin to that employed in labor-management disputes, in which divorcing spouses would negotiate directly with one another with the help of a trained third party (or parties). Ideas of this type were suggested by three of the respondents, two of whom were lawyers. We believe that there is much merit in the approach. Among the possible advantages of having the parties negotiate directly with each other we may include: a better opportunity for their needs to emerge and be accommodated during negotiations; an increase in their sense of competence and mastery; the development of skills in dealing with one another which will be of value in the post-divorce period; the creation of a greater sense of "ownership" of the agreement and hence an increased probability of adherence to it; and an appreciable reduction in legal fees.

It would be naïve, however, to ignore the fact that there are problematic aspects to the mediator role, just as there are to that of the advocate. We have already noted that establishing a working alliance—the prerequisite for effective intervention—is at least as difficult for therapists or clergy acting as mediators as it is for lawyers. Additional light on the advantages of mediation, as well as the challenges, may be shed by a brief discussion of our own most recent research on the process of "Structured Mediation." The primary purpose of this research has been to clarify the principal emotional and interpersonal issues arising in face-to-face divorce negotiations. Data analysis is currently in progress, but certain issues are sufficiently clear to warrant preliminary presentation.

THE RESEARCH PROJECT ON STRUCTURED MEDIATION

Structured Mediation, developed by O. J. Coogler, a lawyer and psychotherapist, is, to our knowledge, the only well-developed and conceptualized mediation approach to divorce negotiations. The process involves divorcing parties in direct negotiations. They are assisted by a mediator (or mediators). An advisory attorney, serving both parties, is available for legal consultation. Written rules of mediation, agreed to by both spouses prior to negotiations, spell out the mediation procedure and the obligations of the mediator, advisory attorney, and the Family Mediation Association (FMA) which administers the program. Since its inception two and a half years ago, the Association has assisted more than 100 Atlanta area couples to arrive at divorce settlements. It has received an interested, if cautious, reception from various legal groups around the country. (More details on Structured Mediation may be found in Coogler, Weber, and McKenry, in press.)

Our investigation consisted of an intensive analysis of nine completed cases. The cases were chosen to represent negotiations of some complexity. All couples were white, middle- to upper-middle-class, and had dependent children. The analyses were based on tape recordings of mediation sessions made by the Association, and two-and-a-half- to four-hour interviews with each of the ex-spouses, three months to a year after the completion of mediation and the obtaining of a divorce. The interviews, conducted by our research team, focused on the mediation experience, post-divorce adjustment, and feelings about the terms of settlement.[7]

THE BENEFITS OF MEDIATION

In the post-divorce interviews, five of the nine couples were generally enthusiastic about mediation. They felt, among other things, that the mediator had made useful suggestions for compromise, kept them issue oriented when anger threatened to become disruptive, reassured them by remaining calm in the face of their own or the spouse's provocation, and left them with a sense of having achieved a settlement that was truly their own.

In two couples the spouses disagreed about the value of mediation, and in two others both spouses regarded the experience as unsatisfactory. The principal complaints were lack of adequate guidance on substantive matters, suspicions of mediator bias, and the belief that the settlement now appeared unfair.

7. We would like to express our thanks to O. J. Coogler for permitting us access to the tapes of mediation sessions and for the cooperative and open spirit with which he has greeted our close scrutiny of his pioneering efforts.

The value of the mediation process is illustrated by the case of Mr. and Mrs. Smith:

Mr. and Mrs. Smith came to the Family Mediation Association with an agreement they had worked out with a lawyer, but had not yet signed. Mrs. Smith had taken this agreement to a lawyer of her own choosing in order to make sure that the agreement was fair. This lawyer had torn the agreement apart, warning Mrs. Smith that her interests were being violated in nearly every clause. Frightened, Mrs. Smith had refused to sign. At this point, Mr. Smith, who had heard about the FMA from a colleague, told Mrs. Smith that it was either going to be resolved through mediation or "he would see her in court."

The Smiths presented their original agreement to the FMA with hopes that it would be examined by an objective party and quickly validated or modified. This, however, did not happen. The agreement, while ultimately not changed in many significant respects, was redone. In the process, some things were added and others were spelled out in greater detail.

From the tapes of the mediation, it appeared that this renegotiation was a constant source of irritation to Mr. Smith, who sounded restless and impatient. Indeed, in the post-divorce interview, Mr. Smith admitted that he had felt great frustration with the process of mediation. However, when asked whether he had any negative experiences during mediation that he later thought had been worthwhile, he admitted that it was precisely the time consuming renegotiation that he now regarded favorably. He was quite convinced that this process had been responsible for producing a much more complete, viable agreement, and that it had made the post-divorce adjustment easier for both of them.

THE DIFFICULTIES OF MEDIATION

The tapes of mediation sessions also bear eloquent testimony to the difficult task faced by the mediator. Among the major problems were the emotional ambivalence and reactivity of the parties and their ignorance on matters of bargaining substance and procedure.

Emotional reactivity. Anger, humiliation, grief, jealousy, and guilt are among the powerful emotions that may have adverse effects on the negotiation process:

Mrs. K. initiated the divorce. Dr. K. claimed repeatedly during mediation that he loved his wife and children very much and did not want the divorce. On the other hand, he was often openly angry and bitter at having been "deserted" by his wife. Mrs. K. was consumed by guilt at ending the marriage. The effect of these conflicting emotions was apparent in the negotiations over division of marital assets, during which Mrs. K. said nothing in her own behalf, and simply acquiesced to her husband's offer to take 25 percent of their $83,000 in assets, although at the time she had no job and the custody of three young children.

Negotiating ignorance. In divorce the negotiating naïveté of the parties is virtually guaranteed. In addition, in nearly all of the cases both spouses were ignorant about basic details of family finances. This ignorance had at least two major consequences for the mediator: in the first instance, the absence of sound information on financial affairs made the search for compromises extremely difficult. Secondly, the mediator spent much time trying to educate the parties about principles of money management in the midst of negotiations, a time when emotional turmoil created strong obstacles to comprehension. Moreover, although husbands were frequently poorly informed, they were paragons of financial expertise in comparison to their wives. Husbands had almost exclusive control of important financial documents and were aware of financial arrangements of which their wives were ignorant. The wife's ignorance combined with her heightened anxiety about her poor post-divorce prospects created strong pressures on the mediator to shore up the wife's side of negotiations:

Mrs. W. had dropped out of college to send her husband through dental school. She was to have custody of their three children and was clearly anxious about how she would manage after the divorce. She was highly suspicious of her husband's reporting of his financial assets during mediation, but also found it difficult to ask informed questions or to follow explanations involving tax and business terminology. She relied increasingly on the mediator to explain matters to her ("What's depreciation?"). Dr. W. acquiesced verbally to repeated requests from the mediator to provide documentation of his assertions as to what he could and could not afford in child support and alimony, but continually failed to provide such information. An adversarial stance gradually developed between Dr. W. and the mediator.

THE FUTURE OF DIVORCE MEDIATION

There are, of course, possible solutions to the problems created by emotional reactivity and negotiating ignorance. Diagnostic intake procedures, individual counseling coordinated with joint bargaining sessions, and pre-negotiation training on the art of bargaining are all possible modifications in Structured Mediation that we have begun to explore as our research enters the stage of systematic clinical implementation and evaluation.

There are also important legal and substantive issues. How can the parties best be provided with the tax, insurance, health care, and other practical information that they need? Is a single advisory attorney sufficient guarantee to each spouse that the agreements reached are equitable and workable? Here too there are possible solutions in the form of expert panels available on some sort of consultative basis.

As one begins to formulate these basic issues of divorce mediation, it becomes clear that its value cannot be determined simply by asking whether "it works" or if "it is better" than the adversary system. This is like asking, "Is psychotherapy good?" It would probably be more useful to ask, "What modes of dispute resolution are likely to be most effective for which types of divorcing couples under what circumstances?"

Structured Mediation remains a promising alternative to the adversary process in divorce. While devising and evaluating alternatives to the adversary system is an important and overdue task, the search for such alternatives must be based on the recognition that every mode of intervention, adversarial or not, is likely to be appropriate under certain conditions and not in others.

PART V

Consequences for Families and Children

THE MAJORITY of American divorces now involve minor children. And a growing proportion of children are finding their parents separating. What is the magnitude of this problem? How does it affect those children? How is child custody determined? And how can children's interests be served best in arranging for their custody during and after the separation process? Each of the following chapters examines a different facet of this set of questions.

The first selection, by Mary Jo Bane, draws on U.S. census statistics and special surveys in order to analyze the magnitude of marital disruption and its impact on children. While the proportion of American children experiencing a parental divorce has increased steadily since 1900, the proportion experiencing the death of a parent decreased until recently by an even larger margin. Thus Bane indicates that children born in the 1901–1910 decade were actually more likely to experience some form of marital disruption before age 18 than were children born in 1951–1960. While the parental death rate is probably stable now, the divorce rate is not; thus considerably more of today's and tomorrow's children (Bane estimates around 40 percent) are likely to experience the breakup of their parents' marriage.

Bane analyzes various consequences of the pattern. She focuses particularly on the economic problems of the single-mother family. The serious income drop for women who leave their marriages leads her to propose income support policies to assist such families. With the increasing numbers of children affected by marital disruption, such ideas may find an increasing public response.

To complement Bane's demographic and economic projections of marital disruption, the next chapter, by Cynthia Longfellow, assesses its psychological impact on children. She begins by noting that the meaning of divorce differs greatly, depending on its familial context and on the child's age. Therefore, she analyzes the important "intermediary links" which tend to condition its effects on children.

Divorce, it is sometimes asserted, affects children because it changes the family structure. Longfellow reminds us that we must inquire about the nature of the change. Mere father absence, for example, may have its most direct impact on the mother and only indirectly affects the child's circumstances. Similarly, the mere fact of single motherhood may be less important than the mother's economic and emotional circumstances, which in turn affect her treatment of the children. Altogether, it seems to be the quality of mother-father and of parent-child interaction that most influences the child's experience. Thus it has been noted that children's adjustment is worse in a conflicted, intact home than in a harmonious separated family.

Longfellow also examines the child's age as an important variable that affects the child's understanding of events surrounding marital separation. She uses a "social-cognitive" analysis of the levels of childhood comprehension to reinterpret previous data on the ways children react to their parents' separation. Both those data and her analysis suggest that younger children are more adversely affected than older children.

The remaining two chapters are concerned with parental custody of children: who gets it, who should get it, and for what reason? How shall it be decided with whom children shall live and how much contact they shall have with either parent?

The mother currently becomes the custodian in over 90 percent of all American divorces (Weiss, chapter 19). That tendency developed during the past 100 years; it appears associated with American males' progressive withdrawal from taking an active father role. Kelin Gersick examines instances from the small minority of cases where fathers actively sought and legally received the custody of their minor children. In chapter 18, he compares the personal and marital characteristics of a group of men who got child custody with those of another group of men who did not.

Gersick finds some significant differences between the custody and the non-custody samples. Fathers who received custody tended to be somewhat older, somewhat longer married, and somewhat higher in socioeconomic status. The custodial fathers were significantly more likely to have been middle or later-born children and to have *both* brothers and sisters in their family of origin; they also were judged to have had a closer relationship with their own mothers than did the non-custodial fathers. The two groups did not differ in how active they had been in their pre-divorce child rearing; nor were there noticeable differences in their scores on a test of sex-role orientation. Important differences, though, pertained to the manner of their marital breakup: fathers were more likely both to seek and to receive custody if their wives had been either extra-maritally involved or "incapacitated" before the divorce than if their breakup was explained in terms of either the "incompatibility" or the immaturity of their marriage. Gersick points out that single-parent fathers have many of the same problems as single-parent mothers: problems concerning finances, child care, lack of social life, and apprehension about the other parent's visitation.

In the midst of the parents' struggle, the interests of the child are frequently neglected. The final chapter, by Robert Weiss, is concerned with precisely that issue. He addresses himself to the legal and paralegal problems of adjudicating child custody. Weiss reviews the changing meaning of the "Best Interest of the Child" doctrine, whether and how one can consider "parental fault," and the degree to which children can and should be consulted as to which parent they want to take care of them.

Studies cited by Weiss suggest that being able to stay in touch with both parents is preferable for children. In general, visits with the "other" parent appear to be beneficial. In making his recommendations, Weiss argues persuasively for a certain degree of shared custody and for the child's access to both parents. He also argues that custody decisions should encourage rather than discourage both parents' future supportiveness of each other's parental efforts.

Despite their diversity, the chapters in Part V all shed new light on important consequences of divorce for families. Each selection subjects a piece of this topic to critical analysis, each reflects on current American social norms; each therefore pertains to future public policy. While the problems faced by broken families will continue to remain difficult, such informed analyses will help to enlighten our awareness of the complexities of their circumstances and of potential solutions.

Marital Disruption and the Lives of Children

Rising divorce rates and increasing numbers of single-parent families raise legitimate public concern for the children involved in marital disruptions. Proposed divorce reform laws, for example, contain explicit and detailed provisions on the custody and support of children (Uniform Marriage and Divorce Act, 1970). Welfare programs, both existing and proposed, also focus on children; the labels "Aid to Families with Dependent Children" and "Family Assistance Plan" reflect public priorities quite clearly. With even more attention likely to be directed to divorce and welfare reform in the next few years, it becomes important to know how many children are affected by marital disruption and how the experience affects them.

This chapter was written at the Center for the Study of Public Policy, Cambridge, Massachusetts, supported by a grant from the Carnegie Corporation of New York. The computer programming was done by Peter Mueser, who also offered extremely helpful comments and suggestions on the analyses and interpretations. Gail Howrigan reviewed and called to my attention the psychological literature on single-parent families, and commented on other sections as well. For reading and commenting on an earlier draft I am grateful to Mary Corcoran, Christopher Jencks, Michael R. Olneck, Robert Weiss, and Kenneth I. Winston.

A previous version of this chapter appeared in *Journal of Social Issues*, 1976, 32 (1).

Numbers of Children Affected

Marital disruption occurs when married adults separate, divorce, or die. If the adults have children, a family remains after the disruption—a family that must settle into a new structure. This may involve setting up a new household of one parent and children, moving in with relatives, or sending the children to live somewhere else. Eventually the family structure changes again. The children may grow up and leave home. If the parents were separated, they may reconcile. If they were divorced or widowed, the parent with whom the children are living may remarry, or the other parent may remarry and the children move in with the new family. After a disruption, children most commonly live with their mother and siblings in a separate household, but other arrangements are not unheard of. The amount of time spent in the single-parent situation can vary widely.

The process of disruption and restructuring is thus complex and highly variable. Ideally, statistics would be available to describe the entire process in all its diversity: incidence, duration, and resolution. The most important pieces of information for public policy, however, are two: the number of children affected by disruption at any time during their childhood years and the amount of time children spend in single-parent homes. The first statistic tells how many different children might be affected by policy or need services; the second indicates the length of time services to single-parent families might have to be provided. Various sources of data can be used to estimate these two pieces of information.

SHORTCOMINGS OF EXISTING DATA

Information on the total number of children affected by marital disruption and on the duration of the disruption is not readily available from published sources. The Census Bureau publishes statistics from the decennial census and the annual Current Population Surveys on the number of children living in various kinds of arrangements at the time of the surveys. These surveys show that the proportion of children under 18 living with both parents has declined from 85.0 percent in 1968 to 80.0 percent in 1976. Of those not living with both parents in 1968, 10.7 percent lived with their mothers, 1.1 percent with their fathers, and 3.2 percent with neither parent. In 1976, the proportion living with their mothers was up to 15.8 percent, the proportion with fathers was up only slightly to 1.2 percent, and the proportion with neither parent was down to 3.0 percent (U.S. Bureau of the Census, 1969, 1977a). The annual Current Population Survey does not include children (or anyone else) in institutions. The decennial census, which does collect such data, reported that 0.4 percent of children under 18 in 1970 were living in institutions (U.S. Bureau of the Census, 1973b).

One problem with these numbers is that they are "net" numbers—added to by children who come into the single-parent state in a given year and subtracted from by children who turn 18 or whose parents reconcile or remarry. The static numbers might be concealing extensive annual turnover—for example, that all children are involved in at least one year-long disruption and some are involved two or three times—or they might be concealing very little annual turnover. The numbers give no hint of what the underlying process actually is.

PROCEDURES

To obtain better data on the number of children affected by disruption and the length of time spent in disrupted family states, I have relied on a survey conducted by the U.S. Bureau of the Census (1971) that collected data not only on current living arrangements but also on marital history. The Survey of Economic Opportunity (SEO), conducted in 1967, surveyed a stratified random sample of approximately 26,500 households. The survey collected a wide variety of information on social, economic, and background characteristics of the households and has been extensively analyzed by sociologists and economists. It also collected information on the marital history and birth dates of children for all the women in the sample households. This information can be used to estimate the incidence and duration of marital disruptions which affected the children of the sample women.

The SEO is the major source of estimates in this article. The SEO does not, however, include all the relevant pieces of information—for example, no information is available on the death of mothers. Nor is it completely up to date. I will therefore use other sources of data to supplement the SEO in making estimates of the number of children now being affected by disruption.

INCIDENCE AND DURATION OF MARITAL DISRUPTION

The SEO gathered information on 20,989 women who had borne children. The marital history data on these women reveals that they had experienced a good deal of marital disruption. Many of the older women, of course, had been widowed—60.6 percent of those born before 1900. Widowhood among younger women was less common; for example, 6.5 percent of the women born between 1921 and 1930 had been widowed by 1967. About 15 percent of the entire sample of women had been divorced. The proportion varied by age, and was highest (16.6 percent) among women born 1911–1920. Most of the divorced women and many of the widowed women remarried. Of women born 1901–1910, 21.2 percent had been married more than once, as had 19.2 percent of those born 1911–1920, 16.1 percent of those born 1921–1930, and 12.3 percent of those born 1931–1940. The younger women, of course, had lived fewer years in which to be divorced, widowed, or remarried.

The data can be used to make a very rough estimate of the number of women involved in long-term separations. These separations can be considered as substitutes for divorces, the recourse for those who, for financial, religious, or other reasons, do not get a legal divorce. My estimates—based on the SEO duration data, divorce data for 1967–1972, and the reported durations of predivorce separations (NCHS, 1973)—suggest that between 2 and 3 percent of all women experience such long-term separations. There is no indication that the proportion has gone up or down over the century.

Table 16-1 summarizes the extent to which marital disruptions affected the children of the women in the sample. It shows the proportion of children in the sample whose parents had died (Rows 1 and 2), divorced (Row 3), separated (Row 4), or never married (Row 6). It also shows the duration of the disruption as it affected the children (Row 8): the number of years between either the disruption and the remarriage of the mother, or the disruption and the child's eighteenth birthday.

Over the entire century the proportion of children affected by disruption has been large—between 25 and 30 percent (Row 7, Table 16-1).

TABLE 16-1
Children Involved in Marital Disruption before Age 18
(Percentages)

	Disruption	Children Born					
		1901-1910	1911-1920	1921-1930	1931-1940	1941-1950	1951-1960[a]
(1)	by death of father	11.9	11.7	9.2	8.5	6.4	5.4
(2)	by death of mother	10.7	10.5	7.4	6.0	3.8	3.2
(3)	by divorce	5.2	4.9	7.0	9.8	9.2	10.5
(4)	by long term separation	0.7	0.6	0.9	1.4	1.5	1.7
(5)	by "other reasons"	0.2	0.8	0.6	0.9	2.1	2.4
(6)	parents never married	0.2	1.3	1.6	1.8	1.8	1.5
(7)	total, all causes	28.9	29.8	26.7	28.4	24.8	24.7
(8)	mean duration of disruption (years)	6.35	5.49	6.23	5.57	5.15	5.2
	Number in sample	885	2914	5455	6848	11,388	14,592

Note. Row 2 estimated by adjusting Row 1, death of father, for the ratio of female to male death rates for adults aged 25-64 in 1915, 1925, 1935, 1945, 1955, and 1965 (calculated from Grave & Hertzel, 1968). Row 4 estimated by adjusting Row 3 by the ratio of the proportion of women affected by long term separation to the proportion of women affected by divorce. Row 8 based only on data for divorce and death of father.

[a]Extrapolations based on rates by age group in earlier cohort.

Disruption in the earlier cohorts is probably underestimated, since younger and healthier mothers of these cohorts of children would have a better chance of appearing in a 1967 survey and would also have a better chance of a stable marriage during their children's youth. Thus it seems quite certain that the proportion of children affected by disruption declined somewhat from the 1900s to the 1950s. This reflects both falling death rates and smaller families, in which children are more often born to younger parents. The ratio of disruption by divorce to disruption by death has increased considerably; among those born 1941–1950 divorce affected more children than death. As the effects of rising divorce rates overcome the effects of falling death rates, the total proportion of children affected may begin to rise.

The average marital disruption affecting children lasted between five and six years, a figure which also seems to have fallen over the century, though not dramatically. The changing ratio of divorce to death may have produced this change. Divorce tends to affect children who are younger and thus would allow more time in the disrupted state; however, divorced women remarry considerably faster than widows. The duration of disruption will probably remain between five and six years, especially if remarriage rates continue to level off (Norton and Glick, 1976).

Supplementary data on divorce. The extent to which rising divorce rates will overcome falling death rates can be investigated further. The NCHS publishes data on the number of divorces granted each year and estimates the number of children involved in divorces granted, based on information from 29 states which use a standard registration form. These statistics can be used to predict the proportion of children who are likely to be affected by the divorce of their parents.

The number of divorces granted in the United States went from 377,000 in 1955 to 1,090,000 in 1977 (National Center for Health Statistics, 1977b and 1978a). Table 16-2 shows the changes in the number and proportion of children involved. The proportion of divorces involving children went up until the mid-1960s and since then has remained at about 60 percent.

The mean number of children per decree also went up steadily through the early 1960s, reflecting perhaps an increased reluctance to hold unhappy marriages together "for the sake of the children." Recently though, the average has begun to fall, undoubtedly reflecting falling birth rates and smaller families. The proportion of all children under 18 involved in a divorce each year has gone steadily up from 0.6 percent of all children in 1955 to about 1.7 percent of all children in 1976. This rise is likely to continue despite fewer children per decree, since the total number of children (the denominator in the ratio) is declining as well.

These figures can be used to estimate the proportion of a given birth cohort involved in a divorce. My estimates suggest that about 14 percent of all children born in 1955 had parents divorce before their eighteenth

TABLE 16-2

Children Involved in Divorce, 1955-1975

	Percentage of Divorces Involving Children	Mean Number of Children/ Decree	Number of Children under 18 Involved in Divorce	Percentage of All Children under 18 Involved Annually in Divorce
1955	48.1	0.92	347,000	0.6
1960	56.7	1.18	463,000	0.7
1965	59.8	1.32	630,000	0.9
1970	59.9	1.22	870,000	1.3
1971	59.9	1.22	946,000	1.4
1972	60.1	1.20	1,021,000	1.5
1973	59.5	1.17	1,079,000	1.6
1974	58.0	1.12	1,099,000	1.6
1975	57.1	1.08	1,123,000	1.7
1976	57.3	1.03	1,117,000	1.7

Source: National Center for Health Statistics, 1977b, 1978b.

birthday. This figure is somewhat higher than that derived from the SEO data for the 1951–1960 birth cohort, and may reflect recent rises in the divorce rate which did not show up in the SEO.

Making predictions for children born later is difficult. One way to arrive at an estimate is to assume that the proportion of children involved each year during the next two decades will be the same as in the early 1970s, a fairly conservative assumption given rising rates. For children born during 1970 and later, the proportion involved in a divorce at some point during their childhood is about equal to the proportion involved each year multiplied by 18, assuming that most children are involved in only one divorce. Using this logic, the 1971 rate gives an estimate that 23.4 percent of the children born around 1970 will be involved in a divorce. The 1976 rate predicts 30.6 percent.

Other causes of disruption. In contrast to divorce rates, death rates have been falling over the past two decades. The death rate for males 35–44 years old, for example, was 4.3/1000 in 1950 and 3.5/1000 in 1975 (U.S. Bureau of the Census, 1977h). Illegitimacy rates, like divorce rates, have been rising. In 1950, for example, 3.9 percent of all live births were to unmarried mothers, compared to 14.2 percent in 1975 (U.S. Bureau of the Census, 1977h). Rates of long-term separation and desertion cannot be calculated, since no data are collected. Cross sectional data on the proportions of men and women who report themselves as separated suggest that long-term separations may be decreasing as divorce increases.

These changes in the relative importance of different causes of dis-

ruption are reflected in shifts in the marital statuses of female single
parents at different points in time. In 1968, of children living with female
single parents, 6.2 percent had mothers who were single, 32.3 percent
separated, 21.4 percent widowed, and 27.2 percent divorced. In 1976,
11.1 percent had mothers who were single, 31.1 percent separated, 13.2
percent widowed, and 38.9 percent divorced (13.0 percent in 1968 and
5.8 percent in 1976 had fathers absent for other reasons.) (U.S. Bureau
of the Census, 1969 and 1977a).

TOTALS

A rough estimate based on recent divorce rates is that about 30 percent
of children growing up in the 1970s will experience a parental divorce.
Another 15 to 20 percent may spend time in a single-parent family
because of death, long-term separation, or birth to an unmarried mother,
bringing the total to 45 or 50 percent.

This estimate is consistent with the proportion of children living in
single-parent families in 1976. If the average duration of disruption is
five or six years, then the number of children in single-parent families
at a given time is about a third of the number who will be in such
families over an 18-year period. Since about 17 percent of all children
were in single-parent families in 1976, 51 percent might be involved at
some point during their childhood.

The number of children likely to be affected by marital disruption is
large, larger even than earlier in the century. The durations are also substantial, implying that children in disrupted marriages will be an important part of the social landscape of the next few decades.

With such a large number of children affected by marital disruption—
and with an increasing proportion of these affected by divorce—public
attention might well be directed toward the special needs of these
children. Policy could be enlightened by an understanding of the effects
of marital disruption on children and of the ways various services might
help.

Another paper in this volume (Longfellow, chapter 17) reviews what
is known about the effects of divorce on children's psychological well-
being and illustrates the difficulty of understanding, much less intervening to solve, problems in that area. The effects of marital disruption
on economic well-being, however, are clearer, and suggest the appropriateness of public intervention.

ECONOMIC PROBLEMS

In 1975, the median family income of husband-wife families with
children (calculated using the child as the unit of analysis) was $15,534;
the median income of female-headed families with children was $5,501

(U.S. Bureau of the Census, 1977e). In 1976, 52 percent of children in female-headed families were in families with incomes below the poverty level, compared with 8.5 percent of children in male-headed (mostly husband-wife) families (U.S. Bureau of the Census, 1977g).

There are a number of reasons why women with children but without husbands find themselves in such desperate economic straits. The data suggest the following causes: loss of "economies of scale"; greater prevalence of divorce and death among poor families; low and irregular levels of alimony, child support, and public assistance; fewer adult earners; fewer opportunities for female heads of families to work; lower wages than men when they do work.

Most children in the single-parent families of the 1970s are living with one parent rather than two because of the divorce or separation of their parents. Only 13 percent in 1976 were living with a widowed mother or father; the rest presumably have two living parents. In theory, only the children of widowed parents should suffer severe economic deprivation, since only in families broken by death has the number of adults capable of earning money decreased.

The children of divorced and separated parents do, of course, lose the benefits of economies of scale in family living. These economies are not trivial. The poverty threshold for a family made up of husband, wife, and two children was set at $5,456 in 1975. The poverty threshold for that same family if the parents separated and the mother had custody would equal that for a female-headed family with two children, set at $4,307, plus that for a man living alone, set at $2,906, for a total of $7,209—about a third more than for the intact family (U.S. Bureau of the Census, 1977f). The loss of economies of scale would in itself cause the proportion of children below the poverty level in female-headed families to be approximately double that in male-headed families. But in fact, the proportion is six times greater, a much larger difference than would be expected by economies of scale alone. What accounts for the rest?

Part of the answer is that couples who divorce are likely to have had lower incomes to begin with. The greater incidence of divorce among low-income compared with high-income families is well documented (Goode, 1956; Carter and Glick, 1976; Cutright, 1971). Death rates are also related to income (Kitagawa and Hauser, 1973). Thus one would expect both men and women in disrupted marriages to be somewhat worse off than other families.

An eight-year study of income dynamics conducted at the University of Michigan (Hill and Hoffman, 1977) shows, however, that the disruption itself has an important effect on the ratio of family income to family needs. (The measure of family needs used in the study is similar to that used by the Census in setting the poverty level. The income to needs ratio is 1.00 at the poverty line, 2.00 at twice the poverty line, and so on.) Women fare much worse than men. For men who were divorced or separated between 1968 and 1975, the ratio of income to needs rose by 0.93 from 1967 to 1974 if their family size was reduced by more than one as a result of the disruption (for example, if they had children who went to live with the wife) and fell by 0.01 if family size was reduced by one. For women, the ratio of income to needs fell by 0.58 if family size was reduced by more than one (children with the husband) and fell by 0.35 if family size was reduced by one (Hill and Hoffman, 1977).

In some cases, a father's ability to support his children is stretched to the limit by his remarriage and assumption of the financial burdens of a new family. In other cases, the husband's income is simply too low to share. The median income for divorced men aged 25–64 was $10,009 in 1975, and for separated men was $7,683; many men, therefore, do not seem well enough off to do without a large proportion of their income (U.S. Bureau of the Census, 1977e).

The earning potential of female family heads is thus crucial to their families' economic well-being. One obvious and important difference between one- and two-parent families is in the number of adults able to earn money. Virtually all two-parent families with children have one adult working full time and about half have two adult earners. In contrast, many single-parent families have no earners at all. The labor force participation rates of female family heads are high: in 1977, 42.7 percent for never married mothers, 54.8 percent for separated mothers, 52.3 percent for widowed mothers, and 77.1 percent for divorced mothers. Unemployment rates, however, are also high: 30.8 percent for never married mothers, 16.5 percent for separated mothers, 8.4 percent for widowed mothers, and 9.5 percent for divorced mothers (Hayghe, 1978).

Those female family heads who did work suffered the effects of wage discrimination, occupational segregation, and lack of training. Female family heads were concentrated in low paying occupational groups: clerical workers (32.1 percent of female family heads in 1977), operatives (14.7 percent), and service and private household workers (25.2 percent) (Johnson, 1978).

INCOME SUPPORT POLICIES

Improvements in wages and work opportunities for women could ease the economic problems of female-headed families somewhat. Free public day care could help women take advantage of work opportunities, though at a very high—perhaps too high—cost (Bane, 1974). Attempts could be made to require greater contributions from the noncustody parent. But the loss of economies of scale is inherent to single-parent families, and the expense of day care, the scarcity of jobs, and the difficult circumstances of many fathers must also be faced. It would appear, in short, that single-parent families need more income than they are capable of earning or collecting, at least during the difficult periods when children are young or when the father's remarriage precedes the mother's.

A general income redistribution scheme—tax credit or negative income tax—is one solution to the economic problems of all poor families, including single-parent families (Kenniston, 1977). A scheme with a high enough base level to support no-earner or partial-earner families would, however, be enormously expensive and probably politically unacceptable (Moynihan, 1973; Jencks, 1974).

It may, therefore, be worth considering income support schemes that focus explicitly on the needs of single-parent families. Many European countries have such programs. Sweden, for example, supports single-parent families from a number of different sources. All families with children receive children's allowances and housing allowances. Widows receive pensions. Divorced and separated women receive a major part of their income in the form of a guaranteed maintenance allowance. The woman receives a standard support payment from the government regardless of her husband's ability or willingness to pay. The government assumes the responsibility of recovering the allowance, to the extent it can, from the husband (Cockburn and Helco, 1974).

A guaranteed maintenance allowance, or something like it, could dramatically improve the situation of single-parent families in the United States. It would take from women the burden of collecting alimony and child support and ensure that payments were steady and adequate. It would take most single-parent families off welfare, and if designed correctly would provide strong incentives to work. It would, of course, cost a good deal of money, but not nearly as much as a full-fledged income maintenance scheme covering everyone.

Conclusion

Guaranteed maintenance allowances for single-parent families are not the only way of meeting their needs. Other countries use other plans, and an almost infinite variety can be imagined. But some sort of income support policy is clearly needed. Two-fifths of American children born in the next decade are likely to experience a marital disruption. They are likely to live in a single-parent situation for an average of five years. During these years, their families will probably be extremely poor, suffering from the combined disadvantages of low earnings and little outside help. No matter how thrifty, resourceful, and supportive their mothers are, children cannot help being affected by family poverty. Their physical well-being ordinarily suffers and they are subjected to all the tensions and frustrations which come from not having enough money.

These economic problems ought to be the main concern of policymakers who worry about the children of marital disruption. They are real problems, and they are solvable. General programs to aid all the poor would help, and something like a guaranteed maintenance allowance for separated, divorced, and widowed mothers would be a great help. The need for such reforms is compelling.

Divorce in Context:
Its Impact on Children

Divorce and separation are affecting the lives of an ever increasing proportion of children. Bane (chapter 16) estimates that over 30 percent of the current generation of children will witness the breakup of their parents' marriages. As the ranks of such children swell, it becomes necessary to focus more sharply on the effects of divorce on children. A substantial body of research has been conducted to assess the impact of divorce on children. It has tried to demonstrate, with limited success, that divorce directly causes some harmful consequences to children, such as poor academic performance, juvenile delinquency, and confusion over sex roles (Herzog and Sudia, 1973). The findings to date are equivocal; they do not permit assertions that divorce has any single, broad-reaching impact on children. Nor should they encourage further pursuit of the question: does divorce have negative effects? Instead, our questions should be phrased to discover what it is about divorce that troubles children. Here previous research is instructive. This chapter will reexamine the literature to determine what aspects of divorce and the divorcing family's situation influence children's reactions to the event. Consideration is given first to the conventional argument that it is the father's absence which lies at the heart of children's troubles. Rejecting this oversimplified explanation, I will suggest a number of other factors which have been implicated in the child's adjustment: the life-event changes that coincide with divorce, the single mother's emotional health, and the quality of the family's interrelationships and outside support. Often overlooked is the fact that the degree to which any experience affects a child depends in part on the way it is assimilated and understood by the child. The final section of the chapter presents a cognitive developmental analysis of children's understanding of divorce. Overall, the chapter catalogues the kind of information needed to more accurately anticipate the impact of divorce on children.

The Change in Family Structure

The impact of divorce on children is most often attributed to the fact that there is a change in structure from a two-parent to a one-parent family. Departure of one parent is indeed a salient aspect of divorce and is an obvious starting point for the search for effects of divorce on children. Since in over 90 percent of the cases, the father leaves and the mother remains, it is this situation that will be considered. Much of the research has emphasized that it is the loss or the absence of the father which is directly detrimental to the child's healthy social and cognitive development. Some of the limitations to such a line of reasoning will be demonstrated in the section that follows. More recently, research on divorce has approached the issue of the absent father from a different perspective, emphasizing the reorganization process that is an inevitable result of the family's structural change. In this context, the departure of the father is seen as just one of a number of events to which the child must adjust.

EFFECTS OF FATHER'S ABSENCE

There appears to be a cherished notion that prolonged absence of a father from a household does irreparable psychological harm to the growing child. Divorce is but one of a number of events that precipitate the state of affairs known as father absence. Studies of the effects of father absence on samples of children of separation or divorce have entered some of the following claims: father-absent boys show inappropriate sex-role behaviors, have a less adequate sex-role identification (Biller, 1969; Biller and Bahm, 1971), and have a lower level of moral development (Santrock, 1975); father-absent girls behave inappropriately in their heterosexual relationships (Hetherington, 1972); and both boys and girls from father-absent homes have lower academic performance (Sutton-Smith, Rosenberg, and Landy, 1968; Tuckman and Regan, 1966). In general, the father-absence position assumes that fathers have a direct effect on the psychological well-being of their children—particularly their sons.

In a comprehensive review of research on father absence, Herzog and

Sudia (1973) point out two ways in which it is assumed that fathers directly affect their children. First, fathers are supposed to serve as sex-role models for their sons. Social learning theory states that identification with a male sex-role model is necessary for the male child's development of a healthy masculine self-image and appropriate sex-typed behaviors (Mischel, 1966). It is hypothesized that the absence of the father results either in increased "feminized" behavior, or in overly aggressive behavior —a kind of reaction formation or overcompensation for the lack of a male model. In their comprehensive review of father-absence studies, Herzog and Sudia (1973) find little support for this assumption. Not only are the findings contradictory as to the degree of impaired sex-role development in father-absent children, but it is not even clear what importance to attach to significant differences. What does it mean, for example, that father-absent boys are more likely to choose "feminine" toys or games to play with than father-present boys (Biller, 1969)?

Secondly, a father's absence is considered detrimental to the child's development because of the lack of paternal supervision and discipline (Herzog and Sudia, 1973). This lack of supervision is associated with the child's increased aggressive behavior and reduced impulse control. Parental supervision is known to be related to a child's social adjustment (Baumrind, 1967), but it need not be provided by the father. There is evidence to suggest that firm control and supervision by any consistent adult—by a mother or even a grandmother—is sufficient to keep a boy out of trouble (Herzog and Sudia, 1973).

"Reconstituted" families. That father-absence alone cannot account for the negative impact of divorce on children is further demonstrated by the findings on "reconstituted" families. It seems that any consistent adult male can provide the essentials—an appropriate male role-model, and a firm source of supervision and control. Therefore, in cases of marital separation one would expect that any detriment to children's development created by a father's absence would be reversed if the custodial parent remarried; normality and psychological well-being would then be restored. It seems, however, that remarriage and the presence of a stepfather tend to create more problems than they solve.

Most studies have found *no* differences between the adjustment or development of children with no fathers and of those with stepfathers (Biller and Bahm, 1971; Blanchard and Biller, 1971; Bohannan, 1975; Nye, 1957; Kalter, 1977; Burchinal, 1964). Several investigations have actually found that children living with a stepfather were negatively affected, compared to those living with no father at all. McCord, McCord, and Thurber (1962) found that a higher percentage of children from broken homes with a "parent substitute" had delinquent gang reference groups and later became criminals, compared to children from broken homes with no parent substitute. The authors reanalyzed the data from Glueck and Glueck's (1950) study of juvenile delinquents and found the same trend. Rosenberg (1965) found that low self-esteem and psychosomatic symptoms were more often reported by children living with a stepfather than by those living with their single-parent mothers. Zill (1978) reported that children living with mothers and stepfathers were significantly more likely to be seen as "needing help" than were children in mother-father or single-parent homes. Although the investigation by Kalter (1977) showed more similarities than differences between the two groups, when differences occurred, it was always the children living with stepparents who had the higher frequency of problem behaviors.

Cause of father absence. If it is the *direct* effect of a father's absence that is the overriding cause of children's reactions to divorce, then one would expect it to exert a similarly strong effect in the case of a father's death, desertion, or prolonged absence. While there are many similarities among all children who have lost a father, there are also some striking differences—especially between children who have experienced a father's death and those whose parents have divorced. The main difference between the two groups is the type of behavioral problems and psychiatric symptoms they manifest. In clinical samples, for example, children from divorced homes have more problems of an aggressive, antisocial type, whereas children of widows have a greater frequency of anxiety, moodiness, and neurotic problems (Tuckman and Regan, 1966; Felner, Stolberg, and Cowen, 1975). Studies of non-clinical samples also confirm this "acting out" pattern in reaction to divorce and the anxiety and moodiness responses to paternal death (Santrock, 1975; Hetherington, 1972; Nye, 1957). In a study of the impact of father-absence on lower- and middle-class white adolescent girls, Hetherington (1972) found that daughters of divorce did significantly more sexual acting-out than did either daughters of widows or girls from intact families. The daughters of widows were shy, withdrawn, and extremely nervous during their interviews with a male interviewer; they also reported the least amount of heterosexual activity of any of the adolescent girls. Zill's recent survey (1978) found that parents' and teachers' ratings of aggressive behavior were much higher for children whose parents were separated or divorced than for those whose mothers were widowed or never married.

Evidence of this kind makes it difficult to support the claim that only the absence of the father lies at the heart of the children's response to divorce. One explanation for the different reactions is that the "child introjects the predominant behavior 'modeled' for him during a given crisis, and this becomes a guiding framework for his later behavior and coping" (Felner et al., 1975, p. 309). In the case of death, the model is the mother's grief: her mourning, withdrawal, and depression. In a divorce, the model may often be the parents' hostile and aggressive conflicts.

This brief review of the father-absence research indicates how limited its contribution is to an understanding of what it is about divorce that affects the child. Yet there is something powerful about the departure and prolonged absence of a parent from a family. It may be that the absence of the father has its most *direct* impact—not on the child—but on other factors—such as the economic and social position of the family, and most significantly, the situation of the now single parent-mother— her behavior, outlook, and mental health. In other words, the absence of the father may exert its most direct effects on the mother which in turn affects how she behaves toward her child. The influence of father-absence on the *mother* may be a more powerful determinant of the child's adjustment.

EFFECTS OF SINGLE MOTHERHOOD

An alternative to the father-absence arguments is presented in re-search which emphasizes the reorganization that the family must undergo when the father departs. The assumption underlying this approach is that adaptation is required of all family members in order to continue the tasks of family maintenance (Weiss, in press; Brandwein, Brown, and Fox, 1974). In spite of the structural change, the functions facing the family remain the same: income is needed for subsistence, emotional and physical care must be provided to the children, and the household must be kept in an acceptable state of order and repair. Following divorce, the important change is in who does what and how the tasks are accom-plished (Weiss, in press). For example, the single-parent family may rely on welfare payments in order to obtain income previously provided by the father, or the mother may take a full-time job, relinquishing her role as child-caretaker to a day care center. Children are also expected to become more responsible and participate more in routines of household and personal care.

Viewing divorce as a reorganization process from a two-parent to a single-parent family unit suggests several factors that may affect chil-dren's adjustment. In the first place, one adult trying to perform the same functions formerly done by two adults will inevitably lead to some short-changing somewhere along the line. For example, the single mother has only a limited amount of emotional energy and time available for her chil-dren, especially if her responsibilities entail being the sole provider and caretaker. Second, change often leads to stress (Brown, Bhrolcháin, and Harris, 1975) and as the changes demanded of the new single-parent family mount, so do the stresses, and with them an increased vulner-ability to psychiatric problems. One of the most common stresses experienced by single-parent mothers is lack of money. Bane (chapter 16) points out that not only is divorce more likely to occur in families with lower incomes, but also that divorce itself can *cause* reduced income, though only for the single-parent mother. Financial support from the

departed father is forthcoming less than half the time, and even if
alimony payments are made, the majority of the recipients still must
work full- or part-time to make ends meet (Zill, 1978). The strain of
living under economic hardship, as the majority of single, female-
headed families do (Bane, chapter 16), may take a psychological toll on
mothers and children alike.

Some of the stresses that accompany divorce may more directly affect
the child. For example, following the divorce, the single-parent family
may move: the child leaves old friends, enters a new school, and has to
make new friends. If the mother takes a full-time job, the child's entire
daily routine may have to change. If the mother remarries, the child
must adjust to a new adult male in the house. (This might help to explain
the consistent finding that children living with stepfathers have as
many, if not more, behavioral problems as do children remaining in a
single-parent household.)

Although there is a good deal of research on life events, stress, and
the emotional health of adults (see Makosky, forthcoming), little is
known about what effect life-event changes have on children's adjustment. Departure of the father is probably only one of the many changes
that the child of divorce encounters. If it is true of children, as it is for
adults, that an increase in life-event changes produces greater risk for
psychiatric problems, then knowledge of the major changes that accompany the divorce would enable us to make a more accurate prediction of
its impact on children.

The Quality of Family Relationships

MARITAL CONFLICT

It is not enough merely to focus on the structural changes inherent in
divorce. Each divorce occurs in the context of a particular family with
its own interpersonal dynamics. It would be easy to avoid the debate on
effects of divorce by arguing that each case is unique. That is indeed true.
However, some interesting patterns of family relationships have been
observed to be related to the child's adjustment. One aspect of family
relationships that characterizes many divorces is the strained relationship
between the two parents before, during, and even after separation. One
might suspect that conflict or tension between parents is as salient in the
children's eyes as the departure of the father. Marital discord also
distinguishes families undergoing separation and divorce from other

types of father-absent families, and might help to explain the differences between these two groups of children, noted earlier.

Nye (1957) questioned a group of randomly selected high school students about their parents' marital status, the amount of parental quarreling and arguing in their homes, and their parents' marital happiness. He also asked questions concerning the children's own adjustment in school, family, and community. Nye found no significant differences between reported school adjustment or church attendance of children from single-parent homes and of those from unhappy and conflict-ridden two-parent homes. However, other differences between these two groups were significant. Children from single-parent homes reported a lower incidence of psychosomatic illness and of delinquent behavior than did children from unhappy two-parent homes. Children from single-parent homes also indicated superior parent-child adjustment. Nye's study makes a strong case that parental conflict alone is sufficient to produce both delinquent and psychosomatic reactions in children, while living with a single parent does not count as an automatic strike against the child. Equally important in Nye's study is the finding that even when socioeconomic status was controlled, the differences between the two groups of children were still apparent; at all socioeconomic levels, children from unhappy, unbroken homes reported more problems of adjustment than did children from single-parent homes.

McCord et al. (1962) also found a connection between conflict in the home and juvenile delinquency. Their findings, based on a prospective observational study of lower-income boys aged ten to fifteen and their families, revealed that boys from intact homes where the parents constantly and openly quarreled reported the highest frequency of delinquent gang association (43 percent); boys from single-parent homes and those from harmonious two-parent homes reported only half that rate.

In a review of previous research, Rutter (1971) concluded that *separation* from a parent did not have consistently negative effects on children's adjustment, but *conflict* did. A poor marital relationship characterized by conflict and a lack of warmth was associated with a high incidence of children's antisocial disorder, no matter what a family's social class status. Zill's (1978) survey of over two thousand children reported that the need for psychiatric help was greatest among children from family types where marital conflict would most likely have been witnessed— unhappily married and divorced homes. Children whose parents were separated did not have as great a need for help—a puzzling finding, especially since on all other counts, these children were very similar to the divorced sample. Nor was the need for help as great among children from family types where marital conflict would be unlikely to occur: happily married, widowed, and never-married families.

All of these studies suggest that living with two parents whose relationship is conflict-ridden is much more damaging to the child's adjustment than simply living with a single parent. It is not clear, though, if separation of the two parents immediately alleviates the stress associated with conflict, or if the effects of the conflict are more longlasting. Wallerstein and Kelly (1975) found that the degree of conflict *prior* to their parents' divorce was *not* related to the post-divorce adjustment of a sample of normal, middle-class preschool children. But, following the divorce, if the parents continued to interact in a conflict-ridden vein, their children's adjustment was negatively affected.

PARENT-CHILD RELATIONSHIPS

Rutter's (1971) important study of children in intact families suggests a second aspect of family relationships that should be considered when weighing the impact of divorce on children: the quality of the parent-child relationship. He discovered that children who had a good relationship with one or both parents, whose marriage was stable, had a low incidence of behavior problems (5 percent). Poor parent-child relationships in families where the marital relationship was stable were associated with a higher incidence of behavioral problems (25 percent). However, even a good relationship between the child and one or both parents failed to mitigate the ill effects of a *poor* marriage: 40 percent of the children in situations of this type showed signs of antisocial behavior. And a poor marriage combined with a poor relationship with both parents was a double whammy: 90 percent of these children had antisocial behavior problems!

A study of the reactions to parental divorce of a group of normal, lower-middle and middle-class preschoolers offers the most clearcut evidence for the connection between the adjustment of the child and the quality of the parent-child relationship (Wallerstein and Kelly, 1975). The investigators found that fifteen children had more serious psychological problems at the time of the follow-up (one year later) than they had at the time of the divorce. The quality of the mother-child relationship had deteriorated in 10 of the 15 cases. In the course of a year the ten mothers had become less supportive and nurturant, and more anxious and tense in their relationships with their children. Interestingly, although many of the relationships between the preschoolers and their departed fathers had improved during the first year of separation, this factor was not related to the child's subsequent adjustment.

Hetherington also noted certain patterns in parent-child interaction in divorced families. Compared to widowed and married mothers, divorced mothers reported the greatest amount of conflict with adolescent daughters, and were the most punitive, yet the most inconsistent disciplinarians (Hetherington, 1972). And in another study, Hetherington and her colleagues (1976) found that divorced mothers, especially mothers of preschool boys, continued to feel angry, depressed, and incompetent two years after their divorces. Compared to married parents both divorced mothers and divorced fathers had much greater difficulty in controlling and disciplining their children. One of the implications of these investigations is that the quality of the parent-child relationship itself is susceptible to some of the ill effects of divorce.

PARENTS' MENTAL HEALTH

Earlier reference was made to the possibility that parental divorce may influence a child's adjustment by affecting the mental health of the single parent. The studies on parent-child relationships suggest that following divorce, mothers may be less attentive, more punitive, or less consistent in their behavior towards their children. Of special concern is the finding that divorced and separated mothers are more likely to have psychiatric symptoms, such as anxiety or depression, than married mothers (Briscoe, Smith, Robins, Marlens, and Gaskin, 1973; Guttentag and Salasin, in press; Hetherington, 1972; Pearlin and Johnson, 1975). In terms of their children, what are the implications of the single parent's increased risk for mental health problems? Surprisingly, little evidence is available to answer this question.

Rutter (1971) reported that a parent's personality disturbance was associated with the child's antisocial behavior only when the marriage was unhappy and conflict-ridden. Another study found that the mother's emotional disturbance affects a son's adjustment only if there is no father present in the family (McCord et al., 1962). Zill's (1978) survey draws the clearest connection between a mother's mental health and her child's report of happiness. Children whose mothers were psychologically distressed were more likely to feel unhappy and rejected than children whose mothers were more positive in their outlook on life and parenthood. And the survey found that the mothers who were most likely to be depressed were either single (excepting widows) or unhappily married. In short, one significant change in children's lives following their parents' divorce may be that their mother's emotional well-being is in greater jeopardy. This in turn may cause a turn for the worse in the parent-child relationship.

SUPPORT NETWORKS

Pearlin and Johnson (1975) noted not only that single parents are vulnerable to depression, but that this vulnerability is compounded by the degree of their social isolation. For all persons, married and single, depressive symptoms were associated with a lack of social contacts.

Single persons had fewer social contacts than did married persons. Finally, even when both had the same amount of social contact, single persons were still more vulnerable to depression, especially when the lack of social participation was extreme. In other words, not only were the unmarried more likely to be socially isolated, but the conditions of their social isolation were more highly associated with depression than for the married.

Those survey findings point to yet another aspect of the family's social situation that is related to the child's adjustment—contacts with persons outside the family. There are numerous ways in which social contacts are important to the mother: they function as a source of emotional support and as an exchange for goods, services, and advice (Pearlin, 1975). They also contribute to a woman's sense of maternal competence and increase her positive attitudes towards her family (Abernethy, 1973).

The role of the social network in adjustment takes on greater significance in the divorcing family's situation because so much of the research suggests a real loss of contact with others as a direct result of divorce. For example, following divorce, the single mother usually maintains or increases her frequency of contact with her own kin, but she significantly decreases her contact with her former husband's kin (Anspach, 1976; Spicer and Hampe, 1975; Marsden, 1969). A sample of low-income mothers interviewed by Marsden (1969) reported that their relationships with friends outside the family suffered a real setback following divorce. One-fifth of that sample seemed to have no outside friends at all, and many others said their social life was severely limited. Marsden also found that a very large proportion of the single mothers had to relocate one or more times following their marital separation; this suggests the possibility that residential mobility is an important factor in the breakdown of social relationships of divorced women. Goode (1956) reported that the divorcees least likely to keep up their old friendships were those who began working after separation. Here is a case where the new financial pressures associated with divorce force a woman to go back to work, thus affecting the single mother's ability to maintain contacts with her friends.

Only the study by Hetherington, Cox, and Cox (1976) looked for a connection between the support available to the parent and the quality of her relationship with her children. They found that the parent-child relationship was least threatened in cases where the divorced mother continued to have the support of her ex-husband. Mothers who failed to have this type of support had greater difficulty in effectively controlling their preschool children. Support from persons outside the family was also positively associated with the divorced mother's effectiveness as a parent, but their support was less important than the divorced father's continuous involvement with the child.

It seems that social and kin networks function so as to alleviate some of the single mother's stress. They are, therefore, important to her mental health and adequate functioning, and hence to the adjustment of her family. What is less clear is the effect that divorce has on a woman's ability to maintain her social support system. High residential mobility, a characteristic of the divorced population, would disrupt the maintenance of a social network. Employment might also affect it negatively by making excessive demands on the time available for participation in a social network—visiting, chatting on the phone, or trading child-sitting time. However, a woman's fellow employees may be an important source of support. Furthermore, the simple fact that the single mother is solely responsible for all the tasks of family maintenance may mean that she simply does not have time to be in contact with other supportive adults.

In reviewing studies on how divorce affects the quality of family interpersonal relationships, a picture begins to emerge which suggests that divorce exerts considerable influence on all fronts of the family's interpersonal and social contacts. Not only do children suffer from the direct effects of the marital strife of their parents, but they are also likely to endure deteriorating relationships with their single parents who may be depressed or anxious or overburdened by the emotional events in their lives. The problems are not only internal; divorce also intensifies the single mother's need for an external support system, while at the same time it throws up obstacles against her ability to build or maintain such a network. The loss of the benefits of a supportive network to the mother may well be a disadvantage for the child.

The Child's Perspective

Thus far, this discussion has tried to isolate some of the particulars of the child's social environment which may mediate the impact of divorce. In so doing, it has relied on the assumption that divorce is an experience which directly impinges upon the child, subject to modification by certain situational variables. However, there is an additional modifier of the divorce experience: the child himself. In one sense, it is true that each child is unique in his or her response to divorce, based on an interwoven set of individual characteristics—personality traits, tolerance for stress, adaptive behaviors, and areas of competence. In another sense, though, all children are alike; they all proceed along a similar course of physical, emotional, and cognitive development. I will argue that the child's level of development has important implications for how he or she processes the experience of divorce and adjusts to the changes.

THE CHILD'S AGE

A number of studies indirectly suggest the importance of a child's developmental level by comparing the effects of divorce on children at different ages. Age, of course, is a rough indicator of location in a developmental agenda. These studies ask whether the age of the child at the time of divorce affects subsequent social-emotional or cognitive development. In most cases, some aspect of the development of father-absent children is measured at a time later than the actual separation. Typically, age at separation is categorized roughly as during the infancy and preschool years (0–5), latency (6–12), or adolescence (13+). Five of the ten studies that performed an analysis by age found that children who were under the age of 5 at their father's departure were the group most adversely affected. Impairments were noted in the following areas: academic achievement (Santrock, 1972; Sutton-Smith, et al. 1968); self-esteem (Rosenberg, 1965); and development of basic trust (Santrock, 1970). Hetherington (1972) found that adolescent girls whose fathers had left their homes during their early years sought more attention from adults of both sexes and displayed more sexually provocative behavior than did girls whose parents were divorced later.

Two other studies that included an analysis by age found that children whose fathers left during their middle childhood years (age six to twelve) had significantly lower academic performance and more behavioral problems (Ryker, 1971; McCord et al., 1962). Another study found that college students who were in later latency and early adolescence (ages 9–16) at the time of divorce recalled having more difficulty in adjusting to the new home situation than did those who had been 5 to 8 years old (Landis, 1960). And the remaining two studies found no differences related to the child's age at father's departure—either in academic achievement (Blanchard and Biller, 1971) or in moral development and moral behavior (Santrock, 1975).

Two of the above mentioned studies (McCord et al., 1962; Santrock, 1972) also found that the more recent the divorce or separation, the more negative were the behaviors being observed, suggesting that divorce *at any age* may cause some interference (if only temporarily) with the child's normal level of functioning. In other words, divorce seems to have some negative short-term effects on all children's social or cognitive behavior. However, long-term disruptions in development may be more probable only when divorce has occurred during a particular age period.

The weight of these combined findings suggests that the younger child is more vulnerable to the negative effects of divorce than the older child. Corroboration is provided by some data on utilization rates of outpatient psychiatric services (Guttentag and Salasin, in press). They reported that for children living with a "separated" mother the rate of utilization was higher among children under the age of 6 than for those age 6–13. Whereas in other family types, frequency of clinic visits was higher among the 6–13 year-old group.

It is interesting to note that for single parents with children (including the widowed, divorced, separated, and never-married) vulnerability to depression is greatest when children are under 5 years of age (Pearlin and Johnson, 1975). The same does not hold true for married parents. Both for the mother and for the child, then, divorce is more difficult when the child is younger.

An understanding of the child's view of divorce is hindered by two major shortcomings in the empirical work just reviewed. One is the lack of systematic studies on children's reactions *at the very time of divorce*. The literature reviewed thus far has assessed some aspect of the child's development at a later date, often many years later. Those studies which have looked at children's responses at the time of divorce are almost all based on clinical populations (e.g., Despert, 1953; Gardner, 1976), and cannot justifiably be generalized to the normal, non-clinical majority. Only a very few researchers have sampled the non-clinical population of children around the time of their parents' divorce (Hetherington et al., 1976; Kelly and Wallerstein, 1976; Wallerstein and Kelly, 1974, 1975, 1976).

The second problem lies in the interpretation of the findings. Although the studies reviewed do suggest that there are age-related patterns of adjustment, the investigators in general have failed to explain the meaning of these age differences or the reasons they may have occurred. The research suffers from a lack of a theoretical perspective within which to interpret and integrate such findings. In this final section, I will propose one interpretation of the age-related patterns based on a theory of children's social-cognitive development.

A SOCIAL-COGNITIVE DEVELOPMENTAL PERSPECTIVE

A basic tenet of social-cognitive developmental theory is that children themselves are active constructors of the world they experience. As children develop, their reasoning about the social and physical world undergoes changes. Their concepts become increasingly complex, integrated, and abstract, and decreasingly ego-centered and concrete (Kohlberg, 1969; Selman, 1971, 1974; Selman and Byrne, 1974). Accounting for the changes in children's thinking is important to the study of children's reactions to divorce for several reasons. First of all, it is difficult to evaluate the child's response to divorce without knowing what he or she perceives and understands about the situation. Also, knowledge of children's level of reasoning has important practical implications for clinical intervention. For example, "insight therapy" may be of limited usefulness to young children who intellectually are still unable to reflect upon their own feelings. Finally, a developmental analysis of children's response to divorce may shed some light on the age-related findings reported in other studies. It is hypothesized that different levels of social understanding are related to different perceptions of what is happening and consequently to different reactions to the divorce.

To illustrate my point, I have reinterpreted some data on children's reactions to divorce using the social-cognitive developmental framework developed by Selman and his associates (Selman, 1971, 1974; Selman and Byrne, 1974). Selman's levels of interpersonal reasoning are particularly useful because they have been derived from extensive interviews with children of all ages on their views of interpersonal relationships—peer relationships (Selman 1974), group relationships (Jaquette, 1976), and parent-child relationships (Bruss, 1976).

Interviews with children concerning their reactions to divorce were conducted as part of the "Children of Divorce" Project (Kelly and Wallerstein, 1976; Wallerstein and Kelly, 1974, 1975, 1976). The project intensively interviewed 60 families at the time the parents were taking action for a divorce and then again one year later. There were 131 children between the ages of 2½ and 18: none had had previous psychological problems. The sample of families was primarily middle-class and well-educated. The investigators reported their findings by age groups in a clinical descriptive manner. The age groups roughly correspond to the levels of social reasoning in social-cognitive developmental theory, making it possible to reanalyze the findings from a developmental perspective. Table 17-1 presents a summary of the levels of social reasoning and the typical age-related reactions to divorce.

Preschool years—egocentric reasoning. One of the most pervasive reactions of the slightly older preschool child (3½–6) was that of self-blame—an attitude that was found to be "highly resistive to educational interventions by parents or by the clinical staff" (Wallerstein and Kelly, 1975, p. 605). Preschoolers' reactions were also marked by a confusion about the nature of families and interpersonal relationships. Only among the oldest preschool children was there any reasonable grasp of what the divorce meant—in terms of new living arrangements and of altered patterns of parent-child contact. All of the preschoolers, especially the youngest ones, had difficulty expressing their feelings.

A social-cognitive developmental interpretation of these findings would focus on the fact that preschoolers think largely in an egocentric way. In trying to understand why their parents have split up, they look mainly to external, observable actions; they often juxtapose two independent, unrelated events in a causal manner. Because their reasoning is egocentric, these children's explanations are apt to center on themselves. Thus, they conceptualize the divorce as if it has happened between *them* and their parents, or as a result of their *own* wrongdoing. The result is often self-blame, very likely for an illogical reason. For example, "Daddy left home because I was a bad boy—I didn't put away my toys that day."

TABLE 17-1

Levels of Interpersonal Reasoning and Characteristic Reactions to Divorce

Social Perspective Taking[a]	Interpersonal Reasoning[a]	Age	Characteristic Reactions to Divorce[b]
Level 0 – Egocentric: Child fails to distinguish other's viewpoint from own.	Child can identify subjective feelings, but confuses self's and other's subjectivity. Only one subjective state can exist at a time. Child conceptualizes interpersonal relationships in terms of physical aspects. Child fails to differentiate between inner motives and outward actions or appearances.	Preschool 2½-6 Years	Preschool children were frightened, confused and blamed themselves. There was a great need for physical contact with adults. Children expressed fears of being sent away or being replaced. Only 5- and 6-year-olds were able to express feelings and to understand some of the divorce-related changes (Wallerstein and Kelly, 1975).
Level 1 – Subjective: Child understands that all others have subjective perspectives distinct from own.	Different subjective feelings can exist, but not toward the same social object. Child conceptualizes persons in terms of context-specific feelings or actions, and interpersonal relationships in terms of the subjective evaluation of the other's actions.	Early Latency 7-8 Years	Children expressed feelings of sadness and loss, fear and insecurity. They felt abandoned and rejected, although they did not blame themselves. They had difficulty in expressing their anger toward their fathers. They felt angry at their mothers for sending the fathers away but were afraid of incurring their mothers' wrath. They held an intense desire for the reconciliation of their parents, believing that the family was "necessary for their safety and continued growth" (Kelly and Wallerstein, 1976).
Level 2 – Self-Reflective: Child can reflect on own thoughts and behavior from another's point of view.	Conflicting feelings can exist toward the same social object. Inner motives can be differentiated from overt behaviors. Child conceptualizes interpersonal relationships in terms of reciprocal attitudes and actions.	Later Latency 9-10 Years	Later latency children had a more realistic understanding of divorce and were better able to express their feelings of intense anger. They did not feel responsible for the divorce but were ashamed and morally outraged by their parents' behavior. Their loyalties were divided between the parents and they frequently felt lonely and rejected. They used age-appropriate coping mechanisms including a conscious layering of psychological functioning (Wallerstein and Kelly, 1976).
Level 3 – Third Person: Adoption of a third-person viewpoint which can simultaneously consider self's and other's perspectives as they relate to each other.	Child can observe his own self-reflective process. Persons are conceptualized in terms of simple traits. Interpersonal relationships are conceptualized in terms of mutuality — members' subjective attitudes are considered simultaneously and independent of context-specific actions.	Adolescence 13-18 Years	Adolescents were the most openly upset by the divorce. They expressed strong feelings of anger, sadness, shame, and embarrassment. Divorce forced the adolescents to see their parents as individuals and to reassess their relationships with each parent. They also re-examined their own values and concepts about what is a good marital relationship. Most were able to disengage themselves from their parents' conflict by a year following the divorce (Wallerstein and Kelly, 1974).
Level 4 – Qualitative Systems: Coordination of multiple levels of perspectives, e.g., self's, other's, society's, etc.	Adolescent conceptualizes qualitatively distinct "levels" of behavior and feelings. Personalities are viewed as complex systems of values, traits, and feelings. Relationships are seen as existing on qualitatively distinct levels.		

[a] Based on the work of R.L. Selman and Associates (1974).
[b] Findings reported by Wallerstein and Kelly (1974, 1975, 1976; Kelly and Wallerstein, 1976).

Children at this stage do not have a firm sense of continuing family relationships following the divorce, because their conceptions of a family are based on who lives together in the same house. Finally, while aware of their feelings, egocentric preschoolers are unable to reflect on them and this may itself be a source of considerable suffering for children at this age.

Early latency—subjective reasoning. Compared to the preschool children, the early latency children (7–8) were much more aware of their feelings; many were able to openly admit their sadness (Kelly and Wallerstein, 1976). This is indicative of their developing awareness of feeling states (the subjective level of social reasoning—Level 1; Selman, 1974). What they were less able to do was to admit their anger toward their parents, especially their fathers. This finding makes sense from a social-cognitive developmental perspective, which suggests that children at the "subjective level" of social reasoning do not understand that they (or anyone else) can simultaneously hold two opposing feelings (love and anger) towards the same person.

Unlike preschoolers, the early latency children in the project did not blame themselves for the divorce. This change can be interpreted as a result of the increased understanding the primary-school child has that there are inner motives behind outward acts (e.g., father leaves because he is unhappy or angry). However, the seven- and eight-year-olds did share some very strong feelings of abandonment and rejection. While the children felt rejected by their departing father, they were afraid of incurring the wrath of their remaining mother. They were worried that they themselves, like their fathers, could be expelled from the house. Again one sees that these younger children's conceptual understanding of interpersonal interactions is still limited to fairly context-specific situations. They do *not* appear to understand that mother and father are *mutually* unhappy in their marital relationship and that it is their *mutual* dissatisfaction which motivates the divorce. Instead, these children believe that one of the parents got mad and either left or made the other one leave. They may reason that if they make mother similarly mad, they too will suffer these dire consequences. At this age, the children's view of the consequences in interpersonal interactions is absolute. It is based on what they have observed to occur; it fails to take into account the particular nature of the relationship and how it differs from their own relationship with their parents.

Later latency—self-reflective reasoning. Like the primary schoolers, the nine- and ten-year-old "later latency" group rarely indicated that they felt responsible for their parents' divorce; similarly, they felt rejected and abandoned by the departing parent (Wallerstein and Kelly, 1976). Unlike those younger children, they acknowledged their intense feelings of anger toward one or both parents. Most striking was that later latency children would consciously hide their feelings of suffering in order to present a more courageous front to the world. This "conscious layering of psychological functioning" (Wallerstein and Kelly, 1976, p. 258) is indicative of older children's increasing cognitive ability to see themselves as others would see them (the self-reflective level of social reasoning—Level 2; Selman, 1974). Thus, they realize that people can feel or think one way on the inside, but act in a different (not totally consistent) way on the outside.

While many of the nine- and ten-year-olds were able to admit their anger toward their parents, the clinical observations gave the impression that these children were still torn by their feelings of anger and loyalty toward their parents (Wallerstein and Kelly, 1976). The understanding that one can have different feelings toward the same person and the inability to integrate these feelings (e.g., love-hate, ambivalence) is characteristic of the self-reflective level of social reasoning.

The investigators also found that many of the children felt ashamed of their parents' behavior and of their family's dissolution. At this level of social reasoning children should have the ability to view their family's situation from an outsider's perspective and to see that each parent is behaving deplorably—fighting, bickering, and neglecting the children. Children may feel ashamed because they can understand only too well how others may view the family.

Finally, it was observed that nine- and ten-year-old children experienced a feeling of loneliness, derived mainly from their parents being so embroiled in their own struggles that they paid only peripheral attention to their children. These children sensed an erosion in the parent-child relationship resulting from the parents withdrawal of emotional support. At this age, children's conceptions of the parent-child relationship embody love and concern at their base (Bruss, 1976). At a self-reflective level of social reasoning, children are becoming increasingly sensitive to the subjective feelings and intentions of others. Thus their reactions may correspond more closely with the particular emotional states of their parents. Unlike younger children who frequently expressed fear of starvation, the later latency children were *not* afraid of not being fed; they were afraid of not being loved.

Adolescence—third-person reasoning. The reactions of the adolescents (13–18) continued the trend of children becoming increasingly more conscious and expressive of their feelings with age. In fact, the investigators were surprised by the visible upset among the 21 teenagers in their sample (Wallerstein and Kelly, 1974). Anger, sadness, a sense of loss and betrayal, and feelings of shame and embarrassment pervaded these adolescents' reactions. The children seemed painfully aware of their feelings. The ability to consciously reflect on one's own feelings is a further step in the development of social reasoning (third-person perspective taking—Level 3; Selman, 1974).

The most distinguishing reaction of these adolescents was the extent of their reflection about their parents as persons, their parents' marriage (and marital relationships in general), and about their own relationships with their parents. They assumed a much more realistic view of their parents, recognizing each of them as an individual with individual needs and interests. The investigators felt that the divorce actually forced the teenagers to think of their parents as individuals. Their ability to do so is indicative of a "third-person" level of social-cognitive awareness that enables them to view their parents relatively objectively as individuals, independent of the parent-child relationship. Younger children simply do not have this conceptual ability.

The adolescents also had a better understanding of their parents' marriage as a mutually incompatible and unsatisfying relationship. These children were extremely concerned about their *own* future marriages and worried about the possibilities for maintaining a relationship based on mutual concern, respect, and interests. The concerns of the adolescent were consistent with the characteristics of the "third-person" level of social reasoning: the ability to understand others independent of specific contexts of relationships, and the ability to conceptualize interpersonal relationships as mutually based.

While initially about one-half of the adolescents had felt unable to extricate themselves from the conflicts at home, a follow-up one year later found that all of them had succeeded in disengaging themselves from these battles. Of further interest is the fact that those teenagers who had been able to detach themselves emotionally from the start were the ones who seemed best-adjusted one to two years later. The ability to step back from one's interpersonal involvements and to observe them objectively seems at this age to function as a coping mechanism. In fact, it appears to be a fairly successful coping device: the adolescents seemed to be the least affected of all the age groups. It is my contention that their level of understanding of interpersonal relationships contributed to the adolescents' ability to deal successfully with the divorce.

AGE RECONSIDERED

Do children's social-cognitive level of understanding of divorce have any implications for their adjustment to it? In the Divorce Project's follow-up study one year later, 44 percent of the preschoolers showed some deterioration in their behavior; in contrast, 23 percent of the early latency group, 24 percent of the later latency group, and only a few of the adolescents had more problems at follow-up. Thus, relative to the other age groups, the preschoolers had the most difficulty in their adjustment. These are the youngsters whose ability to reflect on the divorce experience is most limited by their egocentric level of interpersonal reasoning or awareness. In contrast, the investigators were impressed with the adolescents' ability to be insightful and concerned, yet also detached. I would contend that the ability to reason from the third-person perspective facilitated the adolescents' relatively good adjustment, just as the inability to do so inhibited the preschoolers' successful resolution of their experience. This hypothesis awaits further validation.

Age, then, appears to be an important mediator of the effects of divorce on children. In two contexts, it is the younger child who is more adversely affected: preschoolers create a greater psychological strain on their divorced parents and at the same time seem cognitively less able to cope with the divorce. In the empirical studies cited earlier, the preponderance of later negative effects noted for children whose parents divorced during the child's first five years may be reverberations of the double-edged effects of early age.

Conclusions

It is apparent from this review that there are many aspects of divorce that contribute to its impact on children. To talk about the effects of *divorce* is too broad to be useful. A more accurate statement of impact is obtained if divorce is placed in the context of the major changes it entails, the quality of the family's relationships, the single mother's mental health, and the child's own viewpoint. At this point it is possible to identify some of the factors associated with divorce that have a distinct impact on children's adjustment, and to suggest other aspects of divorce that merit further investigation.

Evidence accumulated from numerous studies makes a strong case for the negative effects of marital conflict on children's adjustment. It doesn't seem to matter if the conflict leads to separation or divorce: the child who experiences his parents' marital discord is at greater psychiatric risk. Separation or divorce may well reduce the stress produced by marital conflict. On the other hand, if the conflict continues after the divorce, either openly or in the more subtle loyalty battles, the child is likely to experience adjustment problems.

This review has also underscored the importance of the child's age at the time of divorce. Young children are a greater source of stress than older children, and single-parent mothers with young children are among the most highly stressed groups of women. A family with young children is also often at the point in its life cycle when job and financial pressures are the greatest. Therefore, we might expect that a divorce at this time simply overtaxes the family, placing both mothers and children at greater psychiatric risk. I have also argued that the young child is more vulnerable to the negative effects of divorce because he or she is less able to cope with the experience due to limited reasoning abilities. The young child appears to be doubly at risk due to the increased vulnerability of the mother and to his own limited capacity to understand the experience.

A persistent theme in the literature has been the emotional vulnerability of the single mother. Links between the mother's mental health and the child's adjustment have been tentatively established: they suggest that children are more likely to experience problems when their mothers are depressed. Further investigation is needed to determine what influence the mother's emotional state has on her child's adjustment to divorce. It may be that the incidence of children's behavioral problems is more closely associated with their mothers' mental health than it is with the mere occurrence of divorce, separation, or living with a single parent.

Another area deserving more careful investigation concerns the changes to which the divorcing family must adjust. Research on life events has shown that multiple events put people (adults) at risk for psychiatric problems. In many cases, divorce and separation produce more changes than just the mere departure of the father. We need to know what those changes are and their effects on mothers and children alike.

In my review, I have pointed to the threat that divorce poses to the parent's mental health, the child's adjustment, the parent-child relationship, even to the family's relationship with outside social supports. At the same time I should emphasize that the strength of the individuals and their interpersonal relationships help to mitigate the impact of divorce. The research does attest to the beneficial effects of a good parent-child relationship, a supportive network of friends, and an ex-husband who continues to be supportive towards his family. The real impact of divorce on children will be more accurately understood when we know what strains are placed on the family and what strengths protect it.

Fathers by Choice: Divorced Men Who Receive Custody of Their Children

"Father is not a very impressive figure in American life," writes Leonard Benson (1968), and an overview of American family life during the last one hundred years supports his opinion. Family roles were affected dramatically by the industrial revolution. As fathers moved away from the home into industrial and commercial jobs, they abandoned much of their role in the traditional home-centered training of children, and child rearing settled more and more firmly on the shoulders of the mother. The patriarchal family pattern carried over from Europe began to break down, and the father role became increasingly amorphous. Finally, the materialistic boom and increased mobility of the postwar years, while placing emphasis on the nuclear family, further solidified parental role segregation and assigned child rearing to the province of the mother.

In recent years, however, the role of the American father has been enjoying a resurgence. Several factors may be involved: a decrease in the average man's working hours and resulting increase in leisure time; the woman's dissatisfaction with her role limitations and movement toward greater economic and social flexibility; and the spreading disenchantment with material acquisition as the exclusive measure of the good life, along with the espousal of close relationships as a principal measure of happiness. Whatever the reasons, there appears to be a recent upswing in fathers' involvement in their families.

This chapter is an adaptation of the author's Ph.D. dissertation in the Department of Psychology and Social Relations at Harvard University ("Fathers by choice: characteristics of men who do and do not seek custody of their children following divorce," 1976). The study was supported in part by a grant from that department.

It is ironic that renewed interest in fathering in America parallels an accelerating trend toward divorce. The American divorce/marriage ratio is higher than ever before, and in recent years 6 out of every 10 divorces have involved children (see Norton and Glick, chapter 1). Divorce is a crisis which demands immediate decisions affecting all intrafamilial relationships, including those between parents and children. Issues such as sharing and role flexibility come face to face with the legal requirement of determining a permanent caretaking arrangement in the dissolving family.

The divorce process deals with parenting through the determination of custody. In recent decades, the norm has been for custody of minor children to be granted to the mother.[1] It is estimated that mothers receive custody in approximately 90 percent of all cases, a ratio which has been relatively stable for several decades (U.S. Bureau of the Census, 1975; Goode, 1956).

This imbalance cannot be seen as primarily court determined; in fact, a high percentage of couples (approximately 80 percent, as in Kohen, Brown, and Feldberg, chapter 14) jointly agree before their case is heard in court that the wife will have custody. It is likely that the preponderance of custody awards to mothers has arisen from a combination of the parents' desires, the realities facing the parents as they plan their post-divorce futures, and, in disputed cases, the actual or assumed orientation of the courts. Men have been more likely to be employed full time, to be making the larger income, to have higher status jobs, and to be in a career progression. Following the divorce, it has usually been easier for the father to continue his occupation than for a non-working mother to leave the home and start a new career. Regardless of the man's emotional attachment to his children, the couple's pre-divorce division of labor was most likely to have assigned the primary childcare role to the mother. This not only increased her childcare skills and the dependence of the children on her, but also established patterns of many years' standing which would take great effort to reverse, and at best would require a major adjustment for all the family members. In addition, the social pressure on mothers to take custody has been overwhelming (Mindey, 1969).

The rigidity of these post-divorce parental roles appears to be changing to some degree. Working mothers are now the norm rather than the exception. More women are expressing a preference for a post-divorce life that is not centered on single parenthood. More men are angrily demanding that the letter of the law in most states prohibiting bias toward mothers in custody disputes be honored; it is a rare urban area

1. Weiss, in chapter 19, summarizes the reversal of the eighteenth century British family law doctrine ("the legal power over infant children is in the father, the mother has none," III Eng. Rep. 922, 1836) into the twentieth century American assumption that children's best interests are usually served by mothers.

that does not have an active organization of "fathers for equal justice." A number of men, still small but growing, are seeking custody.

The study reported here is an exploratory analysis of interviews with 40 recently divorced fathers, half of whom were awarded custody of their minor children. These particular men are of interest because the breakup of their marriages faced them with the immediate prospect of losing the opportunity to be traditional fathers. One group of these men chose to seek custody, preferring the total responsibility of the single parent to the peripheral role of the visiting parent. The other group, the control sample, took the normative course of agreeing that their wives should receive custody. This study looks for differences and similarities between these two groups, with a special interest in discovering factors which are a part of the fathers' decision making and which lead some men to pursue the counter-traditional role of the single-parent father.

Areas of Investigation

In this exploratory study, I relied primarily on structured interviews to investigate a broad range of fathering behaviors and marital experiences. A review of the limited literature on fathering suggested five areas that might be related to the custody decision. Interviews were designed to gather data in those areas, which include:

1. *Demographic variables.* There is very little empirical basis for predicting the effects of age, race, or religion on fathering behavior. A few researchers have looked at social class and occupation as determinants of the father role in the family (Haavio-Mannila, 1971; Aldous, 1969). Studies comparing fathering styles across socioeconomic status levels (SES) reach conflicting conclusions: some find more involvement by working-class fathers (Gavron, 1966), while others find middle-class fathers more active (Davis and Havighurst, 1946; Radin, 1972). Some newspaper and magazine features suggest that the most active fathers are young, highly educated, and generally liberal.

The interview began with questions about the age, religious preference, occupation, and education of each man and his ex-wife; his race was noted. There were also descriptive questions about the family, including age and sex of the children and the date of the marriage.

2. *Father's families of origin.* Most theories of personality development consider the family of origin to be critically important in the formation of lifelong behavior patterns. In the development of a role such as fathering, one's family of origin seems doubly important as the setting

for both the process of identification that is the core of depth-psychology theories and the modeling of parenting behavior that is stressed in cognitive and learning theories.

The general questions of interest here are: In what kinds of families did these men grow up? Were they intact or separated? Large or small, close or fragmented? Are there any characteristics which can differentiate the custody and non-custody samples?

A more specific question concerns the relative strength of the man's childhood relationships to each of his parents. Would men who seek custody have had especially close identifications with active and loving fathers, or would they model their parenting on mothers who had been their primary caretakers? One psychiatric report (Group for the Advancement of Psychiatry, 1973) suggests that all children learn both fathering and mothering from the mother, but other theorists have felt that the boy's oedipally based relationship with his father is the key factor in his eventual fathering style (Zilboorg, 1931).

The interview included several items asking for descriptions of each member of a man's family of origin. There were additional questions exploring the quality of his relationship with his parents.

3. *Fathers' participation in child rearing.* Behavior in the past, in this case fathering behavior, is usually a good predictor of similar behavior in the present and future. A review of the few studies that exist on what fathers actually do in families quickly points up the tremendous range of behavior that is described. Some men, according to Josselyn (1956), fill a father role best described as a tired worker who shouldn't be bothered: "It is a masculine virtue offering at least some recognition to be too busy to express fatherliness" (p. 270). Rebelsky and Hanks (1971) and Ban and Lewis (1974) report data on fathers whose daily interaction with their children can be counted in minutes, or even seconds. On the other hand, other researchers describe fathers who take over large parts, and in some cases the major share, of the childcare work and "compete" with their wives to be the most involved parent (Burlingham, 1973; Caplan, 1961). While there is developing interest in "new roles for fathers," much of the writing so far has been primarily anecdotal and the empirical data on actual behavioral changes is equivocal (Fein, 1974; Ripin, 1971).

Our goal was to gather information on the history of father-child interactions in the family as a potentially valuable predictor of the custody decision. There are several questions and one "Participation Scale" in the interview asking for specific information about the fathers' caretaking responsibility and shared activities with their children, in infancy and through the years leading up to the divorce.

4. *Sex-role orientation.* The traditional idea that childcare is more naturally a "feminine" activity makes sex-role orientation a logical place to look for predictors of fathering behavior. If a self-image as a child-

care giver is a sex-linked characteristic (as Bernstein and Cyr [1957] put it, "the feminine aspects of parenthood"), then men who actively seek that role should be identifiable as more feminine than those who do not want the caretaker role.

A modified version of the Bem Sex Role Inventory (Bem, 1974) was therefore administered to each father at the end of the interview. This adjective self-rating scale generates scores of masculinity, femininity, and androgyny.

5. *Characteristics of the marital dissolution.* In addition to the intra-psychic and fathering variables, we also wished to test the hypothesis that the spouses' personal characteristics are less important than situa-tional characteristics of the divorce itself in reaching decisions about seeking custody. The reasons for the divorce, the man's evaluation of his wife's competence, the degree of hostility, and the potential for using a custody petition as a bargaining chip in the courtroom may all play a central part in the couple's decisions about custody.

The section of the interview related to these issues began with general questions about the divorce, followed by more directed probes into the areas that seemed most important in each case. In this area in particular, the goal was not to test specific hypotheses, but to look for patterns in the experiences of the participants.

Method

Since the goal was to explore the experiences of a limited number of men in some depth, and to search for predictors of custody decisions, it was decided to interview samples of men who did and of men who did not receive custody. A probate court docket from a large and socio-economically diverse county in Massachusetts was used to locate the samples. The court processes between 4,000 and 5,500 divorce filings per year, and actually grants about 2,500 divorces annually.

The population was identified as all cases filed within the first ten weeks of 1974, chosen so that all of the participating men would have been granted a divorce between nine and twelve months prior to the interview. A total of 583 divorce actions involving minor children had been filed during that period, and 350 of those cases had been awarded decrees by the time of the sample search, six months later. In 25 of those 350 decided cases, complete or joint custody had been granted to the father. To enlarge the sample pool somewhat, 5 additional father-custody cases were added from the few weeks before the original ten-week period. An attempt was made to contact all 30 of these fathers with custody; 21 were reached, and 20 agreed to be interviewed. These men constitute the "custody sample."

In order to create an equal-sized "non-custody sample," a randomizing procedure was used to generate names from the remaining 325 completed cases. An attempt was made to contact each man in turn, until 20 men who agreed to be interviewed could be located. In all, 185 names had to be generated to locate 27 men without custody, leading to 20 interviews.[2]

Once a man from either group was reached, the refusal rate was remarkably low. Ninety-five percent of the men with custody who were located, and 80 percent of the men without custody, agreed to be interviewed. Most interviews were conducted in the evening at the man's residence, although several took place during the day at work or elsewhere at the man's request (e.g., a hotel lobby or a rented room).

The interviews ranged in length from two hours to about five hours. A specific schedule of items was followed, although the man was encouraged to expand on issues as they arose. A 13-item Participation Scale, the modified Bem inventory, and a story writing task were completed by each man at predetermined points in the interview.

To facliitate the comparisons between samples, the responses to each question were coded by two judges whose reliability correlations ranged from .62 to .88, with "effective" reliability coefficients (Rosenthal, 1973) between .82 and .89. After making their independent codes, the judges resolved any disagreements to reach a single score for each item. These scores were used for subsequent t-tests, chi-squares, correlations, and multiple regression analyses.

Results

Demographic variables. The men in the combined samples ranged in age from 24 to 56, with a median of 38 years old. The custody sample averaged five years older than the non-custody sample (t = 2.0, p < .05), with comparably older wives and children. Occupation and education

2. The main reason for the lower success rate in reaching men without custody was their greater mobility. Nearly all of the men in the custody sample remained in their marital residences; the non-custody sample used their "separation" addresses on legal documents (often temporary residences such as boarding houses, motels, or offices). In the great majority of cases, no current address or telephone number was available. Every effort was made to reach each selected name, but many of those men could not be found.

are distributed across the range of social class categories in both groups, but men in the custody sample tended to come from higher categories ($t = 1.7$, $p < .10$). It was not possible to do analyses by race, since the sample was nearly all white (39 out of 40, reflecting the county's overall population). Religious preferences also reflected the county's overall population distribution (48 percent Catholic), and there were no religious differences between the samples.

In all cases but one, this was the first marriage for both spouses. The average family in the combined sample consisted of a couple which had been married nearly fourteen years and had two or three children.[3] In keeping with their older age, the custody sample had been married slightly longer and had somewhat larger families. There were no differences between samples in the gender of the children; the idea that men would be more interested in taking custody of boys was not supported by the data.

The results do not support the hypothesis that men with custody would be a younger, more radical group who would demonstrate alternative life styles in general. If anything, the men in the custody sample were older and more established. Among all men in the combined sample who had ever considered or initiated a custody petition, those of higher socioeconomic status were more likely to be successful; these men could probably afford better legal help, and also may have been viewed more positively by the judges.

Fathers' families of origin. Nine of the 40 men (22.5 percent) reported that their parents were either divorced or separated. Though the number of cases is small, this result is completely in line with the data reported by Pope and Mueller (chapter 6), and is higher than the 15 percent disruption rate one would expect among the parents of a general population of white males of this age group (U.S. Bureau of the Census, 1972b). There are no differences between the custody and non-custody samples in the percentages of disrupted and intact families of origin.

One of the strongest and most surprising findings in this area was the effect of sibling configuration: men in the custody sample were more likely to be middle- or last-born children, and were significantly more likely to have *both* brothers and sisters rather than siblings of only one sex ($x^2 = 4.07$, $p < .05$). These effects hold true even though there were no differences in average family size between the two groups.

The second finding to emerge from the family of origin data was a tendency for men in the custody sample to describe more intense rela-

3. A majority of the men in both groups said that they never used birth control of any kind, perhaps reflecting the high percentage of Catholics. This lack of birth control was implicated in many of the marriages, and might conceivably have had an effect on the men's feelings about their children; somewhere between 35 and 50 percent of the wives were pregnant at the time of the marriage (see Furstenberg, chapter 5).

tionships with their mothers and more distance from their fathers than did men in the non-custody sample. There were three indices of this effect. First, men in the custody sample evaluated their relationship with their mothers as closer than their relationship with their fathers; men in the non-custody sample said they were close to both parents. Second, mothers of men in the custody sample were significantly less often employed outside the home ($x^2 = 6.80$, p $<$ .01), suggesting that they may have been more completely responsible for childcare in the family and more available to their children.[4] Third, if forced as a child to choose one family member to live with, a significantly higher percentage of the custody sample said they would have chosen their mothers ($x^2 = 14.1$, p $<$ .01); men in the non-custody sample preferred their fathers, or said they could not have chosen.

Fathers' participation in child rearing. On several measures the fathers' participation in child rearing varied widely. Overall, the combined sample appeared to be active fathers in comparison with samples described in other published studies (Newson and Newson, 1963; Fein, 1974; Komarovsky, 1962). For the time when the children were infants, 42 percent reported minimal participation in their care, another 42 percent reported giving their wives significant help, and 15 percent reported either an equal or the larger share of the childcare responsibility. For the years when the children were older, they said that they engaged in such activities as playing with the children after school, taking care of them in the wife's absence, and putting them to bed, between once and several times per week.

The most surprising finding is that none of the participation measures discriminates significantly between the custody and non-custody samples. Two possible explanations come to mind. One is that there truly are no differences, and participation in childcare tasks is unrelated to the desire for custody. Divorce may be such a dramatic interference in family relationships that its impact overwhelms the pattern of past interactions. A second possibility is that this is an extraordinary sample of non-custody men, since due to the selection process they all still lived near their marital home. This particular non-custody sample may have had an unusually high pre-divorce involvement in child rearing, not representative of all fathers without custody, which eliminated differences between samples in this study.

Sex-role orientation. Based on the Bem scale, no differences in sex-role orientation were found between the custody and non-custody samples. Overall, the 40 men demonstrated the same balance of masculinity,

4. This is apparently not the result of important economic differences between the families of origin of the custody and non-custody samples. There were no differences between samples in the distribution of the men's fathers' occupations.

femininity, and androgyny scores as Bem's (1974) standardizing sample of college students. These data do not support the hypothesis that men who receive custody would be more feminine in their orientation.

Characteristics of the marital dissolution. In analyzing the 40 interviews it became apparent that the original intention to view "characteristics of the marital dissolution" in the same way as the other four areas of data was too simplistic. The major part of nearly every interview was used by the participant to describe and examine his divorce experience. The complexity of this information meant that too much essential content would be lost in a reduction to a few variables such as, for example, "degree of hostility." In addition, some of the most interesting findings were not essentially a comparison of the custody and non-custody samples. Therefore, to capitalize on the advantage of this kind of interview procedure, a more descriptive approach is used for this set of findings.

The fathers' accounts of the divorce process are here organized into four groups: (1) the incompatibility group, (2) the incapacitated wife group, (3) the provisional marriage group, and (4) the extramaritally involved wife group. It should be kept in mind that the explanations discussed here are not "fact"; no effort was made to find out what "really happened," or to get the wife's side of the story. It is the men's interpretations of their divorce experiences and the effect of those interpretations on the custody decisions that constitute the data.

1. *Incompatibility group* (*n* = 11). Each man in this group attributed his divorce to both parties' failure to meet the other's needs. Typically, he reported that his marriage started off well and the couple was happy for several years. Over the last few years, however, the couple began to drift apart. After a period of unhappiness, and usually without any identifiable precipitating event, the couple decided to get a divorce.

In nine of these eleven cases, there was little rancor between spouses. The divorce decision was described as mutual and calmly reached. However, several of the men said they acceded to the divorce with great reluctance; their final acquiescence stemmed from their realization that their wives were inevitably slipping away from them.

We're still very compatible; we just started growing in different directions. Our marriage was constraining. The romanticism dissolved—there was resentment that we were not understanding each other's needs. . . . Things have continued as a friendship.

In five cases, there was a joint decision that the husband should take custody. Reasons included an agreement that the husband's life was more stable ("She was into experimenting with her life in ways that I wasn't") and that the wife wanted more freedom.

Of the six men who did not take custody, two said that they felt the children would be better off with their mothers. The other four men were intensely ambivalent about custody. They expressed some anger and regret, but felt that they had had no choice.

I just thought it would be unheard of—what causes are there for getting custody? To this day I still feel the children would be better off with me.

In general, the men in the "incompatibility group" experienced the divorce as both a relief and a loss. For some, the dominant feeling was a sense of escape from an increasingly painful marriage. For others, especially those without custody, loneliness and a feeling of having been abandoned have interfered with taking on a comfortable new identity as a single adult; they seemed to consider the loss of their children to be the high price of ending an unsalvageable marriage. As one of them said, "Wherever your children are, there's a home. If you don't have your children, you don't have a home."

2. *Incapacitated wife group (n = 5).* Each man in this group described his ex-wife as somehow incapacitated, either as an alcoholic or as suffering from a severe mental disorder. Each of the alcoholic wives had allegedly been drinking for many years; those three divorces were friendly. The other two women each suffered from a form of psychosis; one wanted the divorce, the other did not.

In only three of these five cases did the husband actively seek custody. The three men had, in fact, been raising their children alone for some time and were determined to have custody; their wives agreed completely. The other two men were ambivalent; both of their wives felt capable of raising the children and would have contested any custody claim by the father. Both men felt the children would have been better off with them, but they reported that their lawyers supported their assumption that they could not win in court, and thus did not file a custody petition.

3. *Provisional marriage group (n = 5).* The cases in this group share an aura of tentativeness, in spite of the presence of at least one child. The five men average under 26 years old, and were married an average of only three years before the filing of divorce papers. In three cases the wife was a pregnant teenager at the time of the marriage; in the other two cases, the wife became pregnant immediately after the wedding. There was a remarkably consistent story in these cases: two young people, not yet truly independent as individuals, married and immediately had children. Soon thereafter the limitations and responsibilities of married life and parenthood became intolerable; the couple divorced, and the woman returned to her prior home with the children, where she shared childcare with her mother.

In these cases the extended families, especially the mothers of both spouses, were very intrusive. The men's accounts give the impression that the couple never successfully created a boundary around their new family unit.

It turned out to be a choice [between my mother and my wife] which I couldn't make one way or the other. Both of them would yell at me when they were alone with me. My wife said, "Who's more important?" I said, "Does it have to be a choice?"

We lived with her aunt [who had raised her] for eight months. We fought all the time about her—she wanted to be in on all our decisions. My wife listened to the aunt more than me, especially about what to do with the baby.

The men in this group were characteristically depressed, and uniformly felt like failures. Custody was awarded to the wife in all five cases. In general the men felt that their wives would be better able to raise the children. Three of the men said that they had considered custody, and two had actually discussed a custody petition with their lawyers. However, neither of them pursued it very aggressively, and they are not sure if the custody petition was ever presented in court.

4. *Extramaritally involved wife group (n = 19)*. This group includes those cases where the man's description is dominated by his ex-wife's extramarital involvement. There are actually three typical stories within this group: either the wife suddenly ran away with another man, or she became involved in one relatively long-term outside relationship, or she developed a pattern of involvement with many men. In these cases, especially, the one-sided source of the report must be kept in mind; none of these nineteen men, for example, admitted any affair of his own.

In two cases, the wife apparently left without notice. Custody was not a choice for either of the men; they suddenly had no alternative. One man said, "Taking care of eight children, the youngest only $3\frac{1}{2}$, I didn't have much time to worry."

In a second subgroup, ten of the men described their wives as having been involved in long-standing affairs, usually unknown to the husbands for many years. At some point each of the husbands discovered that their wives were seeing another man. The wife typically denied any romantic or sexual involvement when first confronted, but soon acknowledged the affair. There was usually a period of uncertainty about the future of the marriage. Efforts at reconciliation failed and the couple separated.

In many of these stories, it is apparent that the wife's extramarital relationship is only one aspect of her general dissatisfaction with the marriage. However, the sequence of events is not clear. It is difficult to tell whether the men feel that a new love made the wife more critical of the marriage, or a general dissatisfaction with the marriage led the wife to seek and find someone else. In every case the wives complained that there was no longer any real communication between the spouses, and that their lives were empty.

I thought things were fine, until out of the blue this happened. I heard her at a cocktail party telling friends that she was considering leaving, was in love with M——, was sick of everything she had, and wanted to start a new life.

The third subgroup includes seven cases where the wife's affairs were allegedly not limited to one relationship, but involved many men. The stories are remarkably similar, and they represent the most bitter descriptions in the entire sample. Typically, after several years of marriage, the wife had begun to see other men openly, and to spend evenings, weekends, and sometimes longer away from home. In almost every case the wife had taken a job, usually the afternoon or evening shift, and frequently did not come home until early in the morning.

She got a job against my wishes, working 3 to 11 P.M. Then she started drinking and carousing, until finally she didn't come back for a whole weekend.

In five instances, there was at least one separation and reconciliation before the final separation and divorce. The repeated separations appear to have had an effect on parenting. These men were not particularly involved in caretaking when the children were younger, and they were happy with their wives' performance of the mother role. However, as the women gradually withdrew from the family (as one man put it, "she just wandered away from parenthood"), the fathers became more active; suddenly the tasks of childcare were "demystified." Several of the men reported significant changes in their orientation toward the children, as the whole family began to change its alignment—the father and the children becoming closer as the mother became more isolated.

The last few years I've changed a lot—become much closer to the kids— enormously so. We did more things together. At first it felt strange; it started as an obligation. Knowing what I do now, I would like to think I'd do it differently from the beginning.

In several of the cases the man's relationship with his children seemed to replace the lost one with the absent, rejecting wife.

[Why did you seek custody of your daughter?] Because I love her. She's the light of my life. If it wasn't for her, I don't know if I could have hacked it. To this day, when the walls close in on me she has a smile for me. It's love, that's all.

Custody was awarded to the father in twelve of these nineteen "extramaritally involved wife" cases. This resolution occurred in eight of the nine instances where the wife suddenly left the family or was openly involved with many men; the wife and the children expected the father to take custody in most of these instances.

In the other ten cases the situation was usually less dramatic. Most of these affairs were more stable and followed a breakdown in the marriage that was more apparent to both spouses. More of the women in this subgroup, and fewer of the men, wanted custody. The four men who did receive custody describe the process almost identically; they presented their wives with a choice, "him or us." "I gave her a choice: Billy and me or the other guy—so she left."

Discussion

Four complex variables appeared to have the strongest effects on the fathers' consideration of custody: their relationships in their family of origin, their feelings toward the departing wife, the wife's intention about custody, and the attitude of their attorneys.

Relationships in the family of origin. Two variables concerning the family of origin differentiated clearly between the samples. Men with custody showed more closeness toward their mothers and less toward their fathers; in addition, they were likely to be later-born children with both male and female siblings. Of the 24 men who ever considered custody (including 4 who did not receive it), 22 fit either the birth order or the relationship-with-parents pattern. Of the remaining 16 men only 5 fit either of those two patterns.

Good research on sibling relationships is sparse, preventing more than speculation on the family configuration effect. One hypothesis is that the combination of birth order and sex of siblings creates a dimension of "variety of sibling models." Those men who followed both brothers and sisters in the family may be less bound by traditional sex-role distinctions, since their parents' definitions of sex-appropriate behavior may have been focused on the first child of each sex in the family. Also, it is likely that to some degree the younger boy was "cared for" by his older siblings of both sexes, and may therefore consider childcare a less sex-typed activity than do men who had only sisters (who would not be sex-role models), or only brothers (whose interactions with their younger brother would be less meaningful as a model with only the mother as a competitive standard). It may also be true that wanting to care for children is an expression of sibling rivalry in these younger brothers, whose older siblings were able to care for them but who themselves did not have younger siblings to care for in turn.

The effects of the man's relationships with his own parents seem particularly strong in those cases where the marital dissolution was least dramatic. Evidence of this comes from the "incompatibility group" of eleven cases where the divorces involved low levels of hostility and recrimination. In this group, the six men without custody came from a mix of family backgrounds. On the other hand, the five men with custody represented an extremely consistent pattern; they all described their parents as filling very traditional, sex-role differentiated family roles. The previously noted "distance from father" actually reflects a relationship that was usually respectful and even admiring, but unemotional. The fathers were formal, sometimes domineering, and very involved in the outside world. The amount of time they spent with their children was typically small, but was generally described as enjoyable.

For the mothers of these men with custody, as one man put it, "her life was her children." In every case the mother was the parent that evoked the more intense emotional response. Most of the men said they felt more similar to their mothers than their fathers. One man made explicit the link between his relationship with his mother and his decision to seek custody: "I guess I'm more similar to my mother. We certainly share an interest in child rearing."

The intriguing aspect of these patterns is the suggestion that men from traditional families are more likely to make the extremely non-traditional decision to seek custody. Although they regret the lack of warmth from their fathers, the men in the custody sample generally feel that they were raised in very competent families. They saw their fathers as able to fulfill their role of material provider and protector completely, if from a distance, and their mothers as skilled at providing great warmth and intimacy.

These fathers' desire for custody in response to the disintegration of their own families seems to express their identification with both parents. First, becoming the single parent satisfies simultaneously the needs both to provide for and to care for children, which he has internalized separately from each parent. Second, by seeking custody the man attempts to assert his competence in running a family, and to avert an admission of failure implicit in the divorce. Third, most of these men struggled during childhood to increase the emotional support they derived from their fathers. They protect the caring part of their relationships with their own children by tightening the family boundary around the children and themselves; the departing wife, not the husband, becomes the outcast.

Feelings about the departing wife. The more wronged, betrayed, or victimized that a man felt, the more likely he was to have sought custody. Most of the men in the custody sample attributed the divorce primarily to the wife's involvement with another man; in contrast, most of the non-custody sample described divorces based on incompatibility or mutual failure. Anger and revenge seemed to be components of many decisions to seek custody; some men had difficulty separating their desire to punish their wives from other motivations, such as affection for the children and attempts to make objective appraisals of which parental environment was likely to be the best for the children in the future. There were cases where a bitter divorce seemed to overwhelm all other considerations so that the father felt compelled to seek custody. There were other cases where the divorce was a mildly disruptive event in the process of family disengagement, so that other factors must be found to explain the man's pursuit of the custodial role.

The wife's intentions concerning custody. In 18 of the 20 cases where fathers took custody, it was with the mothers' pre-trial consent. Many different reasons were offered for the wife's agreement. In some of the cases the wife apparently did not want custody. In several cases the couple decided amicably that the husband could offer the children a more secure home life. In other cases, the husband's fierce determination to have custody seems to have scared the wife out of entering a contest she knew would be bitter and could be publicly humiliating. Finally, in seven cases the children were asked to choose, and their preference for living with their father was honored by the mother. Whatever the reason, in all but two of the 20 cases where the father took custody, the wife agreed before the court hearing.

Attitude of the attorneys. During the divorce procedure most of these men had contact with only one professional from outside the family— their attorneys. The men expressed widespread dissatisfaction with the legal system as a whole and with their own lawyers in particular; 23 of the 40 men had major complaints. Several men felt that their attorneys were incompetent; a few thought that their lawyers were overly sympathetic to their wives.

Unhappiness with the legal aspects of the divorce is clearly related to custody outcome. Seventeen of the 23 dissatisfied respondents were in the non-custody sample. In fact, several of the men who were awarded custody responded to a question about their perception of the fairness of the hearings with answers such as, "How can I complain? I got what I wanted most."

Nineteen of the men said that their attorneys felt it was "impossible" or "extremely difficult" for a man to win custody, and eleven of them went on to say that their attorneys' belief was a major reason they did not file a custody petition. In some of these cases, the attorneys were undoubtedly right and were being blamed for the husband's own disinterest in custody. Some men did file anyway; four of the men who eventually won custody say that they filed despite their lawyers' advice that their chances were very slim. In other cases, however, the lawyers' advice was described as more categorical—not a legal judgment on the merits of the particular case.

My lawyer said it was a foregone conclusion: husbands don't get kids. I would have loved to have them.

I went to the best attorney in the business in this area, and he advised me not to, that nobody has a chance in this state. Nothing I said could have made a difference.

I really wanted custody, so I filed anyway, even though my lawyer said there wasn't any way. . . . In this state, my lawyer says you have to prove the wife unfit. He said he would hire an investigator, but I don't know if he ever did. In fact, I think maybe he withdrew my request. He never told me anything.

It is important to remember that these are reports of complicated legal proceedings through the eyes of laymen. Still, the unevenness of the reported legal advice is noteworthy. There may be a social class effect: professional and middle-class men gave the impression that they used their lawyers, while working-class men more often felt that their lawyers tried to use them.

While the overall influence of the attorneys was clear in most of these cases, it is impossible to assess the quality of the attorneys' advice on the basis of these data alone. There is no way of knowing how many men, if any, failed to pursue strong cases for custody because of their attorneys' reluctance. There is also no way to know whether their attorneys were accurately describing a biased system, or inaccurately maligning a fair one. Both husbands and attorneys may have participated in perpetuating a bias, since inaction because of an assumption of prejudice becomes itself a self-fulfilling prophecy, and itself creates continuing inequities.

Conclusion

These interviews reveal that issues involving children were extremely important aspects of the divorce experience for nearly all of these men, whether or not they had sought custody. Although the interview was presented as being concerned with divorce in general, much of the content of the men's unstructured responses dealt explicitly with emotional needs and attachments to their children. Among the men who received custody, father-child relationships often took on particular intensity and multi-generational meaning; these men were disappointed with their own fathers' emotional distance from them when they were children, and they intend to act differently in their own father-child relationship.

In addition to *caring* deeply about their children, the fathers in the custody sample also felt that *raising* them was important enough to be worth sacrifices in other areas; in some instances, particularly regarding their careers, sacrifices did have to be made. It is interesting to note that many of the difficulties the men faced as a result of taking custody were exactly the same as those widely experienced by single-parent mothers.

Money was tight. Childcare became a problem, which made work more difficult. Visits by the mother were often anticipated with wariness and anxiety. In addition, for some of the men the strain of the divorce, combined with the emotional demands of parenthood, made the development of a new social life very difficult. Yet none of these fathers said he regretted his decision to take custody.

If fathers' interest in custody becomes widespread, it would present the legal system with both an opportunity for increased flexibility and a potential crisis in the evolution of legal precedent. This study suggests that to some degree both women and men now feel freer to let their personal desires and best judgment, instead of social pressure, determine their actions. Broader options may increase the chances that the court can find a custody arrangement suited to all members of a family.

On the other hand, when the practice of giving custody to mothers was almost automatic, the process was often simple. Increasing numbers of fathers interested in custody may now present judges with many complicated cases involving two equally competent parents and children who love them both. At the very least, competition for custody will point out the need for clearer criteria than the vague notions of the "best interest of the child" which are often the court's only guideline (see Weiss, chapter 19). It will be a challenge to both the legal and psychological communities to keep pace with the changing needs of these families, to help them explore new models, and to learn all that we can from the experience of individuals who are at these decision points in their lives.

Robert S. Weiss

Issues in the Adjudication of
Custody When Parents Separate

It is estimated that perhaps a third of the children now growing up in America will, at some point before their eighteenth year, find their parents separating (Bane, chapter 16). If present practice continues, the custody of over 90 percent of these children will be entrusted to their mothers. The majority of separating parents and of those who advise them presume that mothers are more skilled in childcare, are better able to tolerate childcare's interference with freedom to work, are more nurturant, and are more important to the well-being of the children (Gersick, chapter 18).

Most divorcing parents decide on custody out of court: less than 10 percent fail to reach agreement before the divorce hearing (Freed and Foster, 1974; Jacobson, 1959). Prior agreements between separated parents are almost always approved in court. But although judges themselves decide custody in only a small minority of divorce hearings, the decisions they make affect a much larger proportion of the agreements reached out of court. Many custody disputes are preadjudicated in lawyers' offices or in couples' homes on the basis of anticipations of what would happen were the disputes to be carried to court.

What is absolutely remarkable about American statute law in relation to custody adjudication is how much discretion it leaves to the courts. The statute law in some states does little more than exhort judges to award custody according to the best interests of the child. In other states

Work on this chapter was supported by HEW Contract No. 100-76-0135. The author wishes to thank Miss Ellen Carson of Harvard Law School for her help and Professor Frank Sander for a most useful critique. The author also wishes to thank the editors of this volume for useful comments and suggestions.

there is a listing of issues judges are required to consider, but the judges retain discretion to decide not only how to evaluate each of the issues but also what relative weight to give to each.

In this situation judges are of necessity required to draw on what Donald Schon has called "ideas in good currency," by which he means ideas understood as generally accepted. These ideas can undergo change with time. A major change took place during the nineteenth century, when the preferred parent shifted from father to mother. We are now witnessing still another major change as the sex of the parent is increasingly being defined as irrelevant.

Still other changes in custody adjudication have been proposed. With increasing experience of the consequences of custody decisions, it has been recognized that court decisions do not so much end the disputes of divorcing parents as they change their terms. Where before custody adjudication parents might battle over who might have the children, after custody adjudication they are likely to battle over the times and conditions of visitation. This recognition of the persistence of dispute has brought with it realization that there is inconsistency in the award of full custodial responsibility to one parent and visitation rights to the other. Two quite different responses have developed to this recognition: one that would give the custodial parent control over visitation as well as whatever else affects the child, the other that would seek to protect visitation but to associate custodial responsibility with it. This is a controversy whose resolution is as yet unclear.

But if the present scene regarding custody adjudication is marked by changing understandings and new controversies, it is also marked by an entirely positive development: the emergence of useful results from social science research. These results help make clear the aims to which custody adjudication should aspire, although they leave open the identification of the particular custody arrangement which is most likely to reach them.

These are the concerns of this paper. I begin with a review of the principles that seem to have guided custody adjudication in the past.

CHANGING IDEAS OF HOW TO ACHIEVE THE CHILD'S "BEST INTERESTS"

Until the early part of the nineteenth century, English common law regularly awarded fathers the custody of the children if parents separated (Foster and Freed, 1964). Some English judges asserted in their written opinions that God had designated the father to be the child's natural guardian; others suggested that the organization of social life, because of which men not only were responsible for children's support but also better understood the workings of society, demanded that children be subject to their father's direction.

American judges never fully adopted the doctrine that fathers had an absolute right to children's custody. Although reference to this doctrine can be found in early American judicial decisions, most American judges gave primacy to the interests of the child. In an 1813 case a Pennsylvania judge justified awarding custody of two girls, not yet adolescent, to the mother with whom they had been living because, as the judge put it, "Considering their tender age, they stand in need of that kind of assistance which can be afforded by none so well as a mother" (Commonwealth of Pennsylvania vs. Addicks and Wife, 1813, p. 521).

Until the mid-nineteenth century, however, American judges agreed that the best interests of the child would normally be served by awarding custody to the father because the father could better care for the child. Joseph Story, a leading jurist of the early nineteenth century, commented:

> As to the question of the right of the father to have custody of his infant child, in a general sense it is true. But this is not on account of any absolute right of the father, but for the benefit of the infant, the law presuming it to be for his interests to be under the nurturance and care of his natural protector, both for maintenance and education. [U.S. vs. Green, 1824, p. 15]

In the American society of those years the father alone may well have seemed more capable of caring for children than the mother alone. Women were thought of as themselves requiring the protection of men— fathers, husbands, or, in their absence, more distant kinsmen. And insofar as children were to be prepared for participation in the larger society, women were considered to be too insulated and likely to be too lenient.

During the nineteenth century, ideas about the aims of the family and the raising of children gradually changed. Instead of the family being seen as a place where children were prepared for participation in society, the family was viewed as a place where children were nurtured and protected from the impersonal outside world (Kenniston, 1977, pp. 11–17). Now the mother was likely to be considered as the preferred parent, especially if the child was young. Courts did not change in their fundamental commitment to award the child to the parent likely to serve the child's best interests. But there was a change in the accepted ideas regarding which parent was the more important for the child.

Preference for the mother was the dominant judicial outlook from the time of the Civil War through the 1960s. Extravagant appreciations of mother love can be found in opinions written throughout this hundred-year period.

> For a boy of . . . tender years, nothing can be an adequate substitute for mother love—for that constant ministration required during the period of nurturing that only a mother can give because in her alone is duty swallowed up in desire; in her alone is service expressed in terms of love. She alone has the patience and sympathy required to mold and sooth the infant mind in its adjustment to its environment. [Jenkins v. Jenkins, p. 595]

Because the very young child for whom the mother was believed to be so critically important was regularly referred to as being of tender years, the preference for the mother came to be known as "the doctrine of tender years" (see Bath vs. Bath, 1949; Podell, Peck, and First, 1972; Trenkner, 1976).

At first, judges often held that the doctrine no longer applied once children were of school age. For example, in one case a judge declared that "A boy of three years of age may properly be deemed to be of such tender age that consideration of his welfare calls for his having a mother's care, but the same cannot be said when the child has reached the age of five" (Sinclair vs. Sinclair, 1905, p. 862). With the passage of time the range of children's ages to which "tender years" could be applied appeared to increase, although the upper limit for applicability of the doctrine appears to have been the onset of adolescence (Trenkner, 1976, p. 291). Despite the limited range of applicability of "tender years" in practice, by the beginning of the 1970s a number of State statutes required that the mother be preferred over the father in deciding the custody of a child of any age, so long as other things were equal (Trenkner, 1976, pp. 293–4).

Criticism of the presumption in favor of the mother began to appear in the 1960s and by the early 1970s had gathered enough force to lead to the repeal of some State statutes that had required the mother to be preferred. California, for example, in 1973 repealed an earlier statute that gave preference to the mother, all else equal, and replaced it with one which required that custody be awarded according to the best interests of the child.

A number of elements contributed to the changed view of the mother's comparative importance for the children. One was a growing skepticism regarding the natural superiority in parenting of mothers over fathers. Insofar as fathers might have equal merit as parents, a presumption in favor of the mother would then constitute unfair discrimination on account of sex. Judge Sybil Hart Cooper of the New York Family Court held in an opinion that the presumption in favor of the mother deprived the father of his right to equal protection by the law (Watts vs. Watts, 1973; see also Freed and Foster, 1976). In addition, defenders of fathers' rights pointed out that if men are to have no advantage over women in the competition for jobs, and if most single mothers can be expected to work, then women should not be seen as having more right to the children: "A man can hire a babysitter as well as a woman" (Title, 1974, p. 200).

Judges' courtroom practice may be changing more slowly than statute law. Kram and Frank (1976) report: "One can best conclude that while the current trend is against 'tender years' a healthy skepticism about its complete demise would not be out of place" (p. 15). They believe that for some time to come judges will continue to feel that the mother, all else equal, is the more appropriate custodian for the children.

FAULT AND THE "BEST INTERESTS" PRINCIPLE

The "best interests" principle requires that judges treat as irrelevant the issue of which parent is in the right. As Judge Cardozo put it in an opinion, "The chancellor . . . is not adjudicating a controversy between adversary parties, to compose private differences, he is not determining rights . . . between one parent and another . . . [his] concern is for the child" (Finlay vs. Finlay, 1924, p. 626). The "best interests" principle requires that a behavior be treated as irrelevant to a custody decision unless that behavior bodes ill for the children's future welfare. The custody statute in the Bar Association's Proposed Uniform Marriage and Divorce Act includes the caution that "The court shall not consider conduct of the proposed custodian that does not affect his relationship to the child" (American Bar Association, 1973, p. 162).

Yet the principle that an individual shall not profit from wrongdoing is deeply embedded in judicial thought. It would not be surprising if judges felt more comfortable when they could decide that the interests of a child were best served by awarding the child's custody to an otherwise wronged parent. Louisiana is apparently unique among States in that it requires a presumption in favor of the plaintiff in the divorce action: "In all cases of separation and of divorce the children shall be placed under the care of the parties who shall have obtained the separation or divorce unless the judge shall, for the greater advantage of the children, order that some or all of them shall be entrusted to the care of the other party." But while Louisiana may be the only State that explicitly directs a judge to consider marital fault, the State of Missouri, while adopting the Uniform Custody Code, deleted the caution that the court should not consider conduct of a proposed custodian that had no bearing on the child's situation (Foster and Freed, 1973–4). The idea that marital fault is irrelevant to custody adjudication is clearly not universally accepted.

Even when State statutes would seem to forbid consideration of parental fault, judges are required to decide whether parents are "fit." After all, the best interests of the child could hardly be realized by placing a child with an "unfit" parent. Yet the conditions that lead judges to appraise parents as unfit are highly suggestive of fault: habitual drunkenness, adultery, gross immorality—which often means living with someone without marriage, cruelty or neglect toward the children, and serious social or emotional disability (Foster and Freed, 1964; Podell, Peck, and First, 1972). Judges can be negatively influenced simply by evidence that a parent is sexually active. Although judges today appear less affected by evidence of "immorality" than they were at an earlier time in our national history, an experienced attorney, writing in 1970, suggests that evidence that the other parent is "engaged in immoral conduct" might still be a useful weapon in a divorce dispute (Sproger, 1971). He recommends to his fellow attorneys:

Consideration should be given to the feasibility of employment of a private investigator, especially where your client fears that the custodial parent is engaged in immoral conduct which will have a deleterious effect upon the well-being of children. [P. 23]

We cannot be certain regarding the extent to which matters of fault now enter into custody adjudication. Very likely such issues play only a secondary role in most custody contests. Yet there are undoubtedly contests in which appraisals of fault affect judges' decisions, and in which the best interests of the child are not the judges' only concerns.

DIFFICULTIES IN THE APPLICATION OF THE
PURE "BEST INTERESTS" RULE

There are several ways in which administration of the "best interests" principle differs from other judicial responsibilities. The "best interests" principle requires that judges predict children's futures rather than evaluate evidence or decide facts or apply general legal principles to particular cases. In dealing with other legal issues, judges are required to go no further in their conclusions than evidence warrants; to decide custody they are asked to make long-term extrapolations from the present. Often they must weigh the relative merits of different kinds of life, and so must be willing to base decisions on values rather than evidence. For example, in the famous Iowa case, Painter vs. Bannister (1966), the Iowa Supreme Court decided to leave a boy in his grandparents' home rather than return the boy to his father primarily because the judges preferred the kind of life the grandparents could provide. Because the parent was deprived of custody in favor of the grandparents, the decision received national publicity. Cases in which judges' values decide between mothers and fathers occur frequently and receive no public attention.

Without a presumption in favor of the mother, it is a formidable task to decide with which parent lie the best interests of the child. Many State statutes add to judges' difficulties by offering only the most vague guidelines. The Idaho statute, for example, says only:

In an action for divorce the court may, before or after judgment, give such direction for the custody, care, and education of the children of the marriage as may seem necessary or proper. [Idaho Code Section 32–705]

Other states do provide judges with a fairly detailed list of the factors to be taken into account. Those states that have adopted the custody statute proposed by the American Bar Association direct judges to consider the wishes of the child's parents and of the child, the relationship of the child and the parents, the child's adjustment to home, school, and community, and the mental and physical health of all involved. Some states go still further. Minnesota requires that judges take into consideration the economic capacity of each parent, the cultural background of all concerned, and "any other factor considered by the court to be relevant to the particular child's custody dispute."

Some observers have thought that statutes providing a list of issues to be considered are an advance over statutes that offer less guidance (Robbins, 1974; Benedek and Benedek, 1972). A listing of factors may, perhaps, reduce the likelihood of a judge exaggerating the importance of a single element. Yet it would seem that these detailed statutes offer not much more than a framework for subjectivity. The issues judges must consider include such elusive matters as the quality of the parent-child relationships and the nature of children's adjustments to various settings. Judges must also decide for themselves how much weight to give to each issue.

Many judges use investigations by social workers, probation officers, lawyers, psychiatrists, and others to help them decide with which parent the best interests of the child will lie. Undoubtedly such investigations are in general useful, although they also tend to delay custody adjudication, often utilize hearsay evidence, can bring embarrassment to the contesting parties insofar as they require interviews with relatives or neighbors, and permit free expression in the report for the judge of the biases of the investigators. Lawyers sometimes bring experts into custody hearings, and judges can then add the experts' testimony to the materials on which they will base their decisions. Yet even with the help of investigators and the contributions of experts, the task of deciding custody disputes remains excruciatingly difficult: judges have so much discretion, the decision is so important to those involved, and the task is intrinsically so very difficult. One judge, writing at a time when the presumption in favor of the mother made custody decisions easier than they are today, said: "A judge agonizes more in reaching the right result in a contested custody decision than about any other type of decision he renders" (Botein, 1952, p. 273). In the era we seem now to be entering, in which there will be a presumption in favor of neither parent, it may be anticipated that judges will agonize still more.

SHOULD THE CHILD BE CONSULTED? AND, IF SO, HOW?

If the aim of the custody dispute is to decide with which parent a child would be better off, should not the child be consulted? And if the child is going to participate, should there not be a lawyer to serve as the child's advocate? Indeed, if a child's interests in a custody hearing are distinct from those of either of the child's parents, how else can the child's interests become known? And a child's interests *can* be distinct: a child might, for example, benefit by maintaining close ties with both parents although each parent wants the other to be away; or a child might benefit if some part of the bank account over which the parents are quarreling were to be sequestered for the child's later education. One legal argument for providing children with counsel in custody proceedings is that since custody proceedings will decide the settings in which children live, the Constitutional guarantee of due process requires that children have the opportunity to be heard (Milmed, 1974).

Two states, Ohio and Georgia, now require that, unless there is a strong reason for not doing so, judges honor a statement of preference made by an older child: in Ohio, twelve or older; in Georgia, fourteen or older. States which provide lists of factors that judges are to consider in reaching their decisions on custody regularly include among the factors the preferences of the child. And informal observation suggests that judges give great weight to a child's expressed preference, especially if the child is adolescent or nearly so and appears both mature and determined.

Yet there are problems associated with routinely soliciting children's preferences. To begin with, the parent the child seems to prefer is not necessarily the better parent for the child. This is not so much because the child's preference may have been gained by implicit or explicit promises to the child of a life of indulgence, free from homework and chores. It is more because children are so easily made to feel responsible for parents' well-being and can so easily be convinced that a parent could not survive their loss. In addition, children are easily moved to anger by parental separation and may feel impelled to reject the parent they see as having caused the separation. And even when children's preferences have not been shaped by feelings of guilt or anger, the children may be mistaken in judging with which parent they would be better off. Children in other areas of their lives are recognized as still immature; why should they in this area be assumed to be fully competent?

Some judges fear that a child would endanger its relationship with one parent by voicing a preference for the other. To avoid this, and to avoid imposing a like anxiety on the child, these judges refuse to ask children to express any preference at all. Other judges, while inviting children to talk with them, assure them that nothing they may say will ever be reported to the parents, that their discussions will remain secret.

Most states make it possible for judges to have off-the-record discussions with children by not requiring that such discussions be made a part of the trial records. However, two states, Delaware and Montana, while giving judges the right to interview children in their chambers, require that the interviews be placed on the record. Whether off-the-record or on-the-record, judicial consultation with children poses a dilemma. Discussions that are off-the-record cannot be contested. This means that what may be the most critical testimony in a custody hearing is inaccessible to the lawyers representing the parents. But if discussions are on-the-record, children will be forced publicly to reject one of the parents.

While children now have a right to be heard in the adversary proceedings by which courts decide their custody, participation in the proceedings incurs risks. Among the dilemmas produced by custody disputes is one confronting the older child: to fail to state a preference permits the judge to make an undesired decision; to state a preference risks hurting one of the parents and damaging the child's relationship with that parent. As yet there appears to be no good way to resolve this dilemma within the context of adversary proceedings and the award of custody to one of the parents.

THE INTERNAL CONTRADICTION OF CUSTODY TO ONE PARENT, VISITATION RIGHTS TO THE OTHER

Although no definition of "custody" exists in statute law, the following definition appears in conformity with general usage:

"Custody" of a minor embraces the sum of parental rights with respect to the rearing of the minor and connotes a keeping or guarding of the child. It includes in its meaning every element of provision for the physical, moral, and mental well-being of the minor, including its immediate personal care and control. [*Words and Phrases*, 1968, 10A, p. 506]

Clearly, by the award of custody, courts intend to give to just one of the parents the rights and responsibilities for the children's care and control that had previously been possessed by the two parents together. The separation of the parents is understood by judges to require that one parent relinquish authority over the children. The custodial parent then has full authority, uncompromised by the need to consider the wishes of the other parent.

Yet, in most awards of custody, there is a significant limitation on the authority of the custodial parent: the noncustodial parent is granted "reasonable visitation." Judges rarely acknowledge, however, that the award of visitation to the noncustodial parent is a limitation of custody. One judge, an exception, did award a father "custody on Sunday afternoons" (Lambert vs. Lambert, 1949, p. 548). But it is much more usual for judges to avoid recognizing that a visiting parent can hardly be prevented from exercising normal parental care and control, so long as the other parent is not immediately present: that a visiting parent is a custodial parent for the interval of the visit. In one notable instance an Oregon court awarded custody to the mother but held that the father's visitation right might include having the child live with him from one week after the end of one school year until one week before the beginning of the next (McDonald vs. McDonald, 1953).

Though judges may not recognize the internal contradiction in the award of custody to one parent and reasonable visitation to the other, this contradiction is felt by parents. The custodial parent, although responsible for the children, must relinquish control over them for the interval of the visitation. Some custodial parents try to bridge the contradiction by presenting the visiting parent with directions regarding the children's care. ("Be sure they have their coats on if they go out to play.") Visiting parents, however, tend to resist the implication that they are now required to observe the custodial parents' directives (Weiss, 1975).

A drastic remedy to the contradiction in the award of custody to the one parent and visitation rights to the other has been offered by Goldstein, Freud, and Solnit (1973). Their response, based on the theory that the role of the child's caretaker must be protected, is to place visitation at the option of the custodial parent. The noncustodial parent would then possess only whatever rights were delegated voluntarily by the custodial parent. Here is what they say on the matter:

> Once it is determined who will be the custodial parent, it is that parent, not the court, who must decide under what conditions he or she wishes to raise the child. Thus, the noncustodial parent should have no legally enforceable right to visit the child, and the custodial parent should have the right to decide whether it is desirable for the child to have such visits. [P. 38]

The merit of the Goldstein et al. proposal is that it would end the helplessness of custodial parents to deal with disruptive invasions of their lives by noncustodial parents. Custodial parents would no longer be powerless to defend themselves and their children from what they believe to be upsetting or endangering experiences. Their authority would be equal to their responsibility.

The Goldstein et al. proposal would, however, seem likely to reduce contact between some noncustodial parents and their children. It would make it possible for custodial parents, in embattled situations, to severely limit the access of noncustodial parents to their children. As one family court judge said, "The custodial parent, intent upon punishing a deserting spouse or erasing all connections or identifications with him, may lack a transcending objectivity to make visitation arrangements in the child's interests" (Dembitz, 1974, p. 460). And in addition, noncustodial parents, required to acknowledge the custodial parents' power to end their relationships with their children and subject to whatever might be the interpersonal uses of that power, might react to minimize their investment in their children.

RECENT AND RELEVANT RESEARCH

Recent research has demonstrated that children very much desire free access to noncustodial parents and frequent contact with them. Rosen (1977), in a study of 92 children whose parents had divorced, found 60 percent of them wanting unrestricted contact with their noncustodial parent. Desire for easy access to the noncustodial parent held true whether the noncustodial parent was the father or the mother. Rosen's young respondents repeatedly insisted that being able to see the non-custodial parent whenever they wished, as well as seeing that parent often, made the parental separation tolerable. In another study, Kelly and Wallerstein (1977) report that the usual visiting arrangement in which the noncustodial parent takes the children every other weekend appeared to children to be woefully inadequate. They report: "The only younger children reasonably content with the visiting situation were those seven- and eight-year-olds visiting two or three times per week, most often by pedaling to their father's apartment on a bicycle" (1977, p. 52). Older children, too, wanted easy access and frequent contact with the noncustodial parent, although adolescents appeared more accepting of infrequent visits.

Kelly and Wallerstein found little reason for limiting visitation by the noncustodial parent. They report:

There were surprisingly few incidences where we considered frequent visits to be detrimental to a child, or where such frequent visiting placed that child substantially at risk. [P. 54]

Furthermore, Wallerstein has noted that depression among younger children appeared linked to infrequent visits from the noncustodial parent (Wallerstein, personal communication).

It would appear, then, that easy access to the noncustodial parent is desired by most children, is rarely disruptive to the children's development, and may even be essential to the continued functioning of younger children. But what of the custodial parent? What are the consequences for the custodial parent of not limiting the other parent's visitations?

Hetherington, Cox, and Cox (1976) report, on the basis of an intensive study of 48 divorced couples and their children, that, except where there was conflict and ill-will between the parents or psychological disturbances in the father, the frequency of the father's contact with the child was associated not only with more positive adjustment of the child but also with better functioning of the mother. They found that no other support relationship was as valuable for the mother raising children on her own as "the continued, positive, mutually supportive relationship of the divorced couple and continued involvement of the father with the child" (p. 426). Although this work does not demonstrate that custodial parents are always better off if noncustodial parents have easy access to the children, it does show that the custodial parent profits to the extent that it is possible for the noncustodial parent to be constructively involved with the children. The more closely the custodial and noncustodial parents can work together for the benefit of the children, the better for the custodial parent as well as for the children.

THE "JOINT CUSTODY" ALTERNATIVE

Research suggests that the aims of custody adjudication should include achieving, as far as possible, the protection of the child's relationships with both parents, easy access to both parents, and the fostering of a relationship between the parents in which each is supportive of the other's parental efforts.

It is, as yet, uncertain how these aims may best be realized. Present practice, in which custody is awarded to one parent and visitation rights to the other, appears often to lead to unsatisfactory conclusions. The approach advocated by Goldstein et al. seems unlikely to better matters, but there is not yet any research that would establish the consequences of the application of the Goldstein et al. principle.

Stack (1976) and others have advocated an approach diametrically opposed to that of Goldstein et al. They would have the two parents retain their custodial rights and responsibilities despite divorce from each other. As Stack has put it, "The legal custodians of a child during their marriage would retain their shared custody after the marriage is dissolved" (1976, p. 511). Insofar as the children lived with one parent, they would be governed by that parent's rules. If they moved to the other parent's home, they would be required to accept the other parent's rules. Both parents would be entitled to access to the children's school reports; both parents would have to agree on the children's education, on optional medical treatments such as orthodonture and psychotherapy, and, most important, on where the children would live and how their access to the two parents would be maintained.

"Joint custody" or "shared custody" is sometimes associated with alternating residences, in which the children live part of the time with one parent and part of the time with the other. But this is not a necessary implication of joint custody. All that is necessary is that the parents each continue to retain responsibility for the children's care and control.

Does joint custody work? There are impressionistic studies that insist that it does. (Some are listed in Roman and Haddad, 1978.) Parents who are quarreling with each other in other spheres appear able to agree on issues affecting their children's well-being. And the provision of mediation or binding arbitration for insoluble quarrels seems effective in preventing an impasse.

It may be the case that joint custody is desirable only if both parents want it or only if couples are affluent enough to afford occasional resort to mediation. Or it may be the case that joint custody has been effective only because it is new and those who have adopted it are enthusiasts. We do not yet know the answers to these questions, and it is clear that further research is necessary.

We do not know nearly enough about the implications for children and their parents of different approaches to the management of custody and visitation after parental separation and divorce. The courts will always be vehicles for the expression of societal values. It would be most useful if custody decisions could be informed by empirical findings on the consequences of various arrangements.

REFERENCES

Aberle, D. F., and Naegele, K. D. 1952. Middle-class fathers' occupational role and attitudes toward children. *American Journal of Orthopsychiatry*, 22, 366–378.

Abernethy, V. 1973. Social network and response to the maternal role. *International Journal of Sociology of the Family*, 3, 86–92.

Ackerman, C. 1963. Affiliations: Structural determinants of differential divorce rates. *American Journal of Sociology*, 69, 12–20.

Albert, S., and Kessler, 1976. Processes for ending social encounters. *Journal for the Theory of Social Behavior*, 6, 147–170.

Aldous, J. 1969. Occupational characteristics and males' role performance in the family. *Journal of Marriage and the Family*, 31, 707–712.

American Bar Association. 1973. Proposed revised uniform marriage and divorce act. *Family Law Quarterly*, 7, 135–165.

American Law Reports, Annotated. 2d ed. 1963, 92, 692–745. Rochester: Lawyer's Cooperative.

Anspach, D. F. 1976. Kinship and divorce. *Journal of Marriage and the Family*, 38, 343–350.

Bachrach, L. L. 1973. Marital status of discharges from psychiatric inpatient units of general hospitals, United States 1970–1971: I. Analysis by age, color and sex. *Statistical note 82: National Institute of Mental Health.* Washington, D.C.: U.S. Government Printing Office.

———. 1975. Marital status and mental disorder: An analytical review. *Department of Health, Education and Welfare* Pub. No. (ADM) 75–217. Washington, D.C.: U.S. Government Printing Office.

Baguedor, E. 1972. *Separation: Journal of a marriage*. New York: Simon and Schuster.

Ban, P. L., and Lewis, M. 1974. Mothers and fathers, girls and boys: attachment behavior in the one-year-old. *Merrill-Palmer Quarterly of Behavior and Development*, 20 (3), 195–204.

Bandura, A. 1969. Social-learning theory of identificatory processes. In D. A. Goslin (Ed.), *Handbook of socialization theory and research*. Chicago: Rand McNally.

Bane, M. J. 1974. Who cares about child care? *Working Papers*, 2, 33–40.

———. 1975. *Economic influence on divorce and remarriage.* Cambridge, Mass.: Center for the Study of Public Policy.

———. 1976. *Here to stay: American families in the twentieth century.* New York: Basic Books.

Bath v. Bath. 1949. *Nebraska Reports*, 150, 591–614.

Baumrind, D. 1967. Child care practices anteceding three patterns of preschool behavior. *Genetic Psychological Monographs*, 75, 43–88.

Becker, G. 1973. A theory of marriage: Part I. *Journal of Political Economy*, 81, 813–847.

Becker, H. 1960. Notes on the concept of commitment. *American Journal of Sociology*, 66, 32–40.

Bell, R. R. 1971. *Marriage and family interaction* (3rd ed.). Homewood, Ill.: Dorsey Press.

Bem, S. L. 1974. The measurement of psychological androgyny. *Journal of Consulting and Clinical Psychology*, 42, 155–162.

Bendix, R. 1962. *Max Weber: An intellectual portrait*. New York: Doubleday.

Benedek, E. B., and Benedek, R. S. 1972. New child custody laws: Making them do what they say. *American Journal of Orthopedic Medicine*, 42, 825–834.

Benson, L. 1968. *Fatherhood: A sociological perspective*. New York: Random House.

Bernard, J. 1966. Marital stability and patterns of status variables. *Journal of Marriage and the Family*, 28, 421–439.

————. 1972. *The future of marriage.* New York: World.

————. 1976. Homosociology and female depression. *Journal of Social Issues,* 32(4).

Bernstein, R. and Cyr, F. E. 1957. A study of interviews with husbands in a pre-natal and child health program. *Social Casework, 38,* 473–480.

Biller, H. B. 1969. Father absence, maternal encouragement, and sex role develop-ment in kindergarten-age boys. *Child Development, 40,* 539–546.

Biller, H. B., and Bahm, R. M. 1971. Father absence, perceived maternal behavior, and masculinity of self-concept among junior high boys. *Developmental Psychology, 4,* 178–181.

Bishop, J. October 14, 1977. Jobs, cash transfers, and marital instability: A review of the evidence. Written testimony to the Welfare Reform Subcommittee of the Committees on Agriculture, Education and Labor, and Ways and Means of the U.S. House of Representatives.

Blair, M. 1970. Divorcées' adjustment and attitudinal changes about life. *Disserta-tion Abstracts, 30,* 5541–5542. (University Microfilms No. 70–11, 099.)

Blanchard, R. W., and Biller, H. B. 1971. Father availability and academic per-formance among third grade boys. *Developmental Psychology, 4,* 301–305.

Blau, P. M. 1964. *Exchange and power in social life.* New York: Wiley.

———— and Duncan, O. D. 1967. *The American occupational structure.* New York: Wiley.

Blood, R. O. Jr., and Wolfe, D. M. 1960. *Husbands and wives: The dynamics of married living.* New York: Free Press.

Bloom, B. L. *Changing patterns of psychiatric care.* 1975. New York: Behavioral Publications.

Bloom, B. L., Asher, S. J., and White, S. W. 1978. Marital disruption as a stressor: A review and analysis. *Psychological Bulletin, 85,* 867–894.

Boehm, F. 1930. The femininity complex in man. *International Journal of Psycho-analysis, 11,* 444–469.

Boekestijn, C. 1963. The significance of value-concordance and value-relevance for group cohesion. In M. Mulder (Ed.). *Mensen, groepen, en organisaties* (Deel 2). Van Gorcum: Assen.

Bohannan, P. 1970. (Ed.). *Divorce and after.* Garden City, N.Y.: Doubleday and Co.

————. 1975. Stepfathers and the mental health of their children. Final report sub-mitted to the Department of Health, Education and Welfare.

Boland, B. 1973. Participation in the Aid to Families with Dependent Children Program (AFDC) (Working Paper 971–02). Washington, D.C.: The Urban Institute.

Botein, B. 1952. *Trial judge.* New York: Simon and Schuster.

Bott, E. 1971. *Family and social network* (2nd ed.). London: Tavistock.

Bowen, W. G., and Finegan, T. A. 1969. *The economics of labor force participation.* Princeton: Princeton University Press.

Bowlby, J. 1969. *Attachment and loss, I: Attachment.* New York: Basic Books.

————. 1973. *Attachment and loss, II: Separation.* New York: Basic Books.

Brandwein, R. A., Brown, C. A., and Fox, E. M. 1974. Women and children last: The social situation of divorced mothers and their families. *Journal of Marriage and the Family, 36,* 498–514.

Brickman, P. 1974. *Social conflict.* Lexington, Mass.: D. C. Heath.

Briscoe, C. W., Smith, J. B., Robins, E., Marlens, S., and Gaskin, F. 1973. Divorce and psychiatric disease. *Archives of General Psychiatry, 29,* 119–125.

Brown, G. W., Bhrolcháin, M. N., and Harris, T. 1975. Social class and psychiatric disturbance among women in an urban population. *Sociology, 9,* 225–254.

Brown, P. 1976. A study of women coping with divorce. In *New research on women and sex roles.* University of Michigan: Center for Continuing Education.

Bruss, E. 1976. *Children's conceptions of parents and the parent-child relationship.* Special qualifying paper, Harvard University.

Bumpass, L., and Sweet, J. 1972. Differentials in marital instability: 1970. *American Sociological Review, 37,* 754–766.

Burchinal, L. G. 1960. Research on young marriage: Implications for family life education. *The Family Life Coordinator, 9,* 6–24.

————. 1964. Characteristics of adolescents from unbroken, broken, and reconstituted families. *Journal of Marriage and the Family, 26,* 44–51.

————. 1965. Trends and prospects for young marriages in the United States. *Journal of Marriage and the Family, 27,* 243–254.

Burgess, E. W., and Cottrell, L. S. Jr. 1939. *Predicting success or failure in marriage.* New York: Prentice-Hall.

Burgess, E. W., and Wallin, P. 1953. *Engagement and marriage.* Philadelphia: Lippincott.

Burlingham, D. 1973. The preoedipal infant-father relationship. *Psychoanalytic Study of the Child.* New Haven: Yale University Press, *28,* 23–47.

Burr, W. R. 1970. Satisfaction with various aspects of marriage over the life cycle. *Journal of Marriage and the Family, 32,* 26–37.

Byrne, D. 1971. *The attraction paradigm.* New York: Academic Press.

Cain, G. G. 1966. *Married women in the labor force.* Chicago: University of Chicago Press.

Campbell, A. May, 1975. The American way of mating: Marriage si, children only maybe. *Psychology Today,* pp. 37–43.

Caplan, G. 1961. *An approach to community mental health.* New York: Grune & Stratton, Inc.

Carter, H., and Glick, P. C. 1976. *Marriage and divorce: A social and economic study.* 2nd ed. Cambridge: Harvard University Press.

Carter, H., and Plateris, A. September 1963. Trends in divorce and family disruption. *HEW Indicators,* pp. v–xiv.

Cavanagh, R. C., and Rhode, D. L. 1976. The unauthorized practice of law and *Pro Se* divorce: An empirical analysis. *The Yale Law Journal, 86,* 104–184.

Chapsky, v. Wood. 1881. *Kansas Reports, 26,* 650–664.

Cherlin, Andrew. 1976. Social and economic determinants of marital separation. Ph.D. dissertation, University of California, Los Angeles.

————. 1977. The effect of children on marital dissolution. *Demography, 14,* 265–272.

————. 1978. Employment, income, marriage and divorce in two cohorts of women. Final report to the Employment and Training Administration, U.S. Department of Labor.

Chesser, E. 1957. *The sexual, marital, and family relationships of the English woman.* New York: Roy.

Chilman, C. S. 1966. *Growing up poor.* Washington, D.C.: U.S. Government Printing Office.

Christensen, H. T. 1953. New approaches in family research: The method of record linkage. *Marriage and Family Living, 20,* 38–42.

————. 1960. Cultural relativism and premarital sex norms. *American Sociological Review, 25,* 31–39.

————. 1963. Timing of first pregnancy as a factor in divorce: A cross-cultural analysis. *Eugenics Quarterly, 10,* 119–130.

Christensen, H. T., and Meissner, H. H. 1953. Studies in child spacing: Premarital pregnancy as a factor in divorce. *American Sociological Review, 18,* 641–644.

Clausen, J. 1972. The life courses of individuals. In M. W. Riley, M. Johnson, and A. Foner (Eds.), *Aging and society* (vol. 3). New York: Russell Sage.

Cline, D. W., and Chosy, J. J. 1972. A prospective study of life changes and subsequent health changes. *Archives of General Psychiatry, 27,* 51–53.

Cline, D. W., and Westman, J. C. 1971. The impact of divorce on the family. *Child Psychiatry and Human Development, 2,* 78–83.

Cockburn, C., and Helco, H. 1974. Income maintenance for one-parent families in other countries. In M. Finer (Ed.), *Report of the Committee on One-Parent Families* (Vol. 2). London: Her Majesty's Stationary Office.

Cohen, L. J. 1974. The operational definition of human attachment. *Psychological Bulletin, 81,* 207–217.

Commonwealth of Pennsylvania v. Addicks and Wife. 1813. *Binney's Pennsylvania Reports, 5,* 520–522.

Constantine, L., and Constantine, J. 1973. *Group marriage.* New York: Macmillan.

Coogler, O. J., Weber, R. E., and McKenry, P. C. Divorce mediation: A means of facilitating divorce adjustment. *Family Coordinator,* forthcoming.

Coombs, L. C., and Freedman, R. 1970. Pre-marital pregnancy, childspacing, and later economic achievement. *Population Studies, 24,* 389–412.

Coombs, L. C., and Zumeta, Z. 1970. Correlates of marital dissolution in a prospective fertility study: A research note. *Social Problems, 18* (Summer), 92–101.

Cott, N. F. 1976. Divorce and the changing status of women in eighteenth-century Massachusetts. *The William and Mary Quarterly, 33,* 586–614.

Crago, M. A. 1972. Psychopathology in married couples. *Psychological Bulletin, 77,* 114–128.

Crain, R. L., and Weisman, C. S. 1972. *Discrimination, personality, and achievement: A survey of northern blacks.* New York: Seminar Press.

Crumley, F. E., and Blumenthal, R. S. 1973. Children's reactions to temporary loss of the father. *American Journal of Psychiatry, 130,* 778–782.

Cutright, P. 1971. Income and family events: Marital stability. *Journal of Marriage and the Family, 33,* 291–306.

Cutright, P., and Scanzoni, J. 1973. Income supplements and the American family. In Joint Economic Committee (Ed.). *The Family, poverty, and welfare programs: Factors influencing family instability.* (Studies in Public Welfare, Paper no. 12, part 1). Washington, D.C.: U.S. Government Printing Office.

Dager, E. Z. 1964. Socialization and personality development in the child. In H. T. Christensen (Ed.), *Handbook of marriage and the family.* Chicago: Rand McNally.

Davis, A., and Havighurst, R. J. 1946. Social class and color differences in child-rearing. *American Sociological Review, 11,* 698–710.

Davis, K. 1972. *The American family in relation to demographic change.* Report of the U.S. Commission on Population Growth and the American Future, C. F. Westoff and R. Parke, Jr. (Eds.), vol. 1, Demographic and Social Aspects of Population Growth. Washington, D.C.: U.S. Government Printing Office.

Davis, M. S. 1973. *Intimate relations.* New York: Free Press.

Day, L. H. 1964. Patterns of divorce in Australia and the United States. *American Sociological Review, 29,* 509–522.

Dembitz, N. 1974. Beyond the best interests of the child: A review and critique. *The Record of the Association of the Bar of the City of New York, 29,* 457–463.

DeRougemont, D. 1949. The crisis of the modern couple. In R. N. Anshen (Ed.). *The family: Its function and destiny.* New York: Harper & Row.

Despert, J. L. 1953. *Children of divorce.* Garden City: Doubleday & Co.

Dizard, J. 1968. *Social change in the family.* Chicago: Community and Family Study Center.

Dohrenwend, B. P. 1975. Sociocultural and social-psychological factors in the genesis of mental disorders. *Journal of Health and Social Behavior, 16,* 365–392.

Dohrenwend, B. S., and Dohrenwend, B. P. 1974. (Eds.). *Stressful life events: Their nature and effects.* New York: Wiley.

Driscoll, R., Davis, K. E., and Lipetz, M. A. 1972. Parental interference and romantic love. *Journal of Personality and Social Psychology, 24,* 1–10.

Duncan, B., and Duncan, O. D. 1969. Family stability and occupational success. *Social Problems, 16* (Winter), 272–306.

Duncan, G. J., and Morgan, J. N. 1976. *Five thousand American families—Patterns of economic progress,* vol. 4. Ann Arbor: Institute for Social Research.

Duncan, O. D. 1975. *Introduction to structural equation models.* New York: Academic Press.

Elder, G. H. 1974. *Children of the great depression.* Chicago: University of Chicago Press.

————. 1977. Family history and the life course. *Journal of Family History, 2,* 279–304.

English v. English. 1880. *New Jersey Equity Reports, 32,* 738–754.

Farber, B. 1967. Introduction to Willard Waller, *The old love and the new.* Carbondale: Southern Illinois University Press.

Fein, R. A. 1974. Men's experiences before and after the birth of a first child: Dependence, marital sharing and anxiety. Unpublished Ph.D. dissertation, Harvard University.

Felner, R. D., Stolberg, A., and Cowen, E. L. 1975. Crisis events and school mental health referral patterns of young children. *Journal of Consulting and Clinical Psychology, 43,* 305–310.

Ferri, E. 1973. Characteristics of motherless families. *British Journal of Social Work, 3,* 91–100.

Festinger, L., Schachter, S., and Back, K. 1950. *Social pressures in informal groups.* New York: Harper.

Figley, C. R. 1973. Child density and the marital relationship. *Journal of Marriage and the Family, 35,* 272–282.

Finlay v. Finlay. 1925. *Northeastern Reporter of the National Reporter System, 148,* 624–627.

Foa, U. G. 1971. Interpersonal and economic resources. *Science, 171,* 345–351.

Fogarty, M. P., Rapoport, R., and Rapoport, R. N. 1971. *Sex, career and family.* Beverly Hills: Sage.

Foster, H. H., Jr., and Freed, D. J. 1964. Child Custody. *New York University Law Review, 39,* 423–443.

———. 1973–4. Divorce reform: brakes or breakdown? *Journal of Family Law, 13,* 443–493.

Fox, A. 1974. *Beyond Contract: Work, power and trust relations.* London: Faber and Faber.

Freed, D. J., and Foster, H. H., Jr. 1974. The shuffled child and the divorce court. *Trial, 10,* 26–41.

———. 1976. Taking out the fault but not the sting. *Trial, 12,* 10–19.

Furstenberg, F. F. 1974. Work experience and family life. In J. O'Toole (Ed.). *Work and the quality of life: Resource papers for work in America.* Cambridge, Mass.: The MIT Press.

———. 1976. *Unplanned parenthood: The social consequences of teenage childbearing.* New York: Free Press.

Furstenberg, F. F., Masnick, G. S., and Ricketts, S. 1972. How can family planning programs delay repeat teenage pregnancies? *Family Planning Perspectives, 4,* 54–60.

Gadlin, H. 1977. Private lives and public order: A critical view of the history of intimate relations in the U.S. In G. Levinger and H. L. Raush (Eds.). *Close relationships: Perspectives on the meaning of intimacy.* Amherst: University of Massachusetts Press.

Gardner, R. A. 1976. *Psychotherapy with children of divorce.* New York: Jason Aronson, Inc.

Gavron, H. 1966. *The captive wife: Conflicts of housebound mothers.* London: Routledge and Kegan Paul.

George V., and Wilding, P. 1972. *Motherless families.* London: Routledge and Kegan Paul.

Gersick, K. E. 1975. *A review of selected literature on sibling relationships.* Unpublished paper, Yale University.

Gerson, E. M. 1976. On 'quality of life.' *American Sociological Review, 41,* 793–806.

Gillespie, D. L. 1971. Who has the power? The marital struggle. *Journal of Marriage and the Family, 33,* 445–458.

Glick, I. O., Weiss, R. S., and Parkes, C. M. 1974. *The first year of bereavement.* New York: Wiley-Interscience.

Glick, P. C. 1957. *American families.* New York: John Wiley & Sons.

Glick, P. C., and Mills, K. M. 1975. *Black families: marriage patterns and living arrangements.* Proceedings of the W.E.B. DuBois Conference on American Blacks.

Glick, P. C. and Norton, A. J. 1971. Frequency, duration, and probability of marriage and divorce. *Journal of Marriage and the Family, 33,* 307–317.

———. 1976. Number, timing, and duration of marriages and divorces in the United States: June 1975. U.S. Bureau of the Census, *Current Population Reports,* Series P-20: 297. Washington, D.C.: U.S. Government Printing Office.

———. 1977. Marrying, divorcing, and living together in the U.S. today. *Population Bulletin, 32*(5).

Glueck, S., and Glueck, E. 1950. *Unraveling juvenile delinquency*. Cambridge, Mass.: Harvard University Press.

Goethals, G. W. 1973. Symbiosis and the life cycle. *British Journal of Medical Psychology, 46,* 91–96.

Goldberger, A. 1964. *Econometric theory*. New York: Wiley.

Golden, J. 1954. Patterns of Negro-White intermarriage. *American Sociological Review, 19,* 144–147.

Goldstein, J., Freud, A., and Solnit, A. 1973. *Beyond the best interests of the child*. New York: Free Press.

Goode, W. J. 1949. Problems in post-divorce adjustment. *American Sociological Review, 14,* 394–401.

———. 1956. *After divorce*. New York and Chicago: Free Press.

———. 1959. The theoretical importance of love. *American Sociological Review, 24,* 38–47.

———. 1961. Family disorganization. In R. K. Merton and R. A. Nisbet (Eds.). *Contemporary social problems*. New York: Harcourt, Brace.

———. 1962. Marital satisfaction and instability: A cross-cultural analysis of divorce rates. *International Social Science Journal, 14,* 507–526.

———. 1963. *World revolution and family patterns*. New York: Free Press.

———. 1964. *The family*. Englewood Cliffs, N.J.: Prentice-Hall.

Goody, E. N. 1962. Conjugal separation and divorce among the Gonja of Northern Ghana. In M. Fortes (Ed.), *Marriage in tribal societies*. Cambridge: Cambridge University Press.

Gordon, D. M. 1972. *Theories of poverty and underemployment*. Lexington, Mass.: Lexington Books.

Goslin, D. A. 1969. (Ed.). *Handbook of socialization theory and research*. Chicago: Rand McNally.

Gove, W. R. 1972a. The relationship between sex roles, marital status, and mental illness. *Social Forces, 51,* 34–44.

———. 1972b. Sex, marital status, and suicide. *Journal of Health and Social Behavior, 13,* 204–213.

———. 1973. Sex, marital status, and mortality. *American Journal of Sociology, 79,* 45–67.

Gove, W., and Tudor, J. 1973. Adult sex roles and mental illness. In Joan Huber (Ed.). *Changing women in a changing society*. Chicago: University of Chicago Press.

Grad, J., and Sainsbury, P. 1966. Evaluating the community psychiatric service in Chichester: Results. *Milbank Memorial Fund Quarterly, 44,* 246–278.

Grave, R. D., and Hertzel, A. M. 1968. *Vital statistics rates in the United States 1940–1960* (U.S. Public Health Service, National Center for Health Statistics). Washington, D.C.: U.S. Government Printing Office.

Group for the Advancement of Psychiatry. 1973. *The joys and sorrows of parenthood*. New York: Charles Scribner's Sons.

Gurin, G., Veroff, J., and Feld, S. 1960. *Americans view their mental health*. New York: Basic Books.

Guttentag, M., and Salasin, S. Forthcoming. *Families abandoned: Mental health in today's society*. New York: Academic Press.

Haavio-Mannila, E. 1971. Satisfaction with family, work, leisure and life among men and women. *Human Relations, 24* (6), 585–601.

Hannan, M., Tuma, N., and Groeneveld, L. P. 1977a. Income and marital events: Evidence from an income maintenance experiment. *American Journal of Sociology, 82,* 1186–1211.

———. 1977b. Income and independence effects on marital dissolution: Findings from the Seattle-Denver income maintenance experiments. Paper presented at American Sociological Association meetings, August.

Harmsworth, H. C., and Minnis, M. S. 1955. Nonstatutory causes of divorce: The lawyer's point of view. *Marriage and Family Living, 17,* 316–321.

Hauser, Philip M. 1975. *Social statistics in use*. New York: Russell Sage Foundation.

Havighurst, R. J. 1961. Early marriage and the schools. *The School Review, 36–47.*

Hayghe, H. 1975. Marital and family characteristics of the labor force, March 1974. Special labor force report 173. Washington, D.C.: U.S. Department of Labor Statistics.

————. 1978. Marital and family characteristics of workers, March 1977. *Monthly Labor Review, 101*, 51–54.

Heath, A. 1976. *Rational choice theory and social exchange.* New York: Cambridge University Press.

Hedges, J. N., and Barnett, J. K. 1972. Working women and the division of household tasks. *Monthly Labor Review, 95*, 9–14.

Heer, D. M. 1974. The prevalence of black-white marriage in the United States, 1960 and 1970. *Journal of Marriage and the Family, 36*, 246–258.

Heider, F. 1958. *The psychology of interpersonal relations.* New York: Wiley.

Heiss, J. 1972. On the transmission of marital instability in black families. *American Sociological Review, 37*, 82–92.

Herzog, E., and Sudia, C. E. 1973. Children in fatherless families. In B. M. Caldwell and H. N. Ricciuti (Eds.), *Child development and social policy.* Chicago: University of Chicago Press.

Hetherington, E. M. 1972. Effects of paternal absence on personality development in adolescent daughters. *Developmental Psychology, 7*, 313–326.

Hetherington, E. M., Cox, M., and Cox, R. 1976. Divorced fathers. *Family Coordinator, 25*, 417–428.

————. 1977. The aftermath of divorce. In J. H. Stevens, Jr. and M. Matthews (Eds.). *Mother-child, father-child relations.* Washington, D.C.: National Association for the Education of Young Children.

Hetzel, A. M., and Cappetta, M. 1971. Marriages: trends and characteristics. National Center for Health Statistics, *Vital and health statistics:* Series 21:21. Washington, D.C.: U.S. Government Printing Office.

————. 1973. Teenagers: Marriages, divorces, parenthood, and mortality. *Vital and health statistics: U.S. Dept. of Health, Education, and Welfare,* Series 21:23.

Hill, C. T. 1974. *The ending of successive opposite-sex relationships.* Unpublished doctoral dissertation, Harvard University.

Hill, C. T., Rubin, Z., and Willard, S. 1972. *Who volunteers for research on dating relationships?* Unpublished manuscript, Harvard University.

Hill, D., and Hoffman, S. 1977. Husbands and wives. In G. J. Duncan and J. N. Morgan (Eds.). *Five thousand American families,* vol. 5, pp. 29–70. Ann Arbor: University of Michigan Institute for Social Research.

Hill, R., and Aldous, J. 1969. Socialization for marriage and parenthood. In D. A. Goslin (Ed.). *Handbook of socialization theory and research.* Chicago: Rand McNally.

Hines v. Hines. 1921. *Iowa Reports, 192*, 569–572.

Hirschi, T. 1969. *Causes of delinquency.* Berkeley: University of California Press.

Hodges, W. F., Wechsler, R. L., and Ballantine, C. 1978. Divorce and the preschool child. Unpublished manuscript, University of Colorado, Boulder.

Hoffman, S., and Holmes, J. 1976. Husbands, wives and divorce. In G. J. Duncan and J. N. Morgan (Eds.), *Five thousand American families—Patterns of economic progress,* vol. 4. Ann Arbor: Institute for Social Research.

Hollingshead, A. B., and Redlich, F. C. 1958. *Social class and mental illness.* New York: Wiley.

Holmes, T. H., and Masuda, M. 1974. Life change and illness susceptibility. In B. S. Dohrenwend and B. P. Dohrenwend (Eds.), *Stressful life events: Their nature and effects.* New York: Wiley.

Holmes, T. H., and Rahe, R. H. 1967. The social readjustment rating scale. *Journal of Psychosomatic Research, 11*, 213–218.

Holmstrom, L. 1973. *Two career family.* New York: Schenkman.

Honig, M. 1973. The impact of welfare payment levels on family stability. In Joint Economic Committee (Ed.). *The family, poverty, and welfare programs: Factors influencing family instability.* (Studies in Public Welfare, no. 12, part 1). Washington, D.C.: U.S. Government Printing Office.

Hostetler, J. A. 1974. *Hutterite society.* Baltimore: Johns Hopkins University Press.

Houseknecht S. K., and Spanier, G. B. 1978. Marital disruption among highly educated women: an exception to the rule. Unpublished paper.

Hunt, M. 1966. *The world of the formerly married.* New York: McGraw-Hill.

Hunt, M., and Hunt, B. 1977. *The divorce experience.* New York: McGraw-Hill.

Hurley, J. R., and Palonen, D. P. 1967. Marital satisfaction and child density among university student parents. *Journal of Marriage and the Family, 29,* 483–484.

Ilgenfritz, M. P. 1961. Mothers on their own—widows and divorcées. *Marriage and Family Living, 23,* 38–41.

Institute for Social Research. 1974. Measuring the quality of life in America. *Newsletter,* 2 (2), University of Michigan.

Jacobson, P. H. 1959. *American marriage and divorce.* New York: Holt, Rinehart and Winston.

Jaffe, D. T. 1975. *Couples in communes.* Unpublished doctoral dissertation, Yale University.

Jaquette, D. 1976. *Developmental stages in peer group organization: A cognitive-developmental analysis of peer group concepts in childhood and adolescence.* Qualifying paper, Harvard Graduate School of Education.

Jencks, C. 1974. The poverty of welfare. *Working Papers, 4,* 5.

Jenkins, C. D. 1976a. Recent evidence supporting psychologic and social risk factors for coronary disease (part 1). *New England Journal of Medicine, 294,* 987–994.

———. 1976b. Recent evidence supporting psychologic and social risk factors for coronary disease (part 2). *New England Journal of Medicine, 294,* 1033–1038.

Jenkins v. Jenkins. 1921. *Wisconsin Reports, 173,* 592–596.

Johnson, B. L. 1978. Women who head families: Their numbers rise, income lags. *Monthly Labor Review, 101,* 32–37.

Johnson, W. D. 1977. Establishing a national center for the study of divorce. *Family Coordinator, 26,* 263–268.

Jones, C. A., Gordon, N. M., and Sawhill, I. V. 1976. *Child support payments in the United States.* Washington, D.C.: The Urban Institute.

Josselyn, I. M. April 1956. Cultural forces, motherliness and fatherliness. *American Journal of Orthopsychiatry, 26,* 264–271.

Kalter, N. 1977. Children of divorce in an outpatient psychiatric population. *American Journal of Orthopsychiatry, 47,* 40–51.

Kanter, R. M. 1972a. *Commitment and community: Communes and utopias in sociological perspective.* Cambridge, Mass.: Harvard University Press.

———. 1972b. Getting it all together: Some group issues in communes. *American Journal of Orthopsychiatry, 42,* 632–643.

———. 1973a. (Ed.) *Communes: Creating and managing the collective life.* New York: Harper & Row.

———. 1973b. Utopian communities. *Sociological Inquiry, 43,* 263–290.

Kanter, R. M., and Halter, M. 1975. De-housewifing women, domesticating men: Equality between the sexes in urban communes. In J. Heiss (Ed.), *Marriage and Family Interaction (2nd ed.).* Chicago: Rand McNally.

Kanter, R. M., Jaffe, D. T., and Weisberg, D. K. 1975. Coupling, parenting, and the presence of others: Intimate relationships in communal households. *The Family Coordinator, 24,* 433–452.

Kantner, J. F., and Zelnik, M. 1973. Contraception and pregnancy: Experience of young unmarried women in the United States. *Family Planning Perspectives, 21,* 21–35.

Kelley, H. H., and Schenitzki, D. P. 1972. Bargaining. In C. G. McClintock (Ed.). *Experimental social psychology.* New York: Holt, Rinehart & Winston.

Kelly, E. L. 1941. Marital compatibility as related to personality traits of husbands and wives as rated by self and spouse. *Journal of Social Psychology, 13,* 193–198.

Kelly, J. B., and Wallerstein, J. S. 1976. The effects of parental divorce: Experiences of the child in early latency. *American Journal of Orthopsychiatry, 46,* 20.

———. 1977. Part-time parent, part-time child: Visiting after divorce. *Journal of Clinical Child Psychology, 6,* 51–54.

Kenniston, K. 1977. *All our children: The American family under pressure.* New York: Harcourt Brace Jovanovich.

Kephart, W. M. 1955. Occupational level and marital disruption. *American Sociological Review, 20,* 456–465.

Kerckhoff, A. C. 1974. The social context of interpersonal attraction. In T. L. Huston (Ed.). *Foundations of interpersonal attraction.* New York: Academic Press.

Kerckhoff, A. C., and Davis, K. E. 1962. Value consensus and need complementarity in mate selection. *American Sociological Review, 27,* 295–303.

Kim, S., Roderick, R. D., and Shea, J. R. 1972. *Dual careers—A longitudinal study of labor market experience of women,* vol. 2. Columbus: Center for Human Resource Research, Ohio State University.

Kirkpatrick, C. 1937. Community of interest and the measurement of adjustment in marriage. *The Family, 18,* 133–137.

Kitagawa, E. M., and Hauser, P. M. 1973. *Differential mortality in the United States: A study in socioeconomic epidemiology.* Cambridge: Harvard University Press.

Kobrin, F. E., and Hendershot, G. E. 1977. Do family ties reduce mortality? Evidence from the United States, 1966–1968. *Journal of Marriage and the Family, 39,* 737–745.

Kohlberg, L. 1966. A cognitive-developmental analysis of children's sex-role concepts and attitudes. In E. E. Maccoby (Ed.). *The development of sex differences.* Stanford, Calif.: Stanford University Press.

———. 1969. Stage and sequence: The cognitive-developmental approach to socialization. In D. A. Goslin (Ed.). *Handbook of socialization theory and research.* Chicago: Rand McNally.

Komarovsky, M. 1940. *The unemployed man and his family.* New York: Dryden Press. Reprint. ed. Arno Press and The New York Times, New York, 1971.

———. 1964. *Blue-collar marriage.* New York: Random House.

Komisar, L. 1973. *Down and out in the U.S.A.: A history of social welfare.* New York: Watts.

Kotelchuck, M. 1973. The nature of the infant's tie to his father. Paper presented at the Society for Research in Child Development Meetings, Philadelphia, Pa., April.

Kraditor, A. S. 1968. *Up from the pedestal.* Chicago: Quadrangle Books.

Kram, S. W., and Frank, N. 1976. The future of 'tender years.' *Trial, 12* (4), 14–15.

Kramer, M. 1966. *Some implications of trends in the usage of psychiatric facilities for community mental health programs and related research.* Public Health Service Pub. no. 1434. Washington, D.C.: U.S. Government Printing Office.

Kreps, J. 1971. *Sex in the marketplace: American women at work.* Baltimore: The Johns Hopkins Press.

Kressel, K., and Deutsch, M. 1977. Divorce therapy: An in-depth survey of therapists' views. *Family Process, 16,* 413–443.

Kriesberg, L. 1970. *Mothers in poverty: A study of fatherless families.* Chicago: Aldine.

Lambert v. Lambert. 1949. Decision of the St. Louis Court of Appeals. *Southwestern Reporter, Second Series, 222,* 544–548.

Landis, J. T. 1949. Marriages of mixed and non-mixed religious faith. *American Sociological Review, 14,* 401–406.

———. 1960. The trauma of children when parents divorce. *Journal of Marriage and the Family, 22,* 7–13.

———. 1963. Some correlates of divorce or nondivorce among the unhappily married. *Marriage and Family Living, 25,* 178–180.

Lantz, H. R. 1976. *Marital incompatability and social change in early America.* Beverly Hills: Sage.

Lawrence, W. 1968. Divided custody of children after their parents' divorce. *Journal of Family Law, 8,* 58–68.

Levinger, G. 1964. Task and social behavior in marriage. *Sociometry, 27,* 433–448.

———. 1965. Marital cohesiveness and dissolution: An integrative review. *Journal of Marriage and the Family, 27,* 19–28.

————. 1966a. Sources of marital dissatisfaction among applicants for divorce. *American Journal of Orthopsychiatry, 36,* 803–807.

————. 1966b. Systematic distortion in spouses' reports of preferred and actual sexual behavior. *Sociometry, 29,* 291–299.

————. 1967. *The stickiness of cohesiveness.* Unpublished manuscript, University of Massachusetts, Amherst.

————. 1972. Little sand box and big quarry: Comment on Byrne's paradigmatic spade for research on interpersonal attraction. *Representative Research in Social Psychology, 3,* 3–18.

————. 1974. A three-level approach to attraction: Toward an understanding of pair relatedness. In T. L. Huston (Ed.). *Foundations of interpersonal attraction.* New York: Academic Press.

Levinger, G., Senn, D. J., and Jorgensen, B. W. 1970. Progress toward permanence in courtship: A test of the Kerckhoff-Davis hypotheses. *Sociometry, 33,* 427–443.

Levinger, G., and Snoek, J. D. 1972. *Attraction in relationship: A new look at interpersonal attraction.* Morristown, N. J.: General Learning Press.

Lévi-Strauss, C. 1969. *The elementary structures of kinship.* Boston: Beacon Press.

Lewin, K. 1951. *Field theory in social science.* New York: Harper.

Linder, F. E., and Grove, R. D. 1943. *Vital statistics rates in the Unitel States, 1900–1940.* Washington, D.C.: U.S. Government Printing Office.

Litman, R. E., and Farberow, N. L. 1961. Emergency evaluation of self destructive potentiality. In N. L. Farberow and E. S. Shneidman (Eds.). *The cry for help.* New York: McGraw-Hill.

Lloyd, C. B. (Ed.). 1975. *Sex, discrimination, and the division of labor.* New York: Columbia.

Locke, H. J. 1951. *Predicting adjustment in marriage: A comparison of a divorced and a happily married group.* New York: Holt.

Lopez-Morillas, M. 1977. *The role of the divorce lawyer: An in-depth survey of matrimonial lawyers.* Unpublished manuscript, Social Psychology Laboratory, Teachers College, Columbia University.

Lowrie, S. H. 1965. Early marriage: Premarital pregnancy and associated factors. *Journal of Marriage and the Family, 27,* 49–56.

Luckey, E. B., and Bain, J. K. 1970. Children: A factor in marital satisfaction. *Journal of Marriage and the Family, 32,* 43–44.

Lynch, J. J. 1977. *The broken heart: The medical consequences of loneliness.* New York: Basic Books, Inc.

McCall, G. J., and Simmons, J. L. 1966. *Identities and interactions.* New York: Free Press.

Maccoby, E. E., and Jacklin, C. N. 1974. *The psychology of sex differences.* Stanford, Calif.: Stanford University Press.

McCord, J., McCord, W., and Thurber, E. 1962. Some effects of paternal absence on male children. *Journal of Abnormal and Social Psychology, 64,* 361–369.

McDonald v. McDonald. 1953. *Oregon Reports, 197,* 275–282.

Mace, D., and Mace, V. 1960. *Marriage: East and West.* New York: Doubleday.

McMurray, L. 1970. Emotional stress and driving performance: The effect of divorce. *Behavioral Research in Highway Safety, 1,* 100–114.

Makosky, V. P. Forthcoming. Stress and the mental health of women: A discussion of research and issues. In M. Guttentag and S. Salasin (Eds.). *Families abandoned: Mental health in today's society.* New York: Academic Press.

Malzberg, B. 1956. Marital status and mental disease among Negroes in New York State. *Journal of Nervous and Mental Disease, 123,* 457–465.

Marschall P. H., and Gatz, M. J. 1975. The custody decision process: Toward new roles for parents and the state. *North Carolina Central Law Journal, 76,* 50–72.

Marsden, D. 1969. *Mothers alone: Poverty and the fatherless family.* London: Allen Lane, The Penguin Press.

Maslow, A. H. 1954. *Motivation and personality.* New York: Harper.

Mason, K. O., Czajka, J., and Arber, S. 1976. Change in U.S. women's sex-role attitudes, 1964–1975. *American Sociological Review, 41,* 573–465

Messner, M. B. 1928. *The family in the making.* New York: Putnam.

Meyers, J. C. 1976. *The adjustment of women to marital separation: The effects of sex-role identification and stage in family life.* (Available from Judith C. Meyers, Dept. of Psychology, Univ. of Colorado, Boulder, Colorado.)

Miller, A. A. 1970. Reactions of friends to divorce. In P. Bohannan (Ed.). *Divorce and after: An analysis of the emotional and social problems of divorce.* New York: Doubleday.

Mills, C. W. 1959. *The sociological imagination.* London: Oxford University Press.

Milmed, P. K. 1974. Due process for children: A right to counsel in custody proceedings. *New York University Review of Law and Social Change, 4,* 177–189.

Mincer, J., and Polachek, S. 1974. Family investments in human capital: Earnings of women. *Journal of Political Economy, 82,* S76–S108.

Mindey, C. 1969. *The divorced mother.* New York: McGraw-Hill Book Co.

Mischel, W. 1966. A social-learning view of sex differences in behavior. In E. Maccoby (Ed.). *The development of sex differences.* Stanford, Calif.: Stanford University Press.

———. 1970. Sex-typing and socialization. In P. H. Mussen (Ed.) *Carmichael's manual of child psychology* (3rd ed., vol. 2). New York: Wiley.

Moles, O. C. 1976. Marital dissolution and public assistance payments: Variations among American states. *Journal of Social Issues, 32* (1), 87–101.

Mollenkott, V. 1977. Milton on divorce. Unpublished paper, Department of English, Paterson State College, Paterson, N.J.

Monahan, T. P. 1952. How stable are remarriages? *American Journal of Sociology, 58,* 280–288.

———. 1955. Divorce by occupational level. *Marriage and Family Living, 17,* 322–324.

———. 1960. Premarital pregnancy in the United States. *Eugenics Quarterly, 7,* 140.

Moore, K., and Waite, L. J. 1978. Marital dissolution, early marriage, and early child bearing: Evidence from the national longitudinal survey of young women. Paper presented at meeting of American Sociological Association, San Francisco.

———. The consequences of age at first childbirth: Divorce and separation, forthcoming.

Morrison, D. F. 1967. *Multivariate statistical methods.* New York: McGraw-Hill.

Morrison, D. G. 1972. Upper bounds for correlations between binary outcomes and probabilistic predictions. *Journal of the American Statistical Association, 67,* 68–70.

Moynihan, D. P. 1965. *The Negro family: The case for national action* (U.S. Department of Labor, Office of Policy Planning and Research). Washington, D.C.: U.S. Government Printing Office.

———. 1973. *The politics of a guaranteed income.* New York: Random House.

Mueller, C. W., and Pope, H. 1974. *The intergenerational transmission of marital instability.* Unpublished manuscript, University of Iowa.

———. 1977. Marital instability: A study of its transmission between generations. *Journal of Marriage and the Family, 39,* 83–93.

Murstein, B. I. 1971. A theory of marital choice and its applicability to marriage adjustment. In B. I. Murstein (Ed.). *Theories of attraction and love.* New York: Springer.

Mussen, P. H. 1969. Early sex-role development. In D. A. Goslin (Ed.). *Handbook of socialization theory and research.* Chicago: Rand McNally.

Myers, J. K., Lindenthal, J. J., and Pepper, M. P. 1971. Life events and psychiatric impairment. *Journal of Nervous and Mental Disease, 152,* 149–157.

———. 1974. Social class, life events, and psychiatric symptoms. In B. S. Dohrenwend and B. P. Dohrenwend (Eds.). *Stressful life events: Their nature and effects.* New York: Wiley.

———. 1975. Life events, social integration and psychiatric symptomatology. *Journal of Health and Social Behavior, 16,* 421–427.

Myers, J. K., Lindenthal, J. J., Pepper, M. P., and Ostrander, D. R. 1972. Life events and mental status: A longitudinal study. *Journal of Health and Social Behavior, 13,* 389–406.

National Center for Health Statistics. 1970a. Mortality from selected causes by marital status. Series 20:8A and 8B. Washington, D.C.: U.S. Government Printing Office.

———. 1970b. Selected symptoms of psychological distress: United States. *Vital and health statistics*, Series 11:37. Washington, D.C.: U.S. Government Printing Office.

———. 1973. Divorces: Analysis of changes. United States. 1969. *Vital and health statistics*, Series 21:22. Washington, D.C.: U.S. Government Printing Office.

———. 1976. Differentials in health characteristics by marital status: United States, 1971–1972. *Vital and health statistics*, Series 10:104. Washington, D.C.: U.S. Government Printing Office.

———. 1977a. Births, marriages, divorces, and deaths for 1976. *Monthly vital statistics report*, 25:12. Washington, D.C.: U.S. Government Printing Office.

———. 1977b. Marriage and divorce. *Vital statistics of the United States 1973*, III: Washington, D.C.: U.S. Government Printing Office.

———. 1977c. Summary report, final divorce statistics, 1975. *Monthly vital statistics report*, 26:2, Supplement. Washington, D.C.: U.S. Government Printing Office.

———. 1977d. Final divorce statistics, 1975. *Monthly vital statistics report*, 26:2, Supplement 2, May 1977. Washington, D.C.: U.S. Government Printing Office.

———. 1978a. Births, marriages, divorces, and deaths for 1977. *Monthly vital statistics report*, 26:12. Washington, D.C.: U.S. Government Printing Office.

———. 1978b. Summary report, final divorce statistics, 1976. *Monthly vital statistics report*, 27:2. Supplement. Washington, D.C.: U.S. Government Printing Office.

National Center for Social Statistics. 1974a. Findings of the 1973 AFDC study: part 1. Demographic and program characteristics. Washington, D.C.: U.S. Government Printing Office.

———. 1974b. Public assistance statistics: September 1974. Washington, D.C.: U.S. Government Printing Office.

Nerlove, M., and Press, S. J. 1973. *Univariate and Multivariate Log-Linear and Logistic Models*. Santa Monica: The Rand Corporation.

Neugarten, B. L. 1968. (Ed.). *Midlle age and aging*. Chicago: University of Chicago Press.

Newson, J., and Newson, E. 1963. *Infant care in an urban community*. London: George Allen & Unwin, Ltd.

Norton, A. J., and Glick, P. C. 1976. The changing American household. *Intercom*, 4 (10), 8–9.

Nye, F. I. 1957. Child adjustment in broken and in unhappy unbroken homes. *Marriage and Family Living*, 19, 356–360.

Nye, F. I., and Berardo, F. M. 1973. *The family: Its structure and interaction*. New York: Macmillan.

Nye, F. I., Frideres, J., and White, L. August 1968. *Marital dissolution: One strategy for theory development*. Paper presented at the meeting of the American Sociological Association, Boston.

O'Gorman, H. J. 1963. *Lawyers and matrimonial cases: A study of informal pressures in private professional practice*. New York: The Free Press.

O'Neill, W. L. 1973. *Divorce in the progressive era*. New Haven: Yale University Press.

Painter v. Bannister. 1966. *Iowa Reports, 258*, 1390–1400.

Parke, R., Jr., and Glick, P. C. 1967. Prospective changes in marriage and the family. *Journal of Marriage and the Family*, 29, 249–256.

Parkes, C. M. 1972. *Bereavement*. New York: International Universities Press.

Parnes, H. S., Shea, J. R., Spitz, R. S., Zeller, F. A. 1970. Dual careers: A longitudinal study of labor market experience of women, vol. 1. Washington, D.C.: U.S. Government Printing Office.

Parsons, T., and Bales, R. F. 1955. *Family, socialization, and interaction process*. Glencoe, Ill.: Free Press.

Paulker, J. D. 1969. *Girls pregnant out of wedlock*. In *Illegitimacy today*. New York: National Council on Illegitimacy.

Pearlin, L. I. 1975. Sex roles and depression. In N. Datan and L. Ginsberg (Eds.). *Life-span developmental psychology: Normative life crises.* New York: Academic Press.

Pearlin, L. I. and Johnson, J. S. 1977. Marital status, life-strains, and depression. *American Sociological Review, 42,* 704–715.

Phillips v. Phillips. 1943. *Florida Reports, 153,* 133–137.

Plateris, A. A. 1969. Divorce statistics analysis: United States 1964 and 1965. National Center for Health Statistics, *Vital and Health Statistics,* Series 21:17. Washington, D.C.: U.S. Government Printing Office.

Podell, R., Peck, H. F., and First, C. 1972. Custody—to which parent? *Marquette Law Review, 56,* 51–68.

Pohlman, E. H. 1969. *Psychology of birth planning.* Cambridge, Mass.: Schenkman.

Radin, N. 1972. Father-child interaction and intellectual functioning of four-year-old boys. *Developmental Psychology, 6,* 353–361.

Radloff, L. 1975. Sex differences in depression: The effects of occupation and marital status. *Sex Roles: A Journal of Research, 1,* 249–265.

———. 1978. Risk factors in depression. Unpublished.

Rainwater, L. 1966. Marital stability and patterns of status variables. *Journal of Marriage and the Family, 28,* 442–445.

———. 1970. *Behind ghetto walls.* Chicago: Aldine.

Ramey, J. 1972. Emerging patterns of innovative behavior in marriage. *The Family Coordinator, 21,* 435–456.

Rapoport, R. N. 1964. The male's occupation in relation to his decision to marry. *Acta Sociologica, 8,* 68–82.

Raschke, H. J. 1974. Social and psychological factors in voluntary postmarital dissolution adjustment. Unpublished doctoral dissertation, University of Minnesota.

Ravich, R. A. 1972. The marriage/divorce paradox. In C. J. Sager and H. S. Kaplan (Eds.). *Progress in group and family therapy.* New York: Brunner/Mazel.

Rebelsky, F., and Hanks, C. 1971. Fathers' verbal interaction with infants in the first three months of life. *Child Development, 42,* 63–68.

Redick, R. W., and Johnson, C. 1974. Marital status, living arrangements and family characteristics of admissions to state and county mental hospitals and outpatient psychiatric clinics, United States 1970. *Statistical note 100: National Institute of Mental Health.* Washington, D.C.: U.S. Government Printing Office.

Reid, D. D. 1961. Precipitating proximal factors in the occurrence of mental disorders: Epidemiological evidence. In E. M. Gruenberg and M. Huxley (Eds.). *Causes of mental disorders: A review of epidemiological knowledge, 1959.* New York: Milbank Memorial Fund.

Rheinstein, M. 1972. *Marriage stability, divorce and the law.* Chicago: University of Chicago Press.

Riley, M. W., Johnson, M., and Foner, A. 1972. *Aging and society: A sociology of age stratification* (vol. 3). New York: Russell Sage.

Ripin, A. 1971. Fathers and sons. *Journal of Emotional Education, 11,* 157–163.

Robbins, N. N. 1974. There ought to be a law! Legal standards for determining 'best interests of child.' *Family Coordinator, 23,* 87–90.

Robertson, N. C. 1974. The relationship between marital status and the risk of psychiatric referral. *British Journal of Psychiatry, 124,* 191–202.

Roby, P. 1973. *Child care—who cares? Foreign and domestic infant and early childhood development policies.* New York: Basic Books.

Rodgers, R. F. 1973. *Family interaction and transaction.* Englewood Cliffs, N.J.: Prentice Hall.

Rollins, B., and Feldman, H. 1970. Marital satisfaction over the family life cycle. *Journal of Marriage and the Family, 32,* 20–27.

Roman, M., and Haddad, W. 1978. *The disposable parent: The case for joint custody.* New York: Holt, Rinehart, & Winston.

Rosen, R. 1977. Children of divorce: What they feel about access and other aspects of the divorce experience. *Journal of Clinical Child Psychology, 6* (2), 24–27.

Rosenberg, M. 1965. *Society and the adolescent self-image*. Princeton, N.J.: Princeton University Press.

Rosenblatt, S. M., Gross, M. M., Malenowski, B., Broman, M., and Lewis, E. 1971. Marital status and multiple psychiatric admissions for alcoholism: A cross-validation. *Quarterly Journal for the Study of Alcoholism, 32*, 1092–1096.

Rosenthal, R. 1973. Estimating effective reliabilities in studies that employ judges' ratings. *Journal of Clinical Psychology, 29* (3), 342–345.

Rosow, I., and Rose, K. D. 1972. Divorce among doctors. *Journal of Marriage and the Family, 34*, 587–598.

Ross, E. A. 1920. *Principles of sociology*. New York: Appleton.

Ross, H. L., and Sawhill, I. V. 1975. *Time of transition: The growth of families headed by women*. Washington, D.C.: The Urban Institute.

Rossi, P. H., Sampson, W. A., Bose, C. E., Jasso, G., and Passel, J. 1974. Measuring household social standing. *Social Science Research, 3*, 169–190.

Rowbotham, S. 1973. *Women's consciousness, man's world*. London: Pelican.

Rubin, J. Z., and Brown, B. R. 1975. *The social psychology of bargaining and negotiation*. New York: Academic Press.

Rubin, Z. 1969. The social psychology of romantic love. Doctoral dissertation, University of Michigan. (University microfilms No. 70–4179)

———. 1970. Measurement of romantic love. *Journal of Personality and Social Psychology, 16*, 265–273.

———. 1973. *Liking and loving: An invitation to social psychology*. New York: Holt, Rinehart, & Winston.

———. 1975. Loving and leaving. Unpublished manuscript, Harvard University.

Rubin, Z., and Levinger, G. 1974. Theory and data badly mated: A critique of Murstein's SVR and Lewis's PDF models of mate selection. *Journal of Marriage and the Family, 36*, 226–230.

Rubin, Z., and Mitchell, C. 1976. Couples research as couples counseling: Some unintended effects of studying close relationships. *American Psychologist, 31*, 17–25.

Rubin, Z., Peplau, L. A., and Hill, C. T. Unpublished. Becoming intimate: The development of male-female relationships.

Rutter, M. 1971. Parent-child separation: Psychological effects on the children. *Journal of Child Psychology and Psychiatry, 12*, 233–260.

Ryder, R. G., Kafka, J. S., and Olson, D. H. 1971. Separating and joining influences in courtship and early marriage. *American Journal of Orthopsychiatry, 41*, 450–464.

Ryder, N. B., and Westoff, C. F. 1971. *Reproduction in the United States, 1965*. Princeton, N.J.: Princeton University Press.

Ryker, M. J. 1971. Six selected factors influencing educational achievement of children from broken homes. *Education, 91*, 200–211.

Sandell, S. H., and Shapiro, D. 1975. *The theory of human capital and the earnings of women: A reexamination of the evidence*. Columbus: Center for Human Resource Research, The Ohio State University.

Santos, F. P. 1972. *Some economic determinants of marital status*. Doctoral dissertation, Columbia University.

———. 1975. The Economics of marital status. In C. B. Lloyd (Ed.). *Sex, discrimination, and the division of labor*. New York: Columbia.

Santrock, J. W. 1970. Influence of onset and type of paternal absence on the first four Eriksonian crises. *Developmental Psychology, 3*, 273–274.

———. 1972. Relation of type and onset of father absence to cognitive development. *Child Development, 43*, 455–469.

———. 1975. Father absence, perceived maternal behavior and moral development in boys. *Child Development, 46*, 753–757.

Sarrel, P. M. 1967. The university hospital and the teenage unwed mother. *American Journal of Public Health, 57*, 308–313.

Sauber, M., and Corrigan, E. M. 1970. *The six-year experience of unwed mothers as parents*. New York: Community Council of Greater New York.

Sawhill, I. V. May 1975. Discrimination and poverty among women who head families. Paper given at Conference on Occupational Segregation, Wellesley College.

Sawhill, I. V., Peabody, G. E., Jones, C. A., and Caldwell, S. B. 1975. Income transfers and family structure. Washington, D.C.: The Urban Institute.

Scanzoni, J. 1970. *Opportunity and the family*. New York: Free Press.

———. 1972. *Sexual bargaining: Power politics in American marriage*. Englewood Cliffs, N.J.: Prentice-Hall.

———. 1975a. Sex roles, economic factors, and marital solidarity in black and white marriages. *Journal of Marriage and the Family, 37*, 130–145.

———. 1975b. *Sex roles, life-styles, and childbearing: Changing patterns in marriage and family*. New York: Free Press.

———. 1976. Sex role change and influences on birth intentions. *Journal of Marriage and the Family, 38*, 43–60.

———. 1978. *Sex roles, women's work, and marital conflict*. Lexington, Mass.: Lexington Books, D. C. Heath.

Scanzoni, L. and Scanzoni, J. 1976. *Men, women, and change: A sociology of marriage and family*. New York: McGraw-Hill.

Schlesinger, B. 1969. The one-parent family in perspective. In B. Schlesinger (Ed.). *The one-parent family*. Toronto: University of Toronto Press.

Schneider, D. M. 1968. *American kinship: A cultural account*. Englewood Cliffs, N.J.: Prentice-Hall.

Schorr, A. L. 1965. The family cycle and income development. *Social Security Bulletin, 29*, 14–25.

Schultz, T. W. 1975. (Ed.). *The economics of the family*. New York: National Bureau of Economic Research.

Schwartz, A. C. 1968. Reflection on divorce and remarriage. *Social Casework, 49*, 213–217.

Selman, R. L. 1971. Taking another's perspective: Role-taking development in early childhood. *Child Development, 42*, 1721–1734.

———. 1974. *The development of conceptions of interpersonal relations: A structural analysis and procedures for the assessment of levels of interpersonal reasoning based on levels of social perspective-taking*. Cambridge, Mass.: Harvard-Judge Baker Social Reasoning Project.

Selman, R. L. and Byrne, D. K. 1974. Structural-developmental analysis of levels of role-taking in middle childhood. *Child Development, 45*, 803–806.

Shneidman, E. S., and Farberow, N. L. 1961. Statistical comparisons between attempted and committed suicides. In N. L. Farberow and E. S. Shneidman (Eds.). *The cry for help*. New York: McGraw-Hill.

Sinclair v. Sinclair. 1905. *New York Supplement of the National Reporter System, 95*, 861–862.

Slater, P. E. 1970. *The pursuit of loneliness*. Boston: Beacon Press.

Smelser, N. J. 1962. *Theory of collective behavior*. New York: Free Press.

Smith, C. E. 1966. Negro-White intermarriage: Forbidden sexual union. *Journal of Sex Research, 2*, 169–173.

Smith, W. G. 1971. Critical life-events and prevention strategies in mental health. *Archives of General Psychiatry, 25*, 103–109.

Spicer, J. W., and Hampe, G. D. 1975. Kinship interaction after divorce. *Journal of Marriage and the Family, 37*, 113–119.

'Split,' 'divided,' or 'alternate' custody of children. 1963. *American Law Reports, Annotated, Second Series, 92*, 695–745.

Sproger, C. E. 1971–2. How to win a child custody action. *Illinois Bar Journal, 60*, 122–128.

Srole, L., Langner, T. S., Michael, S. T., Opler, M. K., and Rennie. T.A.C. 1962. *Mental health in the metropolis*. New York: McGraw-Hill.

Stack, C. 1974. *All our kin*. Chicago: Aldine.

———. 1976. Who owns the child? Divorce and custody decisions in middle-class families. *Social Problems, 23*, 505–515.

Stein, P. 1976. *Single*. Englewood Cliffs, N.J.: Prentice-Hall.

Stein, R. L. 1970. The economic status of families headed by women. *Monthly Labor Review*, *93* (December), 3–10.

Stevenson, M. 1973. Women's wages and job segregation. *Politics and Society*, *4*, 83–96.

Stewart, C. W. 1963. Counseling the divorcée. *Pastoral Psychology*, *14*, 10–16.

Story, J. 1824. U.S. v. Green. 26, Fed. Case 30.

Sutton-Smith, B., Rosenberg, B. G., and Landy, F. 1968. Father absence effects in families of different sibling compositions. *Child Development*, *39*, 1213–1221.

Swift, M. G. 1958. A note on the durability of Malay marriages. *Man*, *208*, 155–159.

Taube, C. A. 1970a. Admission rates by age, sex and marital status: State and county mental hospitals, 1969. *Statistical note 32*. Washington, D.C.: National Institute of Mental Health.

———. 1970b. Admission rates by marital status: Outpatient psychiatric services, 1969. *Statistical note 35*. Washington, D.C.: National Institute for Mental Health.

Thibaut, J. W., and Kelley, H. H. 1959. *The social psychology of groups*. New York: Wiley.

Thomas, D. S., and Locke, B. Z. 1963. Marital status, educational and occupational differentials in mental disease. *Milbank Memorial Fund Quarterly*, *41*, 145–160.

Thwing, C. F., and Thwing, C. F. B. 1887. *The family: An historical and social study*. Boston: Lee and Shepard.

Ticknor divorce: custody of the children. 1868. *Chicago Legal News*, *1*, 89–90, 98–99.

Title, P. 1974. The father's right to child custody in interparental disputes. *Tulane Law Review*, *49*, 189–207.

Trenkner, T. R. 1976. Modern status of maternal preference rule or presumption in child custody cases. *American Law Reports, Annotated, Third Series*, *70*, 262–303.

Tuckman, J., and Regan, R. A. 1966. Intactness of the home and behavioral problems in children. *Journal of Child Psychology and Psychiatry*. *7*, 225–233.

Udry, J. R. 1967. Marital instability by race and income based on 1960 census data. *American Journal of Sociology 72*, 673–674.

———. 1974. *The social context of marriage* (3rd ed.). Philadelphia: Lippincott.

Uniform Marriage and Divorce Act. 1970. Chicago, Ill.: National Conference of Commissioners on Uniform State Laws.

United Nations. 1976. *Demographic yearbook 1975*. New York: United Nations.

United States v. Green. 1824. *Federal Cases*, 26, 30–32.

U.S. Bureau of the Census. 1964. *1960 Census of Population*. School enrollment. Final Report PC(2)–5A. Washington, D.C.: U.S. Government Printing Office.

———. 1967. *1960 Census of Population*. Marital status. Final Report PC(2)–4E. Washington, D.C.: U.S. Government Printing Office.

———. 1969. *Current Population Reports*, Series P–20:187. Marital status and family status: March 1968. Washington, D.C.: U.S. Government Printing Office.

———. 1971. *Current Population Reports*, Series P–20:223. Social and economic variations in marriage, divorce, and remarriage: 1967. Washington, D.C.: U.S. Government Printing Office.

———. 1972a. *1970 Census of Population*. Marital status. Final Report PC(2)–4C. Washington, D.C.: U.S. Government Printing Office.

———. 1972b. *Special Reports: Marital status 1970 Census*. Washington, D.C.: U.S. Government Printing Office.

———. 1973a. *1970 Census of Population*. Age at first marriage. Final Report PC(2)–4D. Washington, D.C.: U.S. Government Printing Office.

———. 1973b. *1970 Census of Population*. Persons by family characteristics. Final Report PC(2)–4B. Washington, D.C.: U.S. Government Printing Office.

———. 1973c. *1970 Census of the Population, vol. 1, part 23–Massachusetts*. Washington, D.C.: U.S. Government Printing Office.

———. 1975. *Household and family characteristics*, Series P–20. Washington, D.C.: U.S. Government Printing Office.

———. 1976. *Current Population Reports*, Series P–20:297. Number, timing, and duration of marriages and divorces in the United States: June 1975. Washington, D.C.: U.S. Government Printing Office.

———. 1977a. *Current Population Reports*, Series P–20:306. Marital status and living arrangements: March 1976. Washington, D.C.: U.S. Government Printing Office.

———. 1977b. *Current Population Reports*, Series P–20:309. School enrollment—social and economic characteristics of students: October 1976. Washington, D.C.: U.S. Government Printing Office.

———. 1977c. *Current Population Reports*, Series P–20:312. Marriage, divorce, widowhood, and remarriage by family characteristics: June 1975. Washington, D.C.: U.S. Government Printing Office.

———. 1977d. *Current Population Reports*, P–20:314. Educational attainment in the United States: March 1977 and 1976. Washington, D.C.: U.S. Government Printing Office.

———. 1977e. *Current Population Reports*, Series P–60:105. Money income in 1975 of families and persons in the United States. Washington, D.C.: U.S. Government Printing Office.

———. 1977f. *Current Population Reports*, Series P–60:106. Characteristics of the population below the poverty level: 1975. Washington, D.C.: U.S. Government Printing Office.

———. 1977g. *Current Population Reports*, Series P–60:107. Advance Report, Money income and poverty status of families and persons in the United States: 1976. Washington, D.C.: U.S. Government Printing Office.

———. 1977h. *Statistical Abstract of the United States*: 1977. (98th edition). Washington, D.C.: U.S. Government Printing Office.

U.S. Department of Health, Education and Welfare. 1973. One hundred years of marriage and divorce statistics. Series 21:24. Rockville, Maryland: National Center for Health Statistics.

———. 1976. *Monthly vital statistics report*, 24:13.

———. 1977a. *Monthly vital statistics report*, 25:13.

———. 1977b. *Monthly vital statistics report*, 26:8.

U.S. Department of Labor. 1976. *Women workers today*. Washington, D.C.

Vincent, C. E. 1961. *Unmarried mothers*. New York: Free Press.

Waller, W. 1938. *The family: A dynamic interpretation*. New York: Dryden.

Wallerstein, J. S., and Kelly, J. B. 1974. The effects of parental divorce: The adolescent experience. In E. J. Anthony and C. Koupernik Eds.). *The child in his family: Children at psychiatric risk. volume 3*. New York: Wiley.

———. 1975. The effects of parental divorce: Experiences of the preschool child. *Journal of the American Academy of Child Psychiatry*, *14*, 600–616.

———. 1976. The effects of parental divorce: Experience of the child in later latency. *American Journal of Orthopsychiatry*, *46*, 256–269.

Wallin, P., and Clark, A. L. 1958. Marital satisfaction and husbands' and wives' perception of similarity in their preferred frequency of coitus. *Journal of Abnormal and Social Psychology*, *47*, 370–373.

Watt, L. 1964. The new woman: Samuel Richardson's Pamela. In R. L. Coser (Ed.). *The family: Its structure and functions*. New York: St. Martin's Press.

Watts v. Watts. 1973. *New York Supplement of the National Reporter System, Second Series*, *350*, 285–291.

Wechsler, H., Thum, D., Demone, H. W., Jr., and Dwinnell, J. 1972. Social characteristics and blood alcohol level. *Quarterly Journal for the Study of Alcoholism*, *33*, 132–147.

Weeks, H. A. 1943. Differential divorce rates by occupation. *Social Forces*, *21*, 334–337.

Weinglass, J., Kressel, K., and Deutsch, M. 1978. The role of the clergy in divorce: An exploratory survey. *Journal of Divorce*, *2*, 57–82.

Weiss, R. S. 1973. *Loneliness*. Cambridge, Mass.: MIT Press.

———. 1975. *Marital separation*. New York: Basic Books.

————. Forthcoming. *The single parent.* New York: Basic Books.

Welter, B. 1966. The cult of true womanhood: 1820–1860. *American Quarterly, 18,* 151–174.

White, S. W., and Asher, S. J. 1976. *Separation and divorce: A study of the male perspective.* Unpublished paper, University of Colorado, Boulder.

Winch, R. F. 1971. *The modern family* (rev. ed.). New York: Holt, Rinehart and Winston.

Winch, R. F., and Greer, S. A. 1964. The uncertain relation between early marriage and marital stability: A quest for relevant data. *Acta Sociologica, 8,* 83–97.

Words and Phrases. 1968. St. Paul: West Publishing, *10A,* 506–507.

Zablocki, B. 1971. *The joyful community.* Boston: Penguin.

————. 1973. *Comparative study of West coast communes.* Paper presented at the meeting of the American Orthopsychiatric Association, New York.

Zautra, A., Beier, E., and Cappel, L. 1977. The dimensions of life quality in a community. *American Journal of Community Psychology, 5,* 85–97.

Zilboorg, G. 1931. Depressive reactions related to parenthood. *American Journal of Psychiatry, 10,* 927–962.

Zill, N. 1978. Divorce, marital happiness and the mental health of children: Findings from the Foundation for Child Development National Survey of Children. Paper prepared for National Institute of Mental Health workshop on Divorce and Children. Bethesda, Md.

NAME INDEX

SUBJECT INDEX